D0299401

Collins Bird Guide

A Chanticleer Press Edition

Collins Bird Guide

A photographic guide to the birds of Britain and Europe

Stuart Keith and John Gooders

Photographs assembled by John and Su Gooders of Ardea London

Collins, 8 Grafton Street, London W1

Published by William Collins Sons & Co Ltd:
London · Glasgow · Sydney · Auckland · Toronto · Johannesburg.

Prepared and produced by Chanticleer Press, Inc., New York.

Colour reproductions by Fontana & Bonomi, Milan, Italy.
Printed and bound by Dai Nippon Printing Co., Ltd., Tokyo, Japan.

Third Printing 1984

ISBN 0-00-219119-9

CONTENTS

INTRODUCTION

Bird-watching is enjoying an ever-increasing popularity. More films, magazines, books, and prints, as well as societies and sanctuaries, are now devoted to birds than ever before. The more urbanized the world becomes, the more we appreciate the beauty, flight and song of birds. That appreciation is often accompanied by a desire to know more about them: this book is designed to satisfy that wish and, incidentally, to be in itself a treasury of bird photographs.

Geographical Scope This guide covers all of Europe including that part of Russia west of the 30th meridian (see map). Iceland is included as well as the larger Mediterranean islands and the part of Turkey lying west of the Bosphorus. We have "bent" the 30th meridian to include those small areas of Norway and Finland that lie to the east of the line.

Choice of Species 464 bird species are fully described and illustrated in this guide. As a rule, we have included a species if it has occurred in Europe more than thirty times. A few birds, such as American Bittern and Pallas's Sandgrouse, which occurred more frequently in the past but very rarely in recent years have been omitted. Others, such as Little

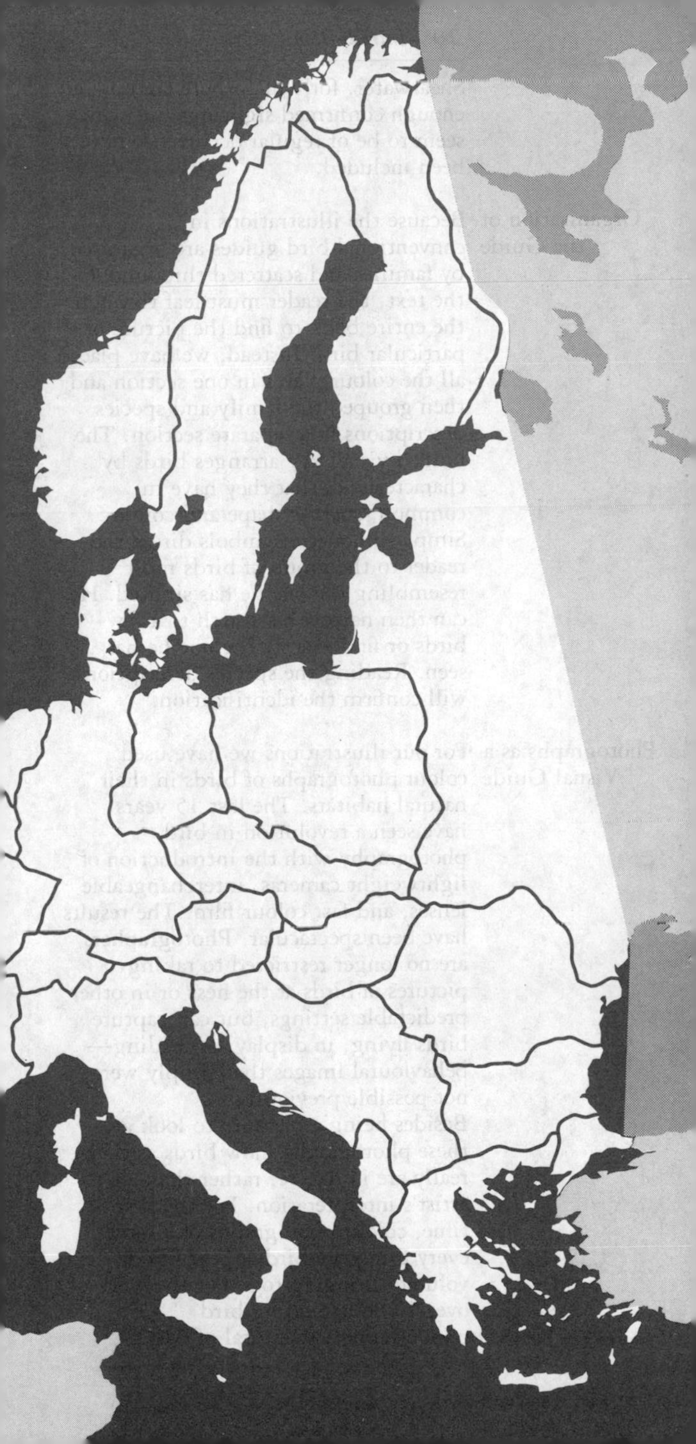

Shearwater, for which there are not yet enough confirmed sightings but which seem to be of regular occurrence have been included.

Organisation of the Guide

Because the illustrations in conventional bird guides are organised by families and scattered throughout the text, the reader must leaf through the entire book to find the picture of a particular bird. Instead, we have placed all the colour plates in one section and then grouped the family and species descriptions in a separate section. The unified visual key arranges birds by characteristics that they have in common, such as shape and colour. Simple silhouette symbols direct the reader to the group of birds most resembling the one he has sighted. He can then narrow his search to a few birds or find exactly the one he has seen. Reading the species descriptions will confirm the identification.

Photographs as a Visual Guide

For our illustrations we have used colour photographs of birds in their natural habitats. The last 15 years have seen a revolution in bird photography with the introduction of lightweight cameras, interchangeable lenses, and fast colour film. The results have been spectacular. Photographers are no longer restricted to taking pictures of birds at the nest or in other predictable settings, but can capture birds flying, in display, or feeding—behavioural images that simply were not possible previously.

Besides being a pleasure to look at, these photographs show birds as they really are in nature, rather than an artist's interpretation. For the first time, colour photographs of almost every European bird appear in one volume, bringing together the work of over 100 outstanding bird photographers in a total of 613 photographs. The result is a book that is a delight to look at as well as to use.

How the Visual Guide Works

Unlike traditional field guides, where the illustrations appear in a strict scientific order, we have organised the birds by size, shape, and colour—the features a bird-watcher sees in the field. Thus the group called Heron-like Birds also includes the unrelated cranes, which share the group's characteristic long bill and very long legs. Similarly the Swallow-like Birds include the unrelated swifts as well as swallows and martins because all are small, fast fliers usually seen in the air.

Sometimes distinctive behaviour and habitat have influenced our groupings. All tree-clinging birds—the treecreepers, nuthatches, and woodpeckers—are placed in a group called Woodpecker-like Birds. The Gannet, Fulmar, Albatross, shearwaters, and petrels are found in the section on Birds of Open Sea because they all share that distinctive habitat.

The perching birds are by far the largest category. We have placed most of them in eight groups based on such generally recognised types as Thrush-like, Flycatcher-like, and Sparrow-like Birds. Within each group, we have arranged the photographs by colour and plumage pattern. Thus the Sparrow-like group begins with birds with primarily red plumage like the crossbills and then progresses to those with rusty-orange, yellow, yellowish-brown, brown, and brown streaked with black plumage, ending with grey and black buntings. At the end a group called Exotic-looking Birds includes brightly plumaged birds that are the sole representatives of their families in Europe, such as the Hoopoe, the Bee-eater, and the Golden Oriole.

Groups The colour plates are arranged in the following groups:

Divers and Grebes
Birds of Sea Cliffs
Birds of Open Sea
Gull-like Birds
Waders
Heron-like Birds
Pelicans
Wildfowl
Rails, Gallinules, and Coots
Game Birds
Hawk-like Birds
Owls
Pigeons and Doves
Cuckoos and Nightjars
Swallow-like Birds
Woodpecker-like Birds
Tits
Warblers
Thrush-like Birds
Flycatcher-like Birds
Wagtails, Larks, and Pipits
Sparrow-like Birds
Crow-like Birds
Exotic-looking Birds

What the Photographs Show Most of the photographs show adult males in breeding plumage, since the males are usually the most brightly coloured and easiest to identify. Many females and birds in winter plumage that differ appreciably from the breeding males are also illustrated. A few distinctive juveniles are included. As often as space has allowed, we have also included flight shots of birds such as swifts and raptors that are usually seen in the air. Beneath each colour plate is a caption giving the bird's common name, size, and the page number of the text description. The age, sex, or plumage is also given whenever the photograph is of other than a breeding male. In a few instances, when a species is confined to inaccessible areas or is very rare, it is illustrated only by a drawing next to the text description. Also included are drawings of some wing patterns, bill shapes, and other features that help to distinguish similar species.

Key to the Colour Plates The organisation of the colour plates is summarised in a chart preceding the photographic section. Silhouettes of the main types of birds within each group are shown on the right of the chart. A silhouette of the most typical bird within each group has been selected to represent the entire group. It appears on the left of the chart and is repeated as a thumb-tab on the left side of each double page of colour plates that illustrate that group. Thus, a silhouette of a Shearwater represents the group called Birds of Open Sea, and a silhouette of a hawk represents the group of Hawk-like Birds that also includes eagles, vultures, harriers, kites, falcons, buzzards, and ospreys.

Text Organization In the text the bird descriptions are arranged in systematic or scientific order. The families are arranged on an evolutionary time scale: birds believed to be the oldest (divers and grebes) are placed first, while the much younger passerine families, which are still rapidly evolving, appear at the end. Families are grouped in a larger category, the order, and within each family, birds are arranged in a "family tree," according to their evolutionary relationships. Thus, the species *Anthus campestris,* Tawny Pipit, is placed in the genus *Anthus* along with other pipits. *Anthus* is one of several genera included in the pipit and wagtail family, Motacillidae, which in turn belongs with other families in the order Passeriformes, the perching birds.

Family Descriptions Each group of species descriptions is preceded by a general paragraph on the family. Characteristics common to all species within that family are given in addition to the number of species worldwide and the number that occur in Europe.

Common and Scientific Names

We have adopted the common names used in the 1978 *British Birds' List of Birds of the Western Palearctic*. At present there is considerable overlap and confusion in names, and many ornithologists believe that a standard list of English names for all birds of the world is desirable. *Charadrius alexandrinus,* for example, is known as Snowy Plover in North America, Kentish Plover in Europe, and Red-capped Dotterel in Australia. Three quite different duck species, one in North America, one in Africa, and one in Australia, are all known as the Black Duck in their respective ranges. To help minimize confusion in cases where a species is commonly known by two names, we have given the alternative name as well as the one in the *British Birds'* list. Thus, Andalusian Hemipode is also called Little Button-Quail, and Black Vulture is also called Cinereous Vulture. In the case of some birds whose principal range is outside Europe, we have provided both the European name and the name used in the greater part of the range. Thus, two African species, the Crested Coot and the Fan-tailed Warbler, are also given their African names, Red-knobbed Coot and Zitting Cisticola respectively. To avoid the confusion of different common names, every bird has a scientific name that is recognized throughout the world. It consists of two Latinized words: the first is the genus, the second is the species. Thus the Latin name of the Grey Wagtail, *Motacilla cinerea,* identifies it as a member of the genus *Motacilla* with the species name *cinerea,* meaning "grey." We have used the scientific names and systematic order of the *List of Recent Holarctic Bird Species* by K. H. Voous, as published in *Ibis* (vol. 115, 1973, pp. 612–638, and vol. 199, 1977, pp. 223–250, 376–406). We have however retained Scottish Crossbill (*Loxia curvirostra scotica*) as a subspecies of Crossbill.

Species Descriptions We have avoided technical terms wherever possible. Occasionally, such terms have been necessary; they are defined in the glossary. The reader should also familiarize himself with the drawings in these pages labelled to show the various parts of a bird's body.

Measurements The size of a bird as given in the text and captions is the average overall length from the tip of the bill to the tip of its tail. When significant, the wingspan, length of bill, or length of tail also appears.

Shape and Colour The description of each species includes the key features by which it is identified, in italics. In the waders, the key characteristics are the rump, tail, and wing patterns; in gulls, the wing-tip pattern and bill and leg colours; in leaf warblers, wing and head patterns; and so on. When the plumage within a species varies, the text first describes the appearance of the breeding male, followed by seasonal changes and the female and juvenile plumages. In some birds, such as the Skylark and the Carrion Crow, the sexes are similar and change little during the year. In others, such as ducks and finches, the sexes have a very different plumage. Still others, like the divers and grebes, have a change of plumage from summer to winter. In many species the young are very different from the adults. The adult Robin has a red breast, whereas the juvenile is mottled-brown and is in fact driven from the adult's territory as soon as its red breast develops. While most young birds moult into adult plumage during their first year, some, such as large gulls and birds of prey, take several years to acquire full adult plumage, and in each year the plumage becomes progressively nearer to the adult's. When distinctive subspecies occur in Europe, these are also described. The colour plates likewise show as many plumage variations for each species as space has allowed. In the case of easily confused species, the text helps distinguish one from the other.

Voice Birds use their voices for a variety of purposes—to defend a territory, to attract a mate, to maintain contact with other birds, or as an alarm. Some have a wide vocabulary; the Great Tit has been credited with 57 different calls. To identify most species, however, it is sufficient to learn the common contact notes and the song. In fact some birds are so similar in appearance that they are best distinguished by their voices. While certainly helpful, descriptions of voices, no matter how phonetic, are no substitute for hearing the actual songs and calls. A number of very good recordings of bird songs are available, but by far the best way to learn songs is to go into the field with someone who knows them.

Habitat Birds are mobile and adaptable and some may occupy a wide range of habitats. Nevertheless, most species have a preferred breeding habitat, and this is featured in the text. When the winter habitat is different, this is also described. For example, geese nest in the arctic tundra but feed in fields and arable land in winter. Petrels, shearwaters, and other seabirds spend most of their lives at sea, coming to land only to nest.

Nesting A description of the eggs, nest, and nest site is given for each species. The number of eggs cited is that normally found in a nest, although the number can vary considerably according to geographical location, whether the eggs are of a first or second brood, and other factors. Some birds construct elaborate nests: The Egyptian Vulture, breeding in caves or holes in cliffs, builds a nest of sticks, bones, fur, paper, and dung, and lines it with hair, wool, and rags. Others, including many waders, lay their eggs in a bare scrape. Some birds, like the Gannet, nest in vast colonies; others, such as the Nightingale, nest as a solitary pair.

Range The geographic range given for each bird focuses on its distribution within Europe and supplements the information in the individual range maps. The range description generally moves from west to east and north to south. Breeding range appears first; winter range is also given if different. This is followed by a brief description of world range. For species that appear in Europe only as migrants, information on their general route is given. In some cases, range can help confirm identification of a species. Thus, a nightjar seen in Britain has to be the Nightjar because the Red-necked Nightjar, the only other European species, is confined to the Iberian Peninsula. The ranges of species are constantly changing: the White-rumped Swift, for instance, is a relative newcomer to Europe, having extended its range northward from Africa into southern Spain in the last decade. A number of Asian species, such as the Paddyfield Warbler and the Azure Tit, are expanding their ranges west into Europe.

Range Maps Maps accompany each range description except for those species whose range is so restricted that a written description suffices or for those that appear in Europe only as migrants. The maps show both breeding and winter ranges, using the following key:

Breeding range

Winter range

Permanent range—areas in which a species occurs in both winter and summer.

Comments At the end of each species description, additional notes discuss behaviour, feeding habits, population status, migration, conservation, origin of names, and other points of general interest. There, for example, we describe the dramatic courtship display of the Great Crested Grebe, the Egyptian Vulture's habit of breaking Ostrich eggs by dropping rocks on them, the 5,000 mile (8,000 km) migration route of the Pallid Harrier, and the fact that swifts sometimes sleep in flight.

How to Find Birds Some advance planning will enable you to increase the number of birds seen on a field trip. Since many species remain more or less in one habitat, you should plan to visit as many habitats as possible. A good system is to begin a field trip very early in the morning and go first to freshwater marshes, since many of the species there are most active shortly after dawn. As the day progresses, you can move to woodland and then to open fields and coastal and aquatic habitats, where most species are active and conspicuous all day.

While many species are rather tame, others are shy or secretive. Learn to move slowly and quietly. Avoid sudden movements and bright-coloured clothing, which serve to make an observer more visible to shy or wary species. Some of these elusive birds can be lured into view by "squeaking," or "pishing," an imitation of the sound of a bird in distress. Rails and certain elusive forest species can be attracted by tape recordings of their songs and calls.

Information on particularly good bird-watching areas in the British Isles and on the Continent is available in books and articles. In addition, it is wise to contact members of the local bird club in an unfamiliar area, since they can provide specific, up-to-date information on the birds of their area and the best places to see them. Many bird-watchers also belong to their own local bird club or natural history society, where they can make contact with fellow aficionados and join group excursions to the best bird-watching areas.

Appendices Information on bird-watching equipment, a list of accidentals, and notes on conservation are included in the appendices.

Parts of a Bird

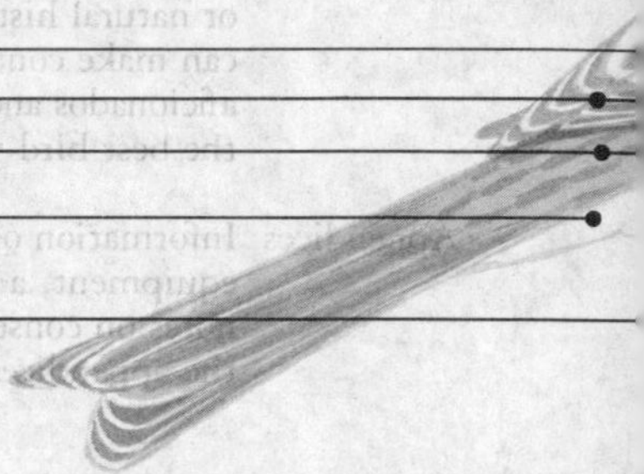

crown

forehead

nape

ear coverts/ bill

back / chin

throat

shoulder

breast

tertials

secondaries / primaries

rump/ flank

upper tail coverts / belly

under tail coverts

tail feathers (rectrices)/ tibia

tarsus

claw/ toe

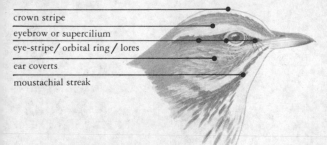

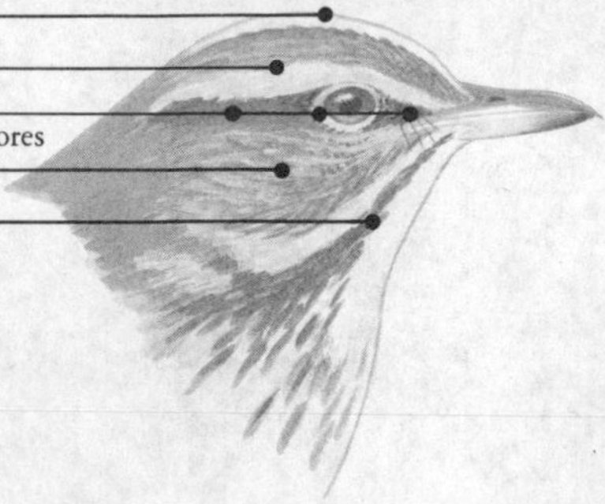

crown stripe

eyebrow or supercilium

eye-stripe/ orbital ring / lores

ear coverts

moustachial streak

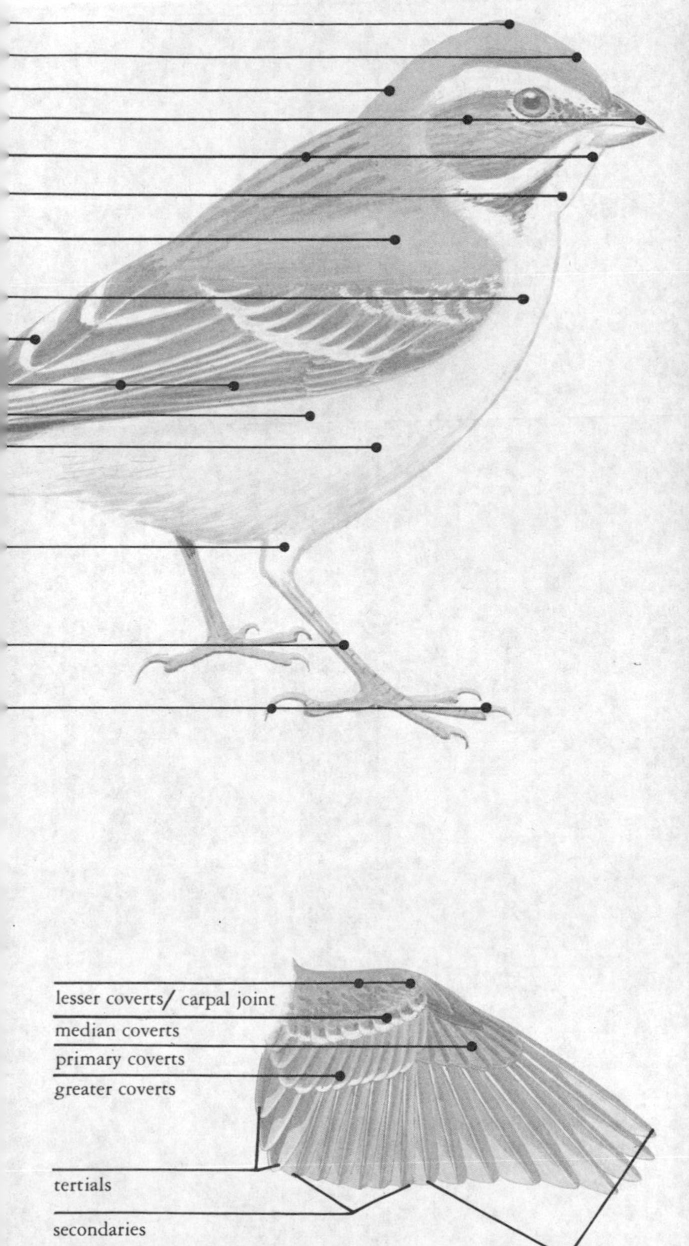
lesser coverts/ carpal joint
median coverts
primary coverts
greater coverts
tertials
secondaries
primaries

HOW TO USE THIS GUIDE

Example
A Thrush-like
Bird

It is early winter and you see a medium-small bird hopping around your garden. Its back and wings are brown, and it has dark speckles on its chest and belly. Its shape and upright stance remind you of the familiar thrush that nests behind the ivy, but it is slightly smaller and has a white eyebrow and rusty colour along the flanks.

1. Turn to the spread of silhouettes that precedes the colour plate section and find the silhouette that fits a thrush-like bird.
2. Look for the thumb tab with the thrush silhouette in the colour plate section.
3. Among the 40 colour photographs of thrush-like birds, you will find there are only three birds with the combination of plain brown above and dark spots below: the Song Thrush, the Mistle Thrush, and the Redwing. Only the Redwing has a white eyebrow and rusty flanks.
4. Under the photograph you will find the page number that refers you to the text description of the Redwing. Reading the description confirms your identification of the Redwing, an autumn migrant from Scandinavia.

Part I
Colour Plates

Key to the Colour Plates

The colour plates on the following pages are divided into 24 groups:

Divers and Grebes
Birds of Sea Cliffs
Birds of Open Sea
Gull-like Birds
Waders
Heron-like Birds
Pelicans
Wildfowl
Rails, Gallinules, and Coots
Game Birds
Hawk-like Birds
Owls
Pigeons and Doves
Cuckoos and Nightjars
Swallow-like Birds
Woodpecker-like Birds
Tits
Warblers
Thrush-like Birds
Flycatcher-like Birds
Wagtails, Larks, and Pipits
Sparrow-like Birds
Crow-like Birds
Exotic-looking Birds

Silhouette and Thumb Tab Guide

To help you learn to recognise birds by their general shape, silhouettes of the different types of birds within each group appear on the following pages. The silhouette that best typifies its particular group has been inset as a thumb tab at the left-hand edge of each double page of plates, thus providing a quick and convenient index to the colour section.

Captions

The caption under each colour plate gives the bird's common name, size, and the number of the page on which it is described. Photographs are of males in breeding plumage unless otherwise indicated.

Thumb Tab	Group
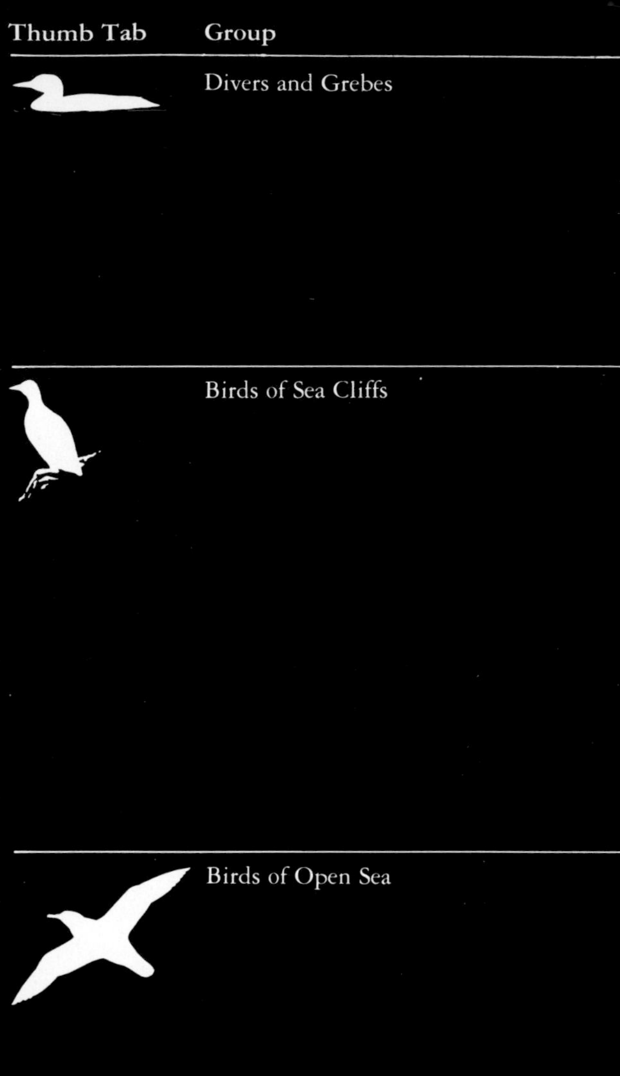	Divers and Grebes
	Birds of Sea Cliffs
	Birds of Open Sea

Birds	Plate Numbers
divers	1–4, 14 16
grebes	5–13
cormorants	26–28
guillemots, auk, puffin, razorbill	17–25
gannet	30, 33
fulmar, shearwaters, albatross	29, 31, 32, 34, 36, 37, 40
petrels	35, 38, 39

Thumb Tab	Group
	Gull-like Birds
	Waders

Birds		Plate Numbers
	gulls	41–72
	terns	73–82
	skuas	83–88
	pratincoles, courser	147, 148
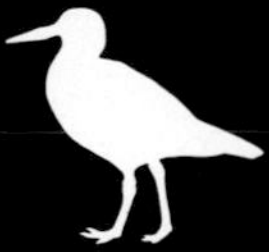	oystercatcher	158
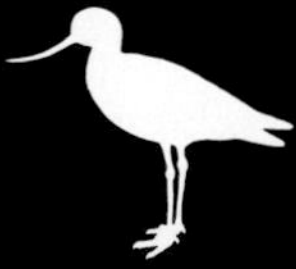	avocet, stilt	159, 160
	stone-curlew, plovers, turnstone	99, 101–103, 118, 121, 124, 144, 145, 149–157

Thumb Tab	Group
	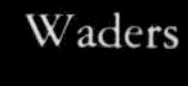 Waders
	Heron-like Birds

Birds		Plate Numbers
	sandpipers	89–98, 100, 107–117, 119, 120, 125–143, 146, 161–163
	phalaropes	104–106, 122, 123
	herons, egrets	165, 167–169, 171, 172, 174, 177, 179
	bitterns	173, 175, 176, 178
	cranes	164, 166
	spoonbill	170
	ibis	182

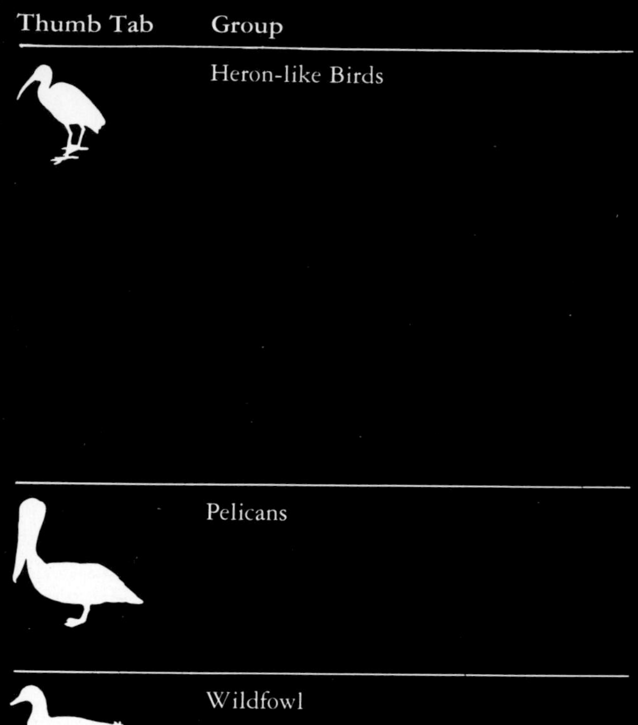

Thumb Tab	Group
	Heron-like Birds
	Pelicans
	Wildfowl

Birds		Plate Numbers
	flamingo	180
	storks	181, 183
	pelicans	184–187
	swans	188–190, 193
	geese	191, 192, 194–203
	shelducks	210, 212
	surface-feeding ducks	205–209, 217, 221–224, 227, 230–233, 235–237, 244

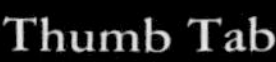

Thumb Tab	Group
	Wildfowl
	Rails, Gallinules, and Coots
	Game Birds

Birds		Plate Numbers
	stiff-tailed ducks	213, 214, 239
	diving ducks	204, 215, 216, 225, 226, 228, 229, 234, 238, 240–243, 245–250, 252–255, 257–262
	mergansers	211, 218–220, 251, 256
	rails, crakes	263–267
	gallinules	268, 269
	coots	270, 271
	grouse, ptarmigan, capercaillie	272–274, 280, 281, 283–285, 287, 288

Thumb Tab	Group
	Game Birds
	 Hawk-like Birds

Birds		Plate Numbers
	bustards	275, 282
	partridges, quail, pheasants	276, 277, 286, 289–295
	sandgrouse	278, 279
	vultures	296–299, 360–362, 365
	eagles	300–305, 307, 313–315, 345, 349–353, 363, 364
	buzzards	306, 308, 310, 311, 347, 348, 355, 356
	hawks	309, 322–324

Thumb Tab	Group
	Hawk-like Birds
	Owls
	Pigeons and Doves

Birds		Plate Numbers
	osprey	312, 346
	kites	316, 317, 330, 339, 340
	harriers	318–321, 331, 354, 357–359
	falcons	325–329, 332–338, 341–344
	barn owls	367, 369
	true owls	366, 368, 370–381
	pigeons, doves	382–387

Thumb Tab	Group
	Cuckoos and Nightjars
	Swallow-like Birds
	Woodpecker-like Birds

Birds		Plate Numbers
	cuckoos	388, 391–393
	nightjars	389, 390
	swallows, martins	396, 398–402
	swifts	394, 395, 397
	woodpeckers	404–414
	wryneck	403
	nuthatches	415, 416

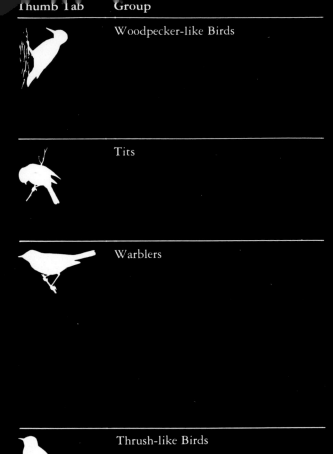

Thumb Tab	Group
	Woodpecker-like Birds
	Tits
	Warblers
	Thrush-like Birds

Birds		Plate Numbers
	creepers	417, 418
	tits	419–430
	wren	460
	warblers	431–459, 461–466
	thrushes, robins, chats, wheatears	467–483, 485, 486, 488–502, 505
	dipper	484
	starlings	487, 503, 504

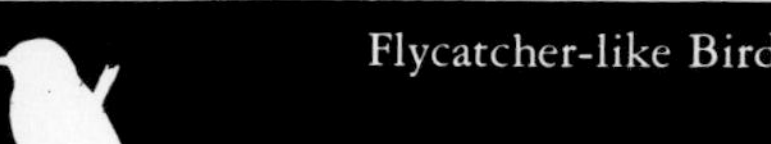

Thumb Tab	Group
	Flycatcher-like Birds
	Wagtails, Larks, and Pipits
	Sparrow-like Birds

Birds		Plate Numbers
	flycatchers	506, 512–514, 517
	shrikes	507–511, 515, 516
	wagtails	518–525
	pipits	530–537
	larks	526–529, 538–541
	accentors	585, 586
	sparrows, buntings, finches	542–584, 587–595

Thumb Tab	Group
	Crow-like Birds
	Exotic-looking Birds

Birds		Plate Numbers
	crows, jays, nutcracker	596–602, 605–607
	magpies	603, 604
	kingfisher	610
	hoopoe	613
	waxwing	612
	roller, oriole	608, 611
	bee-eater	609

The colour plates in the following pages are numbered to correspond with the description of each species in the text. Unless otherwise indicated by the caption, the photographs are of adult males in summer plumage.

Divers and Grebes

These compact, surface-diving birds are rarely seen on land; they nest on fresh water. Divers winter on salt water, grebes on both salt water and fresh water. They dive for food, often remaining submerged for considerable periods.

1 White-billed Diver, 75–90 cm, *p. 318*

2 Great Northern Diver, 68–90 cm, *p. 317*

3 Black-throated Diver, 55–73 cm, *p. 316*

4 Red-throated Diver, 53–68 cm, *p. 315*

5 Great Crested Grebe, 48 cm, *p. 320*

6 Little Grebe, 26 cm, *p. 319*

7 Red-necked Grebe, 43 cm, *p. 321*

8 Little Grebe, 26 cm, *winter*, *p. 319*

9 Slavonian Grebe, 33 cm, *p. 322*

10 Black-necked Grebe, 30 cm, *p. 322*

11 Slavonian Grebe, 33 cm, *winter*, *p. 322*

12 Black-necked Grebe, 30 cm, *winter*, *p. 322*

13 Red-necked Grebe, 43 cm, *winter, p. 321*

14 White-billed Diver, 75–90 cm, *winter, p. 318*

15 Red-throated Diver, 53–68 cm, *winter, p. 315*

16 Great Northern Diver, 68–90 cm, *winter, p. 317*

Birds of Sea Cliffs

During the breeding season these birds perch on coastal cliffs and rocks (cormorants sometimes in trees) in an upright posture. They winter at sea (cormorants sometimes inland), where they surface-dive for food.

17 Razorbill, 40 cm, *p. 523*

18 Black Guillemot, 34 cm, *p. 524*

19 Puffin, 30 cm, *p. 526*

20 Razorbill, 40 cm, *p. 523*

21 Brünnich's Guillemot, 41 cm, *p. 523*

22 Guillemot, 41 cm, *p. 522*

23 Little Auk, 20 cm, *p. 525*

24 Little Auk, 20 cm, *winter, p. 525*

25 Guillemot, 41 cm, *winter, p. 522*

26 Cormorant, 90 cm, *p. 335*

27 Shag, 75 cm, *p. 336*

28 Pygmy Cormorant, 48 cm, *p. 337*

Birds of Open Sea

These pelagic birds come to land only to nest; most live on open ocean far from land (Gannet also appears inshore). Gannet, Albatross, and Fulmar have gull-like plumage but are distinguished by their stiff-winged, gliding flight.

29 Black-browed Albatross, 78–93 cm, *p. 324*

30 Gannet, 90 cm, *p. 333*

31 Fulmar, 46 cm, *light phase, p. 325*

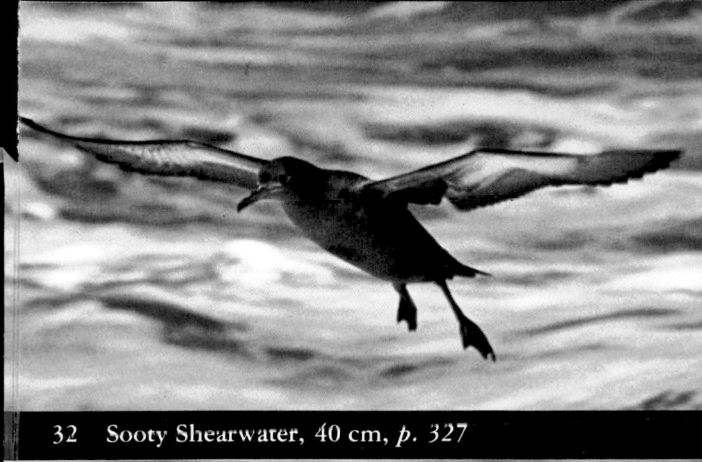
32 Sooty Shearwater, 40 cm, *p. 327*

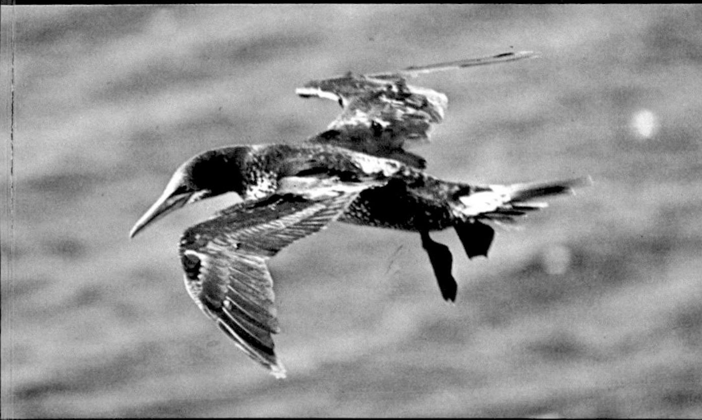
33 Gannet, 90 cm, *juv., p. 333*

34 Fulmar, 46 cm, *dark phase, p. 325*

35 Wilson's Petrel, 18 cm, *p. 330*

36 Great Shearwater, 45 cm, *p. 326*

37 Cory's Shearwater, 45 cm, *p. 326*

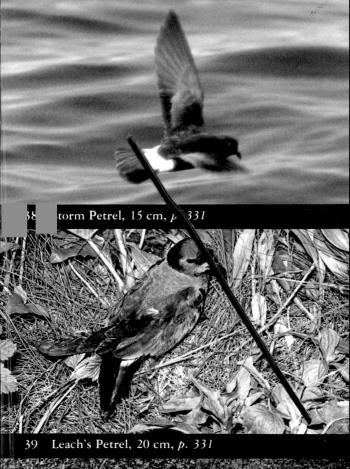

38 Storm Petrel, 15 cm, *p. 331*

39 Leach's Petrel, 20 cm, *p. 331*

40 Manx Shearwater, 35 cm, *p. 328*

Gull-like Birds

These are chiefly coastal water birds, although some gulls and terns appear inland and skuas nest inland and winter at sea. Terns plunge-dive for fish; gulls feed only from the surface. Young gulls are wholly or partly brown.

41 Bonaparte's Gull, 30–35 cm, *p. 504*

42 Little Gull, 28 cm, *p. 503*

43 Sabine's Gull, 33 cm, *p. 503*

44 Black-headed Gull, 35–38 cm, *p. 505*

45 Mediterranean Gull, 38 cm, *p. 502*

47 Great Black-backed Gull, 65 cm, *p. 511*

48 Lesser Black-backed Gull, 53 cm, *p. 508*

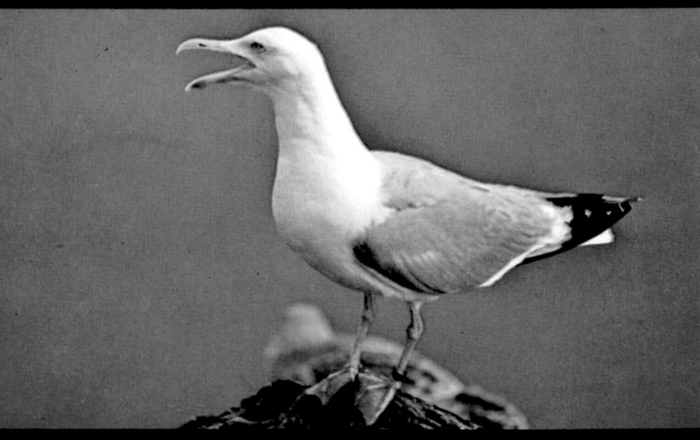

49 Herring Gull, 55 cm, *p. 508*

50 Kittiwake, 40 cm, *p. 512*

51 Common Gull, 40 cm, *p. 507*

52 Glaucous Gull, 63 cm, *p. 510*

53 Slender-billed Gull, 43 cm, *p.* 505

54 Audouin's Gull, 49 cm, *p.* 506

55 Kittiwake, 40 cm, *p.* 512

56 Iceland Gull, 55 cm, *imm.*, *p. 509*

57 Ivory Gull, 44 cm, *p. 513*

58 Ivory Gull, 44 cm, *imm.*, *p. 513*

59 Common Gull, 40 cm, *juv.*, *p.* 507

60 Little Gull, 28 cm, *juv.*, *p.* 503

61 Black-headed Gull, 35–38 cm, *juv.*, *p.* 505

62 Glaucous Gull, 63 cm, *imm.*, *p.* 510

63 Herring Gull, 55 cm, *juv.*, *p.* 508

64 Great Black-backed Gull, 65 cm, *juv.*, *p.* 511

65 Slender-billed Gull, 43 cm, *winter, p. 505*

66 Black-headed Gull, 35–38, *winter, p. 505*

67 Great Black-headed Gull, 65 cm, *winter, p. 501*

68 Ross's Gull, 31 cm, *p. 511*

69 Kittiwake, 40 cm, *imm., p. 512*

70 Bonaparte's Gull, 30–35 cm, *imm., p. 504*

71 Bonaparte's Gull, 30–35 cm, *winter, p. 504*

72 Little Gull, 28 cm, *winter, p. 503*

73 White-winged Black Tern, 23 cm, *winter, p. 521*

74 Gull-billed Tern, 38 cm, *p. 514*

75 Sandwich Tern, 40 cm, *p. 516*

76 Caspian Tern, 53 cm, *p. 515*

77 Roseate Tern, 38 cm, *p. 516*

78 Common Tern, 35 cm, *p. 517*

79 Arctic Tern, 35 cm, *p. 518*

80 Little Tern, 24 cm, *p. 519*

81 Whiskered Tern, 23 cm, *p. 519*

82 Black Tern, 24 cm, *p. 520*

83 Arctic Skua, 45 cm, *p. 498*

84 Long-tailed Skua, 50–55 cm, *p. 499*

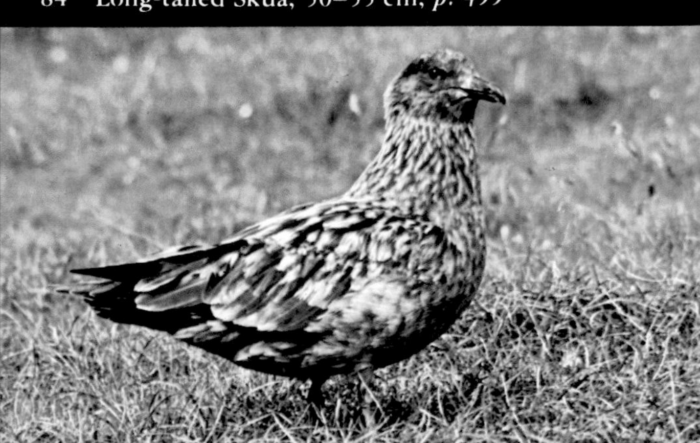

85 Great Skua, 58 cm, *p. 499*

86 Arctic Skua, 45 cm, *p. 498*

87 Pomarine Skua, 50 cm, *imm.*, *p. 497*

88 Great Skua, 58 cm, *p. 499*

Waders

This large group of small to medium-sized birds, with slender bills and often with long legs, usually wades in mud or shallow coastal and inland water. However, the Stone-curlew, pratincoles, Courser, and some plovers are often on dry land far from water.

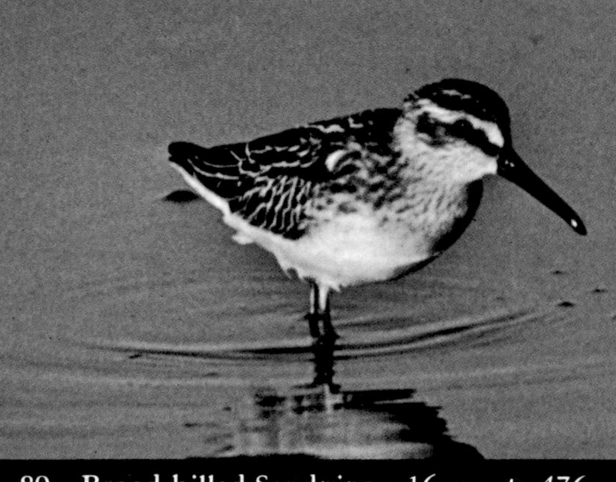

89 Broad-billed Sandpiper, 16 cm, *p. 476*

90 Dunlin, 18 cm, *juv. p. 475*

91 Little Stint, 13 cm, *winter, p. 470*

92 Sanderling, 20 cm, *1st winter*, p. 469

93 Curlew Sandpiper, 19 cm, *juv.*, p. 474

94 Temminck's Stint, 14 cm, *p. 471*

95 Greenshank, 30 cm, *juv.*, *p. 488*

96 Ruff, 29 cm, *winter*, *p. 477*

97 Knot, 25 cm, *juv.*, *p. 468*

98 Purple Sandpiper, 21 cm, *winter*, *p. 475*

99 Turnstone, 23 cm, *1st winter*, *p. 493*

100 Pectoral Sandpiper, 21 cm, *p. 473*

101 Golden Plover, 28 cm, *juv., p. 463*

102 Lesser Golden Plover, 25 cm, *winter, p. 463*

103 Grey Plover, 28 cm, *winter, p. 464*

104 Wilson's Phalarope, 23 cm, *winter, p. 494*

105 Grey Phalarope, 20 cm, *juv., p. 495*

106 Red-necked Phalarope, 18 cm, *winter, p. 495*

107 Terek Sandpiper, 23 cm, *p. 492*

108 Bar-tailed Godwit, 38 cm, *winter, p. 483*

109 Black-tailed Godwit, 40 cm, *winter, p. 482*

110 Redshank, 28 cm, *1st winter, p. 487*

111 Spotted Redshank, 30 cm, *juv., p. 486*

112 Long-billed Dowitcher, 29 cm, *winter, p. 481*

113 Semipalmated Sandpiper, 15 cm, *juv.*, *p. 470*

114 White-rumped Sandpiper, 19 cm, *p. 472*

115 Baird's Sandpiper, 18 cm, *juv.*, *p. 473*

116 Buff-breasted Sandpiper, 20 cm, *p. 477*

117 Dotterel, 21 cm, *juv.*, *p. 462*

118 Stone-curlew, 40 cm, *p. 455*

119 Sanderling, 20 cm, *p. 469*

120 Curlew Sandpiper, 19 cm, *p. 474*

121 Dotterel, 21 cm, *p. 462*

122 Grey Phalarope, 20 cm, *p. 495*

123 Red-necked Phalarope, 18 cm, ♀, *p. 495*

124 Turnstone, 23 cm, *p. 493*

125 Little Stint, 13 cm, *p. 470*

126 Purple Sandpiper, 21 cm, *p. 475*

127 Woodcock, 34 cm, *p. 482*

128 Snipe, 26 cm, *p. 479*

129 Great Snipe, 28 cm, *p. 480*

130 Jack Snipe, 19 cm, *p. 478*

131 Short-billed Dowitcher, 28 cm, *p. 480*

132 Marsh Sandpiper, 23 cm, *p. 488*

133 Green Sandpiper, 23 cm, *juv.*, *p. 490*

134 Black-tailed Godwit, 40 cm, *p. 482*

135 Whimbrel, 40 cm, *p. 484*

136 Curlew, 53–58 cm, *p. 485*

137 Wood Sandpiper, 20 cm, *juv.*, *p. 491*

138 Lesser Yellowlegs, 25 cm, *juv.*, *p. 490*

139 Greater Yellowlegs, 35 cm, *juv.*, *p. 489*

140 Upland Sandpiper, 28 cm, *p. 486*

141 Redshank, 28 cm, *p. 487*

142 Spotted Redshank, 30 cm, *p. 486*

143 Dunlin, 18 cm, *p. 475*

144 Golden Plover, 28 cm, *p. 463*

145 Grey Plover, 28 cm, *p. 464*

146 Common Sandpiper, 19 cm, *p. 493*

147 Collared Pratincole, 25 cm, *p. 457*

148 Cream-coloured Courser, 23 cm, *p. 456*

149 Little Ringed Plover, 15 cm, *juv., p. 459*

150 Ringed Plover, 19 cm, *juv., p. 460*

151 Kentish Plover, 16 cm, *winter, p. 461*

152 Little Ringed Plover, 15 cm, *p. 459*

153 Ringed Plover, 19 cm, *p. 460*

154 Kentish Plover, 16 cm, *p. 461*

155 Killdeer, 25 cm, *p. 460*

156 Spur-winged Plover, 26 cm, *p. 465*

157 Lapwing, 30 cm, *p. 467*

158 Oystercatcher, 43 cm, *p. 452*

159 Avocet, 43 cm, *p. 454*

160 Black-winged Stilt, 38 cm, *p. 453*

161 Ruff, 29 cm, *p.* 477

162 Ruff, 29 cm, *p.* 477

163 Ruff, 29 cm, *p.* 477

Heron-like Birds

These medium- to large-sized birds have long bills and long legs adapted for wading in fresh or salt water. Most prefer warm climates and are most common in southern Europe. Plumage varies from all white in egrets to brown, grey, and black.

164 Demoiselle Crane, 95 cm, *p. 449*

165 Grey Heron, 90 cm, *juv.*, *p. 346*

166 Crane, 113 cm, *p. 448*

167 Purple Heron, 78 cm, *p. 347*

168 Little Egret, 55 cm, *p. 344*

169 Great White Egret, 88 cm, *p. 345*

170 Spoonbill, 85 cm, *p. 351*

171 Cattle Egret, 50 cm, *p. 343*

172 Night Heron, 60 cm, *p. 342*

173 Little Bittern, 35 cm, ♀, *p. 341*

174 Night Heron, 60 cm, *p. 342*

175 Little Bittern, 35 cm, *p. 341*

176 Little Bittern, 35 cm, *juv.*, *p. 341*

177 Night Heron, 60 cm, *juv.*, *p. 342*

178 Bittern, 75 cm, *p. 340*

179 Squacco Heron, 45 cm, *winter*, *p. 343*

180 Greater Flamingo, 125 cm, *p. 352*

181 White Stork, 100 cm, *p. 349*

182 Glossy Ibis, 55 cm, *p. 350*

183 Black Stork, 95 cm, *p. 348*

Pelicans

Huge water birds with an enormous bill and pouch, pelicans have a heavy body and broad wingspan. They are usually seen in groups resting on land or fishing on the water's surface. They also plunge-dive from the air.

184 White Pelican, 138–178 cm, *p. 338*

185 Dalmatian Pelican, 158–178 cm, *p. 339*

186 White Pelican, 138–178 cm, *p. 338*

187 Dalmatian Pelican, 158–178 cm, *p. 339*

Wildfowl

Included here are duck-like birds found on both salt and fresh water. Swans are huge and all white, with long necks; geese are large and mainly brown, grey, and black, with shorter necks; ducks are medium-sized and variably coloured.

188 Bewick's Swan, 120 cm, *p. 354*

189 Whooper Swan, 150 cm, *p. 355*

190 Mute Swan, 150 cm, *p. 353*

191 Snow Goose, 63–75 cm, *white phase*, p. 359

192 Snow Goose, 63–75 cm, *blue phase*, p. 359

193 Mute Swan, 150 cm, *juv.*, p. 353

194 Greylag Goose, 75–88 cm, *p. 358*

195 Bean Goose, 70–88 cm, *p. 355*

196 Pink-footed Goose, 60–75 cm, *p. 356*

197 White-fronted Goose, 65–75 cm, *p. 357*

198 Lesser White-fronted Goose, 53–65 cm, *p. 357*

199 Egyptian Goose, 63–70 cm, *p. 363*

200 Barnacle Goose, 58–68 cm, *p. 361*

201 Brent Goose, 55–60 cm, *p. 361*

202 Canada Goose, 90–100 cm, *p. 360*

203 Red-breasted Goose, 53–55 cm, *p. 362*

204 Harlequin Duck, 43 cm, *p. 380*

205 Mandarin, 43 cm, *p. 365*

206 Teal, 35 cm, *p. 368*

207 American Wigeon, 45 cm, *p. 366*

208 Mallard, 58 cm, *p. 369*

209 Shoveler, 50 cm, *p. 372*

210 Shelduck, 60 cm, *p. 364*

211 Red-breasted Merganser, 58 cm, *p. 386*

212 Ruddy Shelduck, 63 cm, ♀, *p. 363*

213 Ruddy Duck, 40 cm, *p. 388*

214 White-headed Duck, 45 cm, *p. 389*

215 Pochard, 45 cm, *p. 374*

216 Red-crested Pochard, 55 cm, *p. 373*

217 Wigeon, 45 cm, *p. 366*

218 Goosander, 65 cm, ♀, *p. 387*

219 Red-breasted Merganser, 58 cm, ♀, *p. 386*

220 Smew, 40 cm, ♀, *p. 385*

221 Gadwall, 50 cm, *p. 367*

222 Garganey, 38 cm, *p. 370*

223 Pintail, 65 cm, *p. 370*

224 Blue-winged Teal, 38 cm, *p. 371*

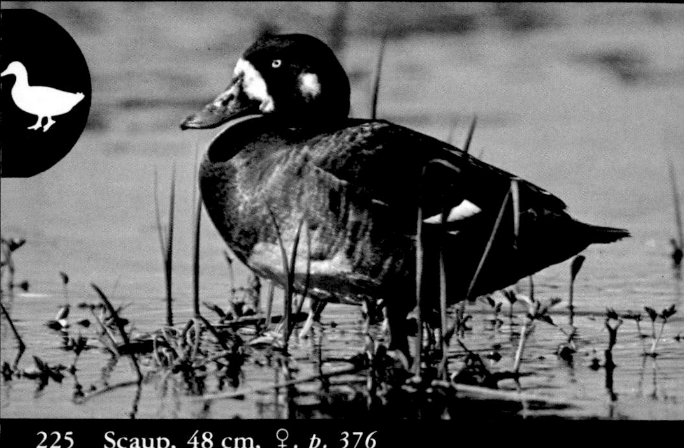

225 Scaup, 48 cm, ♀, *p. 376*

226 Surf Scoter, 53 cm, ♀, *p. 382*

227 Mandarin, 43 cm, ♀, *p. 365*

228 Ferruginous Duck, 40 cm, *p. 375*

229 Tufted Duck, 43 cm, ♀, *p. 376*

230 Mallard, 58 cm, ♀, *p. 369*

231 Gadwall, 50 cm, ♀, *p. 367*

232 Pintail, 55 cm, ♀, *p. 370*

233 Shoveler, 50 cm, ♀, *p. 372*

234 King Eider, 55 cm, ♀, *p. 378*

235 Wigeon, 45 cm, ♀, *p. 366*

236 Teal, 35 cm, ♀, *p. 368*

237 Garganey, 38 cm, ♀, *p. 370*

238 Eider, 58 cm, ♀, *p. 377*

239 Ruddy Duck, 40 cm, ♀, *p. 388*

240 Common Scoter, 48 cm, ♀, *p. 381*

241 Long-tailed Duck, 40 cm, ♀, *p. 380*

242 Pochard, 45 cm, ♀, *p. 374*

243 Red-crested Pochard, 55 cm, ♀, *p. 373*

244 Marbled Duck, 40 cm, *p. 373*

245 Goldeneye, 45 cm, ♀, *p. 385*

246 Barrow's Goldeneye, 53 cm, ♀, *p. 384*

247 Velvet Scoter, 55 cm, *imm.*, *p. 383*

248 Steller's Eider, 45 cm, *p. 379*

249 King Eider, 55 cm, *p. 378*

250 Eider, 58 cm, *p. 377*

251 Smew, 40 cm, *p. 385*

252 Long-tailed Duck, 53 cm, *winter, p. 380*

253 Long-tailed Duck, 53 cm, *p. 380*

254 Tufted Duck, 43 cm, *p. 376*

255 Scaup, 48 cm, *p. 376*

256 Goosander, 65 cm, *p. 387*

257 Barrow's Goldeneye, 53 cm, *p. 384*

258 Goldeneye, 45 cm, *p. 385*

259 Harlequin Duck, 43 cm, ♀, *p. 380*

260 Surf Scoter, 53 cm, *p. 382*

261 Velvet Scoter, 55 cm, *p. 383*

262 Common Scoter, 48 cm, *p. 381*

Rails, Gallinules, and Coots

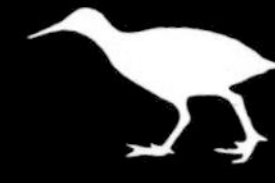

This group includes marsh birds and the Corncrake, which occurs on dry land. Rails are shy and secretive; coots and gallinules are often seen on open water. Flight appears weak, with legs dangling.

263 Water Rail, 28 cm, *p. 440*

264 Baillon's Crake, 18 cm, *p. 443*

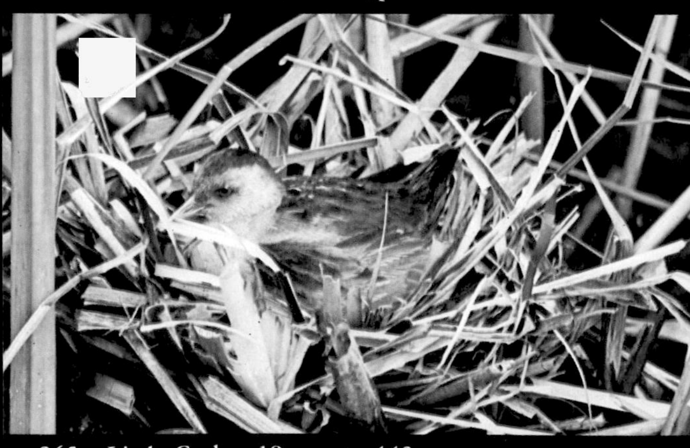

265 Little Crake, 19 cm, *p. 442*

266 Spotted Crake, 23 cm, *p. 441*

267 Corncrake, 26 cm, *p. 444*

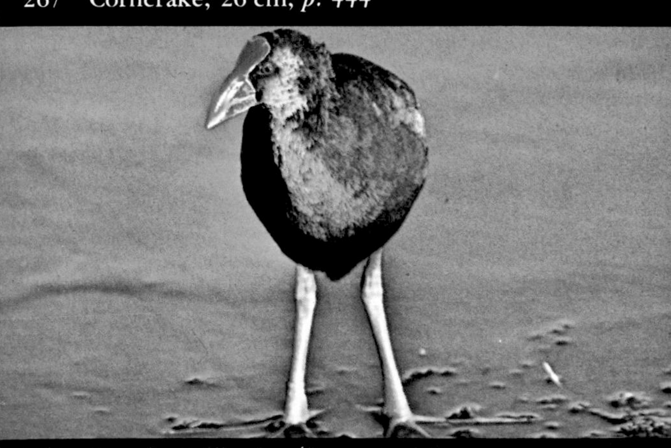

268 Purple Gallinule, 48 cm, *p. 445*

269 Moorhen, 33 cm, *p. 444*

270 Crested Coot, 40 cm, *p. 447*

271 Coot, 38 cm, *p. 446*

Game Birds

Game birds include plump, chicken-like birds of various sizes that are generally seen feeding on the ground in pairs or groups, in both woodland and open country. When flushed they rise with a whirr of rapidly beating wings.

272 Capercaillie, 85 cm, *p. 428*

273 Black Grouse, 53 cm, *p. 427*

274 Red Grouse, 38–40 cm, *p. 425*

275 Great Bustard, 100 cm, *p. 451*

276 Red-legged Partridge, 34 cm, *p. 431*

277 Chukar, 33 cm, *p. 429*

278 Black-bellied Sandgrouse, 34 cm, ♀, *p. 527*

279 Pin-tailed Sandgrouse, 36 cm, ♀, *p. 528*

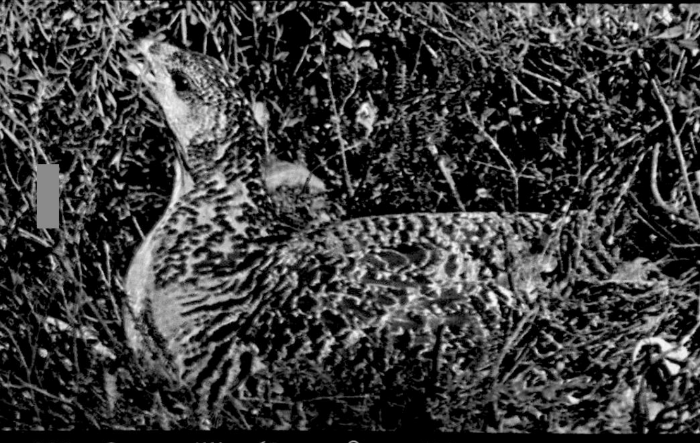

280 Capercaillie, 60 cm, ♀, *p. 428*

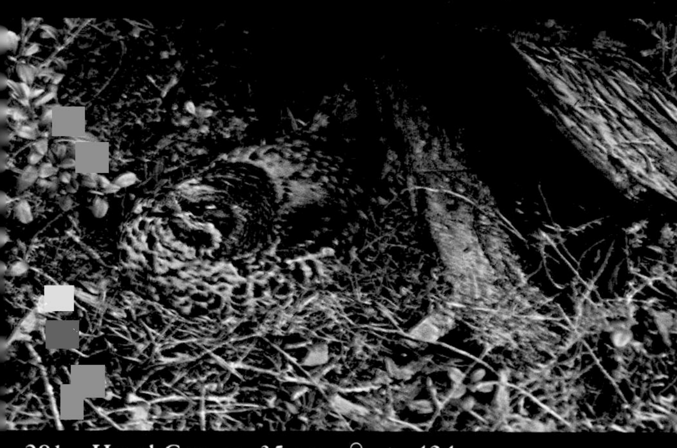

281 Hazel Grouse, 35 cm, ♀, *p. 424*

282 Little Bustard, 43 cm, ♀, *p. 450*

283 Willow Grouse, 38–40 cm, ♀, *p. 425*

284 Willow Grouse, 38–40 cm, *spring, p. 425*

285 Ptarmigan, 35 cm, *p. 426*

286 Quail, 18 cm, *p. 433*

287 Willow Grouse, 38–40 cm, ♀, *winter*, *p. 425*

288 Ptarmigan, 35 cm, *winter*, *p. 426*

289 Grey Partridge, 30 cm, *p. 432*

290 Golden Pheasant, 63–65 cm, ♀, *p. 436*

291 Pheasant, 53–63 cm, ♀, *p. 435*

292 Pheasant, 76–88 cm, *p. 435*

293 Reeve's Pheasant, 208 cm, *p. 434*

294 Lady Amherst's Pheasant, 128–168 cm, *p. 437*

295 Golden Pheasant, 98–108 cm, *p. 436*

Hawk-like Birds

These meat-eating birds of prey have sharply hooked bills and powerful feet and claws. Many species are often seen soaring high in the air. Wings may be rounded, as in the hawks and vultures, or pointed, as in falcons.

296 Egyptian Vulture, 58–65 cm, *p. 395*

297 Griffon Vulture, 95–103 cm, *imm. p. 396*

298 Lammergeier, 102–113 cm, *p. 394*

299 Black Vulture, 98–105 cm, *imm.*, *p. 397*

300 Steppe Eagle, 65–78 cm, *p. 408*

301 Lesser Spotted Eagle, 60–65 cm, *p. 407*

30? Imperial Eagle, 78–83 cm, *imm.*, *p. 409*

304 Golden Eagle, 75–88 cm, *p. 410*

305 Imperial Eagle, 78–83 cm, *Spanish race, p. 409*

306 Long-legged Buzzard, 60–65 cm, *p. 405*

307 White-tailed Eagle, 68–90 cm, *p. 393*

308 Honey Buzzard, 50–58 cm, ♀, *p. 390*

309 Goshawk, 48–60 cm, *juv., p. 402*

310 Rough-legged Buzzard, 50–60 cm, *juv.*, *p. 406*

311 Buzzard, 50–56 cm, *p. 404*

312 Osprey, 50–58 cm, *juv.*, *p. 413*

313 Short-toed Eagle, 63–68 cm, *juv.*, *p. 398*

314 Booted Eagle, 45–53 cm, *p. 411*

315 Short-toed Eagle, 63–68 cm, *p. 398*

316 Black Kite, 55 cm, *p. 392*

317 Red Kite, 60 cm, *p. 393*

318 Hen Harrier, 43–50 cm, ♀, *p. 399*

319 Montagu's Harrier, 40–45 cm, ♀, *p. 401*

320 Marsh Harrier, 48–55 cm, ♀, *p. 399*

321 Pallid Harrier, 43–48 cm, *imm.*, *p. 400*

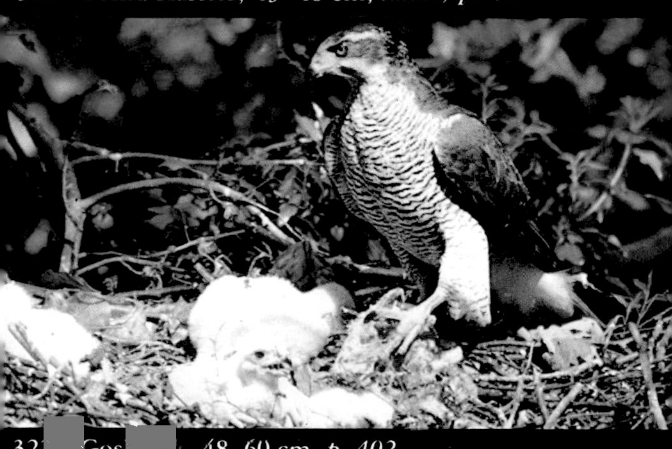

32[illegible] Gos[illegible]k, 48–60 cm, *p. 402*

323 Sparrowhawk, 28–38 cm, ♀, *p. 403*

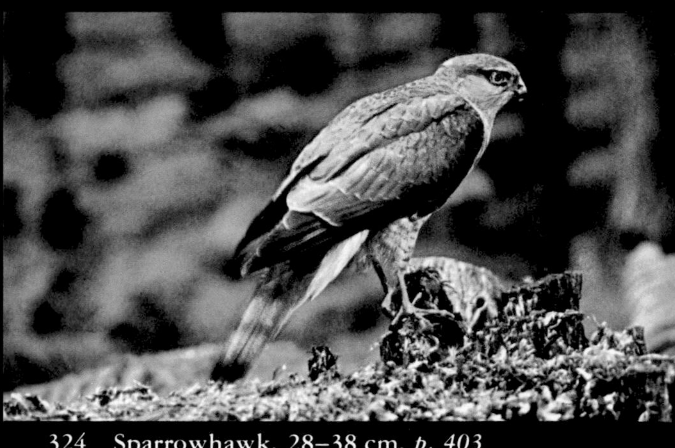

324 Sparrowhawk, 28–38 cm, *p. 403*

325 Lanner, 43 cm, *juv.*, *p. 420*

326 Hobby, 30–35 cm, *p. 418*

327 Eleonora's Falcon, 38 cm, *light phase, p. 419*

328 Eleonora's Falcon, 38 cm, *dark phase, p. 419*

329 Peregrine, 38–48 cm, *p. 423*

330 Black-shouldered Kite, 33 cm, *p. 391*

331 Pallid Harrier, 43–48 cm, *p. 400*

332 Red-footed Falcon, 30 cm, *p. 417*

333 Gyrfalcon, 50–56 cm, *p. 422*

334 Saker, 45 cm, *juv.*, *p. 421*

335 Merlin, 26–33 cm, ♀, *p. 417*

336 Red-footed Falcon, 30 cm, *juv.*, *p. 417*

337 Lesser Kestrel, 30 cm, *p. 415*

338 Kestrel, 34 cm, *imm.*, *p. 416*

339 Red Kite, 60 cm, *p. 393*

340 Black Kite, 55 cm, *p. 392*

341 Kestrel, 34 cm, ♀, *p. 416*

342 Peregrine, 38–48 cm, *p. 423*

343 Merlin, 26–33 cm, ♀, *p. 417*

344 Hobby, 30–35 cm, *p. 418*

345 Short-toed Eagle, 63–68 cm, *p. 398*

346 Osprey, 50–58 cm, *p. 413*

347 Rough-legged Buzzard, 50–60 cm, *juv.*, *p. 406*

348 Long-legged Buzzard, 60–65 cm, *p. 405*

349 Golden Eagle, 75–88 cm, *imm.*, *p. 410*

350 White-tailed Eagle, 68–90 cm, ♀, *p. 393*

351 Bonelli's Eagle, 65–73 cm, *p. 412*

352 Imperial Eagle, 78–83 cm, *imm., p. 409*

353 Steppe Eagle, 65–78 cm, *juv., p. 408*

354 Marsh Harrier, 48–55 cm, *p. 399*

355 Honey Buzzard, 50–58 cm, *p. 390*

356 Buzzard, 50–56 cm, *p. 404*

357 Montagu's Harrier, 40–45 cm, *p. 401*

358 Marsh Harrier, 48–55 cm, ♀, *p. 399*

359 Pallid Harrier, 43–48 cm, *juv.*, *p. 400*

360 Egyptian Vulture, 58–65 cm, *p. 395*

361 Lammergeier, 102–113 cm, *p. 394*

362 Griffon Vulture, 95–103 cm, *p. 396*

363 Lesser Spotted Eagle, 60–65 cm, *p. 407*

364 Spotted Eagle, 65–73 cm, *p. 408*

365 Black Vulture, 98–105 cm, *p. 397*

Owls

Small to large birds with large, round heads, owls have loose, fluffy plumage and disc-like faces. Many are nocturnal and usually roost quietly in trees during the day, but a few, such as the Snowy Owl, hunt by day and may be seen in the open.

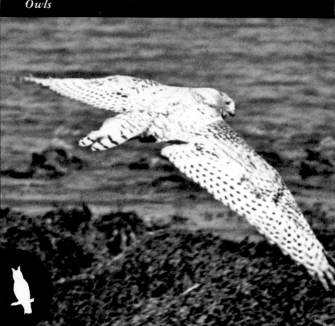

366 Snowy Owl, 53–65 cm, ♀, *p. 540*

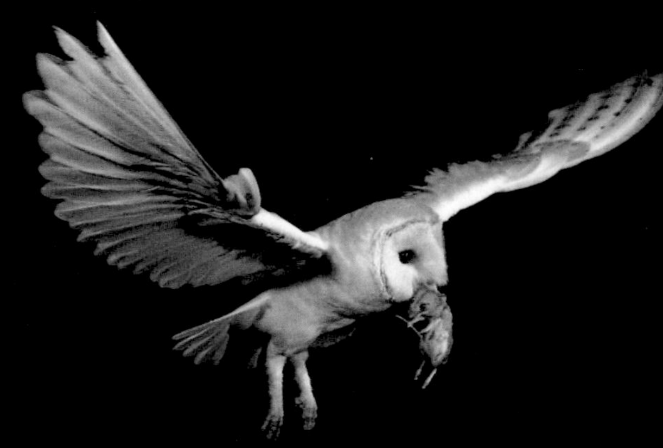

367 Barn Owl, 34 cm, *p. 537*

368 Snowy Owl, 53–65 cm, *p. 540*

369 Barn Owl, 34 cm, *p. 537*

370 Eagle Owl, 65–70 cm, *p.* 539

371 Eagle Owl, 65–70 cm, *p.* 539

372 Long-eared Owl, 35 cm, *p. 545*

373 Short-eared Owl, 38 cm, *p. 546*

374 Ural Owl, 60 cm, *p. 543*

375 Great Grey Owl, 69 cm, *p. 544*

376 Hawk Owl, 35–40 cm, *p. 540*

377 Tawny Owl, 38 cm, *p. 542*

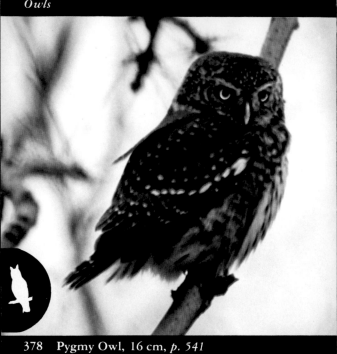

378 Pygmy Owl, 16 cm, *p. 541*

379 Little Owl, 21 cm, *p. 542*

380 Tengmalm's Owl, 25 cm, *p. 546*

381 Scops Owl, 19 cm, *p. 538*

Pigeons and Doves

These medium-sized land birds have small, rounded heads and plump bodies. The tail is fairly short and rounded in pigeons, longer and often graduated in doves. Plumage is mainly grey and brown.

382 Woodpigeon, 40 cm, *p. 531*

383 Stock Dove, 33 cm, *p. 530*

384 Rock Dove, 33 cm, *p. 529*

385 Laughing Dove, 26 cm, *p. 533*

386 Collared Dove, 31 cm, *p. 531*

387 Turtle Dove, 28 cm, *p. 532*

Cuckoos and Nightjars

Medium-sized land birds with long tails, cuckoos are usually found in trees. They are inconspicuous, except when calling. Nightjars are cryptically coloured and rest on the ground during the day, feeding by night on flying insects.

388 Cuckoo, 33 cm, *juv.*, *p. 535*

389 Nightjar, 26 cm, ♀, *p. 548*

390 Red-necked Nightjar, 30 cm, *p. 549*

391 Cuckoo, 33 cm, *p.* 535

392 Great Spotted Cuckoo, 39 cm, *juv.*, *p.* 534

393 Great Spotted Cuckoo, 39 cm, *p.* 534

Swallow-like Birds

Included here are swallows and martins and the similar but unrelated swifts. All are small aerial birds with long, pointed wings used in graceful flight to pursue their insect prey.

394 Alpine Swift, 21 cm, *p. 551*

395 Swift, 16 cm, *p. 550*

396 Sand Martin, 12 cm, *p. 573*

397 Pallid Swift, 16 cm, *p.* 551

398 House Martin, 13 cm, *p.* 576

399 Sand Martin, 12 cm, *p.* 573

400 Red-rumped Swallow, 18 cm, *p.* 575

401 Swallow, 19 cm, *p.* 574

402 Swallow, 19 cm, *p.* 574

Woodpecker-like Birds

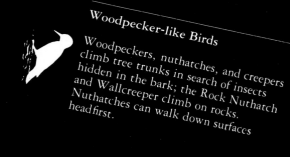

Woodpeckers, nuthatches, and creepers climb tree trunks in search of insects hidden in the bark; the Rock Nuthatch and Wallcreeper climb on rocks. Nuthatches can walk down surfaces headfirst.

403 Wryneck, 16 cm, *p.* 557

404 Black Woodpecker, 45 cm, *p.* 560

405 Grey-headed Woodpecker, 25 cm, *p.* 558

406 Green Woodpecker, 31 cm, *p.* 559

407 Lesser Spotted Woodpecker, 14 cm, *p. 564*

408 White-backed Woodpecker, 25 cm, *p. 563*

409 Great Spotted Woodpecker, 23 cm, *p. 560*

410 Middle Spotted Woodpecker, 21 cm, ♀ *p. 562*

411 Great Spotted Woodpecker, 23 cm, ♀, *p. 560*

412 Syrian Woodpecker, 23 cm, ♀, *p. 561*

413 Three-toed Woodpecker, 22 cm, *p.* 564

414 Lesser Spotted Woodpecker, 14 cm, ♀, *p.* 564

415 Rock Nuthatch, 14 cm, *p. 657*

416 Nuthatch, 14 cm, *p. 656*

417 Treecreeper, 13 cm, *p. 661*

418 Wallcreeper, 16 cm, *p. 659*

Tits

Small, active, arboreal birds, tits are often seen hanging upside down from a small branch or twig. Included here is the marsh-dwelling tit-like Bearded Tit, actually a member of the babbler family.

419 Coal Tit, 11 cm, *p. 651*

420 Marsh Tit, 11 cm, *p. 647*

421 Willow Tit, 11 cm, *p. 648*

422 Great Tit, 14 cm, *p. 653*

423 Blue Tit, 11 cm, *p. 651*

424 Blue Tit, 11 cm, *juv.*, *p. 651*

425 Siberian Tit, 13 cm, *p. 649*

426 Long-tailed Tit, 14 cm, *p. 645*

427 Bearded Tit, 16 cm, ♀, *p. 643*

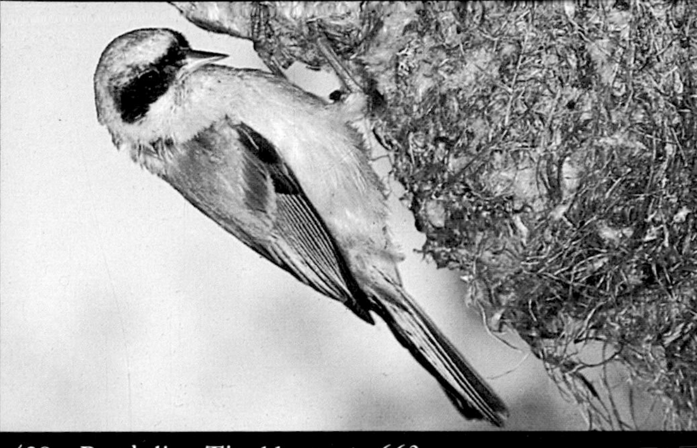
428 Penduline Tit, 11 cm, *p. 663*

429 Crested Tit, 11 cm, *p. 650*

430 Bearded Tit, 16 cm, *p. 643*

Warblers

Small, slim, insectivorous birds with thin bills, warblers are rather drably coloured brown, green, or grey. Their voices are loud and melodious. Included here is the similar-looking but unrelated Wren.

431 Blyth's Reed Warbler, 13 cm, *p. 618*

432 Garden Warbler, 14 cm, *p. 630*

433 Bonelli's Warbler, 11 cm, *p. 634*

434 Chiffchaff, 11 cm, *p. 636*

435 Willow Warbler, 11 cm, *p. 636*

436 Wood Warbler, 13 cm, *p. 635*

437 Melodious Warbler, 13 cm, *p. 623*

438 Icterine Warbler, 13 cm, *p. 622*

439 Greenish Warbler, 11 cm, *p. 632*

440 Goldcrest, 9 cm, *p. 637*

441 Arctic Warbler, 12 cm, *p. 632*

442 Firecrest, 9 cm, *p. 638*

443 Marsh Warbler, 13 cm, *p. 619*

444 River Warbler, 13 cm, *p. 614*

445 Reed Warbler, 13 cm, *p. 619*

446 Great Reed Warbler, 19 cm, *p. 620*

447 Savi's Warbler, 14 cm, *p. 614*

448 Whitethroat, 14 cm, ♀, *p. 630*

449 Whitethroat, 14 cm, *p. 630*

450 Spectacled Warbler, 12, cm, *p. 625*

451 Lesser Whitethroat, 13 cm, *p. 629*

452 Orphean Warbler, 15 cm, *p. 628*

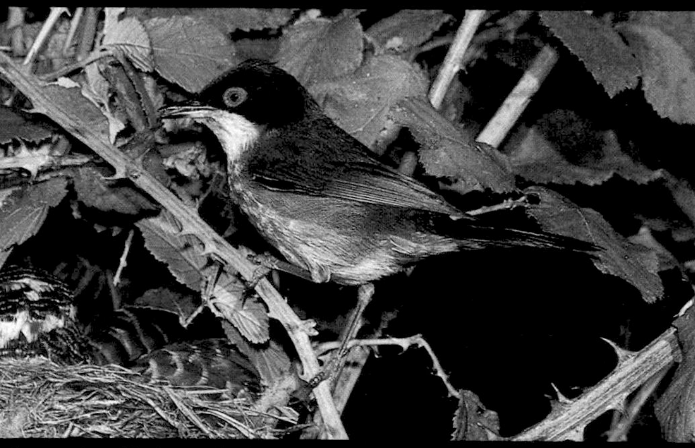

453 Sardinian Warbler, 13 cm, *p. 626*

454 Rüppell's Warbler, 14 cm, *p. 627*

455 Dartford Warbler, 13 cm, ♀, *p. 624*

456 Blackcap, 14 cm, *p. 631*

457 Marmora's Warbler, 12 cm, ♀, *p. 623*

458 Subalpine Warbler, 12 cm, *p. 625*

459 Cetti's Warbler, 14 cm, *p. 612*

460 Wren, 9 cm, *p. 590*

461 Moustached Warbler, 13 cm, *p. 615*

462 Sedge Warbler, 13 cm, *p. 617*

463 Aquatic Warbler, 13 cm, *p. 616*

464 Fan-tailed Warbler, 10 cm, *p. 613*

465 Grasshopper Warbler, 13 cm, *p. 613*

466 Barred Warbler, 15 cm, *p. 628*

Thrush-like Birds

This group includes medium-small, plump land birds with an upright stance. The Robin and Blackbird are true thrushes; starlings and the Dipper are thrush-like in appearance. Larger thrushes are common on lawns, where they eat worms; others feed in trees.

467 Bluethroat, 14 cm, *white-spotted race*, *p.* 597

468 Bluethroat, 14 cm, *red-spotted race*, *p.* 597

469 Red-flanked Bluetail, 14 cm, *p.* 598

470 Robin, 14 cm, *p. 595*

471 Rock Thrush, 19 cm, *p. 606*

472 Stonechat, 13 cm, *p. 601*

473 Black Redstart, 14 cm, *p. 598*

474 Redstart, 14 cm, *p. 599*

475 Redstart, 14 cm, ♀, *p. 599*

476 Black Redstart, 14 cm, ♀, *p. 598*

477 Blue Rock Thrush, 20 cm, ♀, *p. 607*

479 Wheatear, 14 cm, *p. 602*

480 Black-eared Wheatear, 14 cm, *p. 604*

481 Black-eared Wheatear, 14 cm, *p. 604*

482 Rose-coloured Starling, 21 cm, *p. 681*

483 Ring Ouzel, 24 cm, *p. 607*

484 Dipper, 18 cm, *p. 589*

485 Black Wheatear, 18 cm, ♀, *p. 605*

486 Blackbird, 25 cm, ♀, *p. 608*

487 Starling, 21 cm, *juv.*, *p. 680*

488 Ring Ouzel, 24 cm, ♀, *p. 607*

489 Robin, 14 cm, *juv.*, *p. 595*

490 Fieldfare, 25 cm, *p. 609*

491 Stonechat, 13 cm, ♀, *p. 601*

492 Whinchat, 13 cm, ♀, *p. 600*

493 Whinchat, 13 cm, *p. 600*

494 Wheatear, 14 cm, *juv.*, *p. 602*

495 Isabelline Wheatear, 16 cm, *p. 602*

497 Rufous Bush Robin, 15 cm, *p. 594*

498 Nightingale, 16 cm, *p. 596*

499 Thrush Nightingale, 16 cm, *p. 595*

500 Redwing, 21 cm, *p. 610*

501 Song Thrush, 23 cm, *p. 609*

502 Mistle Thrush, 26 cm, *p. 611*

503 Starling, 21 cm, *winter, p. 680*

504 Starling, 21 cm, *p. 680*

505 Blackbird, 25 cm, *p. 608*

Flycatcher-like Birds

Flycatchers and shrikes are insectivorous birds that sit on a prominent perch watching for prey. Flycatchers catch insects in the air, often returning to the same perch; shrikes capture most prey on the ground; they also take lizards and small birds.

506 Red-breasted Flycatcher, 11 cm, *p. 640*

507 Woodchat Shrike, 17 cm, *p. 668*

508 Red-backed Shrike 17 cm, *p. 665*

509 Great Grey Shrike, 24 cm, *p. 667*

510 Masked Shrike, 17 cm, *p. 669*

511 Lesser Grey Shrike, 20 cm, *juv.*, *p. 666*

512 Pied Flycatcher, 13 cm, *p. 642*

513 Collared Flycatcher, 13 cm, *p. 641*

514 Pied Flycatcher, 13 cm, ♀, *p. 642*

515 Woodchat Shrike, 17 cm, *juv.*, *p. 668*

516 Red-backed Shrike, 17 cm, ♀, *p. 665*

517 Spotted Flycatcher, 14 cm, *p. 639*

Wagtails, Larks, and Pipits

This group includes small, insectivorous birds found on the ground. The closely related wagtails and pipits both wag their tails, unlike larks. Pipits and larks are streaked brown; wagtails are patterned in combinations of black, white, grey, and yellow.

518 Yellow Wagtail, 16 cm, *p. 583*

519 Yellow Wagtail, 16 cm, ♀, *p. 583*

520 Yellow Wagtail, 16 cm, *blue-headed race*, *p. 583*

521 Grey Wagtail, 18 cm, *p. 584*

522 Yellow Wagtail, 16 cm, *grey-headed race, p. 583*

523 Yellow Wagtail, 16 cm, *black-headed race, p. 583*

524 Pied Wagtail, 18 cm, *p.* 585

525 White Wagtail, 18 cm, *p.* 585

526 Shore Lark, 16 cm, *p.* 572

527 Thekla Lark, 16 cm, *p.* 569

528 Crested Lark, 17 cm, *p.* 568

529 Skylark, 18 cm, *p.* 571

530 Tree Pipit, 15 cm, *p. 580*

531 Meadow Pipit, 14 cm, *p. 580*

532 Red-throated Pipit, 14 cm, *p. 581*

533 Rock Pipit, 16 cm, *p. 582*

534 Water Pipit, 16 cm, *p. 582*

Water Pipit, 16 cm, *winter*, *p. 582*

536 Tawny Pipit, 16 cm, *p.* 579

537 Richard's Pipit, 18 cm, *p.* 578

538 Woodlark, 15 cm, *p.* 570

539 Lesser Short-toed Lark, 14 cm, *p. 568*

540 Short-toed Lark, 14 cm, *p. 567*

541 Calandra Lark, 19 cm, *p. 566*

Sparrow-like Birds

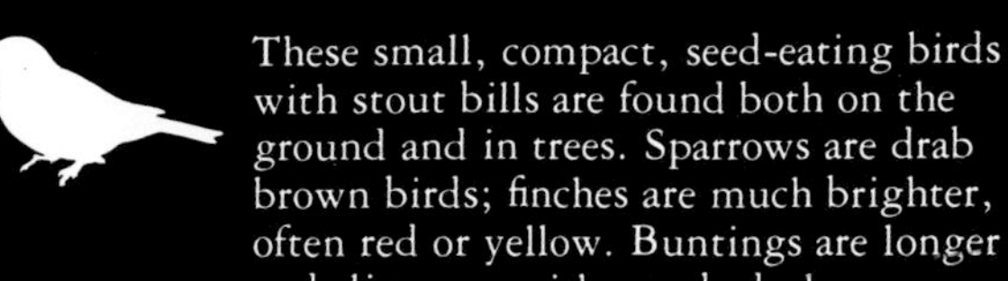

These small, compact, seed-eating birds with stout bills are found both on the ground and in trees. Sparrows are drab brown birds; finches are much brighter, often red or yellow. Buntings are longer and slimmer, with streaked plumage.

542 Two-barred Crossbill, 14 cm, *p. 697*

543 Pine Grosbeak, 20 cm, *p. 701*

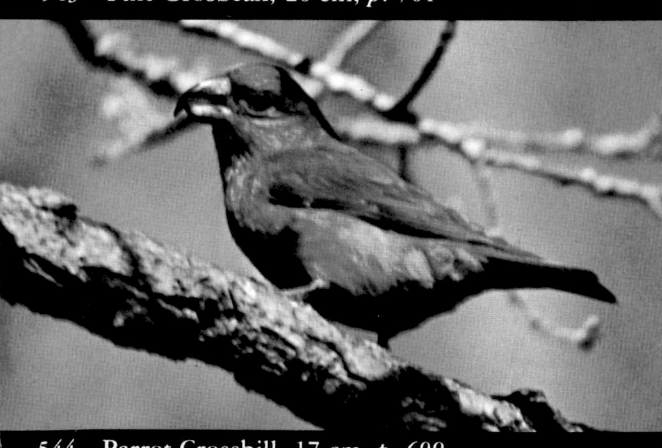

544 Parrot Crossbill, 17 cm, *p. 699*

545 Scarlet Rosefinch, 14 cm, ♀ *(l.)*, ♂ *(r.)*, *p. 701*

546 Linnet, 13 cm, *p. 694*

547 Crossbill, 16 cm, *p. 698*

548 Redpoll, 13–15 cm, *p. 695*

549 Arctic Redpoll, 13 cm, *p. 696*

550 Goldfinch, 12 cm, *p. 692*

551 Brambling, 14 cm, *winter*, *p. 689*

552 Chaffinch, 15 cm, *p. 688*

553 Bullfinch, 14–16 cm, *p. 702*

554 Hawfinch, 18 cm, *winter*, *p. 703*

555 Brambling, 14 cm, ♂ *(l.)*, ♀ *(r.)*, *p. 689*

556 Bullfinch, 14–16 cm, ♀, *p. 702*

557 Pine Grosbeak, 20 cm, ♀, *p. 701*

558 Chaffinch, 15 cm, ♀, *p. 688*

559 Two-barred Crossbill, 14 cm, ♀, *p. 697*

560 Black-headed Bunting, 16 cm, *p. 715*

561 Yellow-breasted Bunting, 14 cm, *p. 713*

562 Siskin, 12 cm, *p. 693*

563 Citril Finch, 12 cm, ♀ *(l.)*, ♂ *(r.)*, *p. 690*

564 Serin, 11 cm, ♂ *(l.)*, ♀ *(r.)*, *p. 690*

565 Yellow-breasted Bunting, 14 cm, ♀, *p. 713*

566 Greenfinch, 14 cm, *p. 691*

567 Greenfinch, 14 cm, ♀, *p. 691*

568 Crossbill, 16 cm, ♀, *p. 698*

569 Cirl Bunting, 16 cm, *p. 708*

570 Yellowhammer, 16 cm, *p. 707*

571 Siskin, 12 cm, ♀, *p. 693*

572 Twite, 13 cm, *winter, p. 695*

573 Corn Bunting, 18 cm, *p. 716*

574 Cirl Bunting, 16 cm, ♀, *p. 708*

575 Linnet, 13 cm, ♀, *p. 694*

576 House Sparrow, 14 cm, ♀, *p. 683*

577 Rock Sparrow, 14 cm, *p. 686*

578 Ortolan Bunting, 16 cm, *p. 710*

579 Little Bunting, 13 cm, *p. 713*

580 Snow Bunting, 16 cm, *winter*, *p. 706*

581 Snow Bunting, 16 cm, ♀, *p. 706*

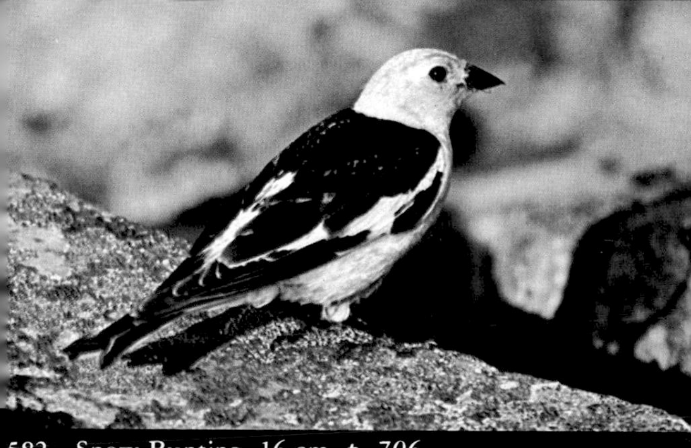

582 Snow Bunting, 16 cm, *p. 706*

584 Cretzschmar's Bunting, 16 cm, *p. 711*

585 Alpine Accentor, 18 cm, *p. 593*

586 Dunnock, 14 cm, *p. 592*

587 House Sparrow, 14 cm, *p. 683*

588 Spanish Sparrow, 14 cm, *p. 684*

589 Tree Sparrow, 14 cm, *p. 685*

590 Rock Bunting, 16 cm, *p. 708*

591 Lapland Bunting, 15 cm, ♀, *p. 705*

592 Reed Bunting, 15 cm, ♀, *p. 714*

593 Rustic Bunting, 14 cm, *p.* 712

594 Lapland Bunting, 15 cm, *p.* 705

595 Reed Bunting, 15 cm, *p.* 714

Crow-like Birds

Crows, magpies, and jays are large, perching birds with stout bills; all are intelligent and wary. Crows are entirely or mainly black; magpies are long-tailed and more colourful; jays are also colourful but have shorter tails.

596 Chough, 38 cm, *p. 675*

597 Alpine Chough, 38 cm, *p. 674*

598 Rook, 45 cm, *p. 676*

599 Raven, 63 cm, *p. 678*

600 Carrion Crow, 46 cm, *p. 677*

601 Jackdaw, 33 cm, *p. 676*

602 Hooded Crow, 46 cm, *p. 677*

603 Magpie, 45 cm, *p. 672*

604 Azure-winged Magpie, 34 cm, *p. 672*

605 Nutcracker, 31 cm, *Slender-billed, p. 673*

606 Jay, 34 cm, *p. 670*

607 Siberian Jay, 30 cm, *p. 671*

Exotic-looking Birds

Included here are birds with exotic colouration or peculiar shape that might be hard for the novice to assign to any other group. All six are the sole representatives of their families in Europe.

608 Golden Oriole, 24 cm, *p. 664*

609 Bee-eater, 28 cm, *p. 554*

610 Kingfisher, 16 cm, *p. 553*

611 Roller, 30 cm, *p.* 555

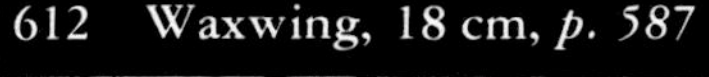

612 Waxwing, 18 cm, *p.* 587

613 Hoopoe, 28 cm, *p.* 556

Part II
Family and Species Descriptions

The number preceding each species description in the following pages corresponds to the plate number in the colour section. If the description has no plate number, it is illustrated by a drawing that accompanies the text.

DIVERS
(Gaviidae)

4 species: northern Eurasia and North America. Three breed in Europe, one is a winter visitor. Large aquatic birds with long, pointed bills and webbed feet. Legs set far back on body, making them expert swimmers and divers but clumsy on land. Able to stay underwater for long periods, traveling considerable distances before surfacing. Frequently swim with their backs awash. In flight, head and neck extended and inclined downward, giving a hump-backed look. Breed on freshwater lakes and rivers and winter mainly on coasts. Diet consists chiefly of fish. Silent except during breeding season. Sexes similar.

4, 15 Red-throated Diver
(*Gavia stellata*)

Description: 21–27″ (53–68 cm). Slimmest diver, with *slender, upturned bill*. Head typically held tilted up. In breeding plumage head and neck grey with red throat patch, upperparts plain grey-brown. At a distance throat patch looks black, causing confusion with Black-throated Diver, but latter has black chin and upperparts patterned black and white. In winter, upperparts finely spotted white, and face and eye-ring white.

Voice: A repeated, rapid, duck-like quacking, often uttered in flight; a long, high-pitched wail; and a variety of cackling and growling notes.

Habitat: Breeds mainly on small lakes and ponds on moorland and tundra. In winter, mainly on coast, but occasionally also on lakes and reservoirs inland.

Nesting: 2 dark-spotted, olive eggs, in grass-lined depression or mass of damp vegetation at water's edge. Both sexes incubate and feed young.

Range: Holarctic, breeding in Iceland,

Scotland, northern Ireland, Fenno-Scandia, and Baltic states, and in northern Asia and North America. Winters from breeding range south to Iberia, western Mediterranean, northern Adriatic, and Black Sea.

It is more sociable than other divers, sometimes forming quite large flocks at sea in winter and on migration. In courtship ceremony, several birds swim together with stiff necks and partly submerged bodies.

3 Black-throated Diver

(*Gavia arctica*)

winter

Description: 22–29″ (55–73 cm). Slightly larger and stockier than Red-throated Diver, but considerably slimmer and smaller than Great Northern. Bill likewise intermediate in size, *less stout* than Great Northern, nearly as slim as Red-throated, but *straight.* In breeding plumage *head and hindneck grey; chin* and *throat black;* sides of neck and breast striped black and white; upperparts black with patches of white stripes. In winter, darker above than Red-throated, lacking white around eye. Resembles Great Northern, but *crown and hindneck generally paler than back;* head more rounded, less angular; upperparts more uniformly dark (scaly in young birds).

Voice: A deep, guttural *kow-hoo* and a mournful, rising wail.

Habitat: Breeds on large lakes in open and wooded country, in hills or in lowlands. Winters on coast; occasionally also on inland lakes and reservoirs.

Nesting: 2 olive-green to dark brown eggs with black, widely scattered spots, laid in shallow scrape close to water, usually on an islet.

Range: Holarctic, breeding in Scotland, Fenno-Scandia, Baltic states, and northern Poland; and northern Asia and North

America. Winters from breeding range south to northern Iberia and Adriatic, Aegean, and Black seas.

It remains submerged from 30 seconds to 1 minute, though some dives last as long as 2 minutes. Divers move fast underwater and often surface 100 yards (90 m) or more from where they submerged.

2, 16 **Great Northern Diver**
(*Gavia immer*)

Description: 27–36" (68–90 cm). Large, goose-sized bird with *heavy, straight bill*. In breeding plumage head and neck black, with necklace and throat band of vertical white stripes; upperparts black, spotted with white. Bill black. In winter, dark above and light below, when *heavier build, thicker neck and bill, steeper forehead, and flatter crown* distinguish it from smaller species. Bill paler in winter, often extensively bluish-white, causing confusion with White-billed Diver.

Voice: A long, mournful wail becoming louder in middle and trailing away at end; a shorter, high-pitched *hee-oo-ee;* a curious hollow "laugh"; and a flight note, *gek*.

Habitat: Breeds on small islets and promontories on deep lakes both in mountains and lowlands. Winters mainly along coasts, rarely on lakes and reservoirs.

Nesting: 2, occasionally 1, olive to dark brown eggs with small dark spots, on mound of vegetation by water's edge.

Range: Breeds in Iceland, Greenland, and across northern North America to Alaska. Winters on coasts of northern and western Europe from Iceland and Norway to Iberia.

The wailing cries and maniacal "laughing" of divers account for their name in North America, where this species is called Common Loon. Divers dive from the water's surface. In their pursuit of fish they are sometimes caught in fishing nets and have been taken at depths of 200′ (60 m).

1, 14 **White-billed Diver**
(*Gavia adamsii*)

Description: 30–36″ (75–90 cm). Largest and heaviest diver; similar to Great Northern in breeding plumage except for *whitish* or *ivory-yellow bill.* In winter, *bill remains completely pale* (Great Northern has dark ridge along top of pale bill). *Head and bill often tilted upward,* like Red-throated Diver (Great Northern holds head straight). In winter, *cheeks and sides of neck* paler than Great Northern.

Voice: Wailing and "laughing" calls like those of Great Northern.

Habitat: Nests on lakes of high Arctic tundra, beyond tree limit; winters on coasts.

Nesting: 2 olive to brown eggs with dark, widely scattered spots. Nest like Great Northern but sometimes uses mud platform.

Range: Holarctic, breeding in northern Asia and North America. Winters on coast of northern Norway; vagrant elsewhere in Europe.

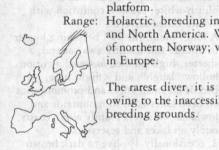

The rarest diver, it is little known owing to the inaccessibility of its Arctic breeding grounds.

GREBES
(Podicipedidae)

21 species: worldwide. Five species in Europe, all breeding. Small to medium-sized aquatic birds with thin, pointed bill and lobed toes. Neck longer than divers' and body more squat, giving a tailless appearance. Legs set far back on body, making swimming and diving efficient but walking difficult. Head and neck extended in flight and inclined downward, giving a humped appearance. Fly with rapid wingbeats on rather small wings. Most species display white patches on wings in flight. Sexes similar. Juveniles have striped head and neck. Some species have ornamental head plumes during breeding season, used in elaborate courtship displays. Breed on freshwater lakes, ponds, and slow-flowing rivers and winter on both fresh water and coasts.

6, 8 Little Grebe
(*Tachybaptus ruficollis*)

Description: 10½" (26 cm). Smallest grebe in Europe, with *short neck and rounded body.* In summer, dark brown above, lighter on flanks, with *chestnut cheeks and front of neck* and *pale streak at base of bill;* bill dark with pale tip. In winter, throat, front of neck, and flanks buffy; no bill patch. In flight, wings show no white. Juvenile has dark stripes on sides of head and neck.

Voice: A loud, high-pitched, rippling trill. Alarm, *whit, whit.*

Habitat: Breeds on lakes, ponds, and reservoirs, and along slow-flowing rivers and canals. Winters in similar habitat, but also on coast in estuaries and bays.

Nesting: 4–6 white eggs in a floating heap of rotting vegetation in shallow water, among aquatic plants or under overhanging branches.

Range: Breeds over most of southern and central Europe, retiring from eastern parts of its range in winter. Also breeds in central and southern Asia; Africa.

The Little Grebe is a common species whose whinnying call is a familiar sound in spring and summer. Rather shy during the breeding season, it spends much time in cover but is more visible in winter, when it is often seen in open water, sometimes in considerable flocks.

---

5 Great Crested Grebe
(*Podiceps cristatus*)

Description: 19″ (48 cm). Largest European grebe. Breeding adults have *black crest, broad frills—chestnut tipped with black—on sides of head,* white face, and *pink bill;* grey-brown above, neck and underparts white. In winter, frills and crest disappear. Distinguished from smaller Red-necked Grebe by *longer, thin white-fronted neck,* long pink-based bill, and *white line between eye and bill.*

winter

Voice: A wide repertoire of barking, growling, croaking, and clicking calls.

Habitat: Breeds on large lakes, reservoirs, and canals with some fringe vegetation. Winters on both fresh water and salt water in sheltered situations.

Nesting: 3–6 white eggs placed in a shapeless mass of aquatic vegetation in reeds near edge of water, either floating or resting on shallow bottom.

Range: Breeds in most of Europe except north; local in Mediterranean area. Moves away from northern and eastern parts of range in winter. Also breeds across central Asia to China, locally in Africa, and in Australasia.

Though slaughtered by plume hunters in the 19th century, it has since increased in many countries through protective laws and the creation of new habitats. It is known for striking courtship displays in which the crest is raised and facial plumes spread to form a ruff. In one phase of the display, the pair face each other with stretched necks and shake their heads from side to side.

7, 13 Red-necked Grebe
(*Podiceps grisegena*)

Description: 17″ (43 cm). A stocky grebe, easily identified in summer by *reddish-chestnut neck, pale grey cheeks, and black crown; yellow bill with black tip.* Two small ear tufts give head a square look. Back grey-brown, underparts white, flanks mottled brown. In winter, neck becomes grey, but cheeks remain noticeably whiter. Smaller than winter Great Crested Grebe, with shorter, dark-fronted neck, *black crown extending below eye,* and dark bill with yellow base. Flight pattern similar to Great Crested Grebe.

Voice: Whinnying and wailing calls during breeding season; also quacking notes.

Habitat: Breeds on small, shallow inland lakes and ponds, wintering chiefly along sheltered coasts, sometimes on larger lakes and reservoirs.

Nesting: 4–5 white eggs, laid in mound of decaying aquatic plants built in shallow water with some vegetation cover.

Range: Holarctic. Breeds in eastern Europe, west to Denmark and Balkans, wintering west and south to Britain, Italy, and Greece; also breeds in western and eastern Asia, and in North America.

During the breeding season the Red-necked Grebe is found chiefly in lowland areas. In summer it eats mainly insects; in winter, small fish.

9, 11 Slavonian Grebe
(*Podiceps auritus*)

Description: 13″ (33 cm). Slightly larger and longer-necked than Black-necked Grebe. Summer adults have black head with projecting *tuft of golden feathers behind eye, forming two bumps or "horns." Neck, breast, and flanks bright reddish-chestnut;* back dark brown; rest of underparts white. In winter, distinguished from similar Black-necked Grebe by *straight bill,* flat forehead, *dark crown not extending below eye,* and white front to neck.

Voice: A rippling trill and a variety of cackling and other calls during breeding season.

Habitat: Breeds on inland lakes and ponds. Winters mainly on coast in sheltered bays and estuaries, sometimes on large inland lakes.

Nesting: 3–5 white eggs in low mound of aquatic plants, built in shallow water among tall vegetation.

Range: Holarctic, breeding from Iceland, Scotland, and Scandinavia across northern Asia to eastern Siberia, and in North America. Winters mainly in coastal waters south to France, Italy, and the Black Sea.

The Slavonian replaces the Black-necked Grebe in the north in summer; their breeding ranges overlap only in the Baltic States. In winter, they are often found together, though the Black-necked favours fresh water while the Slavonian prefers salt.

10, 12 Black-necked Grebe
(*Podiceps nigricollis*)

Description: 12″ (30 cm). Breeding adults have *black head, neck, and upperparts* with *tuft of golden feathers fanning out behind eye.* Underparts white, sides of breast and flanks chestnut. Bill short and slender with distinct *upward tilt.* Crown feathers often raised, giving it a high forehead, in silhouette different from Slavonian Grebe. In winter, similar to Slavonian, but bill shape different, and black crown extends below eye to *dark ear coverts,* and front of neck dusky.

Voice: A plaintive, slurred *poo-eee;* also some trilling and chittering calls during breeding season.

Habitat: Breeds in small, loose colonies on shallow, well-vegetated lakes and ponds, moving in winter to larger, more open waters and to sheltered bays and estuaries along coasts.

Nesting: 3–5 white eggs in low mound of aquatic plants, usually in cover of reeds or other waterside vegetation.

Range: Breeds locally in east-central Europe and in scattered colonies west to Spain, France, and Scotland, moving west and south in winter. Also breeds in central and northeast Asia, North America, locally in Africa.

The location of breeding colonies frequently changes, especially in the drier parts of its range, where the availability of suitable pools varies according to shifting rainfall patterns. Feeds on insects and their larvae, catching some on the water's surface.

ALBATROSSES
(Diomedeidae)

14 species: mainly southern oceans. One species a rare visitor to Europe. Huge seabirds with large head; powerful bill with hooked tip; tubed nostrils; webbed feet; and extremely long, narrow wings. Remarkable fliers, gliding long distances on stiff wings. They also alight on water. Feed on marine animals, principally squid. Breed colonially on remote islands; pelagic the rest of the year.

29 Black-browed Albatross
(*Diomedea melanophris*)

Description: 31–37″ (78–93 cm). Wingspan 7–8′ (2.1–2.4 m). Rare visitor from the Southern Hemisphere, resembling Great Black-backed Gull, but is much larger and has *stiff-winged flight.* Back and wings black, body white, bill yellow. *Black tail, black line through eye,* and *dark underwing with broad white central stripe.* Young birds have dark smudge on crown and nape and dark underside of wing; bill grey-black.

Voice: Braying and grunting calls on breeding grounds; peevish croaking notes while feeding at sea.

Habitat: Breeds on remote oceanic islands; spends rest of year on open ocean.

Nesting: 1 white egg sparsely marked with red-brown spots, laid in a mud or earth nest on steep hillside near sea.

Range: Breeds on islands off South America and New Zealand and elsewhere in southern oceans, moving north after breeding. Accidental in northwestern Europe, principally off Britain and Ireland.

The only albatross occurring with any frequency in Europe, it is principally oceanic and regularly follows ships but will also feed around harbours with gulls.

SHEARWATERS, PETRELS, AND FULMARS
(Procellariidae)

56 species: worldwide, but chiefly southern hemisphere. Three species breed in Europe; three others are visitors. Medium-sized seabirds with slender, hooked bill; tubed nostrils; long, narrow wings; and webbed feet. Fulmars stouter and more gull-like than shearwaters. Pelagic, coming to land only to breed. Glide on stiff wings, alternately rising and planing down to "shear" the water's surface. Feed on fish, squid, and plankton and often follow boats for fish scraps.

31, 34 **Fulmar or Northern Fulmar**
(*Fulmarus glacialis*)

Description: 18½" (46 cm). Large, chunky petrel with *short, thick neck.* Light phase, with white head and body and grey back and wings, superficially resembles a gull, but has *stiff-winged gliding flight, grey tail, dark grey primaries with light patch at base,* and *short, yellow bill.* Less common dark (northern) phase is entirely bluish-grey except for distinctive pattern on primaries.

Voice: Grunting and cackling calls while feeding at sea, and a variety of growling and chuckling calls given on breeding cliffs.

Habitat: Pelagic. Breeds colonially on coastal cliffs; also on turf of island. Spends rest of year at sea.

Nesting: 1 white egg, laid on bare rock ledge; sometimes in hollow in earth.

Range: Breeds in Iceland, Norway (local), Britain, and Ireland, and northwest France, wintering at sea within this area. Also breeds in western Atlantic and North Pacific.

Its breeding range in Europe has been expanding for two hundred years, and it is now a common bird in northern waters, some colonies numbering tens of thousands. It follows ships, particularly fishing vessels.

---

37 Cory's Shearwater
(*Calonectris diomedea*)

Description: 18″ (45 cm). Largest European shearwater; same length as Great, but with heavier body, broader wings, and more *lumbering, less stiff-winged flight.* Upperparts grey-brown, lighter than Great; rump and tail usually grey-brown but *sometimes has narrow white band at base of tail* similar to Great. *Grey-brown crown and cheeks merge gradually into white of underparts.*

Voice: On breeding grounds, a snoring *gyawa* and a higher-pitched *aawi* or *eewi;* when produced at night by dozens of birds, has an eerie effect.

Habitat: Breeds on coasts of islands. Largely pelagic; prefers relatively warm waters.

Nesting: 1 white egg, placed in crevice among rocks or in burrow in hard ground.

Range: Breeds on islands in Mediterranean and eastern North Atlantic from Portugal and Azores south. After breeding season, some birds wander north to southwest Ireland; principal wintering grounds off South Africa.

While usually ignoring ships, Cory's Shearwater will sometimes follow fishing boats and feed on oily offal. The diet consists mainly of small squid, fish, and crustaceans. A strong flier, it is seldom blown to land by gales. Also spends much time sitting on the water, often in flocks.

---

36 Great Shearwater
(*Puffinus gravis*)

Description: 18″ (45 cm). A large shearwater, distinguished from similar-sized Cory's by *dark cap sharply contrasting with white cheeks and throat,* variable *pale collar around back of neck,* darker brown upperparts, white band at base of tail (some Cory's also have this), and *dark bill.* Underparts largely white; dark patch on belly. Stiff-winged glides interspersed with rapid wingbeats.

Voice: Croaking calls at night in burrows.

Habitat: Breeds on islands where it can excavate burrows; otherwise pelagic, preferring colder waters than Cory's.

Nesting: 1 white egg, placed in burrow on grassy slope.

Range: Breeds on Gough and Tristan da Cunha islands in South Atlantic, moving to North Atlantic during southern winter. Occurs annually on open ocean off western Europe, occasionally in large numbers; most common July–October.

It migrates annually from its southern breeding grounds across the equator, making a circular tour of the North Atlantic. From Brazil it heads northwest, passing the West Indies and coasts of eastern North America to reach Labrador and Greenland. After turning east to Iceland, Britain, and Ireland, it heads south through the eastern half of the ocean. Breeding birds return to their colonies by September, though nonbreeders may linger later in the north.

---

32 Sooty Shearwater
(*Puffinus griseus*)

Description: 16″ (40 cm). *Uniform dark sooty-brown* except for *pale stripe down centre of underwing;* looks all black at a distance. Slimmer and narrower-winged than dark-phase Fulmar, which is larger and paler, with mottled primaries.

Voice: Guttural, choking noises on breeding grounds. Generally silent at sea.

Habitat: Breeds colonially on islands where it can excavate burrows. Otherwise mainly pelagic, preferring cold waters, but frequently occurring offshore.

Nesting: 1 white egg, placed in long burrow excavated under grass tussock.

Range: Breeds on islands in southern oceans. Annual visitor to waters off western Europe, reaching Iceland, Norway, and North Sea, rarely western Mediterranean. Largest numbers appear in August and September.

Like the Great Shearwater, it circumnavigates the North Atlantic during the northern summer in a clockwise circuit, appearing in European waters in late summer. Diet consists of squid, crustaceans, and fish.

---

40 **Manx Shearwater**
(*Puffinus puffinus*)

Description: 14" (35 cm). Most common European shearwater; *dark above, light below.* Plumage varies geographically. Atlantic birds (*P. p. puffinus*) blackish above and pure white below, including underside of wing. Birds from eastern Mediterranean and Black Sea (*P. p. yelkouan*) browner above with brownish wash on underwing and flanks. West Mediterranean birds (*P. p. mauretanicus,* "Balearic Shearwater") have brown upperparts and light brown body, suggesting Sooty Shearwater, but body always considerably paler than upperparts.

Voice: A variety of loud cackling, cawing, and crooning noises made at night on breeding grounds, swelling into impressive chorus in large colonies.

Habitat: Breeds on earthen areas on offshore islands, sometimes on mainland clifftops. At other times marine, usually in offshore waters rather than deep oceans.

Nesting: 1 white egg, placed in burrow; nest chamber lined with dry grass and other plant material. Also in crevice among rocks.

Range: Breeds in Iceland, Faeroes, Britain and Ireland, northwest France (very rare), and many places in Mediterranean; also Azores and Madeira.

Breeds in the Atlantic in colonies that often number in the tens of thousands, migrating great distances to southeastern South America; small numbers also occur in summer off New England and eastern Canada. Mediterranean birds disperse after breeding, some remaining within the Mediterranean, others moving into the Atlantic, spreading north to Britain and south to Morocco.

Little Shearwater
(*Puffinus assimilis*)

Description: 11″ (28 cm). *Black above and white below;* very similar to Atlantic race of Manx Shearwater but *smaller,* with more *fluttering flight*—rapid wingbeats and fewer glides. Smaller and shorter bill; black of crown does not extend below eye. Race *P. a. baroli* (Madeira and Canaries) has white undertail coverts like Manx; *P. a. boydi* (Cape Verde Islands) has dark undertail coverts.

Voice: A laughing call, *ha-HA-ha-ha-ha-HOOO,* on the breeding grounds.

Habitat: Breeds on islands in rocky or turfy situations. Pelagic, preferring warm waters, usually staying close to breeding sites.

Nesting: 1 white egg, in hole or rock crevice.

Range: Breeds in North Atlantic on Azores, Madeira, Canaries, and Cape Verde islands, and in the South Atlantic, Pacific, and Indian oceans. Ranges north in nonbreeding season to seas off Spain and occasionally Ireland.

It does not make long-distance migrations, spending much of the year near nesting islands, dispersing to some extent after breeding. A few sighting records from seas off Ireland in recent years suggest it may be annual there. It may often be overlooked among flocks of the much more common Manx Shearwater.

STORM PETRELS
(Hydrobatidae)

21 species: worldwide. Two species breed in Europe; one other is a visitor. Small seabirds with thin, hooked bill and tubed nostrils; most species black with white rump and webbed feet. Flight close to water's surface. When feeding, they hover over water and dip down to the surface, occasionally alighting and diving. Diet consists of small fish, crustaceans, and plankton. Breed colonially in crevices and burrows on offshore islands, coming to land only at night. Sexes similar.

35 Wilson's Petrel
(*Oceanites oceanicus*)

Description: 7″ (18 cm). Similar to Storm Petrel, black with white rump and square tail, but *yellow webbed feet usually project beyond tail in flight,* pale wing bar broader. Similar *fluttering flight* but with *longer glides.*

Voice: Chattering calls in nest burrow, similar calls made by feeding flocks at sea. Generally silent outside breeding season.

Habitat: Breeds on remote rocky islands. Otherwise mainly pelagic, but more often found closer to shore than other petrels.

Nesting: 1 white egg in nest chamber lined with root fragments, at end of earthen burrow or in hole among rocks.

Range: Antarctic and subantarctic islands, migrating north into all oceans. Summer visitor to seas off Iberia and Bay of Biscay; vagrant in Britain and Ireland.

Sometimes cited as the world's most abundant seabird—and one of the most abundant birds in the world—Wilson's Petrel numbers in the hundreds of millions. It regularly follows ships and fishing boats and thousands occur around Antarctic whaling stations. It hovers and patters over water like other storm petrels and also "walks on water," planing over the surface with outstretched wings and periodically dipping its feet into the water.

38 **Storm Petrel**
(*Hydrobates pelagicus*)

Description: 6″ (15 cm). *Smaller and blacker* than Wilson's or Leach's petrels, with white rump, *square tail,* and narrow, indistinct, pale bar on upperwing, white bar on underwing. *Flight weak and fluttering,* like Wilson's, but with shorter glides.

Voice: On nest, a sustained, purring "song" ending with hiccoughing *chikka.* Silent at sea.

Habitat: Breeds colonially on bare turfy or rocky islands. Otherwise pelagic.

Nesting: 1 white egg, often with brownish spots at one end, in burrow excavated among rocks or in old rabbit burrow.

Range: Iceland, Faeroes, Britain and Ireland, northwest and southwest France, and various islands in the western Mediterranean. Migrates along west coast of Africa to winter off southern Africa.

A tiny seabird, it regularly follows ships, searching for marine organisms brought to the surface by the churning propellers. It takes most of its food from the surface, hovering and dipping down, sometimes lowering its feet and pattering over the water. Despite its size, it spends most of its life on the open ocean, and is rarely seen from the coast.

39 **Leach's Petrel**
(*Oceanodroma leucorhoa*)

Description: 8″ (20 cm). Larger than Wilson's or Storm petrels, distinguished by *forked tail,* browner plumage, broader and more conspicuous pale wing bar, and, at close range, grey centre to white rump. *Flight very different, bounding and erratic,* with deep buoyant wingbeats, without fluttering or pattering over the water.

Voice: Two principal calls on breeding grounds, a sustained, low purring and a chuckling *tuk-tukatuk-tuk-tukkrrrrrah.* Otherwise silent.

Habitat: Breeds on bare, turfy, or rocky slopes on offshore islands. Otherwise pelagic.

Nesting: 1 white egg with fine reddish spots at larger end, in earthen burrow or hole among rocks. Nest chamber sometimes lined with dry grass and other vegetation.

Range: Isolated colonies off Iceland, Norway, Faeroes, northern Scotland, and possibly Ireland; also breeds on both coasts of North America and islands of northwest Pacific. Winters mainly in tropical waters; a few remain in north.

Though frequently seen at sea, Leach's Petrel does not follow ships, often passing in front of the bow without so much as a backward look. The European population is rather small, and it is generally much scarcer than Storm Petrel in Britain.

GANNETS AND BOOBIES
(Sulidae)

9 species: almost worldwide. One species breeds in Europe. Large, heavy seabirds with long, narrow, pointed wings; long, wedge-shaped tail; stout, pointed bill; and webbed feet. Adapted for plunge-diving for fish from a considerable height. Their rising and falling flap-and-glide flight, with much soaring on stiff wings, is very different from gulls'. Exclusively marine but not oceanic, usually found fairly close to shore. Breed in large colonies, mainly on steep cliffs or small islands.

30, 33 **Gannet**
(*Sula bassana*)

Description: 36″ (90 cm). Large, white seabird, with stout, pointed bill; *long neck; pointed tail;* and *long, narrow wings.* Body shape tapers both fore and aft. *Head and neck buffy-yellow, wings broadly tipped black.* Distinguished from gulls by *stiff-winged flight,* soaring above waves and gliding low over them. Juvenile dark brown speckled white; immatures mixture of brown and white.

Voice: Main call on breeding grounds sometimes given while fishing, a loud, hoarse *urrah.*

Habitat: Breeds on cliffs of offshore islands, infrequently on mainland. Otherwise in offshore waters, some distance from land but seldom going beyond continental shelf.

Nesting: 1 white egg, in shallow nest of seaweed, placed on ledge or flat top of cliff.

Range: Breeds on both sides of North Atlantic: in Canada, and from Iceland and Norway south through Britain and Ireland to Channel Islands and northwest France. Partial migrant, some remaining within breeding range, others wintering off West Africa and in western Mediterranean.

It breeds in large colonies, with nests so closely placed that sitting birds can reach out and touch their neighbours. Once acquired, nest sites are continually occupied and defended by aggressive displays. Paired birds indulge in headshaking, bowing, bill-fencing, and pointing their bills skyward. When a shoal of fish is sighted, many birds gather at the same spot, diving into the water from great heights.

CORMORANTS
(Phalacrocoracidae)

33 species: worldwide. Three species breed in Europe. Large aquatic birds with long neck and tail, hooked bill, and webbed feet; plumage mainly black; posture upright. Fly with neck extended and head held slightly above the horizontal, often in lines or V's. Flight strong after rising laboriously from water. Silhouette when swimming not unlike divers but bill tilted upward and back even more often awash. Often perch with wings held out to dry. Found on both fresh and salt water; at sea never far from land. Dive into water pursuing fish, using feet rather than wings for propulsion. Breed colonially, usually on cliffs or trees. Sexes similar.

---

26 Cormorant or Great Cormorant
(*Phalacrocorax carbo*)

Description: 36″ (90 cm). Largest European cormorant, more heavily built than Shag, with stouter bill. Breeding adults *glossy black and bronze,* with yellow bill and throat pouch, patch of bare orange skin below eye, and *white cheeks, throat, and thigh patch.* Feathers on back of head and neck show varying amounts of white. After breeding season, loses white thigh patch and white head feathers. Juvenile brown with pale brown throat and whitish underparts.

Voice: A variety of deep, guttural calls at nesting colonies; otherwise silent.

Habitat: Coastal waters, estuaries, inland lakes, marshes with open water.

Nesting: 3–5 pale blue eggs, in stick nest lined with seaweed (coastal sites) or leaves and grass (inland sites), situated on cliff ledge, in tree, or on ground on island.

Range: Breeds on coasts of northwest and southeast Europe, locally on lakes and marshes of central Europe; widespread on nearly all European coasts in winter. Also breeds discontinuously in parts of

Asia and in Africa, Australasia, and eastern North America.

It normally fishes close to land, diving from the surface and catching fish by swimming underwater. On the surface, much of the body is submerged, often only the neck projecting from water and the bill typically tilted upward. When not feeding, it often sits on exposed perches, preening and spreading its wings to dry.

27 Shag
(*Phalacrocorax aristotelis*)

Description: 30″ (75 cm). Smaller and slimmer than Cormorant, with relatively small head and thin bill. Breeding adult *entirely black with green gloss; curly crest on forehead;* yellow base of lower mandible; and orange-yellow gape. When not breeding, lacks crest and has some white on chin, resembling Cormorant, which has white extending to cheeks and throat. Juvenile like Cormorant, but darker on breast and belly.

Voice: Grunting and clicking calls on breeding grounds.

Habitat: Marine, confined to rocky coasts and islands; very rare inland or on flat, sandy, or muddy coasts.

Nesting: 2–5 pale blue eggs, in nest of sticks and seaweed lined with finer plants on sheltered cliff ledge, cave, or hole among rocks. Nests colonially.

Range: Confined to western Palearctic, breeding on rocky coasts and islands. Mainly resident; some post-breeding dispersal, especially of young birds. Uncommon in southeastern England.

It is common, though less familiar than Cormorant owing to its restrictions of habitat. It will fish in rough seas but stays close inshore and prefers sheltered bays. Like all cormorants, it spends much time resting on rocks and drying its wings.

28 Pygmy Cormorant
(*Phalacrocorax pygmeus*)

Description: 19″ (48 cm). Smallest of the three European cormorants, with *short bill, large head,* and *long tail.* Breeding adults have *red-brown head and neck* and black body flecked with white. After breeding, loses white flecks and has white throat and brown breast. Juvenile grey-brown above, with white chin, brown throat and breast, whitish belly.

Voice: Croaking calls while breeding, otherwise silent.

Habitat: Lakes, ponds, slow-flowing rivers, marshes, and freshwater areas with dense vegetation. Some birds winter on brackish coastal lagoons or salt water.

Nesting: 3–7 white eggs, in nest of reeds or sticks, in tree or reedbed. Breeds colonially, often together with egrets, Night Heron, and Glossy Ibis.

Range: Confined to west-central Palearctic, breeding from Yugoslavia, Bulgaria, Romania, Greece, and Turkey east to Iraq, Iran, and southwest Siberia. Resident and local migrant.

It uses trees for communal roosts and when resting or drying its wings. More of a marsh bird than other cormorants, it has lost many of its former breeding areas through drainage.

PELICANS
(Pelecanidae)

8 species: nearly worldwide. Two species breed in Europe. Huge aquatic birds with capacious pouch below very large bill; long, broad wings; short tail; and webbed feet. Inhabit large lakes, marshes, and inshore coastal waters, feeding mainly on fish caught by upending from surface or plunge-diving from air. Fish in parties; fly in formation, often soaring like birds of prey on thermals. Nest colonially, in trees or on the ground. Sexes similar.

184, 186 White Pelican
(*Pelecanus onocrotalus*)

Description: 55–70″ (138–175 cm). Huge white bird, best distinguished from similar Dalmatian Pelican by wing pattern in flight. *Upperside white with black tips; underside white with black flight feathers.* Dalmatian has white upperside of wing, with black tips and grey trailing edge; underwing largely white. Breeding adult has pinkish tinge to plumage and shaggy crest. Further distinguished from Dalmatian by *red eye, yellow throat pouch,* and *pink legs.* Bill yellow-grey, breast patch yellow.

Voice: Mooing and grunting calls in breeding colonies. Flight call, a low croak.

Habitat: Large shallow lakes, deltas, brackish coastal lagoons, marshes, sandbanks, small rocky islets.

Nesting: 2–3 white eggs, in shallow scrape lined with reeds and small plants situated in reedbeds or occasionally unconcealed on sandbanks.

Range: Scattered nesting colonies in Danube delta and north shore of Black Sea; also central and southern Asia and Ethiopian Region. European birds migrate south to winter in Egypt and possibly farther.

Formerly more widespread in eastern Europe, it has suffered a marked range reduction owing to the draining of lakes and marshes where it once nested. Very susceptible to disturbance, it requires inaccessible nest sites and large numbers of fish. Protection, essential for its survival, is now provided at sites in Romania and Russia.

185, 187 **Dalmatian Pelican**
(*Pelecanus crispus*)

Description: 63–71″ (158–178 cm). Slightly larger than White Pelican, with *greyish tinge to plumage.* Lacks crest, though curly feathers on head produce bushy effect. *Eye yellow,* bill grey, *throat pouch orange,* breast patch yellow, *legs grey.*

Voice: Hissing, spitting, and grunting calls at breeding colonies; also bill-clattering.

Habitat: Similar to White Pelican's, but accepts smaller lakes at higher altitudes; also occurs along sheltered coasts.

Nesting: 2–5 white eggs, in large pile of sticks, stones, reeds, and grass, usually in cover of thick vegetation. Nests colonially, sometimes with White Pelican.

Range: Scattered colonies in Yugoslavia, Albania, Greece, Bulgaria, Romania (rare in Danube delta), and southern Russia; also in Turkey and southwestern and central Asia. European birds winter in the Balkans, Turkey, and Egypt.

It remains in flocks outside the breeding season. Feeding cooperatively, it forms a line and drives the fish forward. Man's disturbance and the drainage of nesting areas have decreased the numbers and range of both it and the White Pelican.

HERONS, EGRETS, AND BITTERNS
(Ardeidae)

64 species: worldwide. Nine species breed in Europe. Medium- to large-sized water birds with slender body; long neck and legs; long, straight, pointed bill; and long, unwebbed toes. During breeding season, plumage changes colour and many species acquire long plumes on head, back, or breast. In the air they flap slowly on broad, rounded wings, with head and neck retracted and outstretched legs projecting beyond the short tail. Wade in shallow fresh and salt water, feeding mainly on fish. Nest in colonies, often of mixed species, in trees or reedbeds. Sexes generally similar.

---

178 **Bittern**
(*Botaurus stellaris*)

Description: 30″ (75 cm). Large; *yellowish-brown; streaked, mottled, and barred with black.* Crown and narrow moustachial streak black; legs green. In flight, its broad, rounded wings show much barring. Vagrant American Bittern (*B. lentiginosus*) has chestnut crown and black neck patch; in flight, blackish, unbarred primaries and secondaries contrast with paler wing coverts.

Voice: Flight call, *kow.* Song, a deep, resonant boom, audible up to a mile or more, preceded by 2–3 grunts.

Habitat: Dense and extensive reedbeds, tall, rank vegetation in swamps and at lake edges.

Nesting: 4–6 olive-brown eggs in nest of marsh vegetation on ground or in shallow water. Solitary nester; territorial.

Range: Breeds rather locally from southern Sweden, England, Spain, and North Africa east across north-central Eurasia to northern Japan; also southeast Africa. European birds mainly resident except in east.

It remains hidden during the day, but in early morning or late evening it may fly low over the reed tops with slow wingbeats and head hunched into shoulders. When danger approaches, it freezes, with neck stretched and bill pointing upward, the vertical neck stripes blending with the surrounding reeds and forming an effective camouflage. When threatening an intruder, it crouches with spread wings, raising its crest and neck feathers to present a fierce appearance, bill raised and ready to strike.

173, 175, 176 **Little Bittern**
(*Ixobrychus minutus*)

Description: 14″ (35 cm). *Smallest European heron.* Male has *black crown and upperparts; black wings, with large, buffy-white patch;* buffy-white underparts. Female similar but duller and browner, with pale streaks on dark brown back, dark streaks on underparts, less contrasting pale wing patch. Juvenile heavily streaked above and below.

Voice: Flight note, *quer;* alarm, *gack.* "Song," a low, croaking *hoof,* repeated at 2-second intervals for long periods by night or day.

Habitat: Thick vegetation at edges of lakes, ponds, and rivers, reedbeds, swamps with willow and alder.

Nesting: 5–6 white eggs, in shallow nest of reeds and sedges, lined with finer plant material, anchored to floating vegetation, in reeds, or in shrubs and trees over water.

Range: Summer visitor to most of Europe except extreme northwest—Iceland, Britain and Ireland, and Scandinavia. Winters in tropical Africa. Also breeds in Morocco, Egypt, Ethiopian Region, northern India, and Australia.

It spends the day concealed in thick waterside vegetation, venturing forth in evening to feed, when it may be seen making short flights low over the water or skimming the reed tops. It rises laboriously but flies easily with rapid wingbeats, gliding some distance before landing. It climbs reeds and bushes with agility.

172, 174, 177 **Night Heron or Black-crowned Night Heron**
(*Nycticorax nycticorax*)

Description: 24″ (60 cm). Stout-bodied, thick-necked, short-legged heron with short, thick bill. Adult has *black crown and back,* with 2–3 long, white head plumes in breeding season; *grey wings, rump, and tail;* and *white underparts.* Eye red; legs pale yellow. Juvenile dark grey-brown above with buffy-white spots, white below with dark streaks; less yellowish than Bittern.

Voice: Call, given especially in flight, a flat, hoarse *kwok;* various raucous calls at nesting colonies.

Habitat: Tangled vegetation with bushes and trees in swamps, along riverbanks, or at lake and pond margins.

Nesting: 3–5 pale greenish-blue eggs, placed on platform of sticks, in tree or bush near water. Nests colonially with other herons and water birds.

Range: Summer visitor to southern Europe, north (very locally) to Holland and Czechoslovakia; winters in tropical Africa. Also Asia, Africa, and North and South America.

Though crepuscular in habits, with a preference for resting under cover in trees and bushes during the day, it is much less shy than bitterns and sometimes feeds during the day. It flies at dusk to feeding grounds in the open, on mud, or in shallow water, preying on fish, amphibians, snails, worms, and aquatic insects. It also takes mice and young birds.

179 **Squacco Heron**
(*Ardeola ralloides*)

Description: 18″ (45 cm). Small, squat, short-necked heron appearing mainly *buffy-brown on the ground;* but *in flight, shows white wings, rump, and tail.* Breeding adult has pinkish-buff upperparts, yellowish-buff breast, and *long, shaggy crest* of white feathers edged with black; bill blue or greenish, with black tip. In winter, duller and browner, with reduced crest and some streaks on underparts; base of bill greenish. Legs pink in breeding season, otherwise green. Juvenile similar to winter adult, but darker and more streaked.

Voice: Usually silent, sometimes a harsh *karr* at dusk during breeding season.

Habitat: Marshes, lagoons, ponds, ditches, rice fields, usually not far from cover.

Nesting: 4–6 pale greenish-blue eggs, in twig nest placed in tree or bush or in nest of reeds and sedges in marsh. Nests colonially with other herons, Glossy Ibis, and Pygmy Cormorant.

Range: Local summer visitor to southern Europe, north to France (rare), Hungary, and Russia; winters in Africa. Also breeds in southwestern Asia, Morocco, and Ethiopian Region.

It is the European representative of a widespread group known as pond herons or paddybirds in Asia, where their favoured habitat is rice paddies. Even in the open, their brown plumage and crouched stance enable them to blend with the background. When one of these birds is flushed, the sudden burst of flashing white wings can be quite startling.

171 **Cattle Egret**
(*Bubulcus ibis*)

Description: 20″ (50 cm). Small and chunky; *short-necked,* with *heavy jowl,* giving head a more rounded look than other herons. Breeding adult is *white, with buffy crown, back, and chest;* for brief period, bill, eye, and legs become red. At other seasons, plumage all-white, with pale buffy wash on crown; *bill and eye yellow, legs greenish-black.*

Voice: A croaking *RICK-rack* and other harsh calls at breeding colony.

Habitat: Meadows and dry grasslands near cattle and other livestock; also arable land and dry open country.

Nesting: 4–5 whitish-blue eggs, in shallow nest of sticks and other vegetation, in tree, bush, or reedbed. Nests colonially with other herons.

Range: Breeds in Portugal and Spain and recently southern France. Widespread in Africa and southern Asia; recently colonised North and South America.

With a diet of insects rather than fish, it has successfully exploited a niche not used by other members of its family. It attends large antelope and other big game, including elephant and rhinoceros, snapping up grasshoppers and other insects they flush while grazing. By adapting to domestic animals it has greatly expanded its range.

---

168 Little Egret
(*Egretta garzetta*)

Description: 22″ (55 cm). Medium-sized, slim heron, with *thin bill* and *slender neck. Pure white,* with long plumes on head, back, and chest in breeding season. *Bill and legs black; feet yellow,* usually conspicuous in flight. Smaller version of Great White Egret, distinguished by colour of bill and feet and faster wingbeats; in breeding season, by crest.

Voice: Harsh croaking and growling calls at breeding colony.

Habitat: Shallow lakes and pools, banks of slow-flowing rivers, fresh and salt marshes, flooded land, estuaries.

Nesting: 3–5 pale greenish-blue eggs, in a nest of sticks or reeds in tree, bush, or reedbed. Nests colonially, usually with other herons, Glossy Ibis, and Pygmy Cormorant.

Range: Local summer visitor to southern Europe, north to central and western France, Hungary, and southern Russia, wintering around Mediterranean and in Africa. Also breeds in Africa, southwestern and southern Asia, and Australasia.

Aquatic by preference, it feeds in shallow water or on muddy shores, where it catches fish, frogs, crustaceans, and insects. It is closely related to the Snowy Egret (*E. thula*).

169 Great White Egret

(*Egretta alba*)

Description: 35″ (88 cm). Large, all-white heron with *long neck.* In breeding season has long, white scapular plumes; *long, black legs,* yellow above the "knee"; and *black bill with yellow base.* At other seasons lacks plumes and has *all-yellow bill* and *all-black legs.* May be confused with Little Egret at a distance if size comparison not possible; best separated by *black feet* (yellow in Little), bill colour, and slow wingbeats.

Voice: Deep croaking and cawing notes at breeding colony.

Habitat: Shallow lagoons, edges of lakes, riverbanks, estuaries, swamps.

Nesting: 3–5 pale blue eggs, in large nest of reeds built in shallow water of large reedbeds. Nests alone or in small groups.

Range: Worldwide distribution, but scarce in Europe, breeding in scattered localities in Austria, Hungary, Romania, southern Russia, and sporadically in the Balkans. Winters south to Aegean and northern Africa.

It probably has more English names than any other bird, including Great Egret, Great White Heron, Large

Egret, White Egret, Common Egret, and American Egret. Now protected by law because its numbers (like those of other herons) were once severely reduced by plume hunters, its recovery is currently threatened by drainage of its habitat.

165 Grey Heron
(*Ardea cinerea*)

Description: 36″ (90 cm). Largest European heron, with long bill, neck, and legs. *Grey above, head and neck white,* underparts greyish-white. Slender black plumes form *line along sides of crown* and droop over back of neck; line of black streaks down centre of neck and breast. In flight, *black flight feathers contrast with grey coverts* above; underwing uniformly grey. Bill yellow; legs brown.

Voice: Normal call, a loud, harsh *kraaarnk;* a variety of squawking, croaking, and grunting calls at nesting colony; also bill-snapping.

Habitat: Shallow water, both salt and fresh, including shores and marshes, rivers, lakes, reservoirs, canals, damp meadows.

Nesting: 3–6 pale greenish-blue eggs, in large stick nest lined with thin twigs, in tall tree or bush, reedbed, on cliff ledge, or on ground. Normally colonial; sometimes solitary.

Range: Breeds from Scandinavia, Britain, Ireland, and Spain (local) east across most of Eurasia to Pacific and Indian oceans; also in Ethiopian Region. Partial migrant in Europe; eastern and northern birds move to Mediterranean region and Africa in winter.

The most common and familiar heron in Europe, it is often seen at rest, standing motionless with head hunched into shoulders, or fishing in the shallows, with long neck extended, peering intently into the water below. Besides fish it also eats rodents and other small mammals, young birds, amphibians, small snakes, crustaceans, molluscs, and insects. Its flight is heavy, with broad, arched wings and slow flaps.

167 **Purple Heron**
(*Ardea purpurea*)

Description: 31″ (78 cm). Rather tall, slim heron; *long neck when retracted forms a distinct curve or kink.* Smaller and darker overall than Grey Heron, with slate-grey wings and upperparts; pale chestnut shoulder plumes in breeding season. Crown and head plumes black, *sides of neck rufous, breast and upper belly chestnut.* In flight, underwing dark slate with chestnut lining, upperwing more uniform than Grey Heron. Juvenile sandy-brown above, buff below, lacking black marks on head and neck.

Voice: Normal call, like *kraaarnk* of Grey Heron, but higher-pitched and quieter; guttural croaking calls at nesting colony.

Habitat: Extensive marshes with reedbeds; thickly vegetated swamps.

Nesting: 3–6 pale greenish-blue eggs, in nest of reeds or twigs in reedbed, bush, or tree.

Range: Summer visitor to southern Europe (patchily distributed), north to Holland, Czechoslovakia, and southern Russia; winters in Africa. Also breeds widely in southern Africa and warmer parts of Asia.

Shyer than the Grey Heron, it spends much of the day concealed in dense reeds or vegetation, coming out in the morning and evening to feed, close to cover. Most often seen in flight, it can be difficult to distinguish from Grey Heron, though it is always darker. It is best identified by shape: more prominent neck bulge, slimmer wings, longer legs, and less contrasting upperwing pattern.

STORKS
(Ciconiidae)

17 species: mainly in tropical regions. Two species breed in Europe. Large to very large with long neck, long legs, and long, stout, pointed bill; plumage usually black and white. Broad wings aid in frequent soaring. Neck and legs extended in flight. Slow and deliberate walkers. Found in open marshes and on dry land. Feed on large insects, particularly grasshoppers, snails, frogs, and fish. Nest colonially, mainly in trees, sometimes on cliffs or buildings. Sexes similar.

---

183 Black Stork
(*Ciconia nigra*)

Description: 38″ (95 cm). Mostly *black with green and purple gloss; white breast, belly, and undertail coverts.* Bill and legs red. Juvenile has less gloss, brown head and neck, greenish bill and legs.

Voice: At nest area, a soft *chee-lee* and hissing and whistling notes; more vocal than White Stork but clatters bill less.

Habitat: Breeds in swamps, streams, pools, and wet meadows in forested country; open wetlands on migration.

Nesting: 3–5 white eggs, in stick nest with earth and grass lined with moss, grass, and leaves; in fork of large tree; occasionally on cliff ledge.

Range: Partial resident in Iberia; summer visitor from Estonia, Germany, and northern Balkans east across central Eurasia to Pacific. European birds winter in Africa. Also breeds locally in southeastern Africa.

Shy and retiring, unlike White Stork, it avoids man and is seldom found in cultivated country. Mainly solitary, it nests in isolated pairs; some flocking occurs on migration. Like other storks, it prefers to use thermals while migrating and so usually takes land routes to Africa via Spain and around the eastern end of the Mediterranean.

181 **White Stork**
(*Ciconia ciconia*)

Description: 40″ (100 cm). Very large; long-necked and long-legged, with dagger-like bill; *plumage entirely white except for black flight feathers*. Narrow black patch around eye, which gives large-eyed appearance. *Bill and legs red.*

Voice: Only call a weak hissing; bill-clattering frequent at nest.

Habitat: Shallow lagoons, open marshes, damp meadows, farmland, dry grassy plains; near trees or buildings in breeding season.

Nesting: 3–5 white eggs, in large stick nest solidified with clumps of grass and earth, lined with plant material, placed in tree or on building.

Range: Summer visitor, chiefly to Iberia and eastern Europe; now rare in France, Holland, and Denmark and declining elsewhere; winters in Africa, a few also in Iberia. Also breeds in North Africa and southwestern and eastern Asia.

Well-known for adapting to man-made nest sites, it nests readily on roofs of houses, church towers, chimneys, ruins, haystacks, telephone poles, and nest platforms. Although most nests are rigorously protected, populations have declined or even disappeared in some regions. Possible reasons include insecticides, changes of climate or habitat, collisions with wires, and shootings on migration.

IBISES AND SPOONBILLS
(Threskiornithidae)

33 species: mainly in tropical regions. Two species breed in Europe. Medium-large water birds with long bill, neck, and legs; bill decurved (ibises) or straight and spatulate (spoonbills). Neck and legs extended in flight. Wade in shallow water of lakes and marshes, feeding on fish, frogs, snails, crustaceans, and insects. Colonial nesters, in trees, bushes, reeds, or cliffs, often with herons. Sexes similar.

182 Glossy Ibis
(*Plegadis falcinellus*)

Description: 22″ (55 cm). *Bill long and decurved.* In breeding season body *dark reddish-brown;* wings and tail blackish, glossed with green and purple. Duller in winter, with pale streaks on head and neck. *Looks blackish at a distance.* Juvenile similar to winter adult, but paler below.

Voice: Grating, crow-like *graa;* usually silent.

Habitat: Swamps with trees and dense reedbeds; after breeding, found on shallow lakes and lagoons, flooded fields, mud flats.

Nesting: 3–4 deep blue eggs, in small compact nest of reeds or sticks lined with leaves, in reedbed, bush, or tree. Nests colonially.

Range: Breeds locally in southeast Europe from northern Italy, Yugoslavia, and southern Ukraine to northern Greece, wintering mainly in tropical Africa, with a few around Mediterranean. Also western and southern Asia (discontinuously), Australasia, Ethiopian Region, and eastern North America.

It feeds in small flocks and returns at night to a communal roost in trees, often shared with herons. It flies like the White Spoonbill, with quick flaps and glides, and often in lines. Using its long bill, it probes in mud like a curlew. Its range and numbers have been greatly reduced through drainage of habitat and human disturbance.

170 **Spoonbill**
(*Platalea leucorodia*)

Description: 34″ (85 cm). *White,* with *long, spatulate bill.* Breeding adult has *long crest* and *yellow-buff collar at base of neck;* bare yellow skin on throat and lores; black bill with yellow "spoon" at tip; black legs. In winter, loses crest and collar. Juvenile similar to winter adult, but has black wing tips and pink bill and legs.

Voice: Silent except for grunting noises during breeding season and bill-clattering when excited.

Habitat: Reedbeds and marshes with low trees near shallow water. In winter, open marshes, lagoons, estuaries, and shallow coastal waters.

Nesting: 3–5 white eggs with sparse red-brown spots, on platform of reeds or sticks in reedbed or bush. Nests colonially.

Range: Breeds locally in southeast Europe from Austria and southern Russia to northern Balkans, with outlying colonies in southern Spain and Holland. Winters in Mediterranean and northern Africa. Also breeds in Asia east to China and south to India; very locally in northern Africa.

Its unusual bill is adapted for its method of feeding. Wading in shallow water, it immerses the slightly open bill and sweeps it from side to side, snapping it shut on small fish, water beetles, tadpoles, worms, snails, insect larvae, and other favoured foods. It feeds in small parties. In flight, birds usually form a line, flying with measured wingbeats interspersed with gliding; it also soars like a stork. It is distinguished from egrets in flight by its outstretched neck.

FLAMINGOS
(Phoenicopteridae)

6 species: mainly warmer parts of Eurasia, Africa, and New World. One species breeds in Europe. Very tall water birds with long, curving neck, long legs, webbed feet, and thick, heavy bill decurved in middle. Plumage pale pink or red with black flight feathers; bill and legs pink, red, green, or yellow. Good swimmers. Feed in large flocks and nest colonially. Confined to brackish or saltwater lakes and lagoons. Sexes similar.

180 Greater Flamingo
(*Phoenicopterus ruber*)

Description: 50″ (125 cm). *Very tall* and slim with *exceptionally long neck; stilt-like, pink legs;* and a *bulbous, decurved bill* that is pale pink with a broad, black tip. Adult *whitish or pale pink; black and crimson wings.* Juvenile dull brownish-grey and off-white. Flies with neck and legs extended and slightly drooping.

Voice: Very vocal; flocks keep up a continuous goose-like honking and gabbling.

Habitat: Shallow muddy lakes and coastal lagoons with salt or alkaline water; estuaries, tidal mud flats.

Nesting: 1 (occasionally 2) greenish-white eggs, in hollow in conical mud nest built in shallow water. Colonial nester.

Range: Irregular breeder and partial resident in Spain and southern France; some winter in North Africa.

It feeds in large flocks, using its bill, which is equipped with sieve-like plates (lamellae), to strain out small animals and vegetable matter from the mud. It immerses its head in water, with the bill upside down, and moves it from side to side, sometimes stirring up the mud with a treading action. It may go several years without breeding, doing so only when conditions are optimal.

SWANS, GEESE, AND DUCKS
(Anatidae)

150 species: worldwide. Forty-six species occur in Europe: thirty-one breeding, seven regular migrants, and four introduced. Small, medium, and large water birds with blunt, flattened, or triangular bill (except sawbills) and webbed feet; some have long neck. Sexes similar in swans and geese; ducks dissimilar, with males more brightly coloured. After breeding season, flight feathers moult all at once and birds are flightless for several weeks. Typically aquatic, but geese largely terrestrial; some ducks feed partly on land.

190, 193 **Mute Swan**
(*Cygnus olor*)

Description: 60″ (150 cm). All-white, with *orange-red bill with black knob.* While swimming, *holds neck in curve* and beak tilted down, tail often turned up, *wings often partly raised over back.* Juvenile browner than other swans, with black base to dull pink bill.

Voice: Mostly silent but not mute; snorting, grunting, and growling calls given during breeding season; also hissing. Does not honk in flight like other European swans, but wingbeats are loud.

Habitat: Breeds on large or small well-vegetated lakes. Semidomesticated stock often reside in proximity to man.

Nesting: 5–7 pale greyish-green or bluish-green eggs, in large pile of sticks, reeds, plant material, and feathers built at water's edge or in shallow water.

Range: Breeds widely in central and northwest Europe from Britain, Ireland, and France to Estonia and Poland, and discontinuously across Eurasia from northern Greece and Romania to southeast Siberia. Partial migrant, wintering within breeding range and on shores of Black and Aegean seas.

While mainly wild in eastern Europe and Asia, it has long been domesticated in western Europe and is now a familiar sight on reservoirs, ornamental lakes, and ponds in parks. Once used for food, it is now encouraged for aesthetic reasons. It becomes very tame, readily taking food from man, but is extremely aggressive during breeding season.

---

188 Bewick's Swan

(*Cygnus columbianus*)

Description: 48″ (120 cm). Similar to Whooper Swan, with upright neck and black bill with yellow base, but *smaller,* with shorter neck and bill and *more rounded head. Yellow on bill does not extend beyond nostril and is squared or rounded.* Juvenile pale greyish like young Whooper, but different in size and proportions.

Voice: A loud, honking flight call, *bong* or *bung,* and a musical babble from flocks at rest.

Habitat: Nests in Arctic on flat swampy tundra and along rivers and coasts; winters on lakes, rivers, and flooded grasslands and in sheltered coastal bays.

Nesting: 3–5 creamy-white eggs, in large conical nest of moss and lichens, partially lined with down, on ground near water, usually on islet.

Range: Holarctic, breeding in extreme northern Asia and North America. Winters in Britain and from Denmark, Germany, and Holland to France (rare).

Formerly considered separate species, Bewick's Swan of Eurasia (*C. c. bewicki*) and the Whistling Swan of North America (*C. c. columbianus*) have recently been lumped together. While the Whistling usually has just a tiny spot of yellow at the base of its bill, and sometimes an all-black bill, the shape and extent of yellow varies greatly in both birds and thus is not a very reliable means of separating them.

189 Whooper Swan
(*Cygnus cygnus*)

Description: 60″ (150 cm). Same size as Mute Swan, but has *yellow base to black bill. Holds neck upright; calls frequently. Larger than Bewick's Swan,* with longer, flatter head and yellow patch on bill *tapering to a point.* Juvenile greyer than Mute Swan, with pinkish bill lacking black base.

Voice: Very vocal; principal call, a double *whoop-whoop;* other melodious and nasal calls during breeding season.

Habitat: Nests on shallow inland lakes, moorlands, swamps, arctic tundra, coastal lagoons, and estuaries; in winter, coastal, in sheltered bays and estuaries, and inland on lakes and floodlands.

Nesting: 5–6 creamy-white eggs, in large mound of plant material, lined with grass and down, on ground at water's edge, usually on islet.

Range: Breeds broadly across northern Eurasia from Iceland, Scandinavia, and west-central Siberia to Pacific. European birds winter mainly in northwest Europe.

Like the Trumpeter Swan (*C. buccinator*) of North America, it is named for its loud bugle-like calls. The Trumpeter Swan is probably the product of a fairly recent invasion of North America by the Whooper.

---

195 Bean Goose
(*Anser fabalis*)

Description: 28–35″ (70–88 cm). Large, near size of Greylag; *darker* and *browner* than other grey geese, *with head and neck darker than body. Bill orange, with variable amounts of black; legs orange.* Upperside of wing uniformly dark in flight.

Voice: Similar to Pink-footed Goose, but lower: a reedy *ung-ank.*

Habitat: Nests by small lakes and swamps in forested country; winters near water on pastures, stubble fields, croplands.

Nesting: 4–6 creamy-white eggs, in shallow scrape lined with grass, moss, lichens, and down, near water, often sheltered by vegetation. Nests in groups.

Range: Breeds broadly across northern Eurasia from Norway to Bering Sea; winters in Europe from Britain (rare) and southern Sweden south to Spain, Italy, and Balkans; also in Asia.

Each subspecies is associated with a particular habitat. Those nesting in Scandinavia (*A. f. fabalis*) are unique among native European geese in breeding within forests; other races use open, wet tundra; while *A. f. middendorffii*, in Siberia, is a montane form, using damp alpine meadows.

---

196 **Pink-footed Goose**
(*Anser brachyrhynchus*)

Description: 24–30″ (60–75 cm). Smaller version of Bean Goose, with short neck and bill and *dark brown head and neck, contrasting with light grey body and wings;* distinguished from all other grey geese by combination of *pink legs* and *small pink and black bill.* In flight, pale forewing contrasts with darker flight feathers.

Voice: Like Bean Goose but higher-pitched: *ung-unk, ang-ank, wink-wink.*

Habitat: Nests in Arctic on flat tundra, grassy hillsides, rocky outcrops, cliffs, and river gorges. In winter, on stubble fields and pastures.

Nesting: 4–5 creamy-white eggs, in scrape lined with grass, lichens, moss, and down, on ledge, island in river, or tundra.

Range: Breeds in Greenland, Spitsbergen, and Iceland; winters in Britain, and along southern shores of North Sea from Denmark to northern France.

Like other grey geese, it has cultivated a taste for root crops, especially potatoes. While accustomed to man's presence, it is shy and wary, having often been hunted. Sentinels are always on the lookout while the flock is feeding. It used to be considered a subspecies of the Bean Goose.

197 **White-fronted Goose**
(*Anser albifrons*)

Description: 26–30″ (65–75 cm). Medium-sized grey goose, with *broad, white area around base of bill* and extensive blackish barring on underparts. Rest of plumage mainly grey-brown; bill pink in Eurasian race (*A. a. albifrons*) orange in Greenland race (*A. a. flavirostris*); legs orange. Juvenile has orange legs and lacks white around bill and dark barring.

Voice: A high-pitched, ringing *kow-lyow* or *gar-wa-wa*. Flock's chorus sounds like bells.

Habitat: Breeds in Arctic on wet, treeless tundra; winters on grassland, marshes, and bogs, less often on arable land.

Nesting: 4–6 creamy-white eggs, in shallow scrape lined with down and plant material, on hummock in tundra or river island.

Range: Circumpolar, breeding on Arctic mainland and islands of Asia and North America. Winters in Britain, Ireland, and regions bordering North Sea and Channel; also southeastern Europe.

Like other grey geese, they are highly gregarious outside the breeding season, gathering in large feeding flocks. They choose a secure roost, like a river sandbar, where they will be undisturbed and free from predators, and fly at dawn to the feeding grounds, where they remain until evening, when they return to the roost.

198 **Lesser White-fronted Goose**
(*Anser erythropus*)

Description: 21–26″ (53–65 cm). Smaller version of White-fronted Goose, with *shorter neck* and *smaller bill* and head; distinguished by *more extensive white forehead,* reaching to fore-crown, and *orange eye-ring.* Bill pink, legs orange. Juvenile separated from juvenile White-fronted by orange eye-ring and smaller size.

Voice: Faster, higher-pitched, and more squeaky than White-fronted: *kyu-yu-yu* or *kow-yow.*

Habitat: Nests by open boggy places among wooded tundra in foothills; winters on pastures, steppes, and croplands.

Nesting: 4–5 creamy-white eggs, in hollow scrape lined with grass, moss, down, and feathers, on hummock near swamp.

Range: Breeds in narrow band across Arctic Eurasia from northern Scandinavia to eastern Siberia; winters in Europe from Yugoslavia and Ukraine south to northern Greece; also Asia.

Increased sightings in recent years are probably due to keener observation rather than a change in migratory pattern. In England it is now almost annual in very small numbers. On the ground it walks and feeds faster than the White-fronted and in the air may be identified by its faster wingbeat and higher call note.

---

194 **Greylag Goose**
(*Anser anser*)

Description: 30–35″ (75–88 cm). *Largest* and *palest* of the grey geese, with *large head same colour as body* and *large bill,* orange in western form, *A. a. anser,* pink in eastern form, *A. a. rubrirostris.* On the ground, appears uniform light brownish-grey, with a few dark spots on belly; in flight, dark grey flight feathers contrast with *very pale blue-grey forewing. Legs pink.*

Voice: Similar to domestic goose: a loud, nasal *aahng-ung-ung,* gabbling *gaa-gaa,* cackling, and other calls.

Habitat: Breeds on moorlands and tundra in north; elsewhere in wetlands with thick vegetation and nearby grassland. In winter, stubble fields, grassy pastures, marshes, estuaries.

Nesting: 4–6 creamy-white eggs, in scrape lined with down and plant material or in mound of vegetation in reedbed.

Range: Breeds in Iceland, parts of Scandinavia, Scotland, and eastern Europe; also ferally in England. Partial migrant, wintering south to Mediterranean region. Also breeds broadly across central Asia to Pacific.

The ancestor of the familiar barnyard goose, it is slimmer and more graceful than its descendant but resembles it in plumage. It walks in a normal manner, rather than waddling from side to side. It was formerly more widespread in Europe, but its range has been reduced through hunting and disturbance of habitat.

191, 192 **Snow Goose**
(*Anser caerulescens*)

Description: 25–30″ (63–75 cm). Medium-sized goose with two colour phases, formerly thought to be two different species. White phase ("Snow Goose") *all-white with black wing tips;* blue phase ("Blue Goose") has *white head and neck, blue-gray body and wings* with black wing tips, white uppertail coverts, and dark grey tail. Juvenile "Snow" pale grey with brown mottling; juvenile "Blue" like adult but browner, with head and neck same colour as body. Bill and legs identical in both phases, pink in adults and grey in juveniles. Intermediates between two forms occur.

Voice: A harsh *kaak* or *kawk*.

Habitat: Nests near water on flat arctic tundra; winters in coastal marshes, grasslands, stubble fields, croplands.

Nesting: 4–7 white eggs, in hollow on ground lined with grass, down, and moss, among tufts of grass.

Range: Breeds on coasts and islands of arctic

North America, east to Greenland, wintering in coastal United States; accidental in western Europe.

Although a few truly wild Snow Geese wander to Europe from North America each year, some escape from waterfowl collections. It is often impossible to be certain of a given bird's origin, as free-flying escapes will join wild flocks of other geese and behave like wild birds.

---

202 Canada Goose
(*Branta canadensis*)

Description: 36–40″ (90–100 cm). *Largest* of the "black geese," with *longer neck* and *heavier bill.* Head and neck black, with *white throat patch extending onto cheek.* Wings, *body, and breast brown* (Brent and Barnacle have black breasts). Caution: some races of Canada Goose (seldom found wild in Europe) are as small as Brent and Barnacle.

Voice: A loud, resonant double note, *ka-honk,* second syllable higher.

Habitat: Lakes and ornamental waters surrounded by lawns, grassland, and open marsh.

Nesting: 4–7 creamy-white eggs, in low pile of grass and other plant material, lined with down, on ground near water.

Range: Breeds in Britain and Ireland; locally in Norway, Sweden, and Finland. Introduced from North America. European birds mainly resident; some local migration, especially from Sweden south to Germany and Holland.

Introduced into England in the 17th century, it flourished and within 100 years had become a familiar bird in many areas. While still best known as a semidomesticated bird, there is also a considerable feral population. Introduced into Scandinavia about 50 years ago, it is already expanding.

200 Barnacle Goose
(*Branta leucopsis*)

Description: 23–27″ (58–68 cm). Crown, neck, and *breast black,* offset by *broad, white facial area and forehead; upperparts and wings bluish-grey,* with narrow black and white bars; underparts white, with grey barring on flanks.

Voice: A repeated high-pitched, barking call like yapping of small dog.

Habitat: Cliffs and rocky hillsides of arctic islands; winters mainly on coastal marshes and pastures.

Nesting: 3–6 greyish-white eggs, in hollow lined with down in shallow mound of plant material and droppings, on cliff ledge, rocky outcrop, or small island.

Range: Breeds in Greenland, Spitsbergen, and Novaya Zemlya, wintering on coasts of northwestern Britain and Ireland, Holland, and Germany.

The 3 populations of Barnacle Goose lead separate lives in winter as well as in summer. Greenland birds winter in western Scotland and Ireland; birds from Spitsbergen, in the Solway Firth; and birds from Novaya Zemlya, at the southern end of the North Sea. In 1973 the world population was about 75,000. Almost exclusively coastal.

201 Brent Goose
(*Branta bernicla*)

Description: 22–24″ (55–60 cm). *Short-necked* and *small-headed,* about the size of a Mallard; darkest of the "black geese." *Head, neck, and breast black,* with *small white patch on side of neck;* upperparts and wings dark grey-brown; belly dark slate-gray (*B. b. bernicla*) or pale grey-brown (*B. b. hrota*), with variations within each race. Intermediates also occur.

Voice: A growling *grraak* or *grrok.*

Habitat: Breeds in Arctic on flat grassy tundra near coasts or on offshore islets; winters on coastal and estuarine mud flats, occasionally on arable land.

Nesting: 3–5 creamy eggs, in scrape lined with vegetation and down, on tundra hummock or small island.

Range: Circumpolar, breeding on arctic coasts and islands of North America and Asia. Winters on coasts of northwest Europe from Denmark to France and in Britain and Ireland.

Exclusively maritime in winter quarters, it feeds mainly in the intertidal zone in salt marshes and on mud flats. Its numbers fluctuate according to the supply of its favourite food, eelgrass (*Zostera marina*). In the 1930s a disease wiped out most of the eelgrass and the European population of Brent Geese declined roughly 75 percent. The grass has now recovered and so, with protection, have the geese.

---

203 Red-breasted Goose
(*Branta ruficollis*)

Description: 21–22″ (53–55 cm). Very small, with tiny bill and striking plumage pattern. *Fore-neck, breast, and face patch reddish-chestnut* outlined in white; rest of plumage black except for *conspicuous white line on flanks,* white upper- and undertail coverts.

Voice: A shrill, short double note, *kee-kwa* or *ee-ee.*

Habitat: Nests on steep riverbanks in Arctic tundra; winters on grassy steppes and fields with crops.

Nesting: 4–9 white or greenish eggs, in hollow lined with grass and down on riverbank.

Range: Breeds in limited area in northwestern Siberia. Winters near Aral and Caspian seas and in Iraq, Romania, and Bulgaria. Vagrant to western Europe.

Wild populations are endangered and in need of protection. Its limited breeding range and a world population

not exceeding 25,000 make it extremely vulnerable to pressures from hunting, disturbance, and loss of habitat. It places its nest close to that of Peregrine, Rough-legged Buzzard, or other predators and thus its decline may be partly correlated with the decline of raptors.

199 **Egyptian Goose**
(*Alopochen aegyptiacus*)

Description: 25–28″ (63–70). Long-legged and short-necked, with heavy bill; *rich brown to grey above;* head and underparts pale brown to pale grey. *Eye patch, narrow collar, and patch on belly chestnut;* bill and legs pink. In flight, *wing coverts form large, white patch.* Juvenile lacks chestnut markings and has dusky head.

Voice: A harsh, strident *gaa-gaa-gaag.*

Habitat: In Africa: ponds, lakes, and rivers; in England: lakes, ornamental waters, and nearby meadows.

Nesting: 8–9 creamy-white eggs, laid in mound of grass or reeds under bush or protective vegetation, or in bare depression on cliff ledge or cave, or in hole of bank or tree.

Range: Breeds in Ethiopian Region and north along Nile to Egypt; feral population in southeast England, most common in Norfolk. Sedentary.

A native of Africa introduced into England in the 18th century. It is very aggressive toward both its own and other species, driving them off and even killing them.

212 **Ruddy Shelduck**
(*Tadorna ferruginea*)

Description: 25″ (63 cm). Large duck with *orange-brown* body. Male has *cinnamon-buff head* and *narrow black collar;* female has whiter head and no collar. In flight, *white wing coverts contrast with black wing tips* and green wing patch. Tail black.

Voice: A loud, nasal, goose-like *aang*.
Habitat: Inland lakes and pools, rivers, salt lagoons, inland coasts; also fields and dry steppes in winter.
Nesting: 8–12 creamy-white eggs, in depression lined with down in hole in bank, tree, cliff, or abandoned building, near water.
Range: Breeds from southern Russia, Romania, Bulgaria, and northern Greece across Asia to Manchuria and China; also in North Africa. Winters in Turkey, Middle East, and northern Africa; rare in Greece, southern Spain, and western Europe.

Rather goose-like both in shape and habit of grazing, it is more terrestrial than most waterfowl, spending much time on land. It often occurs around small pools and streams in semidesert country that lacks the rich vegetation usually associated with waterfowl habitat. Omnivorous, its diet varies according to habitat and includes young grass shoots, seeds, grain, insects, molluscs, and small crustaceans. Sightings in western Europe mainly involve escapes from captivity.

---

210 Shelduck
(*Tadorna tadorna*)

Description: 24" (60 cm). Large duck *appearing black and white at a distance,* especially in flight. *Head and upper neck dark green;* body white, with *broad, chestnut band around breast and base of neck;* scapulars black; wings white, with black flight feathers and green wing patch. *Bill red* (male with large knob at base), legs pink. Juvenile grey-brown above and white below; bill pink, legs grey.
Voice: Male, whistling notes; female, rapid, nasal *quack*.
Habitat: In Europe: flat sandy and muddy coasts, estuaries, and coastal heaths and sand dunes, wintering in similar habitat.
Nesting: 8–15 creamy-white eggs, in hollow

lined with down in burrow (especially disused rabbit burrows), in hollow tree, under rock or building, or in haystack.

Range: Breeds on coasts of northwest and southeast Europe, chiefly Black Sea, and in the Camargue, Sardinia, and southern Spain. Also breeds across central Asia to Manchuria. Partial migrant in Europe, wintering south to Mediterranean and North Africa.

Almost exclusively maritime in Europe. More terrestrial than most ducks, it feeds mainly in the intertidal zone on molluscs and crustaceans, on open mud or in shallow water, resting on shore between tides. Its flight is goose-like, with slow wingbeats.

205, 227 **Mandarin**
(*Aix galericulata*)

Description: 17″ (43 cm). Male unmistakable, with *shaggy crest, thick neck,* and *gaudy, multicoloured plumage. Orange ruff, orange raised "sails" on wings,* broad white stripe on head, red bill, and maroon breast. Female dull grey-brown, with *white spectacles;* breast and flanks grey-brown, with white spots. Wing patch dark green, with white trailing edge.

Voice: Male, a sharp rising whistle; female, a short *kek* or *ack*.

Habitat: Fresh water—lakes, ponds, ornamental waters, rivers—surrounded by woods.

Nesting: 9–12 creamy-buff eggs, in tree hole lined with down.

Range: Breeds in eastern Asia from southeast Siberia to Japan and northern China. Introduced in England and Scotland, chiefly in southeast.

Feral populations of escapes are now well established, and new areas are being colonised by birds deliberately released. This may prove to be an important conservation step, since its limited Asian habitat is threatened by deforestation and disturbance.

217, 235 **Wigeon**
(*Anas penelope*)

Description: 18″ (45 cm). Compact duck with small, dark bill and pointed tail. Male has *chestnut head* with *yellow-buff crown*, pinkish breast, *grey back*, black stern separated from grey flanks by white patch. In flight, *white forewing* is conspicuous. Female distinguished from other female surface-feeding ducks by small bill, rounded head, pointed tail, and rufous tinge to plumage.

Voice: Male has loud, musical rising and falling whistle, *whee-yoo;* female has low, purring growl.

Habitat: Nests by fresh water on open and wooded tundra, moorlands, and steppes; in winter, prefers low-lying coastal and estuarine marshes; also found on inland lakes and reservoirs.

Nesting: 7–8 creamy eggs, in depression lined with down and plant material, concealed by heather, bracken, or grass.

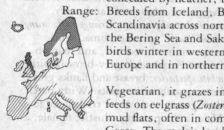

Range: Breeds from Iceland, Britain, and Scandinavia across northern Eurasia to the Bering Sea and Sakhalin; European birds winter in western and southern Europe and in northern half of Africa.

Vegetarian, it grazes in grassy fields or feeds on eelgrass (*Zostera*) on coastal mud flats, often in company with Brent Geese. The male's loud, explosive whistle is one of the most distinctive of all waterfowl calls and announces the presence of a flock long before it comes into view.

---

207 **American Wigeon**
(*Anas americana*)

Description: 18″ (45 cm). Male has *pinkish-brown body, white crown*, and *broad, green stripe* on side of *grey head*. Size, shape, white forewing, and white patch forward of black stern resemble Wigeon. Female very similar to Wigeon female, but *head grey*, not brown, contrasting with brown breast.

Voice: Male has 3-note whistled call, *we-wheeyoo-hoo,* reminiscent of male Wigeon but dry and wheezy, not loud, ringing, or musical; female, similar to female Wigeon's call.

Habitat: Similar to Wigeon, but less maritime in winter; lakes, ponds, marshes, flooded fields, as well as coast.

Nesting: 9–11 creamy eggs, in nest of dry grass and weeds lined with down and feathers, in depression under cover of thick vegetation.

Range: Breeds in North America, wintering south to Central America. Accidental visitor to western Europe, chiefly Iceland, Britain, and Ireland.

Nearly every year some Wigeon wander to America and American Wigeon occur in Europe. Also known as Baldpate, the American Wigeon is popular in captivity and some sightings must inevitably refer to escapes. Nevertheless nearly 100 birds considered wild have now been recorded in Britain and Ireland, including one flock of 13 in Ireland in 1968.

221, 231 Gadwall
(*Anas strepera*)

Description: 20″ (50 cm). Slightly smaller than Mallard. Male *uniform grey,* with *contrasting black stern* formed by black upper- and undertail coverts. In flight, shows *square white patch on trailing edge of wing.* Speckled brown female resembles female Mallard, but has *white wing patch,* sometimes visible at rest, and orange sides of bill; in flight, shows clear-cut pale belly.

Voice: Male, a guttural, reedy *ngek* and some whistled notes; female, a Mallard-like *quack*.

Habitat: Marshes, lakes, pools, and rivers; similar habitat in winter, concentrating on larger lakes and wetlands.

Nesting: 8–12 creamy eggs, in depression lined with down and plant material near water protected by thick vegetation.

Range: Holarctic, breeding discontinuously across Eurasia from Iceland, Britain, and Spain to eastern Siberia, and in North America. Mainly migratory; in Europe, wintering south to Mediterranean and North Africa.

It feeds on the surface like a Mallard, with which it often occurs, but is shyer, not associating with man. Rather scarce and local in Europe, it is absent from many seemingly suitable areas.

206, 236 Teal
(*Anas crecca*)

Description: 14" (35 cm). *Very small,* dark-coloured duck. Male has *grey body,* with *horizontal white stripe* on scapulars and *yellow patch by undertail coverts;* head looks dark at a distance, actually dark chestnut with long, green eye patch. Female is speckled brown, almost featureless at rest. In flight, both sexes appear dark above except for white borders to *dark green wing patch.*

Voice: Male, a plaintive whistled *krrick;* female, a high-pitched *quack.*

Habitat: Nests on small ponds, streams, and marshes in moorlands and heaths. In winter, lakes, reservoirs, and marshes.

Nesting: 8–12 creamy eggs, in ground nest lined with leaves, down, and plant material, placed under heather, bracken, or other ground vegetation.

Range: Holarctic, breeding across northern Eurasia from Iceland and France to Bering Sea and Japan; also North America from Alaska to Newfoundland. European birds winter as far as southern Europe, Mediterranean region, and tropical Africa.

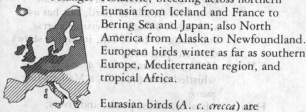

Eurasian birds (*A. c. crecca*) are conspecific with the North American Green-winged Teal (*A. c. carolinensis*). The chief difference between the two, very apparent in the field, is that the male *carolinensis* has a *vertical white stripe* on the side of the breast rather than a horizontal one on the wing; females are indistinguishable. The Green-winged Teal is now a regular visitor to Britain in small numbers.

208, 230 Mallard
(*Anas platyrhynchos*)

Description: 23″ (58 cm). Large, dabbling duck. Male has *green head; narrow, white neck ring; purple-brown breast;* grey body; black-and-white rear end, with *curly tail.* Bill yellow. Female almost featureless speckled brown, with brown-and-orange bill. Both sexes have *bluish-purple wing patch with white border.*

Voice: Male, a rather quiet *reeb;* female, a *quack* like domestic duck.

Habitat: Large lakes, ponds, rivers, streams, marshes, and man-made aquatic habitats. Some movement toward coasts and estuaries in winter.

Nesting: 10–12 pale green eggs, in depression lined with leaves, grass, down, and feathers, on ground under cover of thick vegetation near water.

Range: Holarctic. Breeds throughout Europe and across Asia to Pacific; also northern half of North America and locally in North Africa. Partial migrant in Europe, vacating northern and eastern areas, wintering south and west to northern Africa.

It is one of the most abundant ducks in the world—certainly the most familiar—and the ancestor of our domestic birds. Many farmyard types closely resemble their ancestor, owing to frequent interbreeding with wild birds, except for a few telltale patches of white and a generally overfed and earthbound look. Wild birds adapt readily to man, wintering tamely in parks and joining flocks of captive waterfowl, making it difficult to determine whether a given bird is wild or not.

223, 232 **Pintail**
(*Anas acuta*)

Description: Male, 26″ (65 cm), female, 22″ (55 cm). Slender, long-necked, dabbling duck. Male has *long central tail feathers; chocolate-brown head, throat, and hind-neck;* white underparts and *stripe on side of neck;* grey upperparts and flanks; *pale yellow patch* in front of black stern. Female distinguished from other brown female dabbling ducks by slim shape, thin neck, pointed tail, grey bill, and, in flight, *pale trailing edge to brown wing.*

Voice: Male, a nasal, wheezing *gzeee;* female, quacks and growling notes.

Habitat: Breeds by shallow lakes and pools on tundra, plains, and steppes; in winter, mainly maritime, on coasts, estuaries.

Nesting: 7–9 pale yellow or green eggs, in hollow lined with down, feathers, and plant material, near water, in open or under cover of low vegetation.

Range: Holarctic, breeding from Iceland, Britain, and Ireland across northern Eurasia to Bering Sea, Sakhalin, and North America. European birds winter in western and southern Europe and northern and tropical Africa.

Though a scarce and erratic breeding bird in most parts of Europe, it is extremely numerous in Asia and North America and may be the most abundant duck in the world. Shy and suspicious, it is among the first to take wing in a mixed flock of waterfowl, which may contribute to its success in the face of continuous hunting pressure.

222, 237 **Garganey**
(*Anas querquedula*)

Description: 15″ (38 cm). Small, slender duck. Male mottled brown, with *broad, white streak from eye to nape; greyish sides and white belly* contrast with dark brown breast; *pale blue-grey forewing* conspicuous in flight; green wing patch. Female similar to Teal, but with pale spot at base of bill, more pronounced eyebrow, and paler wings in flight.

Voice: Male, a dry, crackling rattle; female, a short *quack,* like Teal.

Habitat: Breeds and winters on shallow well-vegetated lakes, ponds, marshes, and swampy wetlands.

Nesting: 8–11 creamy-buff eggs, in hollow lined with plant material, down, and feathers, near water.

Range: Breeds from southern Scandinavia, Britain, and France across north-central Eurasia to Sea of Okhotsk. Migratory; European birds winter mainly in tropical Africa.

Unlike other European ducks, it deserts the temperate zone almost completely in winter. By far the most numerous duck wintering in tropical Africa, it is especially abundant in West Africa; 200,000 were present in the Senegal River delta in January 1971. It is subjected to considerable hunting pressure in its winter quarters.

---

224 **Blue-winged Teal**
(*Anas discors*)

Description: 15″ (38 cm). Small duck the size of Garganey, with similar wing pattern in flight. Male has purplish-grey head, with *broad, white crescent in front of eye.* Body, including sides and belly, mottled brown; *white patch on stern.* Female similar to female Garganey but slightly darker, with blue, not grey, forewing, and lacking prominent pale eyebrow.

Voice: Male, a squeaky, toneless *psip;* female, high-pitched *quack,* like Teal.

Habitat: Nests on small freshwater ponds, winters on ponds, lakes, and marshes, seldom on salt water.

Nesting: 10–12 whitish eggs, in hollow on ground, nest lined with dead grass and down, built under concealing vegetation near water.

Range: Breeds in North America. Accidental in

western Europe; most frequent in Britain and Ireland.

The three "blue-winged" teal of the world replace each other geographically, the Garganey occupying Eurasia, the Blue-winged Teal central and eastern North America, and the Cinnamon Teal western North America, with some overlap between the latter two.

209, 233 **Shoveler**
(*Anas clypeata*)

Description: 20″ (50 cm). Squat and short-necked; *long, heavy, spatulate bill* points downward and body is tilted forward on the water. Male has *dark green head; white breast, scapulars, and patch in front of black stern; chestnut belly and flanks.* In flight, both sexes show *pale blue forewing.* Female speckled brown like female Mallard, but distinguished by bill, forewing, and green wing patch.

Voice: Male, a double note, *tsook-took,* and a loud, nasal *paay;* female, loud *quack,* like Mallard, sometimes decrescendo.

Habitat: Reed-fringed lakes and pools with shallow, muddy water; overgrown streams, marshes, wet grassy meadows.

Nesting: 8–12 creamy-buff or olive eggs, in depression lined with plant material, down, and feathers, near water.

Range: Holarctic, breeding from Iceland, Britain, Ireland, and France east across Eurasia to Kamchatka and Manchuria; also North America. Partial migrant in Europe, wintering south to Africa.

It feeds while swimming or wading in shallow water, on surface, or in bottom mud, sweeping its head from side to side and passing water through its bill. Its broad, shovel-like bill is adapted to a diet of small aquatic organisms. As water is sucked through the bill, comb-like strainers (lamellae) filter out plankton, minute animals, and insects.

244 **Marbled Duck**
(*Marmaronetta angustirostris*)

Description: 16″ (40 cm). Small, with long neck and *large, shaggy head;* light grey-brown plumage, *marbled with pale spots;* tail tipped white. *Long, dark, smudgy line through eye* contrasts with pale cheeks and throat. In flight, secondaries paler than rest of wing. Sexes alike.

Voice: Male, a nasal squeak; female, a weak double whistle.

Habitat: Shallow, well-vegetated lakes, pools, marshes, riverbanks, and floodlands.

Nesting: 9–13 creamy-yellowish eggs, in hollow lined with down, feathers, and plant material, near water under thick cover.

Range: Summer visitor and partial resident in southern Spain, some birds moving to North Africa in winter. Also scattered breeding localities in North Africa and southwest Asia.

A little-known bird, it is scarce and local throughout its range. The shallow waters it inhabits frequently dry out, causing it to wander and disperse. Shy and unobtrusive, it requires thick vegetation at the water's edge.

216, 243 **Red-crested Pochard**
(*Netta rufina*)

Description: 22″ (55 cm). Rather large and plump; sits high on water. Male has *crimson bill and legs, orange-chestnut head;* golden-tipped crown feathers form *bushy crest,* giving head rounded appearance. Upperparts brown, with white crescent on shoulder; *underparts and neck black, flanks white.* In flight, both sexes have conspicuous *long, broad white wing bar.* Female dull brown; *pale cheeks* contrast with dark crown; red tip to bill obvious at close range.

Voice: Male, a hoarse *bait,* a hard, sneezing call, and other notes; female, *gock* and *kurr.*

Habitat: Large, reed-fringed freshwater lakes, brackish pools, and lagoons; on open water when not breeding, infrequent on coast.

Nesting: 6–12 pale green or creamy eggs, in nest of reeds and aquatic plants lined with down and feathers, at end of tunnel in vegetation near water.

Range: Breeds in scattered localities in Europe from Spain north to Holland and Denmark, east to Czechoslovakia and Danube delta, and more continuously in west-central Asia from Turkey and southern Russia to Mongolia. Winters mainly in Mediterranean region.

A diving duck with some of the characteristics of a surface-feeder, it feeds both by diving in deep water and by upending in shallower water. More terrestrial than other diving ducks, it walks easily and sometimes grazes.

215, 242 **Pochard**
(*Aythya ferina*)

Description: 18″ (45 cm). Male has *dark chestnut head and neck, black breast and stern,* and *pale grey back and flanks.* Female dull brown; body greyer, with pale areas at base of bill and on throat; sometimes pale streak behind eye. Head rather pointed. Both sexes have *grey-blue band across dark bill,* grey wing with paler grey bar.

Voice: Male, a soft, nasal wheezing call; female, a harsh *brerr* or *karr.*

Habitat: Nests on lakes, ponds, and streams with dense margins of reeds and other aquatic vegetation; in winter, on reservoirs and open water, sometimes estuaries; at sea only if driven by hard weather.

Nesting: 6–11 pale green or grey-green eggs, in heap of plant material lined with down and feathers near or in water among thick vegetation.

Range: Breeds in western and central Eurasia from Iceland, Britain and Ireland, and Spain (very local) east to Lake Baikal. European birds winter in southern and

western Europe and northern and tropical Africa.

Like its North American relatives, the Redhead and Canvasback, it is typically a bird of steppes and open plains. In Asia it inhabits saltwater habitats as well as the freshwater ones it uses in Europe. In recent years it has been expanding its range west in Europe, adapting to new habitats such as reservoirs, where it is often very numerous in winter.

228 Ferruginous Duck
(*Aythya nyroca*)

Description: 16″ (40 cm). Smallest of the European diving ducks; crown rather pointed. Male *rich chestnut,* with dark brown back, *prominent, white undertail coverts,* and *white eye.* Female similar but darker and duller, with brown eye. Both sexes have *conspicuous white wing bar.*

Voice: Male, a rapid, wheezy chatter; female, a loud, croaking *aark.*

Habitat: Nests on shallow, freshwater lakes and pools with margins of reeds and other thick vegetation; also brackish pools and lagoons. In winter, on larger bodies of open water and on coast.

Nesting: 7–11 yellowish eggs, in depression lined with plant material, down, and feathers, by water's edge under cover.

Range: Breeds in west-central Eurasia from Spain, Yugoslavia, Czechoslovakia, and East Germany through southern Russia to Iran and Tibet. Winters south to northern tropical Africa.

Locally numerous on lowland plains and steppes of eastern Europe, it is scarce or absent farther west. It feeds in shallow waters on submerged or surface vegetation, diving and also upending if depth permits it to reach the bottom growth. Outside breeding season it is usually in small parties, mixing infrequently with other species.

229, 254 **Tufted Duck**
(*Aythya fuligula*)

Description: 17″ (43 cm). Male *all-black except for sharply contrasting white flanks and belly;* female dark brown, sometimes with narrow ring of white around base of bill or whitish undertail coverts. Male has *long, narrow tuft of feathers* drooping from back of head; female has shorter tuft. Both sexes show broad white wing-stripe in flight. Bill blue-grey.

Voice: Male, mellow whistled calls during courtship displays; female, a rolling growl, *karr* or *kurr*.

Habitat: Lakes, ponds, slow-moving rivers, and man-made aquatic habitats, usually with some fringing vegetation; in winter, also on larger, more open lakes, reservoirs, and estuaries.

Nesting: 5–12 pale green or grey-green eggs, in hollow lined with grass, down, and feathers near water under cover.

Range: Breeds across northern Eurasia from Iceland, Britain, Ireland, and France to Kamchatka and Japan. Mainly resident in western Europe but birds from north and east winter south to Mediterranean region and Sudan.

The most common diving duck, it is second only to the Mallard in its tolerance of man. Its ability to adapt to man-made habitats has greatly increased its range in western Europe during this century. Its broad and varied diet includes plants, molluscs, crustaceans, and insects, changing according to season and locality. It often joins tame ducks in parks to eat bread and other handouts.

225, 255 **Scaup or Greater Scaup**
(*Aythya marila*)

Description: 19″ (48 cm). Male similar to Tufted Duck, with black head, neck, breast, and stern and white flanks, but *light grey back;* both sexes lack crest. Female dark brown, similar to female Tufted, but with *extensive white patch at base of bill* and a faint pale cheek patch in summer. Both sexes have white wing bar.

Voice: Male gives soft, dove-like *cu-cooo* during courtship; female, a slow, growling *karrr*.

Habitat: Lakes and ponds on open and wooded tundra and moorland; local on Baltic Coast. In winter, chiefly marine, in bays and estuaries, sometimes brackish lagoons and freshwater lakes near coast.

Nesting: 6–15 pale green or grey eggs, in hollow lined with down, feathers, and vegetation in the open by water.

Range: Holarctic, breeding from Iceland and Norway across extreme northern Eurasia to Bering Sea; also northern North America. European birds winter south to France, Yugoslavia, and Black Sea.

The most maritime of the pochard tribe, this hardy species is seemingly unaffected by cold or storms. An accomplished diver, it feeds even in rough seas. It is gregarious at all seasons and often breeds socially, sometimes among colonies of gulls and terns; in winter, it is often found in enormous rafts. It is omnivorous but in winter feeds primarily on molluscs.

238, 250 Eider
(*Somateria mollissima*)

Description: 23″ (58 cm). The heaviest and bulkiest of European ducks, with a long, sloping head profile. Breeding male has *black crown, flight feathers, rump, tail, and belly; rest of plumage white,* with pink tinge on breast and pale green patches on nape that are invisible at a distance. In eclipse becomes dark brown, with white forewing. Female uniform brown with black bars. Immature male mixed black and white, varying with age.

Voice: Male has crooning courtship call, *ah-WOOO;* female, a guttural *krrr*.

Habitat: Almost exclusively marine, breeding

and wintering along coasts and offshore islands; very rare on inland waters.

Nesting: 4–6 pale greenish-grey or olive eggs, in nest of grass and seaweed lined with down and feathers in hollow in open or under cover of vegetation or rocks.

Range: Holarctic, breeding on northern coasts of Eurasia and North America, in Europe south to Britain and Holland. Winters mainly within breeding range, though there is considerable migration from some areas, notably the Baltic.

Female Eiders line their nests with copious amounts of soft down taken from their breasts; this insulates the eggs and chicks in icy conditions. For centuries northern Europeans have harvested the down for commercial use. The species is therefore protected and encouraged. A hardy bird, it spends most of the winter at sea, resting offshore in large rafts or diving in shallow waters for molluscs. It flies low over the water, often in single file or in V formation.

234, 249 **King Eider**
(*Somateria spectabilis*)

Description: 22″ (55 cm). Male has pink breast, black underparts, white forewing, and black flight feathers, all similar to Eider's, but distinguished by *black back* and more rounded, pale blue-grey head with greenish face. *Bill red; broad frontal shield bright orange.* Female very similar to female Eider but more rusty, and dark markings more crescent-shaped; *stubby bill and steeper forehead* give different profile.

Voice: Male, cooing calls during courtship like Eider but coarser and gruffer; female, guttural notes like female Eider.

Habitat: Breeds near freshwater pools and rivers on arctic tundra; winters at sea along coasts.

Nesting: 4–7 pale olive eggs, in hollow lined with down and feathers, among heath or grass tussocks, usually near water.

Range. Circumpolar, breeding on Arctic islands and coastal tundra of Asia and North America. Winters and summers off coasts of Arctic Russia, Norway, and Iceland. Accidental elsewhere, particularly Finland, Sweden, Britain, and Ireland.

Truly arctic, it prefers to remain in northern waters until ice forces it to leave. It is a solitary nester but is very gregarious at other seasons, forming large rafts off the coast, often in mixed flocks with Eiders, scoters, and other sea ducks.

248 Steller's Eider

(*Polysticta stelleri*)

Description: 18″ (45 cm). Compact, with rather flat crown; male has *white head, black and white upperparts,* and *chestnut underparts.* Small green patches on forehead and nape and black eye patch and throat visible at close range. White forewing conspicuous in flight. Female uniform dark brown, mottled rather than barred, with *purple-blue wing patch prominently bordered white.*

Voice: Male, a low growling call; female, rapid guttural calls.

Habitat: Breeds by pools or swampy ground on arctic tundra; winters off rocky coasts.

Nesting: 6–8 pale yellow to olive or greenish eggs, in nest of moss, grass, and lichen lined with down and feathers, in hollow near water.

Range: Breeds on Arctic coasts of eastern Siberia, Alaska, and Mackenzie. Small numbers summer and winter off northern Norway; accidental elsewhere in Europe.

Its shape at rest and slim wings and rapid wingbeats in flight resemble dabbling ducks (*Anas*). It feeds in small flocks; individuals synchronize their diving, all submerging simultaneously.

204, 259 **Harlequin Duck**
(*Histrionicus histrionicus*)

Description: 17″ (43 cm). Small, dark duck with high forehead and short bill. Male has dark grey-blue head and body, with *harlequin pattern of white stripes and spots* and *chestnut flanks.* Female dark brown, similar to but smaller than Velvet and Surf scoters, with 3 small, pale face patches differently positioned—above and below eye and on ear coverts.

Voice: Male, high-pitched squealing and a long, descending whistle ending in a trill; female, a harsh croak.

Habitat: Fast-flowing rivers; winters on rocky coasts.

Nesting: 6–8 pale creamy or buff eggs, in hollow lined with plant material, down, and feathers, on ground under thick vegetation or on rocky island in river. Nests socially.

Range: Holarctic, with large gaps in range. Breeds in Iceland, Greenland, and eastern Canada; mountains of western North America; and in northeastern Asia. Iceland population highly sedentary; accidental elsewhere in Europe.

It spends most of its life in turbulent water: in summer on swift mountain streams, even among rapids and around waterfalls, and in winter on the wildest and rockiest coasts. It rides the surf, diving for mussels, periwinkles, and other shellfish, which it tears from the rocks with its bill. In rivers it feeds mainly on larvae of aquatic insects.

241, 252, 253 **Long-tailed Duck**
(*Clangula hyemalis*)

Description: Male, 21″ (53 cm); female, 16″ (40 cm). Small, agile sea duck, with short bill, steep forehead, and small head. Male has *elongated central tail feathers; in summer, dark brown* with *white face patch* and belly; *in winter, white* with *dark cheek patch, breast band,* back, and wings. Female, in summer dark brown, with whitish face, side neck, and belly, and prominent *dark cheek patch;* in winter, head and neck largely white and cheek patch smaller. Both sexes have uniform dark wing in flight.

Voice: Wide range of far-carrying calls, typically *uh-haaa* or *uh-haaa-haa-OO-WAH*. Female, low, quacking calls.

Habitat: Lakes and pools in open tundra, both lowland and montane; sometimes islands in salt water. In winter, predominantly marine.

Nesting: 5–9 yellowish or greenish eggs, in hollow lined with plant material, down, and feathers, near water under low vegetation or among rocks.

Range: Circumpolar, breeding from Iceland, Spitsbergen, and Norway across extreme northern Eurasia to Bering Sea, and from Alaska to eastern Canada and Greenland. Winters on coasts of northern Europe south to Britain and Ireland, Holland, and Baltic Sea.

It is one of the most vocal of European waterfowl, calling at any time of year, in flight and on water, individually and in flocks. The noise made by a flock of calling and displaying birds has been compared to distant bagpipes or hounds baying. In North America, it is known as Oldsquaw, its cackling calls being likened to the garrulous chatter of a group of old squaws.

240, 262 **Common Scoter or Black Scoter**
(*Melanitta nigra*)

Description: 19″ (48 cm). Male *all-black* except for *orange patch on upper half of bill; knob at base of bill black* (orange in American race, which is accidental in Europe). Female dark brown, with *pale cheeks and throat contrasting with dark crown;* distinguished from female Red-crested Pochard by more blackish upperparts, lack of wing bar, and (usually) saltwater habitat.

Voice: Male, plaintive, piping calls; female, harsh whistle and growling calls.

Habitat: Lakes and slow-moving rivers on tundra and moorland, sometimes at high altitudes; outside breeding season, chiefly marine.

Nesting: 6–9 creamy eggs, in hollow lined with plant material, down, and feathers, near water under cover of heather or other vegetation. Often on small island.

Range: Breeds from Iceland, northern Britain, Ireland, and Norway across northern Eurasia to Bering Sea; also North America. Winters mainly on coasts from Norway and southern Baltic to Spain and northwest Africa.

The name Common Scoter is appropriate only in Europe. In North America it is the least common of the three scoters, and in Asia it has a more restricted range than Velvet Scoter. Most familiar as a winter visitor, it rides offshore waves in large rafts, sometimes with eiders and other sea ducks. It dives in shallow water for molluscs, its principal food.

226, 260 **Surf Scoter**
(*Melanitta perspicillata*)

Description: 21″ (53 cm). *Large head* and *large bill;* male black, with *white patches on forehead and nape* and *red, white, and yellow bill.* Female dark brown, with two pale patches on face like Velvet Scoter, sometimes pale patch on nape; best distinguished at rest by heavier bill. Both sexes separated from Velvet Scoter by *absence of white on wing.*

Voice: Mostly silent, but male in courtship has liquid, gurgling call; female, a guttural croak.

Habitat: Lakes, ponds, and marshes in both wooded and open tundra; winters on coasts, usually close inshore.

Nesting: 5–7 creamy or pinkish-buff eggs, laid in ground depression lined with plant material and down, placed under low branches of trees or grassy tussock in open.

Range: Breeds in North America; accidental in Europe, particularly Britain and Ireland, France, and Scandinavia.

It is sociable, flocking with other scoters and eiders, but stays closer to shore, even among breaking waves, and often enters harbours. It is recorded more frequently in Europe than any other North American waterfowl; with more than 100 records in Britain and Ireland alone. Though most records are of males, many females may have occurred undetected, being difficult to distinguish from female Velvet Scoters.

247, 261 **Velvet Scoter**
(*Melanitta fusca*)

Description: 22″ (55 cm). Large, with heavy bill. Male black, with *small white patch below eye;* bill black, with orange sides. Female dark brown, with *two pale patches on face.* Both sexes have *white patch on trailing edge of wing* prominent in flight, sometimes visible at rest. When no white visible, female distinguished from female Common Scoter by face pattern.

Voice: Male, ringing or piping calls during courtship, and a croaking flight call, *karr;* female, *braaa* or *kjuorrr.*

Habitat: Ponds, lakes, and rivers chiefly in taiga and wooded tundra; also open tundra and alpine moorlands. Outside breeding season, chiefly marine.

Nesting: 7–10 creamy eggs, in nest of grass, twigs, and leaves, lined with down and feathers, in vegetation under bush or tree or by water.

Range: Holarctic, breeding from Norway across Eurasia to eastern Siberia and Kamchatka; also North America. Winters on European coasts from Norway and Baltic and North seas to northern Spain; also Black Sea and some inland lakes.

It winters at sea, often with Common Scoters, even though the Velvet Scoter prefers rockier shores and rougher waters. It is usually found in small parties rather than large flocks and dives in shallow water for food, chiefly shellfish, but also crabs, starfish, worms, and other marine organisms. Diving is often synchronised, all members of party submerging at once.

246, 257 Barrow's Goldeneye
(*Bucephala islandica*)

Description: 21″ (53 cm). Very similar to Goldeneye, but slightly larger; *shape of head different—long and oval,* with low crown and *bushy mane on nape.* Male differs further from Goldeneye in having larger, *crescent-shaped* white mark between eye and bill, *purple gloss* to head, and *black scapulars with row of white spots;* appears blacker above. Female very similar to Goldeneye, but head more oval and bill shorter and deeper, usually with more yellow at tip.

Voice: Rather silent. Male, grunting *ka-KAA* during courtship; female, a low, hoarse *kerr* or *gairr.*

Habitat: Lakes, ponds, and rivers in both wooded and open country; winters in similar habitat and also on coast.

Nesting: 8–14 blue-green eggs, in hole in cliff or wall or among rocks; also in nest box; nest chamber lined with down and feathers.

Range: Breeds in Iceland, Greenland, and North America. Iceland birds highly sedentary; accidental elsewhere in Europe.

In treeless Iceland it has adapted to open country, but in North America it is a woodland bird during breeding season, nesting in tree holes. It is partial to fast-flowing rivers and rapids but on the coast prefers sheltered bays and inlets to rough waters.

245, 258 **Goldeneye**
(*Bucephala clangula*)

Description: 18″ (45 cm). Chunky, with large head and short neck; short bill and steep forehead give triangular shape to head. Male has *black head* with *green gloss* and *round white spot between eye and bill;* white neck and underparts; black upperparts with white lines on scapulars. Female has *chocolate-brown head,* white collar, brownish-grey body, whitish belly. Both sexes have blackish wings, with *large, square white patch.*

Voice: Silent except during courtship, when male has loud, rasping *zeeet* and other nasal and rattling calls; female in flight gives rapid, *kah-kah-kah* . . .

Habitat: Lakes, ponds, and rivers in wooded country, mainly coniferous; winters on inland lakes, reservoirs, rivers, bays, and estuaries.

Nesting: 6–11 blue-green eggs, in tree hole, rabbit burrow, or nest box, lined only with down and feathers, near water in woods.

Range: Holarctic, breeding from Norway and Germany across northern Eurasia to Kamchatka and Manchuria; in North America from Alaska to eastern Canada. European birds winter south to Britain and Ireland, France, Balkans, and Adriatic and Black seas.

It rises more steeply from the water than other ducks on rapidly beating wings, which is perhaps an adaptation to its breeding environment, where it may have to rise almost vertically from a small pond to clear the surrounding trees. In flight the beating wings make a loud, whistling sound audible at a considerable distance. Its diet is chiefly shellfish, and insects and their larvae.

220, 251 **Smew**
(*Mergus albellus*)

Description: 16″ (40 cm). Small, with short bill, differing widely from other sawbills in *size, shape, and plumage.* Male on water appears *all-white, with black eye patch;* other black marks visible only at close range. In flight, looks black and white, with black back, dark tail, and large, white patch on black wing. Female, grey with *white cheeks and throat contrasting with dark chestnut cap;* white wing patches as in male.

Voice: Mainly silent. Male has rattling and grunting calls during courtship; female, a harsh rattle.

Habitat: Small lakes, ponds, and backwaters of rivers in wooded tundra and coniferous forest; winters mainly on fresh water, on larger lakes, reservoirs, and rivers, less often on estuaries and coastal bays.

Nesting: 6–9 creamy eggs, in tree hole or nest box, lined with down and feathers, near water in forest.

Range: Breeds from Sweden and Finland across northern Russia and Siberia to Bering Sea. Winters from southern Scandinavia south to Britain, France, Italy, Balkans, and Black Sea.

Drakes are unmistakable, but a lone female, with its pale cheeks, dark crown, and habit of diving constantly, may at a distance resemble a grebe. At close range the rich chestnut crown, which has caused the duck and eclipse and immature drake to be called "Redheads," becomes obvious. A swift and agile flier and expert diver, it is also quite at home on land.

211, 219 **Red-breasted Merganser**
(*Mergus serrator*)

Description: 23″ (58 cm). Slim-headed sawbill, with *ragged double crest* at back of head; long, thin red bill. Male has dark green head, *broad, white collar, chestnut breast,* and light grey flanks. Female has rusty head *merging gradually* into white throat and neck; *brownish-grey* upperparts. Broad, white patch on wing in flight.

Voice: Mainly silent. Male has wheezy,

rattling call during courtship; female, a harsh *karrrr* and *grraaak*.

Habitat: Lakes and rivers in wooded districts, on open tundra and along coast in quiet bays and inlets. Chiefly marine in winter, preferring sheltered situations to open sea.

Nesting: 7–12 creamy or greenish eggs, in hollow lined with plant material, down, and feathers, near water under cover of thick vegetation or rocks.

Range: Holarctic, breeding from Iceland, Britain and Ireland, Norway, and Denmark across northern Eurasia to Bering Sea and northern Japan; also North America from Alaska to eastern Canada and Greenland. Winters on coasts of Europe south to Mediterranean region and Black Sea.

Mergansers chase their prey underwater, like cormorants; this species uses wings as well as feet. Grasping the slippery fish in their serrated bills, they bring their prey to the surface before swallowing it.

218, 256 **Goosander**
(*Mergus merganser*)

Description: 26″ (65 cm). Larger and bulkier than Red-breasted Merganser, with *heavier, more rounded head;* male has vestigial crest, female has shaggy, drooping crest; both sexes have long red bill. Male has dark green head; *pure white neck and underparts,* often tinged salmon-pink; appears very white on water or in flight. Female has *chestnut head and upper neck, with sharply defined white patch on chin; blue-grey upperparts* and flanks. Broad, white wing patch.

Voice: Generally silent. Male has low croaking and other calls during courtship; female, a hoarse *kar-r-r*.

Habitat: Large lakes and rivers, chiefly in forested regions, but also on open tundra, sometimes by sheltered bays. Winters chiefly on lakes, reservoirs, and large rivers, occasionally on estuaries and protected inlets.

Nesting: 7–14 creamy or yellowish eggs, in cavity lined with down and sometimes plant material, in hole of tree or bank.

Range: Holarctic, breeding from Iceland, Britain, and Switzerland across northern Eurasia to Bering Sea and Sakhalin; also central Asia and northern North America. Winters in northern Europe south to central France, Adriatic, and Black Sea.

It is essentially a freshwater species, while the Red-breasted Merganser is marine for much of the year, though the two may occur together on inland lakes. Persecuted by man as a competitor for fish, it may in fact be beneficial, preventing overpopulation of fish by thinning out their numbers.

213, 239 **Ruddy Duck**
(*Oxyura jamaicensis*)

Description: 16" (40 cm). Slightly smaller than White-headed Duck, without swollen base to bill. Characteristic *stiff tail, usually cocked.* Male has brown crown and nape and *white cheeks and throat;* body rich, uniform chestnut. Female similar to female White-headed, but greyer, with less pronounced dark bar across pale cheeks. Both sexes have blue or blue-grey bill and brown wings.

Voice: Largely silent, though both sexes produce bill-rattling and other nonvocal noises during courtship display.

Habitat: In Britain, breeds on small lakes and pools and winters on larger lakes and reservoirs.

Nesting: 6–10 white eggs, in down-lined nest of reeds and aquatic plants constructed in water among thick vegetation.

Range: New world; feral population now established in western England.

Like the Canada Goose and the Mandarin, it is another introduced exotic that has escaped from captivity and established a self-sustaining breeding population. It feeds by diving in shallow water for insect larvae, seeds, and tubers of aquatic plants, which it obtains by straining mud through its bill.

214 White-headed Duck

(*Oxyura leucocephala*)

Description: 18″ (45 cm). Plump, large-headed, short-necked, with a *swollen base to bill* and long, graduated, *stiff tail, frequently cocked.* Male has *white head, black crown* and neck, and rich, dark brown body almost chestnut on breast and rump. Female's crown and nape dark brown; cheeks and throat white, with *broad, dark bar across cheeks.* Both sexes have blue or blue-grey bill and brown wing.

Voice: Mainly silent. Male, a low, accelerating purr, like the muted winding of a fishing reel; also a high-pitched double piping note. Female, a soft *gek.*

Habitat: Shallow freshwater lakes and pools and brackish lagoons with dense fringe of reeds and other aquatic plants.

Nesting: 5–12 white eggs, in down-lined nest of reeds, leaves, and other plant material in water among reeds, often domed.

Range: Small numbers breed in southern Spain, Romania, and Sardinia, wintering near breeding areas; formerly more widespread. Also breeds in North Africa (scattered) and from Turkey and southern Russia to Mongolia.

It was the only representative in Europe of the distinctive stifftails (*Oxyurini*) until the Ruddy Duck was introduced. Formerly more widespread in central and southern Europe, it now occurs mainly in western Asia, though even there its dependence on very shallow waters makes it vulnerable to shifting rainfall patterns and drought. The world population was recently estimated to be only 15,000.

EAGLES, HAWKS, AND VULTURES
(Accipitridae)

217 species: worldwide. Twenty-seven species breed in Europe. Small, medium, and large birds with broad wings, strong legs, powerful feet, and sharp claws for seizing prey. Bill short, stout, and strongly hooked; used for tearing flesh. Plumage usually brown or grey, often barred and streaked. Sexes usually similar, but female larger than male. Prey on live animals, including mammals, birds, fish, snakes, lizards, frogs, and large insects; some also take carrion. Strong and speedy fliers, soaring often. Usually solitary when not breeding.

308, 355 Honey Buzzard
(*Pernis apivorus*)

Description: 20–23″ (50–58 cm). Adults have sides of head grey; crown, nape, and upperparts dark brown. Underparts extremely variable, ranging from almost wholly brown to white, but typically with heavy brown barring. In flight similar to Buzzard, but has *smaller head, longer neck, heavily barred underparts and underside of wings;* and *longer, round-ended tail,* with *two black bands near base,* as well as black subterminal band. Wings held flat or drooping downward when soaring or gliding. Juvenile has pale head and streaked underparts.

dark juvenile

Voice: Normal call of male, *puihu;* female, *piha*.

Habitat: Mature woodland, chiefly deciduous but also mixed and coniferous.

Nesting: 1–3 white to buff eggs spotted red-brown, in stick nest lined with leaves and twigs; also old nest of crow or hawk, high in tall tree.

Range: Summer visitor to Europe, north to England and north-central Scandinavia; uncommon in Mediterranean areas.

Winters in tropical Africa. Also breeds in western Asia.

It feeds mainly on the larvae of bees and wasps, consuming some honey and part of the nest itself in the process; it also eats the adults, snapping them up skilfully in its bill and nipping off the sting before swallowing the body. On the ground it digs out bees' and wasps' nests with its feet. It also obtains a supplementary diet of mice, frogs, grasshoppers, and termites.

---

330 Black-shouldered Kite
(*Elanus caeruleus*)

Description: 13″ (33 cm). A small, slender bird of prey, with long wings and very short, square tail. Mainly *pale grey above,* with whitish face, underparts, and tail and prominent *black shoulders.* Underside of wings whitish, with contrasting dark primaries. Immature grey-brown above; white below, with pale chestnut wash and brown streaks.

Voice: A variety of weak, whistling and wailing calls.

Habitat: Open country with scattered trees, woodland edge, arid steppes.

Nesting: 3–5 creamy eggs spotted dark brown or pale grey, in a flat, loose nest of thin twigs in a solitary tree.

Range: Scarce resident in southern Spain and Portugal; vagrant elsewhere in southern Europe. Also breeds in Africa, southern Asia, and Indonesia.

It hunts over grassland, fields, and other open country, quartering the ground slowly like a small harrier, hovering frequently. After spotting prey, it descends slowly to earth in a controlled glide until just above the ground, landing with a sudden pounce. It feeds on mice and other small mammals, as well as large insects like grasshoppers and locusts. Much of its day is spent sitting on a dead tree, telephone pole, or other prominent perch.

316, 340 **Black Kite**
(*Milvus migrans*)

Description: 22″ (55 cm). *Dingy, dark brown,* with *shallow forked* tail appearing *almost square* when fully spread. Head lighter brown than body. From below, angular wings appear uniformly dark brown, though somewhat paler at base of primaries. From above, wings also dark except for pale area across coverts, much less prominent than similar mark on Red Kite. Juvenile has pale streaks on underparts; light patch at base of primaries suggests Red Kite, but much less prominent. Could be confused with Marsh Harrier at a distance.

Voice: Noisy; normal call, a high-pitched, complaining whinny similar to a young gull; chattering and rattling calls given during breeding season.

Habitat: In western Europe, lightly wooded country, usually near lakes and rivers; in the east, more open cultivated country, often in towns and villages.

Nesting: Usually 2–3 dull white eggs, unmarked or with red-brown spots and grey-purple marks, in nest of sticks and debris usually in tree, sometimes on rock or building.

Range: Summer visitor to Europe north to France, Germany, and Finland, absent only from the northwest; winters in tropical Africa. Accidental in Britain.

One of the world's most abundant birds of prey, the Black Kite has spread throughout most of the Old World, adapting to a wide variety of habitats, eating almost any kind of animal matter, and living commensally with man. In Africa and Asia it is abundant in cities and towns, performing a very useful function as a scavenger; in warmer waters it takes the place of gulls, feeding on harbour refuse.

317, 339 Red Kite
(*Milvus milvus*)

Description: 24″ (60 cm). Large and long-winged, with long, *deeply forked tail. Head whitish,* with dark streaks; upperparts brown; *rump, tail, and underparts pale reddish-chestnut.* In flight, separated from Black Kite by *prominent white patch on underwing at base of primaries* and *longer, more deeply forked tail.* Juvenile pale rufous-brown with buff streaks on underparts.

Voice: A high-pitched mewing similar to but more shrill than Buzzard, and a whinnying call like Black Kite.

Habitat: Open woodland, chiefly deciduous, in hills and lowlands; parklands, agricultural land.

Nesting: 2–4 white eggs spotted with reddish- or purplish-brown, in nest of sticks and debris, usually built on top of old nest of crow or hawk.

Range: Resident in northwest Africa, southern Europe, Wales, the Caucasus, and northern Iran; summer visitor to central Europe, north to Germany, southern Sweden, and western Russia.

In the 15th century the Red Kite was apparently abundant in towns in Europe and Britain, even in cities like London, acting as a scavenger, just as the Black Kite still does in many parts of the world. Today it has almost disappeared from Britain and is confined to remote wooded hills in Wales. Elsewhere in Europe, it is much less common than the Black Kite and is also a woodland bird.

307, 350 White-tailed Eagle
(*Haliaeetus albicilla*)

Description: 27–36″ (68–90 cm). Very large and bulky, with *very broad wings,* long neck, and *short, wedge-shaped tail.* Adult dark brown, with pale head, neck, and breast and *white tail.* Immature has *dark brown head and tail;* distinguished from

juvenile

young Golden by lack of white on underside of wings and tail.

Voice: Various barking calls, unimpressive for so large a bird: male, *kri-kri-kri;* female, a deeper *gra-gra-gra.*

Habitat: Steep, rocky coasts and offshore islands, large rivers, inland lakes, and marshes.

Nesting: 1–3 (usually 2) dull white eggs, in a bulky stick nest lined with vegetation, twigs, and sometimes wool in top of tall tree, on cliff.

Range: Breeds from Iceland, Scandinavia, Germany, and Balkans across northern Eurasia to Bering Sea and Japan. Adults mainly sedentary; young wander in winter to central and southern Europe and Mediterranean region.

The European representative of an almost worldwide genus of fish-eating eagles that includes the African Fish Eagle and the American Bald Eagle, it is, like most of its relatives, equally at home on fresh or salt water. It catches fish on the surface and also eats stranded or dying fish and carrion. While too cumbersome to catch birds on the wing, it captures ducks and other water birds by cruising low along the edge of a lake and surprising them. It was exterminated in Scotland in the last century, but there have been recent unsuccessful attempts to re-establish it.

298, 361 **Lammergeier**
(*Gypaetus barbatus*)

Description: 40–45" (102–113 cm). Easily distinguished from all other European birds of prey (except much smaller Egyptian Vulture) by *unique flight silhouette:* a combination of *long, narrow wings* and *long, wedge-shaped tail.* Head pale buffy-white, with *broad black mark through eye* to bill; *neck and underparts golden-fulvous;* upperparts, wings, and tail greyish-black. A bunch of black bristles hangs down from bill, producing "bearded" effect. Immature blackish, underparts and head gradually becoming paler with age.

Voice: Mainly silent; in display, a high, thin, descending scream: *peeeee-yoo*.

Habitat: High rocky mountains; in Europe, usually remote from man.

Nesting: 1–2 whitish eggs blotched with brown and purple, in shallow stick nest lined with animal bones in cave or on cliff-face ledge with overhanging rock.

Range: Discontinuous range in high mountains, from Spain, Pyrenees, Balkans, and some Mediterranean islands east through southwestern Asia to central China, and in Africa.

Also known as Bearded Vulture, the Lammergeier is a bird of uncertain affinities. While rare and declining in Europe, it is common in Kashmir, Tibet, and Ethiopia. Where numerous, it becomes commensal with man, living in villages and scavenging. It cracks large bones by dropping them from a height onto a flat rock, to obtain the marrow, its favourite food.

296, 360 **Egyptian Vulture**
(*Neophron percnopterus*)

Description: 23–26″ (58–65 cm). Smallest European vulture. Adult mainly dingy *white, with black flight feathers; yellow bare skin on head;* yellowish-white, shaggy ruff; thin bill. Flight silhouette different from other vultures' (except much larger Lammergeier), with *narrower,* straight-edged wings and *longer, wedge-shaped tail*. Immature uniformly brown, becoming whiter with each moult until fifth year, when it acquires adult plumage.

Voice: Mainly silent, occasionally making whining and mewing sounds and hisses.

Habitat: Open country, both montane and lowland; in some areas around villages.

Nesting: 1–3 white to buff or reddish eggs with red or brown markings, in nest of sticks and debris, including bones and other animal remains, fur, paper, and dung, lined with hair, wool, and rags, in small cave or cliff hole.

Range: Summer visitor to southern Europe, north to southern France, Italy, Yugoslavia, and the Ukraine, wintering in Africa. Also breeds in southwestern Asia and over much of Africa.

While living mainly in the wild in European mountains and countryside, in Asia and Africa it lives in and around towns and villages, eating all kinds of rubbish. It gathers at carcasses with other vultures, staying on the fringes until the larger species have finished. One of the very few known tool-using birds, it breaks ostrich eggs by throwing stones against them with its bill.

297, 362 **Griffon Vulture**
(*Gyps fulvus*)

Description: 38–41″ (95–103 cm). Typical vulture flight silhouette: *broad, straight wings* with spread primaries, *short, square tail*, and small, retracted head. In flight has a *two-tone appearance*, the overall sandy plumage contrasting with blackish flight feathers and tail; white down covering head and neck and creamy-white ruff obvious only on ground. Immature with brown ruff.

Voice: A variety of grunts, whistles, hisses, and other sounds, but usually silent.

Habitat: Open rocky and mountainous country; also eastern plains.

Nesting: 1 white egg with a few red-brown spots, in scanty nest of twigs, grass, and debris, in cave or crevice among rocks or on cliff ledge. Nests in loose colonies.

Range: Local in southern Europe from Portugal to Balkans and southern Ukraine, and through southwestern Asia to northern India; also in Egypt and North Africa. Partial migrant, some birds wintering in northern Africa.

Gregarious, it roosts communally on cliffs at night, spending most of the day soaring at great heights, on the lookout for carrion. Griffons watch each other as well as the ground; when one spots a carcass and descends, others quickly follow, many assembling from all directions around a single dead animal. A hierarchy is established, dominant birds feeding first.

299, 365 **Black Vulture or Cinereous Vulture** (*Aegypius monachus*)

Description: 39–42″ (98–105 cm). Slightly larger than Griffon Vulture, with larger head and more massive bill, distinguished by uniform *dark sooty-brown plumage,* brown ruff, black down on head, and blue-grey bare skin on neck. Immature has paler underparts. From above, *flight feathers appear paler than coverts.* Flight silhouette similar to Griffon; tail somewhat longer and more wedge-shaped, but highly variable according to age. When soaring, holds wings flat; Griffon's silhouette a shallow V.

Voice: Mainly silent; croaks and hisses given at carcasses and mewing notes during breeding season.

Habitat: Open country in plains, foothills, and mountains, with large trees for nesting.

Nesting: 1 white egg with red, brown, or purple marks, in large stick nest lined with bark and green branches, usually in large, isolated tree, sometimes on rock ledge. Nests added to each year and may become enormous.

Range: Southern Iberia, some Mediterranean islands, Balkans east across central Asia to Mongolia. Mainly resident.

The largest Old World vulture, with wingspan of over 10′ (3 m), it dominates all other vultures at a carcass. In spite of this advantage it is uncommon or rare throughout its range, and in most of Europe is considered an endangered species.

Usually solitary or in pairs, it is not gregarious like the Griffon, joining other vultures only to feed. The name Black Vulture is shared by a quite different New World species, *Coragyps atratus*.

313, 315, 345 **Short-toed Eagle**
(*Circaetus gallicus*)

Description: 25–27″ (63–68 cm). Medium-sized eagle, easily distinguished in flight by *largely white underparts,* except for variable amount of *dark brown on throat and upper breast,* black tips to primaries, faint dark barring on underside of wings, and 3 dark bars on tail. Upperparts grey-brown, head rather large and rounded, eye yellow. Immature has light rufous-brown breast and brown barring on white underparts. Often hovers with a distinctive "rowing" wing action, its thick neck giving it an owl-like quality.

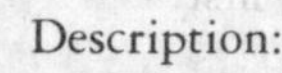

Voice: A variety of high-pitched, mewing and whistling calls.

Habitat: Lightly wooded country, open plains with scattered trees, open rocky hills.

Nesting: 1 white egg in thin nest of twigs, lined with leaves and pine needles, placed on top of low tree, 10–20′ (3–6 m) up. Sometimes reuses old nest.

Range: North Africa, southern and eastern Europe, and through southwestern Asia to India. European birds winter in tropical Africa.

The Short-toed Eagle is replaced in the Ethiopian region by 2 closely related species, possibly only subspecies, the Black-chested Harrier-Eagle (*C. pectoralis*) and Beaudouin's Harrier-Eagle (*C. beaudouini*). All 3 feed largely on snakes, though some lizards, frogs, and a few mammals are also taken. Their legs and feet are covered with heavy scales, believed to be an adaptation to prevent snakebites.

320, 354, 358 **Marsh Harrier**
(*Circus aeruginosus*)

Description: 19–22″ (48–55 cm). Larger and more heavily built than other European harriers, with *broader wings.* Adult male has rusty-brown body, darker on the back, shading to light buff on head; a broad *grey band across the upper wing surface separates brown coverts from black primaries;* tail grey. Adult female *dark chocolate-brown,* with *creamy-buff crown, throat, and shoulders* and dark line through eye. Immatures may be wholly dark, causing possible confusion with Black Kite, but distinguished from it by square-ended tail.

Voice: Display call of male, *kweea* or *kooee;* female, a more drawn-out *beeee-ya.*

Habitat: Swamps and marshes with extensive reedbeds.

Nesting: 4–5 bluish-white eggs, in large nest of sticks and reeds lined with grass, on ground in reedbed.

Range: Europe, north to England and southern Scandinavia, retiring from north and east in winter and migrating as far as tropical Africa. Other races, or closely related species, breed widely in Africa, Asia, and Australasia.

Though confined to marshes over much of its range, in some areas such as Australasia, the absence of competitors allows the Marsh Harrier to live in grasslands and other open country. Marsh breeders stay close to water even on migration, and in tropical Asia they winter commonly among rice fields.

318 **Hen Harrier**
(*Circus cyaneus*)

Description: 17–20″ (43–50 cm). Slimmer than Marsh Harrier, but broader-winged than Montagu's or Pallid harriers. Male *ash-grey,* paler on belly, with indistinct *white rump* (Pallid and Montagu's harriers have grey rumps), with black wing tips, and *indistinct, dark trailing edge to secondaries.* Underparts and underside of wings unmarked. Female dark brown above, with *white rump* and barred tail; buffy-brown below, usually with dark streaks; hard to separate from Pallid or Montagu's, but has more extensive white rump, broader wings, and lacks dark ear coverts. Immature like female, but more rufous on underparts.

Voice: A chattering *chick-ik-ik-ik-ik-ik* and a long-drawn, wailing *peee-ya*.

Habitat: Moorlands, young conifer plantations, grassy steppes, and coastal marshes and dunes; in winter, more open country, especially near coast.

Nesting: 4–6 bluish-white eggs, in shallow nest of sticks and reeds on ground under cover of taller vegetation.

Range: Holarctic, breeding from Britain and Ireland, northern Spain, and Scandinavia across northern Eurasia to Bering Sea, and widely in North America. Partial migrant, wintering south to Mediterranean region.

It is known as the Marsh Hawk in North America, where, in the absence of the Marsh Harrier, it has taken over the wetland habitat. Like other harriers, it quarters the ground when hunting, flying low, with few wingbeats and much gliding, the wings held in a shallow V, and capturing prey with a sudden pounce. About two-thirds of its diet consists of small mammals, especially mice, but small birds, snakes, and insects are also taken.

321, 331, 359 **Pallid Harrier**
(*Circus macrourus*)

Description: 17–19″ (43–48 cm). Slim shape and bouyant flight; male much *paler* than either Hen or Montagu's, with pale ashy-grey upperparts and rump and very pale, *almost whitish head and underparts. Underparts and wings unmarked except for small black patch on outer primaries*. Female almost identical to female Montagu's, but has narrow white collar behind dark ear coverts and more pronounced eye-stripe. Juvenile similar to female, but rufous below.

Voice: A high-pitched, chattering *ki-ki-ki* and a long-drawn *preee-pri-pri*.

Habitat: Open plains and grassy steppes; sometimes standing grain and marshes.

Nesting: 3–6 bluish-white eggs, in grass-lined hollow on ground on a hummock, under cover of tall vegetation.

Range: Breeds from southern Russia east to Lake Baikal and southeast to Iran, wintering in Africa and southwest Asia.

Pallid Harriers leave their breeding grounds on the Asian steppes in September to start the long migration to their winter quarters. Some head south for India, others move west, traveling up to 5,000 miles (8,000 km) to reach Senegal and South Africa. One of the main migration routes follows the Nile Valley and then the Rift Valley of East Africa.

319, 357 **Montagu's Harrier**
(*Circus pygargus*)

Description: 16–18″ (40–45 cm). Slimmer, with narrower wings than Hen Harrier. Male dark ashy-grey, with *grey rump; black bar on secondaries,* visible from *above and below;* and *brown streaks on white belly and underside of wing.* Female slimmer than female Hen, with *dark ear coverts,* but almost indistinguishable from Pallid. Juvenile *unstreaked* rufous-brown below.

Voice: A chattering *yick-yick-yick,* higher-pitched than that of Hen Harrier.

Habitat: Marshes, fens, standing grain, sand dunes, heaths, and moorland, especially with young conifer plantations; in winter, dry open plains.

Nesting: 3–6 bluish-white eggs, in flat nest of reeds, rushes, twigs, and coarse grass, lined with finer material, on ground among taller vegetation.

Range: Summer visitor to Europe, north to England, southernmost Sweden, and Estonia, wintering from Mediterranean region to southern Africa. Also breeds in North Africa and west-central Asia.

Like other harriers, the male has an aerial display during breeding season; he rises in the air, levels off, then folds his wings and dives, swooping upward again and repeating the dive. Sometimes he dives at the female, who turns over on her back and touches claws with him as he passes, and sometimes the two soar together high in the air. Gregarious outside the breeding season, they roost communally on the ground among tall vegetation.

309, 322 Goshawk
(*Accipiter gentilis*)

Description: 19–24″ (48–60 cm). Female larger than male. The largest *Accipiter*, distinguished from similar-sized birds of prey by combination of *short, rounded wings* and *long tail.* Resembles large female Sparrowhawk; dark ashy-brown above, with *pale stripe over eye;* white below, with dark brown barring, white undertail coverts; light *underwing finely barred;* tail has several broad blackish bars. Juvenile lighter brown above; buffy below, with bold spots.

Voice: A shrill, loud, insistent *kew-kew-kew-kew* given by both sexes, and plaintive scream, *hi-aa,* made by female.

Habitat: Coniferous and deciduous forests, especially near clearings and edges; cultivated land with small woods.

Nesting: 2–4 bluish-white eggs, in large stick nest lined with leafy twigs and green conifer needles, placed in tree.

Range: Holarctic, breeding from Morocco, Iberia, Britain (rare), and Scandinavia across Eurasia to Bering Sea and Japan; also in North America. European birds mainly resident; some wander south to Mediterranean region.

A fast and skilful hunter, it is capable of sudden bursts of speed, darting among trees and branches with agility. It catches birds in flight, preying especially on large woodland species, such as game birds, crows, and pigeons, and raids farmyards for chickens and other domestic birds. Rabbits, hares, squirrels, and a variety of small rodents also are a large part of its diet.

323, 324 **Sparrowhawk**
(*Accipiter nisus*)

Description: 11–15″ (28–38 cm). Female larger than male. Over most of European range easily distinguished by combination of *Accipiter* shape (*long tail* and *short, rounded wings*) and small size; in southeast can be confused with Levant Sparrowhawk. Adult male *dark slate-grey above; closely barred red-brown below,* with *rufous cheeks* and pale nape spot; blackish bars on grey tail. Female, grey-brown above, with a long, pale eye-stripe; white below, closely barred dark brown. Immature, dark brown above, with rufous feather edgings; whitish below, with streaks and bars.

Voice: A sharp, rapid *kek-kek-kek* or *kew-kew-kew* and a variety of other calls.

Habitat: Open coniferous and deciduous woodland; farmland with scattered small woods, copses, and plantations.

Nesting: 3–7 bluish-white eggs variably marked with dark brown, in flat stick nest lined with bark and dead leaves, usually fairly high in tree.

Range: Breeds throughout Europe (not Iceland) and across Asia to Pacific, and in North Africa. Partial migrant, some birds wintering south to northern Africa.

Its diet consists chiefly of small birds, which it pursues with great agility. It perches inconspicuously in a woodland tree, dashing out after passing prey, or hunts in open country by hedgehopping, flying low over the ground, barely clearing hedges and fences, coming suddenly on unsuspecting prey, and grabbing it with a quick pounce.

Levant Sparrowhawk
(*Accipiter brevipes*)

Description: 13–15″ (33–38 cm). Similar to Sparrowhawk; male slightly larger, paler bluish-grey above with contrasting dark wing tips, and *grey, not rufous, cheeks;* female somewhat greyer above. Both sexes have *red eye* and *pale underside of wings contrasting with dark wing tips.* Immature similar to Sparrowhawk, but underparts paler and boldly spotted, not barred.

Voice: A high-pitched *kee-wick.*

Habitat: Woodland, mainly deciduous, and wooded river valleys in open country.

Nesting: 3–5 pale bluish or greenish eggs, in shallow stick nest lined with green leaves, placed high in tree.

Range: Summer visitor from central Greece north and east through Balkans, Romania, and Ukraine to southern Russia, and in southwest Asia from Turkey to Iran; winters mainly in Middle East.

Despite similarity to the Sparrowhawk, its closest relative is the Shikra (*A. badius*), an Afro-Asian species with which it is sometimes considered conspecific, though they overlap in Iran.

311, 356 **Buzzard**
(*Buteo buteo*)

Description: 20–22″ (50–56 cm). Very variable in colour, with *basic buzzard shape* of broad, rounded wings and tail and rather short, broad neck. Typically, dark brown, with some white mottling on underparts; brown underwing coverts and black carpal patch contrast with paler secondaries and *whitish patch*

dark

light

at base of primaries. Underside of tail grey, with *fine dark barring and a rather inconspicuous dark terminal band.* Eastern race, "Steppe Buzzard" (*B. b. vulpinus*), usually has rufous underparts and faintly barred rufous tail. Soars and glides with wings held upward in a shallow V.

Voice: A long, high-pitched, mewing call, *peeee-yoo.*

Habitat: Open forest and woodland, both lowland and montane, farmlands with scattered woods, and moorlands; in winter, also on open plains.

Nesting: 2–4 white eggs variably marked with red or brown, in bulky stick nest lined with green leafy twigs, grass, moss, and other fresh vegetation, usually in tree, sometimes on cliff.

Range: Breeds from Iberia, west and north Britain, and Scandinavia across much of Eurasia to the Pacific. Most European birds sedentary, but some winter south to Arabia and Africa.

It is the most common of the buzzards and small eagles, with which it shares a general similarity in size and shape. The wide variety of plumages also makes identification difficult. The best dictum for the birder, watching a soaring hawk of this group, is probably "It's a Buzzard until you can prove it isn't."

306, 348 **Long-legged Buzzard**
(*Buteo rufinus*)

Description: 24–26″ (60–65 cm). Larger than Buzzard, with longer wings and tail. Very variable: either blackish-brown (uncommon); rufous; pale yellowish-brown, with dark streaks on belly; or with whitish head and underparts, streaked light brown. Most have *unbarred pale cinnamon or rufous tail* and *whitish underwings contrasting with dark wing tips, carpal patches, and thighs;* head usually pale.

Voice: A short, high-pitched *mew* like Buzzard's.

Habitat: Open steppes, arid plains, and other dry, treeless areas.

Nesting: 2–5 pale green to white eggs, in large stick nest lined with grass and finer material, placed on rocky outcrop or on ground, usually sheltered by bush.

Range: Sparse resident in Greece; vagrant elsewhere in Europe. Also breeds in North Africa and from Turkey and southern Russia east to Mongolia.

Rather heavy and sluggish, it is often seen perching on a rock or other prominent vantage point, watching for prey. It also hunts from the air, gliding and soaring like other buzzards, hovering on slowly flapping wings as the Rough-legged Buzzard does. It feeds mainly on lizards and small mammals, especially gerbils.

310, 347 **Rough-legged Buzzard**
(*Buteo lagopus*)

Description: 20–24″ (50–60 cm). Longer-winged and slightly larger than Buzzard, with variable plumage. Adults have rather *pale head* and breast variably streaked brown, often contrasting with *blackish belly; underwing whitish* with *black carpal patches and wing tips.* Juveniles paler than adults. In all plumages *white tail with broad, black terminal band* is diagnostic. Often *hovers* or "hangs" in the air.

Voice: A mewing or meowing call like Buzzard's.

Habitat: Open tundra and barren hills, entering forested country only if very open. In winter, on moorlands, fields, marshes, sand dunes, and other open country.

Nesting: 2–4 white eggs marked with red or brown, in large nest of twigs or woody stems, lined with grass and fresh vegetation, on cliff ledge, rocky outcrop, or in tree.

Range: Circumpolar, breeding from Norway

across extreme northern Eurasia to Bering Sea, and from Alaska to Labrador. European birds winter south to Britain and eastern central Europe.

An Arctic species, it fluctuates in number according to the size of the rodent population. In years when lemmings are abundant, much larger clutches are laid and birds remain longer in their northern quarters after the breeding season. In winter, it feeds largely on rabbits, rats, mice, and other small mammals. Tame.

301, 363 **Lesser Spotted Eagle**
(*Aquila pomarina*)

Description: 24–26″ (60–65 cm). Very similar to Spotted Eagle, though slightly smaller and slimmer, with narrower wings and longer tail. Adults generally lighter brown, a few equally black; best distinction is underwing pattern: *coverts lighter than flight feathers* (the reverse being true in Spotted Eagle). Immature has fewer and smaller spots than Spotted Eagle and a *conspicuously pale buffy patch on nape.*

Voice: A high-pitched, yapping *cheuk-cheuk* or *kyeep-kyeep*.

Habitat: Woodlands, often at higher altitudes than Spotted Eagle and less likely near water; in winter, chiefly open savannas.

Nesting: 1–3 white eggs, variably spotted red-brown and grey, in stick nest lined with grass and leafy sprays, high in tree but not at top, usually at forest edge.

Range: Summer visitor from western Russia west to Germany, Hungary, and Balkans, wintering in tropical Africa. Also breeds in Asia.

Though Lesser Spotted and Spotted eagles overlap in part of their breeding ranges, there is some ecological separation between the two, the Lesser Spotted showing no interest in fish or water birds, preferring to hunt for small mammals over dry clearings and open areas at the forest edge.

303, 364 **Spotted Eagle**
(*Aquila clanga*)

Description: 26–29″ (65–73 cm). Rather chunky, with broader wings and shorter tail than those of Golden or Tawny. Head rather small and neck slim; droops wings when gliding. Adult *uniformly blackish-brown,* often with variable amount of *white on upper tail coverts;* from below, *flight feathers appear a shade lighter than wing coverts.* Immature has white upper tail coverts; *upperparts and upper surface of wings broadly spotted with pale buff.*

juvenile

Voice: A barking *tyuck-tyuck* or *kyak-kyak,* lower-pitched than Lesser Spotted.

Habitat: Lowland forest along river valleys, near marshes or lakes; on migration and in winter, over open country, plains, cultivated land, often near water.

Nesting: 1–3 greyish-white eggs, laid in stick nest lined with grass, leaves, and green sprays, usually in woodland tree.

Range: Summer visitor to eastern Europe from southern Finland to Poland and southern Russia, wintering locally and in small numbers west and south to Iberia, Mediterranean region, and northeast Africa. Also breeds across Siberia to Manchuria.

The Spotted Eagle is attracted to water, both on breeding grounds and in winter. It occasionally takes fish but prefers water birds like coots, ducks, and waders, preying especially on injured birds. Rather inactive, it spends much time perched on trees or other vantage points.

300, 353 **Steppe Eagle or Tawny Eagle**
(*Aquila rapax*)

Description: 26–31″ (65–78 cm). Plumage variable, ranging from dark brown through

Steppe Eagle

tawny to pale brown. European race, (*A. r. orientalis,*) usually *uniformly dark brown;* flight feathers black; tail grey-brown, with dark barring; and sometimes a buffy-yellow patch on nape. Immature has *white band on rump* and shows *thin, pale wing bars in flight* from above and below.

Voice: A rather crow-like *kow-kow* or *kwuk kwuk.*

Habitat: Scrubby plains, steppes, savannas.

Nesting: 1–3 white eggs, variably marked with red-brown, in small, shallow, flat stick nest lined with grass, straw, and fur, in tree or bush, sometimes on rock.

Range: Breeds from southern Russia across central Asia to Mongolia and south into India; widely in Africa. European birds winter in Middle East and Africa.

Because of its variability and discontinuous distribution, this species has been divided into a number of subspecies. Central Eurasian birds are often combined into a separate species, the Steppe Eagle, *A. nipalensis,* while elsewhere the birds are known as Tawny Eagles. Omnivorous, it has some uneagle-like feeding habits. It regularly parasitises other birds of prey, pursuing them as a skua pursues a tern, forcing them to disgorge their food. It feeds on carrion and in eastern Asia scavenges around human habitation. Its live prey includes small rodents, birds taken on the ground, snakes, lizards, and locusts.

302, 305, 352 **Imperial Eagle**
(*Aquila heliaca*)

Description: 31–33″ (78–83 cm). Large, heavy, blackish-brown eagle, with *pale yellowish-buff crown, nape, and sides of neck* and *white scapular patches.* Square tail shorter than Golden Eagle, pale grey-brown, with narrow dark bars and broad, dark, terminal band. Upper wing surface dark except in Spanish race, *A.*

h. adalberti, which has white leading edge. Immature tawny-buff, with white lower back and rump and dark streaks on underparts.

Voice: A barking *owk-owk-owk.* Usually silent.

Habitat: Montane and lowland forests, open plains, and steppes and marshes with scattered trees.

Nesting: 2–3 buffy-white eggs laid in huge stick nest lined with twigs, grass, and leafy sprays, in forest or lone tree.

Range: Breeds in Morocco, southern Iberia, and from Balkans and Hungary east across central Asia to Lake Baikal. European birds sedentary.

Rather sluggish, it spends much of the day sitting in a tree or on another perch, although it also soars. It feeds on carrion, as well as mammals, snakes, and birds it catches on the ground. Like many raptors, it reuses its old nests for many years. These often become enormous—up to 8 feet (2.5 m) across and 6 feet (2 m) thick. Since it has no natural enemies, its nest is often highly visible.

304, 349 **Golden Eagle**
(*Aquila chrysaetos*)

Description: 30–35″ (75–88 cm). Large and long-winged, with a tail somewhat longer than that of other *Aquila* eagles. Adult *uniformly dark brown,* sometimes tawny, with *golden-buff crown and nape* and pale buff band across upperwing coverts. Immature has *white base of tail* and *white patch at base of primaries,* visible both above and below.

Voice: Generally silent; a loud yelping *weeeo-hyo-hyo-hyo* and a whistling *tweeo.*

Habitat: Chiefly barren mountainous country, occasionally mountain forests, with broad altitudinal range—800′–7000′ (250–2200 m).

Nesting: 1–2 white eggs marked with brown, red, and pale grey, in bulky nest of branches, sticks, and woody stems, lined with grass, leaves, and pine needles, on cliff ledge.

Range: Scotland, Scandinavia, and northern Russia, and from Iberia through Alps and Mediterranean Europe to Balkans. Also breeds in North Africa, Asia, and North America. Mainly sedentary.

One of the world's most magnificent fliers, it is frequently seen soaring majestically along the face of a mountain, gliding effortlessly along a ridge or quartering a slope. It feeds mainly on mammals, typically large rodents, rabbits, and hares. Its enormous range makes it possibly the most numerous of the genus in the world, despite its declining population in many areas of Europe.

---

314 Booted Eagle
(*Hieraaetus pennatus*)

Description: 18–21″ (45–53 cm). Same size as Buzzard but with narrower wings and longer tail. Dimorphic. Both phases dark brown above, with pale rump and pale buffy band across upper side of wing. Light phase has *white body and underwing coverts contrasting with black flight feathers;* whitish tail with grey tip. Dark phase has *dark body and underside of wings,* and *pale rufous tail;* easily confused with Buzzard. Immatures of both phases very similar to adults.

light phase

dark phase

Voice: Common call, several short notes followed by a downslurred one: *pi-pi-pi-pew;* Also a high-pitched *ki-keee.*

Habitat: Coniferous and deciduous forests, often with nearby clearings or open country, chiefly in mountains but also on plains.

Nesting: 2 white eggs (sometimes 1) marked with brown, in large stick nest lined with leaves and pine needles, usually high in tree, sometimes on rocky outcrop. May reuse old nests.

Range: Summer visitor to Iberia, parts of France, and from northern Greece north to Yugoslavia, Romania, and southern

Russia, wintering in eastern Africa. Also breeds in North Africa and Asia.

A small, active eagle capable of fast flight, it sometimes pursues forest birds and mammals through the treetops like an *Accipiter,* though it spends much of the day soaring, usually in pairs. In open country it feeds on small game birds, mice, and lizards.

351 Bonelli's Eagle
(*Hieraaetus fasciatus*)

Description: 26–29″ (65–73 cm). Considerably larger than Buzzard, with longer, narrower, wings and longer tail. Dark brown above, often showing *pale patch on back; white below,* with variable amount of dark streaks. Tail grey, with *broad black terminal band.* Below, white body and forewing and pale patch at base of primaries contrast with *broad black band across underwing.* Immature lighter brown above and rust-coloured below, with narrow dark bar on underwing and narrow barring on tail, which lacks dark terminal band.

Voice: A mellow *klu-klu-klu,* a whistling *klueee,* a plaintive *klee-ay-o.*

Habitat: Wooded hills and lower mountain slopes, descending to more open country in winter.

Nesting: 2 white eggs lightly spotted and streaked brown and lilac, in large stick nest lined with leafy twigs, on rocky cliff or tree. Nest reused each year.

Range: Local resident in Mediterranean Europe from Iberia to Greece. Also breeds in North Africa and parts of Asia.

Bold and aggressive, it may attack a human approaching its nest. Its large and powerful feet enable it to take a wide range of birds and mammals—as large as hares and game birds, and sometimes storks and herons. It hunts either by a quick dash from cover or by soaring and then stooping on prey.

OSPREYS
(Pandionidae)

1 species: worldwide, breeding in Europe. Large bird of prey with long, pointed wings; short, hooked bill; and strong claws. Outer toe reversible; soles of feet covered with sharp spines for grasping fish obtained by plunge-diving feet first from considerable heights. Sexes similar. Nest in loose colonies; also singly. Food brought to nest by male and fed to young by female.

312, 346 Osprey
(*Pandion haliaetus*)

Description: 20–23″ (50–58 cm). Large, eagle-like bird of prey, *dark brown above and light below,* with long, narrow, *angled wings. Head white, with broad dark line through eye* onto neck; underparts white, with light brown breast band; underside of wing white, with *black carpal patch* and narrow dark bars on flight feathers. Sexes similar.

Voice: A repeated, short, whistled note: *kewk-kewk-kewk . . .* Alarm note at nest, a shrill *peyeee.*

Habitat: Always associated with fresh and salt water—lakes, rivers, seacoasts.

Nesting: 3 creamy or yellowish eggs with red and brown spots, in huge nest of sticks and debris lined with grass and finer material, usually on tree, also cliff or ruin, sometimes in low bush or even on ground.

Range: Cosmopolitan, occurring on every continent. Summer visitor to northern and eastern Europe, west to Scotland and Germany, and rare resident in Corsica and Balearics. In western and central Europe only a passage migrant.

Known also as the "fish eagle" or "fish hawk," the Osprey lives almost exclusively on fish. It circles over the water until it sights one, hovers briefly, then plunges feet first into the water, grabbing the fish with its talons. The underside of its toes are covered with sharp spines, affording a firm grip on its slippery prey. It usually takes fish on or near the surface, but if necessary can submerge completely for an instant. Its numbers have declined in many areas because it has eaten fish contaminated with toxic chemicals and because it has had to abandon nest sites that have been disturbed. Under special protection in Scotland, numbers are gradually increasing.

FALCONS
(Falconidae)

61 species: worldwide. Ten species breed in Europe. Small to medium-sized birds of prey with long, pointed wings, long tail, short neck, rounded head, hooked bill, long toes, and strong claws. Female larger than male. Among the world's fastest birds, using rapid wingbeats alternating with glides; catch birds (their principal prey), bats, and insects in the air.

---

337 Lesser Kestrel
(*Falco naumanni*)

Description: 12″ (30 cm). Smaller than Kestrel, with similar plumage; usually distinguishable by *behaviour.* Male separated by *lack of moustachial stripe; unspotted,* brighter chestnut upperparts; *blue-grey band across upper side of wing,* separating chestnut shoulders from dark primaries; paler, less spotted underparts; and *whitish underside of wing.* Female very similar to Kestrel, with slimmer build and paler underparts and underwing. Immature resembles female.

Voice: A vocabulary of rasping and screeching notes, *jee-jee-jit* or *kee-kee-kee-kick,* and other notes at the breeding colony, where it is very noisy; mainly silent at other times.

Habitat: Grassy plains, cultivated land, and other open country; in breeding season, confined to vicinity of cliffs and old buildings, often in towns.

Nesting: 3–6 white or buffy eggs speckled with yellowish-red, in bare scrape in hole or cavity in cliff face or old building. Nests colonially.

Range: Summer visitor from Iberia through Mediterranean Europe to Balkans and north to Yugoslavia, Romania, and southern Russia. Winters in tropical Africa. Also breeds in North Africa and across central Asia to Mongolia.

Gregarious at all seasons, unlike the Kestrel, it nests in colonies of up to 100 pairs, though 15–25 is more typical. It is very partial to ruined buildings, old walls, church towers, and other edifices that provide nest sites. It hunts in small parties, sometimes hovering. Although it will take a few small mammals, it feeds mainly on insects, many of which are caught in mid-air.

338, 341 **Kestrel**
(*Falco tinnunculus*)

Description: 13½″ (34 cm). One of the most common European birds of prey, readily identified by its *frequent hovering.* Male has *grey head, with black moustachial streak; grey rump and tail,* with black subterminal band and pale tip; chestnut upperparts, with *black spotting;* buffy underparts, with black spots and streaks. Female has brown head, chestnut upperparts, and tail *barred with black.* Immature resembles female.

Voice: A high-pitched, shrill *kee-kee-kee* or *kik-kik-kik.*

Habitat: Moorlands, open fields, rocky coasts, open woodland, and often towns.

Nesting: 4–6 white or yellowish eggs heavily marked with red-brown, in bare hollow on rock ledge, cliff, or building.

Range: Europe except Iceland; most of Asia and Africa. Partial migrant, birds from northern and eastern Europe wintering south to central Africa and Middle East.

When hunting on windy days, the Kestrel heads into the wind and maintains its position with slight movements of wings and tail, but when the air is calm, it hovers on rapidly beating wings. It feeds mainly on mice and other small mammals, which it drops on from a height of about 50′ (15 m). It is a frequent sight hovering above overgrown road and motorway verges.

332, 336 **Red-footed Falcon**
(*Falco vespertinus*)

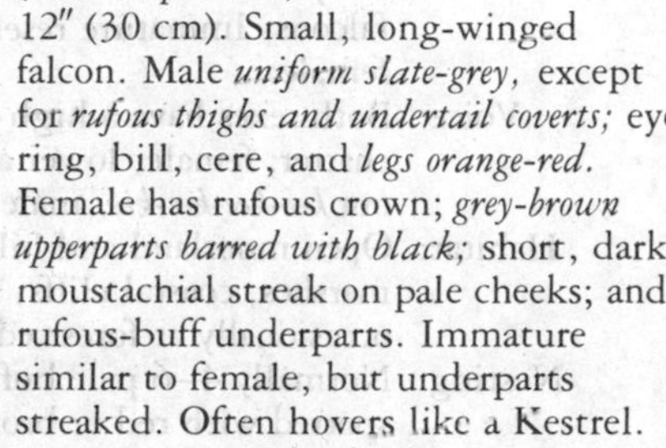

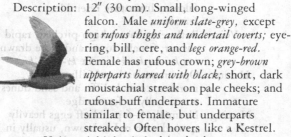

Description: 12″ (30 cm). Small, long-winged falcon. Male *uniform slate-grey,* except for *rufous thighs and undertail coverts;* eye-ring, bill, cere, and *legs orange-red.* Female has rufous crown; *grey-brown upperparts barred with black;* short, dark moustachial streak on pale cheeks; and rufous-buff underparts. Immature similar to female, but underparts streaked. Often hovers like a Kestrel.

Voice: A high-pitched *kee-kee-kee.*

Habitat: Open country and steppes with scattered small woods and scrub, forest edge, farmlands.

Nesting: 3–4 buffy eggs heavily marked with dark red-brown, in old nest of other species, especially Rook.

Range: Summer visitor to eastern Europe, west to Estonia, Poland, Hungary, and Romania, breeding sporadically farther west. During spring migration occurs regularly west to Germany, France, and Spain. Also breeds from Russia east to central Siberia.

Most gregarious of the falcons, they often establish themselves in a rookery while the Rooks are still present, but use vacant nests rather than ejecting the Rooks from active ones. In turn, they are not harassed by the Rooks, an example of mutual tolerance. They migrate in large flocks; in winter, communal roosts may number up to 5,000 birds. Mainly insectivorous.

335, 343 **Merlin**
(*Falco columbarius*)

Description: 10½–13″ (26–33 cm). Smallest European falcon. Male has slate-blue upperparts; grey tail, with *broad black subterminal band;* and *rufous-buff underparts,* finely streaked with black. Larger female has dark brown upperparts, brown tail with pale bars, and whitish or pale buff, streaked underparts. Both sexes *lack white cheeks and prominent moustachial streaks* of other falcons. Immature resembles female.

Voice: Both sexes have a high-pitched, rapid chatter; female, lower and more drawn-out *kee-kee-kee-kee;* male *ki-ki-ki-ki.*.

Habitat: Open moorland and hilly country, marshes, coastal cliffs, and sand dunes; occasionally at forest edge.

Nesting: Normally 4–6 pale buff eggs heavily spotted with red or brown, usually in bare depression on ground, sometimes on cliff ledge or in tree nest of other species.

Range: Northern Holarctic, breeding from Iceland, northern Britain, and Ireland across northern Eurasia to Bering Sea, and in North America. European birds winter south to Mediterranean region.

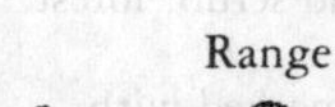

The Merlin hunts low over the ground on rapidly beating wings alternating with short glides, making quick changes of direction, catching small birds—mainly larks, pipits, and other small, open-country ground birds. On migration it often follows coastlines and feeds on migrating passerines. It also takes a few small mammals and some insects.

326, 344 **Hobby**
(*Falco subbuteo*)

Description: 12–14″ (30–35 cm). A *slender* falcon whose *long wings* and relatively *short tail* give it the appearance of a large swift. Adult dark brownish-slate above; *throat and cheeks white,* with pointed black moustachial streak; breast and belly white, heavily marked with black streaks; *thighs and undertail coverts rufous.* Immature darker and browner above; pinkish-buff below, including thighs and undertail coverts, with heavy dark streaks.

Voice: A rapid, high-pitched, complaining *kew-kew-kew,* often repeated.

Habitat: Open country with scattered copses and lines of trees; winters in wooded savannas, bushy country.

Nesting: 2–3 yellowish-brown eggs heavily spotted with red-brown, in old nest of another bird, usually a crow.

Range: Summer visitor to most of Europe, north to southern England, southern Sweden, and Finland, wintering in tropical Africa. Also breeds in North Africa and broadly across Asia.

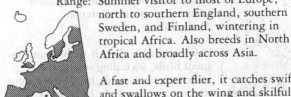

A fast and expert flier, it catches swifts and swallows on the wing and skilfully snatches flying insects from the air, often hunting at dusk. On the breeding grounds it lives mainly on small birds, occasionally taking bats and other small mammals, but in winter quarters in Africa it switches to locusts and flying termites. In display, a pair performs spectacular aerobatics, soaring, stooping, flying upside down, and looping the loop, the male frequently passing food to the female after a sudden dive and upward swoop.

327, 328 Eleonora's Falcon
(*Falco eleonorae*)

Description: 15″ (38 cm). Medium-sized falcon, between Peregrine and Hobby in overall length, with a *slender body, long tail,* and *long, narrow wings.* Dimorphic; light-phase adult, dark sooty-brown above and mainly rufous below, paler on breast, with heavy black streaking. Throat and cheeks white, with broad black moustachial streak; eye-ring, cere, and feet pale yellow. Immature similar to adult, with indistinct rufous barring on wings and tail and heavier streaking on underparts. Dark-phase (about 25% of population) adult, *uniformly dark brown or blackish;*

immature mottled and barred, rufous.

Voice: A repeated, grating, complaining scream, *keeeeya*.

Habitat: Sea cliffs and rocky islands; winters in both forested and open country.

Nesting: 2–3 pinkish-white eggs blotched with shades of brown, in bare scrape or old nest of another species, usually in small cavern or under overhanging rock.

Range: Breeds from the Canaries and Atlantic Morocco through the Mediterranean islands to Cyprus; winters in Madagascar.

A fast and agile flier, it feeds mainly on small birds, including swifts, and insects captured in flight. The breeding season coincides with the autumn migration of passerines across the Mediterranean to Africa, thus assuring a plentiful food supply. Although the falcons arrive at the breeding colonies in late April and remain there all summer, eggs are not laid until late July–early August.

---

325 **Lanner**
(*Falco biarmicus*)

Description: 17″ (43 cm). Similar in shape to Peregrine, but *less bulky* and longer-tailed. *Upperparts slaty-brown,* intermediate between Peregrine and Saker; *underparts pale pinkish,* with variable amounts of *spotting; crown and nape rufous,* with dark streaks. Moustachial streak narrower than Peregrine's but broader than Saker's. Underside of wing whitish, with some spots on wing coverts and grey bands on flight feathers. Immature has heavy dark spots on underparts and underwing coverts.

Voice: A shrill scream: *kri-kri* or *kirr-eeee*.

Habitat: Dry, open country with cliffs and rocky outcrops, mountain slopes, ruins.

Nesting: 3–4 pale creamy-white eggs heavily marked with reddish- or purplish-brown or buff, in bare scrape on rock ledge, sometimes in old tree nest of another species.

Range: Southern Italy, Sicily, and Balkans east to Iraq and Arabia and south through most of Africa. Mainly resident but some wander in winter.

An excellent flier, it is capable of stooping at great speed and is a favourite with falconers. It feeds mainly on birds, many of which are taken in flight. Adaptable and opportunistic in its feeding habits, it preys on migrant passerines in season, game birds when available, lizards in the desert, locusts and flying termites in Africa, and small mammals when birds are scarce.

---

334 Saker

(*Falco cherrug*)

Description: 18″ (45 cm). Large falcon, with broader wings and longer tail than Peregrine, *brown rather than grey upperparts and wings.* Adult has *pale head,* with narrow dark streaks on crown and nape; *very thin moustachial streak;* white underparts, with sparse streaking and spotting; and dark band across white underwings. Immature has darker head and more heavily streaked underparts.

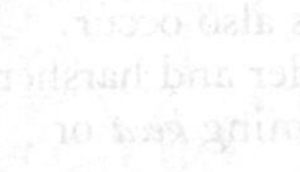

Voice: A harsh *kek-kek-kek,* a long-drawn scream, and other calls during display.

Habitat: Steppes, plains, semideserts, and other flat, open country from lowlands to high plateaux.

Nesting: 3–6 creamy or pale brown eggs heavily spotted with red, purple, and black, in bare scrape on rock ledge or in old tree nest of another species.

Range: Summer visitor to Europe from Czechoslovakia, eastern Austria, and Hungary through Romania to southern Russia, wintering around the eastern Mediterranean and south to Arabia and Ethiopia. Also breeds in central Asia.

It is bold and aggressive, at times attacking animals larger than itself, though it normally prefers a diet of small rodents. When hunting over the plains it sometimes hovers. It feeds on birds, killing larger ones with a Peregrine-like stoop.

333 Gyrfalcon
(*Falco rusticolus*)

Description: 20–22" (50–56 cm). Largest European falcon, with *broader and blunter wings* than Peregrine, slower wingbeats, and longer tail. Plumage variable. Dark phase grey-brown above, with paler mottling and barring; white below, with dark streaks; underside of wings mottled and barred; tail grey, with many narrow dark bars. Distinguished from Peregrine by *more uniform colouration* (less contrast between upper- and underparts), *mottled rather than plain upperparts,* and *poorly marked moustachial streak.* Light phase almost pure white, with black flecks on upperparts, streaks on underparts, and blackish-tipped primaries. Intermediates also occur.

Voice: Like Peregrine, but louder and harsher: *kyek-kyek-keyk* or a screaming *keea* or *heeeeee.*

Habitat: Mountains, cliffs, barren rocky tundra, and rocky coasts and islands.

Nesting: 3–4 pale yellowish or buffy eggs spotted red-brown, either in bare scrape or in old nest of Rough-legged Buzzard or Raven, on cliff or rocky outcrop.

Range: Circumpolar, breeding from Iceland and Scandinavia across arctic Asia to Bering Straits; also arctic North America. Chiefly sedentary, wandering irregularly south to Britain and north-central Europe.

Its breeding success is affected by the cyclical abundance of Ptarmigan and Willow Grouse, which constitute about 90 percent of its diet. In years when these are abundant, Gyrfalcons have large clutches, while in really poor years, they may not breed at all. They take very few mammals, but often hunt along shores and sea cliffs, especially in winter, eating many seabirds.

329, 342 **Peregrine**
(*Falco peregrinus*)

Description: 15–19″ (38–48 cm). Smaller than Gyrfalcon, with narrower, more pointed wings and shorter tail. *Slate-blue* to blue-grey above; *broad black moustachial streak on white cheeks; underparts pale buff, with narrow black bars*. Immature dark brown above; buffy underparts streaked, not barred.

Voice: A rapid, chattering *kek-kek-kek,* a harsh, long-drawn *kaaaak,* and a variety of calls at the nest site.

Habitat: Open country with cliffs and rocky outcrops, mountains, moorlands, tundra. Ranges widely in winter, especially in marshes, estuaries, and flat seacoasts.

Nesting: 2–5 creamy eggs heavily speckled with red, usually in bare scrape on cliff ledge.

Range: Cosmopolitan, breeding on every continent. Occurs throughout Europe except Iceland, but absent as breeder from eastern Britain and from Denmark to France. Partial migrant, northern populations moving south in winter.

Probably the world's most famous bird of prey, the Peregrine's powers of flight make it popular with falconers. Normally it flies with rapid wingbeats interspersed with glides; it also soars and does aerobatics. Kills prey by diving from a great height at tremendous speed, striking feet first in the air. Such dives, or "stoops," have been timed at over 200 mph (320 kph). Peregrines have been greatly reduced in number in recent years by the widespread presence of toxic chemicals in the environment and by illegal taking of young birds for falconry.

GROUSE
(Tetraonidae)

18 species: temperate and arctic regions of Eurasia and North America. Five species breed in Europe. Medium- to large-sized, chicken-like game birds with short, rounded wings that beat rapidly in heavy flight followed by glide. Feathered nostrils, legs, and sometimes toes; legs without spurs. Sexes usually dissimilar; male often larger than female and more brightly coloured. Males often polygamous. Habitat varied; in Europe, mainly tundra and forest. Often roost in trees.

281 Hazel Grouse
(*Bonasa bonasia*)

Description: 14″ (35 cm). Small grouse, with inconspicuous crest. Upperparts vary from grey-brown in north to rufous-brown in south, with darker barring; white underparts mottled with brown and black. *Grey tail with black subterminal band, very conspicuous in flight*. Male's throat *black, with white border;* female's, pale brown.

Voice: Song, a series of high-pitched, sibilant whistles. Calls, also high-pitched.

Habitat: Coniferous and mixed forests with hazel, aspen, and birch thickets and dense undergrowth, usually in mountains, often near rivers and streams.

Nesting: 6–10 yellow-buff eggs spotted with red-brown, in shallow scrape with thin lining of grass, usually under bush or ground vegetation in woods.

Range: Breeds from Scandinavia, Germany, and France to Balkans, Romania, Poland, and western Russia, and across northern Asia. Sedentary, but makes local movements in winter.

Bonasa is a Holarctic genus of three species, all inhabiting dense woodland; the other two are Severtzov's Grouse (*B.*

sewerzowi), of the mountains of western China, and Ruffed Grouse (*B. umbellus*), of North America. Hazel Grouse (also known as Hazel Hen) flushes readily, rather than crouching on the ground, and darts with great agility among trees, frequently perching on branches.

274, 283, 284, 287 **Willow Grouse and Red Grouse** (*Lagopus lagopus*)

Description: 15–16″ (38–40 cm). Plump, with variable plumage. Birds from continental Europe (Willow Grouse) are *pure white with black tail in winter,* retaining white wings in summer. Summer male *rich rufous-brown, with white belly;* female less rufous, with heavier black barring. Birds from Britain and Ireland (Red Grouse) are *rufous-brown* at all seasons, with darker wings and tail, never showing white. Willow difficult to separate from Ptarmigan, but latter tends to be greyer. Also, male winter Ptarmigan has black line from bill to eye (lacking in female and both sexes of Willow).

Voice: A variety of crowing and cackling calls: *kak-kakakakakakak; go-way-ko, go-way-ko; go-bak, go-bak.*

Habitat: Willow lives at lower levels than Ptarmigan on heather moors and tundra with birch and willow scrub; Red inhabits heather moors and peat bogs, moving to lower levels in winter.

Nesting: 6–11 yellowish-white eggs heavily blotched with chocolate and red-brown, in shallow scrape with thin lining of moss, heather, and grass, under cover.

Range: Circumpolar, breeding from Britain and Ireland, Scandinavia, and Lithuania across Russia and Siberia to Bering Sea and Sakhalin; also in North America. Nonmigratory in Europe.

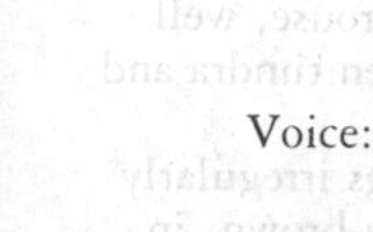

The Red Grouse was formerly classed as a separate species, *Lagopus scoticus,* but is now considered to be a well-marked island subspecies of the wide-ranging

Willow Grouse. Though their plumages are different, they are similar in voice, behaviour, and habitat.

285, 288 **Ptarmigan**
(*Lagopus mutus*)

Description: 14″ (35 cm). Smaller and less plump than Willow Grouse, with more slender bill and different voice and habitat. In winter, both sexes pure white, with black tail; but male has *black line from bill to eye,* distinguishing it from Willow Grouse. In summer, both sexes have white wings and belly; male *dark grey-brown* above, female buffy-brown with dark barring and scalloping. During autumn moult, *mottled grey and white* (Willow Grouse rufous-brown and white).

Voice: Quite different from Willow Grouse, a low, snoring rattle or trill: *kuh-kuh-kurrrrrrrrrrr;* also a short, hoarse croak; male has crowing song during breeding season.

Habitat: Higher than Willow Grouse, well above tree line, in barren tundra and mountain slopes.

Nesting: 5–10 creamy-white eggs irregularly blotched with chocolate-brown, in scrape thinly lined with plants.

Range: Circumpolar, breeding in Iceland, Scotland, Alps, and Pyrenees, and from Scandinavia across northern Asia to Bering Sea and Japan; also in North America and Greenland. Sedentary; makes local movements in severe weather.

Ptarmigan have very effective cryptic colouration; their white winter plumage blends with the snow, helping them to escape the attention of Gyrfalcons, and in mottled-grey summer dress they can easily be mistaken for one of the grey stones among which they live. In winter, they acquire thick feathering on legs and feet that facilitates walking in the snow.

273 Black Grouse
(*Tetrao tetrix*)

Description: Male, 21″ (53 cm); female, 16″ (40 cm). Male (Blackcock) *glossy black,* with *lyre-shaped tail;* large red wattle over eye; *white wing bar, undertail coverts,* and shoulder patch. Female (Greyhen) mottled grey-brown, larger and greyer than Red Grouse, smaller and less barred than Capercaillie, distinguished from both by *notched tail* and *narrow, pale wing bar.*

Voice: Crowing note of male, a sneezing *chu-whee;* "song" on display grounds, a pigeon-like cooing, often in chorus. Note of female, a loud *kuk-kuk.*

Habitat: Forest edge bordering moorland; swampy ground with bushes and scattered trees; rocky hillsides covered with heather; generally avoids open moors, preferring some trees.

Nesting: 6–10 creamy-yellow eggs sparsely spotted with shades of brown, in shallow scrape lined with grass or heather, on damp ground under cover of low vegetation.

Range: Scandinavia, northern Britain, Holland, Belgium, France, and northern Italy east and south to Poland, Romania, and Yugoslavia, and across northern Asia to eastern Siberia and North Korea. Mainly sedentary.

Males and females gather at communal display grounds (leks) in spring. Males stake out and defend territories on which they display, usually at dawn and dusk, raising and fanning the tail, drooping the wings, and distending the red eye wattles. The pigeon-like "rookooing" call, given with head thrust forward and neck swollen, is used in territorial defence. Males make rushes at one another, but fighting is rare. Males are polygamous and mating takes place on the lek. Males also gather on leks in autumn and exhibit territorial behaviour.

272, 280 **Capercaillie**
(*Tetrao urogallus*)

Description: Male, 34″ (85 cm); female, 24″ (60 cm). *Enormous* grouse, distinguished from all native European game birds by size and from all pheasants by heavy build and *broad, fan-shaped tail*. Male *dark slaty-grey,* with glossy blue-green breast, brown wings, black tail, and pale bill. Female grey-brown, with dark barring on upperparts; distinguished from Black and Red grouse by size, *rufous breast,* white mottling on belly, and rounded, *rufous-brown tail*.

Voice: "Song" of male soft for size of bird, yet an extraordinary vocal performance: a series of clicking sounds, accelerating and ending with a *pop* like the drawing of a cork, followed by some grating sounds; also a raucous, guttural call. Female, a loud *kock-kock*.

Habitat: Mature coniferous forests, usually in mountains, locally in lowlands.

Nesting: 5–8 pale yellowish eggs, laid in shallow scrape with thin lining of plants and feathers, among ground vegetation.

Range: Scotland, Pyrenees, and Cantabrian Mountains; central Europe from Germany and eastern France to Romania and northern Greece; and from Scandinavia across Russia and Siberia to Lake Baikal region. Sedentary, moving locally in northern parts of range.

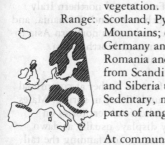

At communal display ground (lek), males "sing" from trees, rocks, or ground with tail fanned, wings drooped, and neck stretched upward. Ground displays include strutting back and forth and jumping into the air with loud wing flaps. Males take no part in nesting. In winter, they feed in trees on buds and shoots of conifers; in summer, they generally feed on the ground, taking berries, seeds, leaves, and some insects.

PHEASANTS, PARTRIDGES, AND QUAILS
(Phasianidae)

189 species: worldwide. Seven species breed in Europe; three others are introduced. Small, medium, and large chicken-like game birds with short, rounded wings that beat rapidly in heavy flight. Bill short and thick; legs stout, unfeathered, some with spurs. Tail long in pheasants, short in partridges and quail. Sexes usually dissimilar, with male more brightly coloured. Ground feeders, often in flocks, eating seeds, fruits, berries, and grain; also insects, snails, worms, and other animals. Often roost in trees; nest on ground.

277 Chukar
(*Alectoris chukar*)

Description: 13″ (33 cm). Similar to Rock Partridge; distinguished by browner upperparts, white lores, black mask broken near eye, broader white eyebrow, buffy wash on throat, broad black band around lower throat, lack of streaking on neck, and *fewer, more widely spaced flank bars*. These characters apparent at close range; at a distance, best identified by *voice*.

Voice: A variety of clucking and cackling notes; song, a rhythmic *chuck-chuck-chuckar,* reminiscent of Red-legged Partridge.

Habitat: Similar to Rock Partridge: stony hillsides and rocky mountain slopes with thin covering of vegetation; generally at lower altitudes in Europe.

Nesting: 8–15 heavily speckled pale russet or yellowish eggs, in grass-lined hollow under rock or small bush.

Range: Breeds from southern Bulgaria, northeast Greece, and Aegean Islands through the Middle East to India and through central Asia to northern China and Manchuria.

Though the Rock Partridge and Chukar were for a long time considered conspecific, a recent study concluded that they are different species. Evidence of overlap is so far only circumstantial, but there is no indication of interbreeding along the zone of probable contact in northeast Greece. The striking difference in their voices is a further indication of specific distinctness.

Rock Partridge

(*Alectoris graeca*)

Description: 13″ (33 cm). Distinguished from Red-legged Partridge by greyer upperparts; more extensive white throat, with *narrow black border not broadening on lower throat;* and *unstreaked breast.* Very similar to Chukar; for differences, see that species.

Voice: Variety of sharp, high-pitched clicking calls, which in breeding season are merged into rhythmical "song" very different from Red-legged Partridge or Chukar: *chivit-tikick* or *chirivit-titikick.* Also a high-pitched, screech.

Habitat: Stony hillsides and rocky mountain slopes with thin covering of grass or scrub; also vineyards. In Alps, in screes and pasturelands up to 8,250′ (2,500 m) or higher.

Nesting: 8–14 pale yellow or buff eggs variably spotted with red-brown, in shallow scrape thinly lined with vegetation, on ground under shrub or rock.

Range: Mountains of central and southern Europe from French Alps through Italy to Austria, south through Yugoslavia to Greece and Bulgaria; also southern Italy and Sicily.

Although the four species of *Alectoris* partridge in Europe are very similar in plumage, field identification is seldom a problem because their ranges are almost entirely separate. Even where there is geographical overlap, they may be ecologically or altitudinally isolated, providing a classic example of identification by range. Both Rock and Red-legged partridges occur in southeast France, but since the Rock lives in mountains and the Red-legged in lowlands, there is little likelihood of their meeting.

276 Red-legged Partridge
(*Alectoris rufa*)

Description: 13½" (34 cm). Larger than Grey Partridge, with different markings, but at long range not easily distinguishable, as both species have brown upperparts and rufous tails. *Throat white, with broadening black border that merges into dark streaks on upper breast.* Upperparts *uniformly brown;* white stripe over eye. Breast lavender-grey; flanks barred black, white, grey, and chestnut; belly rich buff. Bill and legs red.

Voice: "Song" of male long and varied, starting with low notes, followed by a repeated loud, grating *ko-chick-chick,* and ending with a repeated *chuck-chukar* or *chuck-chuck-chukar,* the emphasis always on the final *kar.* Other harsh calls, and a sharp *kuk-kuk* when flushed.

Habitat: Dry, open stony, sandy, or scrubby country, heaths, chalk downs, farmland, waste ground.

Nesting: 10–16 pale yellowish eggs sparingly blotched with reddish-yellow or grey, in shallow scrape thinly lined with leaves and grass, under cover of ground vegetation or bush.

Range: Southwest Europe, from Iberia to western France, northwest Italy, and Corsica. Introduced in Britain, Balearics, and some Atlantic islands.

The Red-legged Partridge is one of the very few species endemic to Europe. Introduced in England around 1770, it is frequently restocked and released in new areas. It had to adapt to damper and lusher habitats than accustomed to in its natural range and still does best in the drier areas of southern and eastern England. Much more reluctant to fly than the Grey Partridge, it prefers to escape by running.

Barbary Partridge
(*Alectoris barbara*)

Description: 13″ (33 cm). Best distinguished from Red-legged by *lack of black-and-white face markings.* Face and throat pale blue-grey, with buffy streak behind eye; *crown and collar chestnut,* latter speckled white.

Voice: A variety of high-pitched, grating, clucking calls and an upslurred whistle. Song, a hoarse *crrick-crrick-crrick-jakar-da.*

Habitat: Scrub-covered rocky hillsides, bushy ravines, woodland, semiarid regions.

Nesting: 8–16 ochre or pale brown eggs blotched with red-brown, in shallow, unlined scrape under low bush.

Range: Sardinia, North Africa, and Canaries; introduced in Gibraltar. Resident.

This species is the North African representative of the genus; Sardinia is its only natural foothold in Europe. It has adapted to a wider range of habitats than the other European *Alectoris,* from woodland to deserts, though in arid country it may not breed in particularly dry years.

289 **Grey Partridge**
(*Perdix perdix*)

Description: 12″ (30 cm). Smallest of the European partridges; distinguished from the *Alectoris* group by *orange-brown face and throat, dark chestnut horseshoe on upper belly,* grey and chestnut barring on flanks, and greyish legs. Upperparts brown, streaked buff; tail rufous; neck and breast grey. Juvenile streaky brown.

Voice: A sharp, grating *keerr* or *keerr-uck* and a cackling *kit-kit* when flushed.

Habitat: A wide variety of open country, especially agricultural land; also heaths, moors, steppes, coastal dunes.

Nesting: 9–20 olive-brown eggs, in shallow scrape lined with grass and leaves under cover of vegetation.

Range: Breeds over most of Europe but absent from Iceland, northern Scandinavia, southern Iberia, southern Greece, and Mediterranean islands. Also breeds in western Asia. Introduced in North America. Mainly sedentary.

The most common and widespread European partridge, it is a favourite with sportsmen. About 300,000 birds are released from captive breeding stock in France each year. A strong flier, it generally keeps low over the ground, hedgehopping and dodging trees and bushes with great skill. Mainly vegetarian, it consumes large quantities of weed seeds, but also eats insects, earthworms, and slugs.

286 **Quail**
(*Coturnix coturnix*)

Description: 7″ (18 cm). Too small to be mistaken for any European game bird except Andalusian Hemipode, but beware of confusion with young partridges or pheasants, which are able to fly when still very small. General colour *sandy, with black mottling and pale lines on upperparts;* buffy breast and flanks, the latter dark-streaked; *pale stripes on head.* Male's throat black and white; female's plain buff.

Voice: A sharp, repeated, rhythmic call of 3 rising notes—*wick—wick-wick*—given both day and night.

Habitat: Grasslands, steppes, rough pastures, and crops; also scrub in semiarid regions.

Nesting: 7–12 pale yellow eggs with bold brown markings, in shallow scrape thinly lined with grass, under cover of vegetation.

Range: Summer visitor in Europe north to England (scarce), Ireland, Denmark, Poland, and Estonia, irregularly farther north; wintering in Mediterranean region and tropical Africa. Also breeds across central Asia to India and Mongolia, and in Africa.

Difficult to see because of its secretive habits; its presence usually revealed only by its distinctive song. It usually escapes by running through low vegetation and is almost impossible to flush. Although the species is present and can be heard calling each year, it apparently is a sporadic breeder.

---

293 **Reeves's Pheasant**
(*Syrmaticus reevesii*)

Description: Male, 83″ (208 cm); female, 30″ (75 cm). Male characterized by *extremely long central tail feathers,* up to 5½′ (165 cm) long, silvery, with yellowish edges and broad brown bars. *Crown and neck white, separated by broad black band* running from forehead through eye and around nape; body plumage chestnut and mustard-yellow, with black scalloping; black belly; wings mottled chestnut, black, and white. Female brown, distinguished from Golden and Lady Amherst's by mottled and streaked, not barred, plumage; crown red-brown; throat and eye-stripe buffy-yellow; tail pointed, with light and dark bars.

Voice: Male, a twittering chuckle or churring noise and a piping note; both sexes, a piercing alarm call.

Habitat: Hills with old trees.

Nesting: 7–15 cream or olive-brown eggs, in shallow scrape thinly lined with plant material, in long grass or under bush.

Range: Northern and central China, southwestern Manchuria, and Inner Mongolia. Introduced in France and

Germany; introduction attempts in Britain have failed.

Reeves's Pheasant, named for the man who imported the first birds into Europe in 1831, has been well-known in China for centuries. Its long and beautiful tail feathers were used in religious ceremonies and for decoration. Though common in captivity and easy to rear, it is powerful and aggressive toward other pheasants; even the chicks quarrel among themselves.

291, 292 Pheasant
(*Phasianus colchicus*)

Description: Male, 30–35″ (76–88 cm); female, 21–25″ (53–63 cm). Plumage of male variable due to large number of introduced subspecies and continuous interbreeding. Standard type has *glossy green head, large red eye wattles,* and small "horns" (ear tufts); plumage basically *coppery-brown,* with fine black markings. Many have white collar ("Ring-necked Pheasant"); others have sandy upperparts and tail, blue or green rump, pale wing patch. Female less variable; generally sandy-brown, with dark mottling. Both sexes have *long, pointed tail.* Juveniles resemble short-tailed female, and are able to fly when still very small.

Voice: Crowing call of male, a far-carrying, explosive *karrk-kock,* followed by thumping of rapid wingbeats.

Habitat: Small woods, forest edges, hedgerows, riverine bush, marshes, and agricultural land, often feeding in open fields.

Nesting: 7–15 olive-brown eggs, in shallow scrape sparsely lined with plant material, under cover of tall vegetation.

Range: Native breeding range from Caspian region across central Asia to Manchuria, Korea, and China. Introduced throughout Europe except in far north and parts of Iberia and Mediterranean region. Resident.

The world's best-known game bird, the Pheasant is very successful as an introduced species. Feral populations are hardy, adaptable, and well established, their numbers continually augmented by birds reared in captivity and released into the wild for the benefit of sportsmen. In France, 2–3 million birds are released each year. While readily eating grain in captivity, wild birds feed mainly on leaves, berries, nuts, and weed seeds, as well as insects and earthworms.

290, 295 **Golden Pheasant**
(*Chrysolophus pictus*)

Description: Male, 39–43″ (98–108 cm); female, 25–26″ (63–65 cm). Male beautifully multicoloured, with *golden crest; black-barred, orange ruff; yellow lower back and rump;* long cinnamon tail, with black marbling; blue and brown wing; and *scarlet underparts.* Female buff, with dark crown and neck; narrow, dark barring on body and broader bars on wings and tail; and bill, legs, and orbital skin yellowish-horn.

Voice: Crowing call of male, a harsh, screeching double note.

Habitat: Native habitat, rocky hillsides covered with dense bush and bamboo scrub; in Britain, woodland and thick brush.

Nesting: The nest in China has never been described. In Britain, lays 5–12 creamy-yellow eggs, in shallow scrape thinly lined with plant material, under thick cover.

Range: Resident in mountains of central China. Feral populations established in a few places in Britain, but introduction failed in France.

One of the most spectacularly coloured birds in the world, the Golden Pheasant is understandably a very popular aviary bird and has been bred successfully in captivity in Britain since 1740. It is a hardy bird, coming from a rugged environment in China, and is inured to cold. Its short wings make it a poor flier, and it prefers to escape on foot. In the wild, it is shy and wary.

294 **Lady Amherst's Pheasant**
(*Chrysolophus amherstiae*)

Description: Male, 51–67″ (128–168 cm); female, 26–27″ (65–68 cm). Multicoloured male has green crown, with red plume; *white erectile ruff, with black scalloping;* black throat; green breast, back, and scapulars; *white belly;* golden rump; long, red tips to uppertail coverts; and very long, *black-barred white tail.* Female similar to female Golden but larger, with darker barring; rufous tinge on head and upperparts; tail feathers with rounded, not pointed, tips; and *bill, legs, and orbital skin blue-grey.*

Voice: Crowing call of male, very similar to Golden: a harsh, screeching double note.

Habitat: Native habitat similar to Golden but at higher elevations; rocky mountain slopes covered with bamboo thickets, scrub, and woods; in England, woods and scrub.

Nesting: 6–12 creamy-buff eggs, in shallow scrape thinly lined with plant material, under ground cover.

Range: Resident in mountains of southeastern Tibet, southwestern China, and northern Burma. Feral population established in central England, though introduction failed in France.

It is closely related to the Golden Pheasant; the two species have been crossed and recrossed in captivity so often that pure Lady Amherst's are now rather rare. Impure males may have scarlet crown, traces of red on the underparts, spots on the tail, or too large a crest.

BUTTON-QUAIL
(Turnicidae)

15 species: warm temperate and tropical regions of Old World. One species breeds in Europe. Small, plump, quail-like birds with only three toes. Bill short and sometimes slender; wings short and rounded; tail very short. Plumage cryptically coloured, patterned brown, black, and grey; female larger and more brightly coloured than male. Terrestrial, feeding on seeds and insects. Female courts males and is polyandrous; males incubate and rear young with only occasional female assistance.

Andalusian Hemipode or Little Button-Quail
(*Turnix sylvatica*)

Description: 6″ (15 cm). Smaller than Quail; distinguished by *orange-rufous breast* and *black spots on flanks and sides of breast,* becoming smaller dark speckling on buffy face. Pale stripes over eye and crown less prominent than Quail, and lacks throat stripes.

Voice: A low, crooning *hoooooo,* mainly at dawn and dusk.

Habitat: Dry grassland, crops, sandy and scrubby plains, especially with palmetto, and brushy wastes.

Nesting: 4 buffy or whitish eggs heavily speckled with black and brown, in shallow depression lined with grass and other plants, on ground well hidden in low vegetation.

Range: Breeds in southern Spain and Portugal, and from eastern Iran and India to southeast Asia; also widely in Africa. Resident.

Although it resembles Quail, it is one of a quite unrelated family, the button-quails. It is like Quail in shape, flight, and secretive behaviour and is usually equally hard to flush or observe. Since both arc mainly seen flying or running away, distinguishing marks on head and underparts are often difficult to see. While very local in Europe, it is abundant in parts of Africa and frequently is seen running along the edges of dusty tracks in dry savanna.

RAILS, GALLINULES, AND COOTS
(Rallidae)

130 species: worldwide. Nine species breed in Europe. Small to medium-sized terrestrial birds with short, rounded wings; short tail often cocked; long legs and slender toes (lobed in coots). Body laterally compressed, aiding progress through thick vegetation. Plumage dull and cryptically coloured in rails but not in gallinules and coots; sexes similar. Dangling legs make flight appear weak, but they are strong fliers, performing long-distance migrations and colonising many oceanic islands.

---

263 **Water Rail**
(*Rallus aquaticus*)

Description: 11″ (28 cm). Distinguishable from crakes by *larger size* and *long, red bill.* Upperparts olive-brown, streaked black; face, throat, and breast slate-grey; flanks barred black and white; conspicuous white undertail coverts; legs brownish-flesh. Juvenile has clear, sandy-brown eyebrow and underparts, with barred flanks and red-barred bill.

Voice: A wide variety of grunting, groaning, purring, and pig-like squealing notes, often heard at dusk, and a series of sharp, ringing notes, *kik-kik-kik* . . . , which also form part of rhythmical call, *kik-kik-kik—tikrreeerrr.*

Habitat: Marshes, reedbeds, swampy vegetation; in winter, also ditches, sewage farms, and other open muddy places with vegetational cover.

Nesting: 6–11 creamy eggs with a few red-brown or blue-grey spots, in cup nest of dead leaves of marsh plants, on or near ground in dense vegetation.

Range: Breeds throughout Europe, including Iceland, except northern Scandinavia. Partial migrant, birds from northeast wintering south to Mediterranean

region and Middle East. Also breeds in North Africa and Asia.

Like most rails, this species is more often heard than seen, frequently calling at night during the breeding season. Its explosive squeal can be startling when heard at close quarters. Though shy and skulking, it is less so than the smaller crakes, and in winter when the marshes freeze over, it is more often seen in the open, even perching in bushes.

266 **Spotted Crake**
(*Porzana porzana*)

Description: 9″ (23 cm). Larger than Little or Baillon's crakes; distinguished by *buffy undertail coverts* and *white spotting on dull grey face and breast;* flanks barred brown and white. Crown and upperparts olive-brown, with white streaks and spots; short bill greenish-yellow, with red at base; legs olive-green. Female duller, with browner breast; juvenile has buffy, white-spotted underparts, brown bill.

Voice: Male's call, a repeated, sharp, whip-like note, *whick—whick—whick* . . . , with a pause between notes. Calls mainly at night.

Habitat: Sedge marshes, swamps, bogs, and thick aquatic vegetation at the edges of ponds, lakes, and rivers; in winter, also ditches and more open marshes.

Nesting: 8–12 olive-buff eggs spotted and blotched with brown and grey, in cup nest of coarse vegetation lined with finer materials and grass, on ground or in grass tussock well hidden.

Range: Breeds locally from Britain and southern Fennoscandia south to France, Italy, and Yugoslavia. Mainly migratory, wintering in Mediterranean region and northern Africa. Also breeds in western Asia.

Though easier to see and identify than Little and Baillon's crakes, it is a shy bird, slinking away at the first hint of danger, threading its way so skilfully through dense vegetation that the observer may not see a single leaf or stem move, even though the bird is very close. When uneasy, it flicks its tail like a Moorhen, displaying buffy undertail coverts. It can swim for short distances. Normally solitary, it is sometimes found in small groups on migration.

---

265 Little Crake
(*Porzana parva*)

Description: 7½″ (19 cm). *Smaller* than Spotted Crake and *lacking white spots on underparts;* very similar to Baillon's Crake. Adult male has brown upperparts, with many dark and a few whitish streaks; brown wings, with *no pale streaks on coverts;* slate-grey face and underparts, with *bars on rear of flanks and undertail coverts.* Bill greenish, with red base; legs green. Female has white throat and eyebrow and *buffy underparts.* Juvenile similar to female, but with more extensive obscure dark barring on flanks and dull brownish legs.

Voice: "Song" of male, a single repeated note, *kurk* or *kook,* accelerating slightly and descending the scale, often fading at end. Other notes include a low double note, *ku-weck,* and an explosive trill, *kek-krrrrr.*

Habitat: Marshes, swamps, ponds with water lilies and other floating vegetation, and swampy edges of lakes and rivers.

Nesting: 7–8 ochreous eggs covered with small brown spots, laid in cup of marsh plants lined with grass and fine material, on ground well concealed in vegetation.

Range: Summer visitor to eastern Europe from Estonia to Yugoslavia and perhaps to Greece, and west to Germany, France (rare), and northern Italy, wintering in Mediterranean region and Africa. Also breeds in western Asia.

To see this or any other shy, skulking crake or rail, a special approach is required. Wading through a marsh is useless because the birds are most reluctant to fly. Even when flushed, they afford a glimpse too brief for identification. Instead, watch from a concealed vantage point beside the marsh at dusk, when crakes and rails often venture from cover for short periods to feed on the open mud, though they always remain close to protective shelter.

264 Baillon's Crake
(*Porzana pusilla*)

Description: 7″ (18 cm). Sexes alike, similar to male Little Crake, but has more *white streaks and spots on back and wings; prominent black and white barring on flanks and undertail; all-green bill; and pale, flesh-coloured legs.* Juvenile like adult female or young Little Crake, but more strongly barred black and white on flanks and undertail.

Voice: "Song" of male, a dry, rattling trill like winding of a watch, all on same pitch, and a 2-part call, *chor-chor-chor-chakakakaka.*

Habitat: Marshes with shallow water and thick growth of sedges and other aquatic plants, swamps, fens, dense vegetation beside rivers, ponds, and small lakes.

Nesting: 6–8 ochreous eggs with yellow-brown spotting and stippling, in small cup of aquatic plant leaves hidden on ground near water.

Range: Summer visitor to Iberia and France (rare) and through northern Italy to Romania, Bulgaria, and southern Russia, wintering in Africa. Also breeds widely in Africa, Asia, and Australasia.

Baillon's and Little Crakes are often confused, owing to their similarity in plumage, their frequently shared habitat, and some overlap in calls;

extreme caution should be used in identifying them.

267 **Corncrake**
(*Crex crex*)

Description: 10½″ (26 cm). *Yellowish-buff* rail, with broad dark streaks on upperparts, *red-brown bars on flanks* and undertail coverts, and *chestnut wing patches* conspicuous in flight. Has short, stubby yellowish bill. Often stands upright. Male has greyish eye-stripe, cheeks, throat, and breast; female less grey; immature same as female, but less barred on flanks.

Voice: "Song" of male, a loud, often repeated, rasping double note: *rrak, rrak,* or *crex, crex.*

Habitat: Grasslands, rough pastures, and cultivated fields; uncommon in cornfields, in spite of name.

Nesting: 8–12 pale greenish-grey or pale reddish-brown eggs with brown, purple, and grey spots, on small pad of dead grass well hidden in vegetation.

Range: Summer visitor to central Europe, north to Scotland, Ireland, southern Scandinavia, and Finland, south to south-central France, northern Italy, northern Balkans, and Ukraine, and east to central Siberia and Iran. Winters mainly in tropical Africa.

Though a land rail, the Corncrake skulks in low vegetation and is as hard to see as the crakes that live in swamps. In a few areas, especially in Ireland, it becomes bolder and may be seen walking along the edge of a country road. It is easily located during the breeding season, when males call very persistently by day and night.

269 **Moorhen or Common Gallinule**
(*Gallinula chloropus*)

Description: 13″ (33 cm). Plumage slaty-black, browner on back, with *white stripe along sides* and *white undertail coverts* with black centre. *Frontal shield red; bill red, with yellow tip;* legs green, with red "garter" above tarsal joint. Flicks tail constantly. Immature browner, with whitish face and greenish-brown bill and frontal shield; distinguished from young Coot by white flank stripe and undertail coverts and much less white on throat.

Voice: A loud *quarrk* and a variety of clucking notes: *kuk-kuk-kuk; kuk-kuttuck; kek-kek-kek.*

Habitat: Ponds, small lakes and slow-flowing rivers with well-vegetated margins, swamps, and reedy marshes, often feeding in grassy meadows near water.

Nesting: 5–11 pale grey, buff, or greenish eggs spotted with red-brown and grey, in flat, bulky nest of dead aquatic plants, near water or among vegetation in water, sometimes in waterside bushes.

Range: Almost worldwide except Australasia. Breeds throughout Europe except Iceland and northern Fenno-Scandia. Mainly resident but birds from north and east move farther south in Europe in winter.

It is the most successful and adaptable member of its family. Though always retaining some of its natural caution, it often becomes fairly tame, adapting to such man-made habitats as parks, ornamental ponds, and farmyards.

268 Purple Gallinule or Purple Swamphen

(*Porphyrio porphyrio*)

Description: 19″ (48 cm). Much larger and heavier than Moorhen or Coot, with *long red legs, stout red bill,* and red frontal shield; plumage *dark bluish-purple,* washed with turquoise on neck and breast. Further distinguished from Moorhen by white undertail coverts without black centre and lack of white flank stripe. Juvenile slaty, with red shield, bill, and legs.

Voice: Loud cow-like mooing, crane-like trumpeting, and a variety of croaking, grunting, and clucking calls.

Habitat: Marshes, reedbeds, lakes, and rivers fringed with dense vegetation.

Nesting: 2–5 creamy or buff eggs spotted with red-brown, purple, or grey, in bulky cup of dead aquatic plants, on ground near water or among plants in water.

Range: Declining in Europe; now confined to southern Spain and Sardinia. Widespread in Old World, from Africa to southern Asia and Australasia.

Rather shy, the Purple Gallinule spends much time inside reedbeds or, in Africa, in papyrus swamps, but also feeds along the fringes, walking in and out of the vegetation at any time of day. In the evening it often clambers up stems of reeds or papyrus and sits up in the open, surveying the landscape.

---

271 Coot
(*Fulica atra*)

Description: 15″ (38 cm). Larger than Moorhen and lacking white side stripe and undertail coverts. Plumage *slaty-black,* pure black on head and neck; *frontal shield and bill white;* legs green. Narrow white trailing edge to secondaries shows in flight. Juvenile dark grey-brown, with whitish throat and front of neck.

Voice: Wide vocabulary. Common call, a loud *kowk, keck,* or *kick,* sometimes combined into a double note.

Habitat: Breeds on large ponds, lakes, and slow-flowing rivers with reed margins and other aquatic vegetation. Winters on lakes, reservoirs, estuaries, and other open water, sometimes in large numbers.

Nesting: 6–9 pale buff eggs spotted dark brown, in large cup of aquatic vegetation near water or built up in water, among vegetation but with little attempt at concealment.

Range: Breeds throughout Europe except

northern Fenno Scandia. Mainly resident, birds from north and east wintering south to Mediterranean and northern Africa. Also breeds in North Africa and Australasia.

The Coot is a common and familiar bird, without the cautious habits of its family. It feeds mainly on underwater plants, diving frequently, but also leaves the water to feed on grass; tame birds will take scraps. It requires a substantial stretch of open water for its laborious takeoff, its feet pattering over the water.

270 Crested Coot or Red-knobbed Coot
(*Fulica cristata*)

Description: 16″ (40 cm). Slaty-black; similar to Coot, but with *2 red knobs on top of white frontal shield* (hard to see at a distance), blue-grey legs, and *no white trailing edge on wing.* Juvenile indistinguishable from juvenile Coot.

Voice: A booming *hoo,* a short, sharp *kerrt,* and some grunting noises.

Habitat: Reed-fringed lakes and ponds.

Nesting: 4–6 pale greyish-buff eggs spotted dark brown, in large nest of leaves and stems of reeds and other aquatic vegetation, near water or built up in water.

Range: Breeds in southern Spain (rare), moving north in winter into southern Portugal and farther into Spain. Also breeds in Morocco, eastern and southern Africa, and Madagascar.

The Crested Coot is an African species that just reaches southern Europe. Scarce and rather shy in Europe, it is abundant in parts of Africa south of the Sahara. Its habits are similar to the Coot: it feeds underwater on stems and shoots of aquatic plants, and also eats some insects and molluscs. During dry years in East Africa, it can be seen on open mud, eating seed pods of water lilies exposed by the receding waters.

CRANES
(Gruidae)

14 species: North America and most of Old World. One species breeds in Europe, another is a scarce visitor. Tall, long-necked, long-legged terrestrial birds with stout, straight bill, broad wings, and elongated secondaries drooping over tail. Despite a superficial resemblance, cranes are not related to either storks or herons. Neck and legs extended in flight and inclined downward, producing humped look. Flocks migrate in line or V with much soaring and gliding.

166 Crane or Common Crane
(*Grus grus*)

Description: 45″ (113 cm). A tall, long-legged, and long-necked bird, with proportionately shorter bill than those of storks or herons and with *drooping, bushy "tail"* formed by elongated inner secondaries. Head and neck black, with *broad white stripe from cheeks down side of neck* and a small, *red crown patch* of bare skin. Remaining plumage grey except for black flight feathers. Immature's head and upperparts brown.

Voice: Contact note, a throaty *krrr,* lengthened during excitement or in flight to a loud, trumpeting *krrooh.*

Habitat: Breeds in open marshes, boggy heaths, and wooded swamps, wintering in open fields, steppes, lagoons, and marshes.

Nesting: 1–2 whitish eggs tinged grey, brown, or buff blotched with brown or purple, in heap of vegetation near or in water.

Range: Summer visitor from Scandinavia, northern Germany, Poland, Baltic States, and western Russia, east to eastern Siberia. European birds winter in Mediterranean region and northeast Africa.

Cranes are famous for their ceremonial "dancing" displays. In this species, a typical dance starts with a pair facing each other and bowing, pumping the head and neck up and down, then leaping into the air with spread wings, giving a few flaps to gain added height. Between leaps they may pick up a stick, stone, or clump of grass and toss it into the air. Single birds may also dance on their own, suggesting that the dance is not only a sexual display but also a response to a general state of excitement.

164 Demoiselle Crane

(*Anthropoides virgo*)

Description: 38″ (95 cm). Much smaller than Crane, with less bushy "tail." *Black face,* neck, and breast, latter with *elongated plumes.* Has *tuft of long, drooping, white feathers behind eye* and *short bill. No red on head.* Rest of plumage grey except for black flight feathers. Immature has grey head and ear tufts.

Voice: A trumpeting call, higher-pitched than Crane.

Habitat: Marshes, grassy steppes, open plains, and semideserts.

Nesting: 2 whitish eggs tinged buff, grey, or brown with brown or purplish-grey spots and blotches, in shallow scrape on dry ground near water.

Range: Summer visitor from the Ukraine eastward to Lake Baikal region and northern Manchuria. Formerly bred in Romania and occasionally in southern Spain. Vagrant elsewhere in Europe. Also breeds locally in northwest Africa. Winters in Middle East, southern Asia, and northeast Africa.

In flight, the Demoiselle Crane has the characteristic family silhouette of extended head and neck and trailing legs held lower than the body, producing a "humped" appearance. Storks differ in having an extended neck and legs level with the body, and herons fly with retracted head and neck.

BUSTARDS
(Otididae)

23 species: warmer regions of Old World. Two species nest in Europe. Medium-sized to very large, heavily built terrestrial birds with short, stout bill, thick neck, and broad wings. Stout legs and broad toes suited to running. Most species have ornamental plumes on head or neck. Sexes dissimilar; males larger than females. Flight ponderous but powerful, with neck and legs extended, but birds prefer to walk or run, and often crouch when alarmed. Males perform remarkable courtship displays. Inhabit open plains and semideserts. Omnivorous.

---

282 Little Bustard
(*Tetrax tetrax*)

Description: 17″ (43 cm). Much smaller than Great Bustard, more like long-necked game bird. Breeding male has *slate-grey face and throat* and *bold black-and-white neck* pattern. Crown, upperparts, and tail sandy-brown, with fine dark vermiculations giving a mottled appearance; white underparts. *Flight feathers mainly white, with black tips.* Male in winter similar to female: sandy head and neck, with dark streaks; pale underparts, with fine dark barring.

Voice: Display note of male, a brief, dry rattle like the winding of a clock: *prritt;* when flushed, a short *dahg*.

Habitat: Grassy plains, clearings in cork plantations, large fields of grain and other crops, and areas with scattered trees or bushes.

Nesting: 3–5 olive-green or olive-brown eggs streaked and blotched with brown, in shallow unlined scrape on bare ground.

Range: Breeds in Iberia, France, Sardinia, southern Italy, and Balkans; also northwest Africa, and in southwestern Asia. Partial migrant, European birds

wintering south to Mediterranean region.

A very shy bird, the Little Bustard crouches motionless on the ground or runs away rapidly at the first sign of danger. When flushed, it flies strongly and swiftly like a game bird, the wings making a whistling sound. When not alarmed, it walks with measured steps and head held stiffly erect. It forms flocks outside the breeding season.

---

275 **Great Bustard**
(*Otis tarda*)

Description: Male, 40″ (100 cm); female, 30″ (75 cm). *Very large, heavy* bird, with thick neck and stout legs. Male has *light grey head and neck,* with *tuft of white "whiskers";* tail and sandy-brown upperparts barred black; rufous breast band and white belly. *Wings white, with black flight feathers.* Female and young males smaller and thinner, lacking "whiskers" and breast band.

Voice: Mainly silent; in breeding season, a low grunting bark.

Habitat: Grassy plains, open steppes, and large fields of grain.

Nesting: 2–3 pale grey, olive, or greenish eggs with brown and grey blotches, in unlined scrape among vegetation.

Range: Breeds very locally in Iberia, Germany, Poland, and from Austria and Czechoslovakia to Romania and Bulgaria, east across central Asia to southeastern Siberia and Manchuria. Mainly resident, some southward movement in winter.

It is declining in numbers and is in need of strict protection in spite of its extraordinary shyness. In its spectacular display, the male, by cocking tail over back, drooping wings, sinking head in shoulders, puffing out throat, and lowering breast to the ground, becomes a huge, fluffy white ball.

OYSTERCATCHERS
(Haematopodidae)

7 species: widespread, on most temperate and some tropical seacoasts, some inland. One species breeds in Europe. Large waders with short neck, long, straight, rather deep bill, and thick legs. Three toes partially webbed. Plumage black and white or all black; legs pink. Red bill is laterally compressed, specially adapted for opening oysters, mussels, and other bivalve molluscs and for prising shellfish off rocks.

158 Oystercatcher
(*Haematopus ostralegus*)

Description: 17″ (43 cm). Large, stocky *black-and-white* shorebird with *long, thick orange bill, orange-red eye,* and *pink legs.* Black above; in flight, shows broad white wing bar and white rump. Solid black throat and breast in summer; white partial throat collar in winter.

Voice: Shrill, piercing *pic-pic,* repeated, and *kleep-kleep* alarm call. Piping displays, often communal, accompanied by prolonged whistling trill.

Habitat: Seashores, beaches, shingle bars, estuaries; inland on moors and agricultural land and along shingle banks of large rivers. Winters on coasts.

Nesting: 3 pale buff eggs boldy blotched and spotted, laid in bare scrape occasionally lined with pebbles or small shells.

Range: Virtually cosmopolitan. Breeds along most European coasts; inland in Scotland and other areas. Absent from parts of Mediterranean. Winters along most European coasts.

Gregarious birds, they are commonly found in large, noisy flocks feeding on mussels and other shellfish. Their bill is adapted to hammering and prising open the shells of their prey.

AVOCETS AND STILTS
(Recurvirostridae)

7 species: worldwide in warmer regions. Two species breed in Europe. Large waders with small head and long bill and neck; bill straight (stilts) or recurved (avocets); legs fairly long (avocets) to extremely long (stilts). Feet of avocets partly webbed. Plumage mainly black and white; sexes similar. Wade and sometimes swim in shallow water, feeding mainly on aquatic insects taken from the surface and underwater, as well as crustaceans, shellfish, and other aquatic animals.

160 Black-winged Stilt
(*Himantopus himantopus*)

Description: 15″ (38 cm). Boldly patterned *black-and-white* wader, with *extremely long, pink legs*. Black above, including crown and nape in summer male; white below. Thin neck, with small head and needle-like bill. Legs extend a third of body length beyond tail in flight, when black underwing shows. Juveniles similar, but browner.

Voice: A loud *kick, kick;* sometimes a double note, *kee-yik, kee-yik, kee-yik.*

Habitat: Marshes, shorelines of lakes, pools, even small ponds. Salt pans a favoured haunt, but seldom found on open shoreline.

Nesting: 4–5 clay-coloured eggs spotted black, laid on ground with varying amounts of nesting materials. Semicolonial nester.

Range: Widespread in the Old World. In Europe patchy; breeding distribution mainly in the Mediterranean, wintering in Africa. Also breeds in central and southern Asia and in Africa. Sometimes overshoots on spring migration and found farther north.

Adapted to wading in deep water, it picks its food from the surface. Its diet consists of insects, small molluscs, and small worms. Like the Redshank, it is a "warden of the marshes," rising with loud, protesting cries at the approach of an intruder.

159 **Avocet**
(*Recurvirostra avosetta*)

Description: 17″ (43 cm). Unmistakable, slim *black-and-white* wader with fine, black *upturned bill*. Black cap and boldly marked black-and-white wings. Long, *blue-grey legs*.

Voice: A high-pitched *kleet*.

Habitat: Prefers salt marshes, both coastal and inland. Breeds on dried-out lagoons and winters on creeks, estuaries, salt pans, salt lakes.

Nesting: 4 clay-buff eggs irregularly spotted with black, laid in shallow depression in sand or dried mud.

Range: Breeds patchily in Europe from Britain and Portugal east across southern Palearctic; also in Africa. Migrant, wintering on Mediterranean and Atlantic coasts, and in Africa.

Difficult to overlook with their piebald plumage and loud cries, they feed along the tide line or in shallow water, swishing their upturned bills from side to side in a nonstop scything motion. They feed mostly on crustaceans, as well as marine worms, insects, shrimps, and fry.

THICK-KNEES
(Burhinidae)

9 species: temperate and tropical regions of Old World and tropical America. One species breeds in Europe. Medium-sized land birds resembling large plovers, with large, broad, rounded head, stubby bill, and extremely large yellow eyes. Legs long with thickened tarsal joint ("knee"). Shy and wary, usually running rather than flying and crouching when alarmed. Feed mainly at night when their large eyes help them to spot prey.

118 Stone-curlew
(*Burhinus oedicnemus*)

Description: 16″ (40 cm). Primitive-looking, with large, round head; *big yellow eye; thick yellow legs;* short, stubby black and yellow bill; and *bold black-and-white mark across closed wing* that becomes a *double wing bar* in flight. Sandy, streaked plumage is an effective camouflage.

Voice: A thin-whistled *coor-lee.*

Habitat: Sandy wastes, bare downland, stony ground, even large shingle beaches; also ploughed fields and bare forestry rides.

Nesting: 2 pale brown eggs blotched or spotted with sepia, laid on bare ground.

Range: Breeds from Europe and North Africa east to Middle East, India, and southwestern Siberia. Rare in southeastern Britain, and absent from much of central Europe and Scandinavia. European birds go southwest to winter.

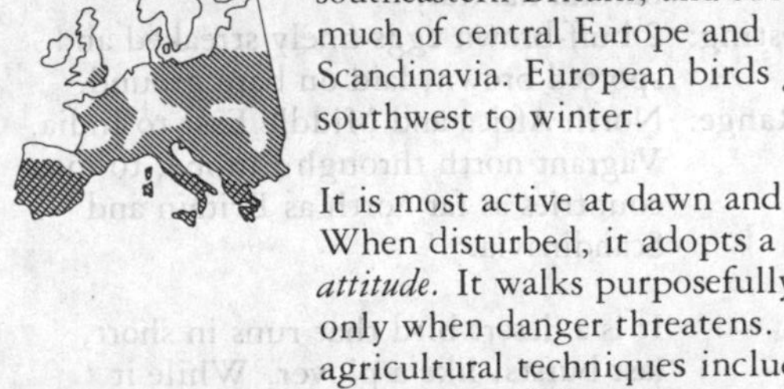

It is most active at dawn and dusk. When disturbed, it adopts a *hunched-up attitude.* It walks purposefully and flies only when danger threatens. Changing agricultural techniques including the cultivation of formerly marginal land or wasteland have destroyed its main habitats over much of Europe.

PRATINCOLES AND COURSERS
(*Glareolidae*)

17 species: widespread in warmer regions of Old World. One species breeds in Europe, and another is a regular migrant. Small to medium-sized plover-like land birds. Pratincoles have short bill and legs; in flight, resemble terns or large swallows. Coursers have longer bill and legs and shorter and broader wings. Plumage mainly brown and grey, often boldly marked on head and breast. Sexes similar. Coursers inhabit bare, dry ground. Pratincoles feed near water, mainly on insects taken in the air; coursers are terrestrial, feeding on insects, seeds, snails, and small lizards.

148 Cream-coloured Courser
(*Cursorius cursor*)

Description: 9″ (23 cm). *Long-legged, fast-running* relative of pratincoles. Sandy-buff plumage, lighter below, relieved only by *head markings of light blue, white, and black* behind eye. Bill short and *downcurved; legs long and yellow*. In flight, underwing black and upperside of wing sandy-buff, with black primaries.

Voice: Call note, a harsh *praak-praak*.

Habitat: Deserts and semideserts. Occasionally wanders north to Europe, where beaches are nearest equivalent of its natural habitat.

Nesting: 2 buff-brown eggs finely streaked and spotted brown, laid on bare ground.

Range: North Africa and Middle East to India. Vagrant north through Europe, to most countries as far north as Britain and Scandinavia.

It is a desert bird that runs in short, fast bursts, like a plover. While it prefers to run rather than fly from danger, it is a swift and strong flier once aloft.

147 Collared Pratincole
(*Glareola pratincola*)

Description: 10″ (25 cm). Strange-looking bird, with *long wings,* white rump, *deeply forked tail,* and tiny, *stubby, red-based bill.* Runs quickly on *short legs.* Plumage brown, with *cream patch on throat boldly bordered with black;* off-white belly. *Strongly resembles a tern,* particularly in flight. In Europe, separated from Black-winged Pratincole by chestnut, not black, axillaries (armpits) and *white trailing edge to secondaries.*

Voice: Tern-like, high pitched *kirri-kitti-kirri.*

Habitat: Dried-out floods, baked mudbanks, sand bars, dry meadows, rocky plains.

Nesting: 2–3 greyish-buff eggs spotted and blotched dark brown-black, laid in scrape on bare ground. Colonial nester.

Range: Breeds locally in Mediterranean and Balkans, east through southern Asia and parts of Africa. European birds migrate into Africa across Sahara.

Gregarious and particularly noisy, they arrive in Europe in large flocks and settle into colonies, screaming and diving to intimidate intruders, as the Mediterranean sun dries out the marshes. With their long wings, forked tails, and noisy behaviour, they closely resemble terns.

Black-winged Pratincole
(*Glareola nordmanni*)

Description: 10″ (25 cm). Almost identical to Collared Pratincole; however, Black-winged has *black, not chestnut, underwing coverts,* though this feature is difficult to see even in good light. Also *lacks white trailing edge to the secondaries.*

Voice: Tern-like *kyik* like Collared Pratincole.

Habitat: Like Collared Pratincole: dried-out floods, baked mudbanks, sand bars, dry meadows, rocky plains.

Nesting: 3–4 eggs similar to Collared Pratincole's but less heavily marked. Generally found in larger colonies, always near water.

Range: Replaces Collared Pratincole to the north, from the Black Sea north of the Danube delta east to central Asia. Migrant through the Middle East, fairly regularly through the Balkans. Elsewhere in Europe a rare vagrant. Winters in Africa.

A bird with chestnut "armpits" is definitely a Collared, but one with dark "armpits" may be either a Collared or a Black-winged. As intermediate birds also occur, there is debate about whether or not the two are simply forms of one hybridising species.

PLOVERS
(Charadriidae)

60 species: worldwide. Seven species breed in Europe, one is a winter visitor, three are vagrants. Small to medium-sized compact waders with short, straight bill, round head, and short neck. Legs proportionally shorter in smaller species and longer in larger species. Plumage mainly brown above and white below; smaller species often have breast bands and bars on the head; larger species often have crests or bare skin and wattles on face. Sexes similar. Run quickly in short spurts, stopping to observe or feed; bob heads when nervous. Found on grasslands, marshes, and coasts. Feed on insects, worms, and small crustaceans.

149, 152 **Little Ringed Plover**
(*Charadrius dubius*)

Description: 6″ (15 cm). Smaller than Ringed Plover, with similar *breast band;* in flight *lacks white wing bar. Bill dark; legs pale yellow; prominent yellow eye-ring.* Juveniles have incomplete breast band and may resemble Kentish Plover but lack white wing bar.

Voice: A distinctive, short *tee-ooo* quite different from Ringed Plover.

Habitat: Rivers, lakes, gravel pits with broad shingle margins. In winter, frequents marshes, lagoons, and coasts.

Nesting: 4 grey-brown eggs speckled with dark brown, laid in scrape on sand or gravel.

Range: Summer visitor throughout Europe except extreme north. Migrates to Africa in winter. Breeds across the Palearctic and Oriental regions.

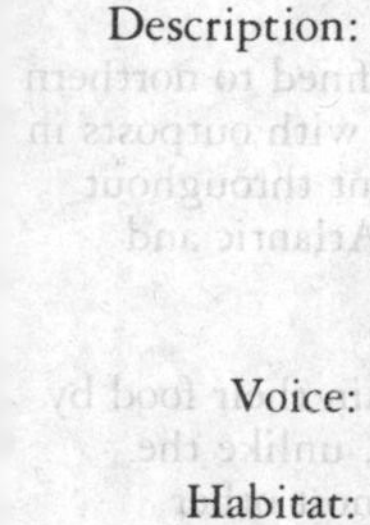

The freshwater equivalent of the Ringed Plover, it is seldom found in large flocks, and even on migration usually travels singly or in pairs. Over the past 40 years it has colonised new areas of Europe by adapting to gravel pits as substitutes for the stony margins of rivers where "improvement" schemes have reduced its numbers.

150, 153 **Ringed Plover**
(*Charadrius hiaticula*)

Description: 7½" (19 cm). Boldly marked with *black band across breast* and black bars through eye and across crown. *Orange legs* and *orange bill with black tip,* and *white wing bar* conspicuous in flight, distinguish it from Little Ringed Plover. In winter and juvenile plumage, breast band may be incomplete, and black on head lacking.

Voice: A musically pleasant *too-lee* and rather more abrupt *coo-weep*. Flight song, a rapid trill.

Habitat: Shingle, sand, and muddy shores, and estuaries. Inland on open tundra. On migration, lakes, and sewage farms.

Nesting: 4 olive-grey eggs speckled and blotched with brown and black, laid in scrape among shingle.

Range: Eurasia. In Europe confined to northern coasts and tundra zone with outposts in Spain and Italy. Migrant throughout Europe, wintering on Atlantic and Mediterranean coasts.

These active birds obtain their food by running and pouncing, unlike the probing technique of most other waders. Common and gregarious, they flock with other waders.

155 **Killdeer**
(*Charadrius vociferus*)

Description: 10" (25 cm). Similar to Ringed Plover but larger, with *two distinct breast bands* and more complex face pattern. *Rust-coloured rump* and uppertail coverts; *long, wedge-shaped tail* marked with distinct black V. *Broad white wing bar* crosses black primaries, becoming bolder as it follows trailing edge of wing.

Voice: A clear *kill-dee* repeated loudly.

Habitat: Grassland and ploughed fields; also coasts and estuaries outside breeding season.

Nesting: 4 light buff eggs boldly marked with black, laid in shallow scrape sometimes lined with wood chips, pebbles, or dried grass in nest or around edge. Usually on open ground some distance from water.

Range: Most of North America south of tree line. Partial migrant, leaving Canada and northern parts of United States. Vagrant across the Atlantic to Europe, mainly in autumn and winter.

The most familiar wader in North America, its loud, insistent calls draw attention to its whereabouts. Like other plovers, it is adept at "distraction displays," drawing danger away from its nest by feigning injury.

151, 154 **Kentish Plover**
(*Charadrius alexandrinus*)

Description: 6¼" (16 cm). A typical plover: *breast band lacking*, but has a *small black patch at either side of breast*. Plumage above paler, *more sandy* than Ringed or Little Ringed plovers, and male has ginger-coloured cap in summer. *White wing bar* and *white outer tail feathers* show in flight. At all ages, distinguishable from juvenile Ringed and Little Ringed (which do not have a complete breast band) by black legs, white tail-sides, paler upperparts, and call.

Voice: A clear *wee-it*, or *wit, wit, wit*. A rolling *priip*.

Habitat: Sandy and muddy shorelines, estuaries, lagoons, and salt pans. Normally not far from the sea; breeds on beaches and dried-out lagoons.

Nesting: 4 grey-buff eggs marked with black streaks and spots, laid in simple scrape and often partially buried in sand for insulation. Both sexes incubate and care for young, probably raising two broods a season.

Range: Found on every continent. Summer visitor to most European coasts north to Denmark and extreme southern Sweden; also breeds inland in eastern Europe. Winters in Africa and parts of southern Europe.

Though named after the English county of Kent, it has been many years since this worldwide species nested in Britain, though it does breed in the Channel Isles.

117, 121 **Dotterel**
(*Charadrius morinellus*)

Description: 8½″ (21 cm). Female slightly larger, similarly but more boldly marked than male. Dark head has prominent *white eyebrow* and white chin. Grey breast separated from *chestnut belly* by narrow but prominent *white chest band;* yellow legs. In winter, both sexes become buff-grey but keep *white eyebrow and chest band*.

Voice: A trill *wee-titi-wee-titi-wee.*

Habitat: Tundra and high stony plateaux; rarely at sea level on bare earth. On migration, sandy wastes, ploughed fields, bare chalk downs.

Nesting: Late breeder. 3 clay-buff eggs heavily blotched with black-brown, laid in hollow in ground with sparse lining of mosses and lichens.

Range: Patchy distribution through Palearctic, mainly in mountain chains. In Europe, confined to extreme north and a few localities in highest mountains. Rarely, at sea level (for example, on Dutch polders). Migrates south to winter in Africa.

The male is not only slightly smaller and duller in colour, but also takes principal responsibility for incubating eggs and rearing young. The female initiates courtship and, having settled one male on a clutch of eggs, may seek out and court another partner. This adaptation to the briefness of the breeding season at high altitudes and high latitudes may produce twice as many young as in a monogamous relationship.

102 **Lesser Golden Plover**
(*Pluvialis dominica*)

Description: 10″ (25 cm). Similar to Golden Plover but smaller, with proportionally *longer legs* and *longer wings* extending well beyond tail at rest. *Grey-buff underwing* and axillaries (white in Golden Plover).

Voice: A melodious *quee-i-lee* or *kl-ui*.

Habitat: Breeds on arctic tundra; on migration found on grasslands and ploughed fields.

Nesting: 3–4 buff eggs spotted with dark brown, laid in depression lined with lichens and mosses on open tundra.

Range: Northern Canada and northeastern Siberia. Winters in South America and in Asia as far as India. Vagrant to Europe, principally Britain and Ireland.

The Lesser Golden Plover is a long-distance migrant that follows the autumn route across arctic Canada to Labrador. After fattening on berries, it sets off on a great-circle route over the Atlantic to South America; some stray off course to Europe.

101, 144 **Golden Plover**
(*Pluvialis apricaria*)

Description: 11″ (28 cm). Dark above, *speckled with golden-yellow*. White line runs from forehead, over eye, bordering cheek, along neck, and below folded wing. Below line entire plumage is *black in summer* (northern populations), or *black-mottled grey* around the white dividing line (southern populations). In winter, loses black underparts, acquires buffy-grey streaking on breast, and has less golden plumage above. No wing bar or only a faint one. Underwing grey with *white axillaries.*

Voice: A mellow *tlui* contact note. Song, a fluty trill uttered in flight.

Habitat: Grass and heather moors in upland Britain and Ireland; also lowlands in Denmark and other Baltic countries. Tundra marshes and arctic heaths farther north. In winter, damp meadows and arable fields, estuaries, and marshes.

Nesting: Usually 4 buff-yellow eggs boldly blotched with black-brown, particularly toward larger end, laid in depression lined with a few heather twigs, lichens, or grasses. Scrape frequently located on a slight hummock.

Range: Northern Europe and adjacent parts of northwestern Siberia. Winters in southern and western Europe.

Large flocks, sometimes mixed with Lapwings, are common on lowland grasslands of southern and western Europe. Both species are affected by frost, which sends worms and other grassland animals deep into the soil beyond their reach. Thus, because of the weather, they often move throughout the winter.

103, 145 **Grey Plover**
(*Pluvialis squatarola*)

Description: 11″ (28 cm). Similar to Golden Plover but bulkier. *Grey-white speckles* on mantle and wings; grey underwing marked at all seasons by *black axillaries* (armpits). In flight, shows *white rump* and *white wing bar.* In winter, rather dumpy, nondescript grey and white; but in summer, black face and belly are prominent.

Voice: A clear, whistling *tee-oo-ee.*

Habitat: Arctic tundra. On passage and in winter prefers open shorelines, estuaries, and mud flats. Seldom found inland.

Nesting: 4 greyish-buff eggs lightly spotted and

occasionally blotched, laid in shallow depression lightly lined with moss or lichen. Placed on top of ridge or bluff with a good view of surrounding tundra.

Range: Circumpolar in high latitudes bordering Arctic Ocean in Alaska, Canada, and Siberia. Migrates south through Europe; winter visitor to North Sea, Atlantic, and Mediterranean coasts.

This large shorebird stands out among the sandpipers and "shanks" with which it frequently associates. It often appears hunched and ungainly, but when feeding it has the quick pounce of the true plover. Though it does not migrate in large flocks, in favoured localities such as the Sado estuary of Portugal it can be exceptionally numerous.

156 Spur-winged Plover
(*Hoplopterus spinosus*)

Description: 10½" (26 cm). A long-legged, medium-sized plover; mantle and folded wings buff-brown, rest of plumage boldly marked *black and white*. *Crown* slightly crested and *black* to below eye; *black chin stripe broadens out over breast* and belly. White cheek extends and broadens on to mantle. In flight, black primaries form *distinctive wing pattern* with buff-brown coverts and back, and has striking black-and-white pattern when seen from below.

Voice: A loud *zeep-zeep-zeep*.

Habitat: Open landscapes with water, fresh pools, riverbanks and sandbars, salt pans, shorelines, estuaries, and deltas.

Nesting: 4 olive-yellow eggs blotched and spotted with brown and black, laid in shallow scrape on sandbar or dried-out water margin, always within short distance of fresh water.

Range: Middle East south to Egypt, sub-Saharan Africa to India.

Spur-winged Plovers are frequently seen alongside crocodiles in Africa and Asia and possibly feed on the smaller animal life these great reptiles disturb. They often adopt a crouched attitude, which, together with their delicate treading gait, gives an impression of embarrassment at having been spotted.

Sociable Plover

(*Chettusia gregaria*)

Description: 11½″ (29 cm). A *large plover;* in breeding plumage has *black crown* and variable *black eye-stripe* offset by *white forehead and eyebrow* completely circling crown. Chest vinaceous pink-grey abutting *deep maroon belly.* Long *legs black.* In winter, bold colours of underparts become nondescript buff-grey, but *dark eye-stripe* retained. In flight, *white underwing* contrasts with black primaries. Striking upperwing pattern of black primaries, white secondaries, and buffy-grey coverts. Tail has white coverts and base and broad, *black subterminal band.*

Voice: A shrill, short whistle; a harsh *ketz.*

Habitat: Sandy, grassy plains, dry steppes; winters in open country and marginal farmland, sometimes beside pools.

Nesting: 4 eggs brownish-buff spotted and streaked with brown-black toward larger end, in shallow scrape lined with grasses.

Range: Breeds north of Caspian east to Siberia. Winters south to Egypt, Arabia, Iran, and India. Occasional visitor to eastern Europe, vagrant farther west.

Sociable Plovers, despite their name, keep to small parties of 6 or 7, forming larger flocks of up to 100 or more only prior to migration.

157 **Lapwing**
(*Vanellus vanellus*)

Description: 12″ (30 cm). A very common *black-and-white* plover. Dark upperparts iridescent green; fine *black crest* rises from crown. In flight, *wings appear remarkably rounded* and tail has white base and black subterminal band. Chestnut undertail coverts easily overlooked. Immatures and winter adults similar to summer plumage but duller, with less clear-cut pattern on face and breast.

Voice: Flight call, a plaintively shrill *pee-wit,* often repeated, from which it gets one of its many English country names, "Peewit." Also calls during spectacular aerial display.

Habitat: Damp meadows, upland grassland, ploughed fields, marshes, moorland; in winter, grasslands, water margins, mud flats, and estuaries.

Nesting: 4 clay-brown eggs blotched and spotted with black, laid in well-hidden scrape lined with grass.

Range: Breeds across temperate zone of Palearctic region extending north to Lofoten Islands of Norway and the Gulf of Bothnia. Leaves northern and eastern part of range in winter, but partial migrant in Europe.

This adaptable bird has occupied almost every open habitat in Europe and is the most common and widespread wader. Its call is one of the most familiar springtime country sounds.

SANDPIPERS, SNIPE, AND PHALAROPES
(Scolopacidae)

93 species: worldwide. Twenty-five species breed in Europe, four are regular migrants. Large and variable family of small to large waders. Bill short to long, straight or decurved (recurved in a few species); legs short to long. Upperparts generally mottled browns and greys, underparts whitish, but many species acquire brighter plumage in breeding season. Sexes similar. Wing bars and rump and tail patterns are important in identification. Inhabit beaches, mud flats, salt and fresh marshes, inland ponds and lakes, and damp meadows. Feed on wide range of aquatic organisms, often probing in mud or sand with bills. Many species breed on arctic tundra and perform long annual migrations in large flocks. Phalaropes, the only truly aquatic waders, differ in having lobed toes, enabling them to swim with ease and spend most of their lives in water, but they also walk well on land. Sex roles reversed; female phalaropes more brightly coloured and maintain territories; males incubate and tend young.

---

97 Knot
(*Calidris canutus*)

Description: 10″ (25 cm). Medium-sized wader, larger than Dunlin, with *stocky build* and short neck, legs, and bill. In summer, deep chestnut-red below. In autumn and winter, grey above and whitish below. White wing bar and *barred grey rump and tail*.

Voice: A low-pitched double *knut-knut* and a whistled flight call.

Habitat: High arctic tundra; in winter, essentially maritime, found on estuaries and along open shores.

Nesting: 4 greyish-olive eggs lightly marked

with spots and streaks, laid in depression thickly lined with lichen

Range: Breeds central Siberia, Alaska, Canadian arctic islands, Greenland. Siberian birds cross to Baltic and on to North Sea and Atlantic coasts to winter.

Named specifically after King Canute, who attempted to turn back the waves—a reference to its maritime life. It does not appear in many European localities, but if an estuary does attract the Knot, it descends in the thousands.

92, 119 **Sanderling**
(*Calidris alba*)

Description: 8″ (20 cm). A *short-billed, active* little wader that *follows breaking waves in and out*. In summer, scalloped, rusty-brown on back; *lacks eye-stripe;* underparts white, with dark, rusty streaks on breast almost forming complete pectoral band. In Europe, usually seen in winter plumage, which is pale grey above and white below, with *dark patch at bend of folded wing*. The *whitest European wader*. In flight, shows very *bold white wing bar*.

Voice: A sharp contact note, *twick, twick*.

Habitat: Tundra. In winter, frequents open sandy or sometimes rocky shores.

Nesting: 4 dull olive-green eggs sparsely marked with small brown spots, laid in hollow lined with dead leaves and protected by tuft of vegetation.

Range: Circumpolar in highest latitudes. Migrant through northern Europe to winter on Atlantic and western Mediterranean coasts.

Sanderlings live on the minute planktonic crustaceans left behind by the tide. They also feed among rocks in company with Turnstones and Purple Sandpipers, but their light colouration makes them easy to spot.

113 **Semipalmated Sandpiper**
(*Calidris pusilla*)

Description: 6″ (15 cm). Similar to Little Stint. In all plumages the best differences are *blunt-tipped bill* (fine-tipped on Little Stint), *webbing between toes* (visible only at close range; Western Sandpiper only other small wader with webbed feet), and voice. Juveniles in autumn further distinguishable by uniform, scaly mantle with usually only *faint white Vs.*

Voice: A low, throaty *chrrup,* quite distinct from call of Little Stint.

Habitat: Grassy marshes in Arctic. In winter, on seashores, estuaries, and salt marshes; also margins of lakes and pools.

Nesting: 4 olive-buff eggs marked with sepia, laid in depression lined with leaves; not hidden in any way.

Range: North America. Vagrant to Europe, especially to Britain and Ireland.

This is one of five small American waders known as "peeps." The others—White-rumped, Baird's, Western, and Least sandpipers—are occasionally seen in Europe. While the first two are relatively distinctive, the others are difficult to distinguish. The Least is slightly smaller than the Semipalmated and Western, with browner plumage, more heavily streaked breast, and yellow or greenish legs. In autumn and winter, some Westerns retain rusty feathers on scapulars and crown, but others are virtually indistinguishable from the Semipalmated.

91, 125 **Little Stint**
(*Calidris minuta*)

Description: 5¼″ (13 cm). A tiny, very active version of a Dunlin. *Short straight bill* and *short black legs.* In summer, feathers of upperparts *boldly edged with rufous and buff;* rufous streaking on breast and white belly. Summer adult and juvenile (which has neatly scaled underparts) both show *white V on back.* In winter, plumage (seldom seen in Britain), upperparts generally grey with dusky feather centres; often *white forehead* and white eyebrow; underparts white with faint streaking on sides of breast. In flight, shows white wing bar and *grey outer tail feathers.*

Voice: Flight note, a high-pitched *tit.*

Habitat: Breeds on dry tundra, open marshes, small pools. In winter and on migration, found on seashore and on coastal marshes, sewage farms.

Nesting: 4 glossy, pale greenish-buff eggs with large blotches and spots of chestnut, laid in neat grass and leaf-lined cup.

Range: From northernmost Scandinavia across Arctic to central Siberia. Passes through most of Europe on migration; winters in parts of Mediterranean and in Africa.

They frequently gather in large flocks on migration and on wintering grounds. Busy feeders, they probe with head down and often seem oblivious of approaching danger. They are the standard small wader against which American "peeps" are compared.

---

94 Temminck's Stint
(*Calidris temminckii*)

Description: 5½" (14 cm). Similar in size to Little Stint; feeding action slower, rather sluggish. Typically rather secretive, keeping to the vegetated margins of freshwater mud flats. Adults in summer uniformly brownish above; juveniles in autumn rather plain grey-brown above, *lacking the striking scaly pattern of Little Stint.* In all plumages has *uniformly dusky patches at sides of breast* (a pattern recalling that of Common Sandpiper) and in flight shows *white outer tail feathers. Legs pale greenish,* not black, and bill finer than Little Stint's.

Voice: A distinctive *priit* in flight.

Habitat: Breeds on shores of tundra lakes and pools. On passage and in winter, usually found along freshwater margins and shoreline pools.

Nesting: 4 greenish-grey eggs evenly spotted with brown, laid in scrape lined with grasses or few leaves.

Range: From Scandinavia across tundra zone to Bering Sea. Passes through most of Europe to winter in Africa south of the Sahara.

Temminck's Stint is a confiding small wader that lacks the robustness and gregariousness of the Little Stint. Though gathering in quite large numbers, it never feeds in flocks like Little Stint. When flushed, it often rises steeply giving its typical call, unlike the Little Stint which flies away low.

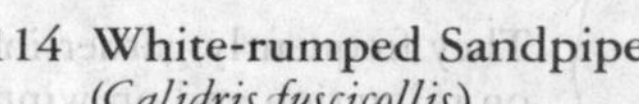

114 White-rumped Sandpiper
(*Calidris fuscicollis*)

Description: 7½" (19 cm). Largest of the American "peeps," about same size as a Dunlin; but wings project well beyond the tail when at rest, giving an elevated rear end. In summer, rufous above; but juveniles that reach Europe in autumn are generally grey-brown above with neat scaly pattern, and rufous at shoulder only. Clear-cut, streaked breast band. Head rounded with *marked eyebrow; bill thin, shorter and straighter than Dunlin's.* Bold *crescent-shaped, white rump patch* (narrower than Curlew Sandpiper) and black tail. Bill shorter than Curlew Sandpiper and straight.

Voice: A squeaking *jeet-jeet*.

Habitat: Tundra; mud flats, estuaries, lagoons, and pools in winter.

Nesting: 4 olive-green eggs spotted with brown, laid in grass-lined depression.

Range: North America. Accidental in Europe, annually in Britain and Ireland.

Though rarely seen in Europe before 1940, improved standards of identification have proved the Wh[illegible] rumped to be an annual transatlant[illegible] vagrant. It breeds in the far northwe[illegible] of North America and migrates east and south to the Atlantic and South America in the autumn, occasionally drifting off course to Europe.

115 **Baird's Sandpiper**
(*Calidris bairdii*)

Description: 7″ (18 cm). A large "peep" that looks strikingly *buff-brown* in all plumages except adult winter. *Upperparts scaly* with *rufous-buff edges to the feathers.* White eyebrow, buffy head and breast band. Belly white; legs *black* and rather *short.* Bill black. In flight, shows faint wing bar and white edges to dark-centred tail. *Long wings* extend well beyond tail-tip when perched, giving *long, low appearance.*

Voice: Mellow *preet-preet* when flying.

Habitat: Tundra; in winter and on passage, frequents grassy pools of inland meadows, lake and river margins, shore pools. Seldom on estuaries.

Nesting: 4 pinkish-buff eggs thickly spotted with rich chestnut, laid in grass-lined depression.

Range: North America. Vagrant to Europe, mostly to Britain and Ireland.

This is one of the most distinctive of the American "peeps" and a rare vagrant to Europe.

100 **Pectoral Sandpiper**
(*Calidris melanotos*)

Description: 8½″ (21 cm). Slightly larger than a Dunlin, recalling a small Ruff in its proportions and stance. Upperparts brown and scaly with prominent *pale stripes* forming double V. Light eyebrow. *Breast streaks end abruptly on lower breast,* forming pectoral line sharply contrasting with *white belly.* Bill straight, legs pale greenish-yellow. Fine wing bar and white ovals at sides of tail-base (in pattern like that of Ruff).

Voice: A distinctive *brrrp*.

Habitat: Meadows with pools, short wet grass areas, golf courses, airports, shore pools.

Nesting: 4 glossy olive-buff eggs spotted and blotched with brown, laid in well-hidden depression lined with grass.

Range: North America. Rare autumn visitor to western Europe.

A long-distance migrant, the Pectoral Sandpiper breeds in Alaska and migrates southeast, flying over the Atlantic to winter in South America. One of the most frequent American birds in Europe, with up to 20 records per year in Britain and Ireland alone.

93, 120 **Curlew Sandpiper**
(*Calidris ferruginea*)

Description: 7½" (19 cm). Medium-sized wader similar to Dunlin but slightly larger and with *prominent white rump.* In summer, has deep chestnut-red underparts. Adults are dull grey above. *Longer neck,* longer legs, more upright posture, *longer, decurved bill,* and more elegant shape *than Dunlin.* Juveniles have warmly-coloured upperparts with striking scaly pattern and usually show a pinky-buff wash across breast.

Voice: A gentle, whistled *chirrup.*

Habitat: Dry arctic tundra in breeding season; in winter and on passage, prefers estuaries and mud flats; also on marshes near shoreline.

Nesting: 4 olive-buff eggs heavily marked with brown blotches and spots, laid in tussock of grass.

Range: Central northern Siberia. Migrates across Europe, a few staying to winter in the western Mediterranean; most pass on to Africa.

Breeding only in remote northern Siberia, with an outpost on the arctic coast of Alaska, it occurs in varying numbers in Europe in autumn, reflecting the varied breeding success from year to year. In autumn, it flocks with Dunlins and other waders.

98, 126 **Purple Sandpiper**
(*Calidris maritima*)

Description: 8¼″ (21 cm). A *squat, stocky, short-legged* wader a little larger than a Dunlin. Drab, dark grey winter plumage. *Legs yellow* and, in winter, *base of bill orange-yellow.* Head and breast streaked with grey. In summer, all brown with heavy streaking on head and breast and totally black bill. Faint wing bar and light uppertail with dark centre show in flight.

Voice: A short *trrit-trrit* in flight.

Habitat: Tundra; winters almost exclusively on wave-washed, *rocky coasts.*

Nesting: 4 greenish eggs fading to olive-buff blotched and spotted with sepia, laid in neat cup lined with leaves and lichens.

Range: Circumpolar, nesting in Iceland, Scandinavia, and high arctic areas of Asia and North America. Winters along coasts of Scandinavia, the North Sea, Britain, and Ireland.

Purple Sandpipers inhabit some of the coldest regions of the world, leaving the far north only when the sea freezes; they then move as far as Britain and the North Sea. Food consists of crustaceans and molluscs.

90, 143 **Dunlin**
(*Calidris alpina*)

Description: 7″ (18 cm). The "standard" small wader. Summer upperparts russet-brown; underparts white with streaked breast and prominent *patch of black on belly.* In winter, grey-brown above, grey-white below. Juveniles have rusty upperparts with white lines forming a V; underparts white, streaked on breast and flanks. *Bill rather long* and slightly *downturned at tip.* In flight, shows faint wing bar, black-centered rump, and tail with grey sides.

Voice: A distinctive *treep.*

Habitat: Moorland, grassland and meadows, tundra; outside breeding season, on estuaries, shorelines, beaches, pools.

Nesting: 4 olive-buff eggs spotted or blotched with chestnut-brown, laid in neat cup lined with grass concealed in tussock of vegetation; almost always close to water.

Range: Holarctic. Breeds in Iceland, Britain, Ireland, Fenno-Scandia and shores of Baltic, and in northern Asia and North America. Winters from southern Scandinavia and Britain to Atlantic and Mediterranean coasts.

These active little waders feed busily, probing this way and that as they wade across shallow pools or follow the tide line. They sometimes gather in immense numbers at favoured feeding grounds and will form dense packs in flight. They alternately show white, then dark, as they twist and turn in unison in the air.

---

89 Broad-billed Sandpiper
(*Limicola falcinellus*)

Description: 6½" (16 cm). Short-legged wader slightly smaller than Dunlin, with *striped head and body pattern* recalling that of Snipe. Dark brown upperparts marked with *double creamy-white* V; head has *pale eyebrow* that may be divided over eye, and distinct dark stripe through eye. Bill longer than head and *drooped or kinked at tip.* Breast streaked, belly white. In greyer winter plumage, head pattern, bill shape, and short legs best distinguish it from Dunlin.

Voice: Contact call, a deep *treek.*

Habitat: Bogs in tundra. In winter, estuaries, marshes, salt pans.

Nesting: 4 white eggs densely covered with

small red-brown spots, laid in tussock of grass in shallow bog or marsh.

Range: In Europe, breeds in Scandinavian mountains and tundra zone. Migrates south and east to winter in Middle East, southern Asia, and Australia. Rare in western Europe.

A high Arctic breeder, it is notoriously difficult to locate once the display-song period is over and thus its geographical range is not fully known. It is generally a solitary bird, seldom mixing with other waders.

---

116 **Buff-breasted Sandpiper**
(*Tryngites subruficollis*)

Description: 8″ (20 cm). *Similar to a small juvenile Ruff* with uniformly orange-buff underparts and face. Neat scaly pattern on back; yellow legs. Small round head on long neck; black eye prominent in featureless buff face; *short needle-like bill. Lacks wing bar* and has *no distinctive rump pattern.* Underwing is white. Underparts uniformly *buff*, unlike Ruff, becoming whitish on belly.

Voice: A low, trilled *preet;* also a sharp *tick.*

Habitat: Short-grassy fields, airstrips, golf courses, open country.

Nesting: 4 greenish-olive eggs boldly marked with black, laid in shallow depression on dry ridge in tundra.

Range: North America. Vagrant to Europe.

Buff-breasted Sandpipers were once hunted nearly out of existence in North America and are still rare. Now annual in Britain and Ireland, they sometimes appear in small parties. Usually tame; when flushed they twist and turn in the air like a Snipe.

96, 161, 162, **Ruff**
163 (*Philomachus pugnax*)

Description: Male, 11½″ (29 cm); female, 9″ (23 cm). For most of the year a remarkably featureless wader; in summer, male (Ruff) sports *extraordinary growth of feathers around neck and head,* including full colourful ruff and ear tufts. Face becomes bare and red-brown; feathered ornaments vary from white through brown and chequered to black. Female (Reeve) dull buffy-brown above and white below. *Upperparts strikingly scaly,* especially juveniles. In flight, base of tail shows *two white oval marks.* Legs yellow, green, or orange; *small head sits on long neck.* Outside the breeding season, adults generally greyish above and white below.

Voice: Practically mute; subdued squeaking sounds in flight.

Habitat: Tundra, grassland, especially water meadows, inland marshes, lakeshores.

Nesting: 4 pale grey-green eggs boldly blotched and spotted with sepia, laid among thick grass in neatly lined hollow.

Range: Across northern Palearctic. Breeds in northern Europe, locally in Britain and France; migrates to Africa. Some winter as far north as England.

Ruff gather at a lek, a traditional display ground, where they engage in mock combat to assert their dominance and the right to mate.

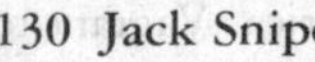

130 Jack Snipe
(*Lymnocryptes minimus*)

Description: 7½″ (19 cm). Similar to but smaller than Snipe, with proportionately *much shorter bill* (about same length as head). When flushed, flies away low, without the erratic zig-zagging of Snipe, and usually drops quickly back into cover. When seen on ground, lacks the barring on flanks and light central crown-stripe shown by Snipe. Silent when flushed.

Voice: On the breeding ground, soft note like a galloping horse.

Habitat: Bogs, marshes, wet meadows, lagoons.

Nesting: 4 creamy-olive eggs spotted sepia, laid on hummock of moss or grass among scrub or marsh.

Range: Breeds from Scandinavia east across Palearctic in scrub and birch zone. Migrant across Europe to Britain, France, Mediterranean, and Africa.

A well-camouflaged, retiring species. Most often encountered when flushed from rank grassland, it is frequently found alongside Snipe in winter but seldom in large concentrations.

128 Snipe or Common Snipe
(*Gallinago gallinago*)

Description: 10½" (26 cm). A heavily streaked and barred, long-billed wader, with highly effective camouflage. *Dark brown above,* with *pale creamy stripes;* whitish below, with dark bars continued to chest and flanks. *Belly white. Long, straight bill* at least 2½ times length of head. Little white at tip of tail. When flushed, has characteristic call and *zig-zag* flight.

Voice: Alarm call, a rasping *schaark.* Spring call, an insistent repeated *chipp-er, chipp-er, chipp-er.* "Song" given by night, a characteristic whinnying *e-e-e-e-e-e,* produced by vibrating outer tail feathers.

Habitat: Overgrown marshes, lagoons, wet meadows, old sewage farms, moors, creeks, rivers.

Nesting: 4 olive-brown eggs boldly blotched and spotted sepia, laid in hollow in tussock near water.

Range: Holarctic. Breeds throughout temperate Europe, including northern Scandinavia; winters in western and southern Europe and Africa.

A shy bird that relies on its cryptic colouration for concealment, it generally rises with a sharp alarm call. During its display flight it produces a drumming sound by diving through the air around its territory at great speed, causing the air to bleat or drum through its outer tail feathers.

129 Great Snipe
(*Gallinago media*)

Description: 11″ (28 cm). Only marginally longer than Snipe, with *shorter bill,* but much bulkier and looks decidedly larger, giving *impression of small Woodcock.* Plumage much like Snipe, but prominent *white corners to tail* (visible only in flight) and almost entirely *barred underparts* are diagnostic. Bill less than twice length of head. Flight more direct than Snipe.

Voice: Silent or a subdued harsh croak when flushed; bubbling chorus in spring.

Habitat: Breeds in marshy country in wooded regions. On migration and in winter, on marshes; also drier ground, fields.

Nesting: 4 stone-buff eggs blotched and spotted brown, laid in depression lined with grass sheltered among birches.

Range: Breeds from Scandinavia east to central Siberia. Migrates through eastern Europe to Africa.

It forms leks at traditional jousting grounds where 50 or more birds engage in bill-clattering, a chorus of calls and ritualised fighting. Females emerge, observe the display, and then fly off with a male.

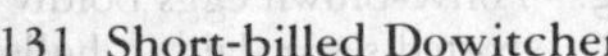

131 Short-billed Dowitcher
(*Limnodromus griseus*)

Description: 11″ (28 cm). Very similar to Long-billed Dowitcher. Underparts rust-red in summer, greyish-white in autumn and winter. Despite name, *length of bill is a notoriously unreliable distinguishing feature.* Short-billed has *thinner black bars on tail* and *spotted, not barred, undertail coverts.* Both dowitchers have bold white V extending up back and white trailing edge to inner wing. Most reliably separated by call. Juveniles are warmer brown above than Long-billed, and have diagnostic barred tertials.

Voice: Rapid, Greenshank-like, mellow whistle, *tu-tu-tu*.

Habitat: Bogs and lakes; prefers mud flats and open shorelines.

Nesting: 4 greenish eggs spotted with brown, laid in a depression lined with grasses and moss in wet ground.

Range: North America. Very rare vagrant to Europe.

A common shorebird in North America, it probes deeply with its bill for worms and crustaceans in the mud.

112 Long-billed Dowitcher
(*Limnodromus scolopaceus*)

Description: 11½" (29 cm). A stocky, long-billed wader. In summer plumage, underparts rust-red; in winter, *greyish-white. Bill is 2½ times length of head* and tail is short, adding to stocky appearance. Difficult to separate from Short-billed Dowitcher, but its voice, *broader black bars on tail,* and *barred (not spotted) undertail coverts* are the best distinctions. In flight, shows white rump extending up back in V and white trailing edge to secondaries. Juveniles are generally greyer above than Short-billed, and have dark tertials with thin pale fringes.

Voice: A single high-pitched *keek* or a series of such notes.

Habitat: Mostly confined to freshwater marshes and lagoons in tundra. On migration, also common on coastal mud flats and estuaries.

Nesting: 4 olive-green eggs spotted with brown, laid in depression lined with grass or moss.

Range: North America. Vagrant in Europe.

Both dowitcher species often occur in the same flock although the Long-billed shows some preference for fresh water and the Short-billed for open mud flats.

127 **Woodcock**
(*Scolopax rusticola*)

Description: 13½" (34 cm). Large, brown bird with most effective camouflage of any wader, a beautiful combination of browns, creams, and buffs, *Transverse band on crown; large eye.* Most often seen in flight, when *rounded wings, dumpy shape,* and *long, straight bill (held pointing downward)* facilitate identification.

Voice: A few grunting croaks followed by a sharp, clear *tissick* produced in flight as male circles its territory (roding) at dawn and dusk.

Habitat: Mixed deciduous woodland, marshy woodland, damp heaths.

Nesting: 4 buff eggs spotted and blotched chestnut, laid in scrape lined with dead leaves at base of tree.

Range: Breeds over most of non-Mediterranean Europe to tree line, east across north-central Asia to Japan. Migrates south and east to winter in western Europe, Mediterranean, and southern Asia.

Seldom encountered casually, they are best searched for in spring, when their roding flight brings them out at dawn or dusk, about the same time as the nightjars begin to call. They feed mainly at night.

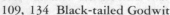

109, 134 **Black-tailed Godwit**
(*Limosa limosa*)

Description: 16" (40 cm). One of the larger European waders, distinctively long-legged with a long, straight bill. In summer, head, neck, and breast are bright chestnut, flanks and belly white with dark barring. Plumage grey in winter. Marked at all seasons by bold *white wing bar* and *black terminal band to white tail,* separating it from similar Bar-tailed Godwit.

Voice: Flight note, *wick-a-wick-a-wick.* Other notes in breeding season.

Habitat: Breeds on wet grassland; winters on marshes, estuaries.

Nesting: 4 olive-green eggs speckled and blotched with varying amounts of dark brown, laid in neat grass-lined hollow among thick grass.

Range: Breeds from Iceland, Britain, and France across Eurasia to Bering Sea; winters on Mediterranean and Atlantic coasts, and in Africa.

Found mostly on fresh water, it is a long-distance migrant that passes over the Mediterranean and Sahara to winter in the marshes of the Sahel zone. Numbers in the Lake Chad and Niger inundation zone are reportedly huge. Often gregarious, they form large, dense flocks.

---

108 **Bar-tailed Godwit**
(*Limosa lapponica*)

Description: 15″ (38 cm). Chestnut-red underparts in summer; whitish in winter. Easily confused with Black-tailed Godwit, except in flight, when finely *barred (not banded) tail* and lack of bold white wing bar are obvious; legs shorter; *bill shorter and slightly upturned.*

Voice: Flight note, a short, nasal *kirrick.*

Habitat: Tundra marshes; outside breeding season, essentially a shorebird frequenting estuaries, beaches, and mudbanks.

Nesting: 4 glossy, brownish-olive eggs spotted and streaked with dark olive-brown, laid in a depression lined with dry leaves on small hillock.

Range: From extreme north of Lapland across the northern Palearctic to western Alaska. Migrates south to winter on coasts of North Sea and Atlantic and to the Old World tropics, including Pacific Islands.

Essentially maritime, the Bar-tailed Godwit forms large flocks that feed and roost together and often perform complex aerial evolutions like the much smaller Dunlin. It uses its long, upturned bill to probe deeply for intertidal creatures in the mud.

---

135 **Whimbrel**
(*Numenius phaeopus*)

Description: 16″ (40 cm). Like the Curlew, but *smaller; decurved bill shorter* and *crown prominently striped.* In flight, shows V-shaped white rump.

Voice: A series of brief whistles (often 7 in number) in rapid succession, distinct from all other curlews.

Habitat: Moors, open tundra; on migration and in winter, shorelines, estuaries, marshes.

Nesting: 4 olive-green eggs blotched and spotted sepia, laid in hollow lined with grasses.

Range: Circumpolar in tundra-alpine zone. In Europe, breeds in Iceland, northern Scandinavia and Russia, Shetland Isles, and extreme northern Scotland. European birds winter in Spain, Portugal, and Africa.

It is known as the "Seven Whistler" among country folk. Mainly a bird of passage through most of Europe, it arrives late, leaves quite early, and is seldom seen in large flocks; can often be heard calling at night.

Slender-billed Curlew
(*Numenius tenuirostris*)

Description: 16″ (40 cm). Smaller version of Curlew, only slightly larger than Whimbrel, but *lacking crown-stripes* and with longer bill and legs. Best separated from Curlew by *bold, heart-shaped spots* on sides of flanks and *whiter barred tail* below white V-shaped rump. Generally *lighter in colour and cleaner-looking* than Curlew or Whimbrel, with *wing showing greater contrast* between dark primaries and lighter inner wing.

Voice: A *coor-lee* similar to Curlew, but higher in pitch.

Habitat: Marshes on steppes; in winter and on migration, on sandy coasts, lagoons, estuaries.

Nesting: 4 olive-brown eggs marked greyish-brown, laid in depression lined with grasses and situated on dry ridge.

Range: Breeds on western Siberian steppes north to borders of taiga zone; winters from Iraq and eastern Mediterranean to western Morocco.

A little-known bird that occurs irregularly in Europe, though it passes through the Mediterranean region twice each year. In Morocco it winters on the Atlantic coast in small numbers and may well pass unreported through southern Spain and Italy.

---

136 Curlew
(*Numenius arquata*)

Description: 21–23″ (53–58 cm). Largest European wader. Brown, speckled plumage shading to white on belly. *Long slate-grey legs* and *very long decurved bill,* over 3 times length of head. In flight, shows white rump extending in V up back.

Voice: A liquid *coor-lee;* in display flight, a bubbling note and more prolonged, trilled extensions of flight note.

Habitat: Upland moors, wet meadows, marshes; in winter and on migration, on estuaries and open shores.

Nesting: 4 greenish-brown eggs spotted sepia, laid in scantily lined hollow.

Range: Breeds from northern and central Europe east across Palearctic. Passage migrant and winter visitor throughout southern Europe.

The largest and longest-billed wader in Europe. Its familiar call has made it popular with country people, though it is still shot along the shoreline in season. Its long bill enables it to secure food that is out of reach of other waders.

140 **Upland Sandpiper**
(*Bartramia longicauda*)

Description: 11″ (28 cm). Medium-sized, Ruff-like bird, with heavily streaked, buff plumage. Remarkably *long neck and small head,* short, straight bill, and upright stance; *long tail* gives it slim look. Breast marked with fine arrows; dark crown. Distinctly barred underwing. Flies with *shallow wingbeats.*

Voice: A beautiful song, with mellow whistles and trills. Alarm, a rapid *quip-ip-ip.*

Habitat: Invariably found on grasslands.

Nesting: 4 cream-coloured eggs speckled red-brown, laid in grass-lined hollow.

Range: North America. Vagrant to Europe.

A very rare vagrant from America, it has occurred in several western European countries, most frequently in Britain and Ireland. Often called Upland Plover and formerly Bartram's Sandpiper, it holds its wings up over its back when alighting.

111, 142 **Spotted Redshank**
(*Tringa erythropus*)

Description: 12″ (30 cm). Summer plumage *sooty-black with white spots on upperparts; red legs;* and *red base on long, straight bill.* In winter, upperparts pale grey with whitish spottings. In this plumage, can be confused with Redshank, but is paler grey and has *longer and finer bill* and *longer legs.* In flight, *legs extend beyond tail* and wing *lacks white trailing edge* of Redshank. Tail finely barred and white rump extends well up back in V.

Voice: A shrill, whistling *tuhu-eet;* also a *chick-chick-chick.*

Habitat: Open areas of conifer and birch forests. In winter, fresh water margins, estuaries, marshes, lagoons, salt pans.

Nesting: 4 greenish-buff eggs boldly blotched with umber, laid in depression lined with grass, leaves, and feathers, hidden among low vegetation.

Range: Breeds across northern Palearctic.

Passes through Europe to winter in Mediterranean, Atlantic coasts, northern equatorial Africa, and southern Asia.

An elegant wader, the Spotted Redshank is distinguished from the similar Redshank by its shape and grace. It frequents marshes more than shorelines and is not generally found in large flocks. A few "black" birds appear in temperate Europe in late summer—presumably unsuccessful breeders making an early return.

110, 141 **Redshank**
(*Tringa totanus*)

Description: 11″ (28 cm). A noisy, greyish-brown wader with *bright orange-red legs.* Bill slightly longer than head, red at base. Upperparts brown in all seasons; underparts white, with breast and flanks boldly streaked. In flight, legs extend beyond barred tail. White rump extends up back in bold V. Broad *white trailing edge to wing.*

Voice: An alarm, *teuk-teuk-teuk;* a flight note, *teu-loo-loo.*

Habitat: Moorland, marshes; in winter, on wet meadows, marshes, estuaries, rocky shores, salt pans.

Nesting: 4 variably-coloured eggs, mostly yellow-brown spotted with dark brown, laid in grass-lined cup hidden in tussock of grass pulled over nest. Side entrance.

Range: Breeds from Iceland, Scandinavia, Britain, and Spain east across central Eurasia to central Siberia. Winters in western and southern Europe, chiefly on coasts; also northern and tropical Africa.

The numerous and widespread Redshank is found almost anywhere there is water. It forms dense flocks on estuaries and will crowd together at high-tide roosts with Knot, Dunlin, and Oystercatcher. On breeding grounds it is the watchdog of the marshes, rising at the first sign of danger and calling loudly as it hovers overhead.

132 Marsh Sandpiper
(*Tringa stagnatilis*)

Description: 9″ (23 cm). A delicate wader similar to a Greenshank but smaller, with shorter, *pencil-slim bill* and *longer, more spindly greenish legs* that extend well beyond the tail in flight. Brownish in summer, but most often seen in *grey winter plumage.* Face and forehead white. In flight, shows barred tail and white rump extending in V up back. No wing bar.

Voice: A *tu, tee, chick,* and a trill.

Habitat: Marshy borders of lakes; freshwater margins and marshes.

Nesting: 4 creamy-buff eggs blotched and spotted with rich brown, laid in hollow among vegetation and lined with grasses.

Range: Steppe regions of central and eastern Palearctic from Romania and Ukraine east. Migrant through eastern Europe on way to Africa; rare in western Europe.

The Marsh Sandpiper is an elegant wader most at home wading in shallow fresh water, picking its food delicately from the surface. It is usually alone or in small parties.

95 Greenshank
(*Tringa nebularia*)

Description: 12″ (30 cm). Slim grey wader with long, *pale green legs* and *long bill slightly upturned* and at least *twice as long as head.* Upperparts grey, flecked with black and white. Breast speckled and streaked, rest of underparts white. Legs extend beyond tail in flight. No wing bar. White rump extends up back in V. Tail lightly barred; looks pale in flight.

Voice: A loud, unmistakable *tu-tu-tu.*
Habitat: Upland moors, open areas in wooded zones; freshwater margins, estuaries.
Nesting: 4 buffy eggs boldly blotched with dark brown, laid in well-lined depression among low vegetation, often near stone, dead tree, or other marker.
Range: Scotland east across Scandinavia and the Palearctic. Passage migrant through rest of Europe, wintering in Mediterranean, along Atlantic coast, and in Africa, Asia, and Australia.

Greenshanks are generally solitary birds, sometimes forming small parties. Though often found on creeks and salt pans, they are much more numerous at freshwater margins and in shallow lagoons. In their winter quarters, they often occur at inland floods and lakes and even at small waterholes and reservoirs. On migration, they may turn up at the smallest wetlands.

139 Greater Yellowlegs
(*Tringa melanoleuca*)
Description: 14″ (35 cm). Slim, elegant wader similar in proportions to Greenshank, but with long *yellow legs.* Grey-brown above with white spots. In summer, white underparts have dark bars and spots, but in winter, barring is confined to flanks. *Bill twice as long as head,* and slightly upturned, distinguishing it from Lesser Yellowlegs. *White rump ends squarely,* not extending in V up back as on Greenshank.
Voice: *Whew-whew-whew,* like Greenshank. Lesser Yellowlegs has shorter, less ringing call of one or two notes.
Habitat: Fresh marshes and mud flats in winter; wooded swamps and tundra in breeding season.
Nesting: 4 olive-buff eggs blotched with chestnut, laid in simple scrape lined with grasses, often among fallen timber in wet marshy areas.
Range: North America. Vagrant to Europe.

A wary and noisy bird, it seldom forms large flocks and is more like the Greenshank than the Redshank. Distinguishable from Lesser Yellowlegs by its call and larger size.

---

138 **Lesser Yellowlegs**
(*Tringa flavipes*)

Description: 10″ (25 cm). Smaller than similar Greater Yellowlegs; *bill thinner and shorter* (1½ times length of head or less). *Yellow legs* proportionately longer. Lacks wing bar; square white rump.

Voice: A short *tu* or *tu-tu;* occasionally three notes like Greenshank.

Habitat: Breeds on lakes and bogs in wooded country; at other times found on ponds, marshes, lakes, river margins, mud flats.

Nesting: 4 greyish-buff eggs spotted with chestnut, laid in depression sparsely lined with leaves, often placed near fallen log.

Range: North America. Vagrant to Europe, mostly Britain and Ireland.

The Lesser Yellowlegs is a more gregarious and approachable bird than its larger counterpart. It frequently forms medium-sized flocks and is much more regularly seen in Europe than the Greater Yellowlegs.

---

133 **Green Sandpiper**
(*Tringa ochropus*)

Description: 9″ (23 cm). Medium-small wader, larger than Dunlin with the elegance and grace of a "shank." *Dark slate-brown above* with light spots giving faintly mottled appearance; white below with dark streaking on breast. In flight, *white rump forms strong contrast with almost black upperparts,* underwing, and barred tail. Legs dark and bill slightly longer than head.

Voice: A penetrating *weet-a-weet.*

Habitat: Breeds in damp, marshy forests; at

other times frequents marshes and freshwater pools but characteristically found along narrow streams and ditches in wooded areas.

Nesting: 4 greenish-buff eggs spotted with brown, laid in old nest of another species, in trees in damp forest.

Range: Palearctic from Scandinavia and central Europe east to eastern Siberia. Passage migrant across western Europe, wintering in south and west, and in the Mediterranean; also in tropical Africa and southern Asia.

A solitary bird, it is seldom seen until flushed from a marshland dyke or shallow stream, when it usually gives a noisy call. The contrasting black-and-white pattern can be confused in poor light with that of the Wood Sandpiper, which has a similar flight pattern but is paler.

137 Wood Sandpiper
(*Tringa glareola*)

Description: 8″ (20 cm). A medium-sized wader resembling Green Sandpiper, but upperparts browner (not blackish) with more prominent white spots. Underparts whitish with dark streaks on breast. Bill about same length as head. *Legs* pale yellowish, longer than Green Sandpiper's, and *extending beyond tail* in flight. Flight pattern similar to Green Sandpiper, with uniform wings and *square white rump;* lacks Green Sandpiper's striking black-and-white appearance; underwing brownish, not black.

Voice: A high, trilling *whit-whit-whit* or *chip-chip-chip.*

Habitat: Breeds in open areas in northern forests, bogs, and tundra; winters on marshes, freshwater margins.

Nesting: 4 variably coloured eggs, usually buff-olive blotched with dark brown, laid in hollow lined with leaves and grasses.

Range: Palearctic from Denmark (and Scotland recently) east to the Pacific. Migrant through most of Europe en route to Africa south of the Sahara.

Though seldom found in flocks, up to 50,000 Wood Sandpipers have been counted in the Camargue in southern France, moulting in autumn. Most nearly double their weight prior to flying across the Sahara.

---

107 Terek Sandpiper
(*Xenus cinereus*)

Description: 9″ (23 cm). A medium-sized wader with tear-shaped dark markings on brown-grey upperparts in summer, but uniformly grey in winter. Short *orange or yellow legs; long, gently upturned bill.* In flight, shows white trailing edge to inner wing. Bobs tail when feeding, like Common Sandpiper.

Voice: A trilled *du-du-du-du-du* and a *wit-a-wit-a-wit.*

Habitat: Breeds on marshes and particularly offshore islets. On passage and in winter, on marshes and mud flats.

Nesting: 4 olive-buff eggs spotted and blotched with sepia, laid in depression lined with oddments found nearby. Usually near floods on rivers, often on islets.

Range: Palearctic from Finland east to eastern Siberia; European birds migrate southeast to Middle East.

The only certain way of seeing a Terek Sandpiper in Europe is to visit its breeding haunts on the Gulf of Bothnia coast in Finland, where it is a regular, if rare, breeder. Elsewhere it is a vagrant, though the chances of seeing it improve the farther east one goes.

146 Common Sandpiper
(*Actitis hypoleucos*)

Description: 7¾″ (19 cm). A slim, medium-sized brown-and-white wader that *typically bobs its tail* when feeding. Patch of brown on sides of breast separated from upperparts by wedge of white; underparts white. Bill as long as head; short, yellowish-green legs. Flies low over water with shallow, rapid beats of downcurved wings alternating with short glides. Prominent *wing bar,* dark rump, and white barred outer tail feathers.

Voice: A high-pitched, down-slurred *twee-wee-wee* flight note.

Habitat: Breeds along lakeshores and fast streams; in winter, frequents most freshwater margins.

Nesting: 4 cream-buff eggs spotted with dark chestnut, laid in scrape lined with grasses and sheltered by tufts of grass, invariably near banks of stream.

Range: Palearctic. Breeds from western Europe to Pacific. Migrates through Europe to winter in Africa. Also winters on Atlantic and Mediterranean coasts in small numbers.

The characteristic bobbing and the stiff-winged flight make this familiar species one of the easiest to identify.

99, 124 Turnstone
(*Arenaria interpres*)

Description: 9″ (23 cm). Unique wader that finds food by turning over seaweed and stones. *Short, stout, slightly upcurved bill* and *short, orange legs.* Summer plumage, bold *tortoiseshell pattern* (rust-brown, black, and white) is highly effective camouflage; in winter, becomes generally duller.

Voice: A rapid *tuk-a-tuk;* also a *kit-it-it-it* trill.

Habitat: Open dry tundra near sea and rocky seashores; offshore and river islands. In winter, along shorelines and mouths of estuaries, occasionally on coastal marshes. Prefers rocky areas between tides.

Nesting: 3–4 greyish-green eggs, streaked, spotted, and blotched with brown, laid in bare scrape or depression lined with lichens, leaves, and grasses. Sometimes nests in loose colonies of several pairs.

Range: Circumpolar, breeding on northern coasts and extending south to southern Scandinavia. Winters on North Sea and Atlantic coast south to Iberia, and in Africa.

Often found along rocky shores with Purple Sandpipers and Redshanks, Turnstones feed among seaweed and jetsam, searching out small crustaceans. Though they *do* turn stones, they will also turn dried mud, plastic bottles, and anything else that may harbour food. Effective scavengers, they eat carrion and will even take bread.

---

104 Wilson's Phalarope
(*Phalaropus tricolor*)

Description: 9″ (23 cm). Larger and longer-necked than the two European phalaropes and *wades more frequently.* Distinctive summer plumage mainly grey above, with broad extension of black eye-stripe down neck turning to chestnut over grey back. Winter or juvenile plumage most often seen in Europe is *very pale grey,* with faint eye-stripe, grey tail, *square white rump,* and *plain* dark wings. Fine bill, longer than other two species'.

Voice: A whistled *tu* flight note.

Habitat: Muddy pools and marshes.

Nesting: 4 pale buff eggs spotted and blotched dark brown, laid in depression lined with grasses near water.

Range: North America. First recorded in Europe in 1954, but now appears annually, usually in Britain and Ireland.

Less maritime than its relatives, it swims well but prefers to find its food

by wading, when it co[illegible]
with a Lesser Yellowlegs[illegible]

106, 123 Red-necked Phalarope
(*Phalaropus lobatus*)

Description: 7″ (18 cm). Small bird that *swims* [illegible] *than wades* and lives mostly *at sea.* Breeding female larger and more bol[illegible] coloured and marked than male. Female's head slate-grey; back has creamy stripes forming prominent Vs; *chin white;* sides of *neck bright orange.* Male similar but paler. Both sexes' winter plumage grey above and white below, with dark mark through eye. Back darker than other phalaropes', always with *pale stripes. Black legs; black, needle-sharp bill.* White wing bar visible in flight.

Voice: A low *prip.*

Habitat: Breeds on tundra marshes and pools; mainly at sea in winter and on migration.

Nesting: 4 buff-olive eggs spotted and blotched dark sepia, laid in tussock along marshy margins of pools or lakes.

Range: Circumpolar in tundra zone, migrating south to tropical seas either overland or by sea. Breeds in Iceland, Shetlands, Orkneys, Outer Hebrides, Ireland, and Scandinavia. Outside breeding areas in Europe, a rare autumn storm-driven migrant.

It picks its food from the surface while swimming in some of the world's richest oceans. For a few brief weeks in summer it comes to land and feeds in a similar way on tundra pools. In its efforts to bring food to the surface in shallow waters, it frequently spins round and round like a child's top.

105, 122 Grey Phalarope
(*Phalaropus fulicarius*)

Description: 8″ (20 cm). Slightly larger than Red-necked Phalarope but with *thicker bill,* ellow with black tip. Female bright *chestnut-red on neck and underparts;* back black with buff scalloping; crown black; *face white.* Male similar but more subdued. In winter, similar to Red-necked Phalarope, but *grey of back much lighter* and lacks V's. Both species show *bold, white wing bar* in flight.

Voice: High-pitched *priip.*

Habitat: High Arctic; breeds even farther north than Red-necked Phalarope on tundra pools. Winters at sea.

Nesting: 3–4 olive-brown eggs blotched and spotted chestnut-brown, laid in tussock or on ridge. Semicolonial nester.

Range: Circumpolar in farthest north; in Europe breeds only in Iceland. Migrates south to winter in tropical seas. Found offshore and on inland waters of western Europe after autumn storms.

A role-reversed breeder, the female takes the initiative in courtship and mating, lays the eggs, and leaves the rest to her mate. Breeding grounds often have small parties of the boldly coloured females loafing about on a pool, while the males are busily incubating or caring for the young.

SKUAS
(Stercorariidae)

5 species, possibly more: higher latitudes of Northern and Southern hemispheres. Three species nest in Europe, one other is a migrant. Medium-large, gull-like water birds with strong, hooked bill; stout body; long, pointed wings; short legs; and webbed feet. Larger species all brown; smaller species have two colour phases —all brown or brown-and-white. All species have variable white patch on wing. Adults of smaller species have elongated central tail feathers; immatures lack these, making specific identification difficult. Predatory; swift and agile in flight, pursuing gulls and terns and forcing them to disgorge their food. Nest on ground on tundra, feeding on rodents and eggs and young of other birds. Migrate along coasts, usually offshore, and winter at sea. Aggressive, vigorously defending their nests.

---

87 Pomarine Skua
(*Stercorarius pomarinus*)

Description: 20″ (50 cm). Overall length includes 2″ (5 cm) extension of central tail feathers. *Thick-set,* and bulkier than Arctic Skua. *Broad and twisted central tail feathers* are diagnostic, but are not always present. Pale phase (most common) has dark cap, yellowish cheek and nape, dark upperparts, and light underparts with a *broad, dark breast band;* immature and dark phase best identified by *size and bulk.* Prominent white flashes on wings.

Voice: Scolding *wish-you, wish-you.*

Habitat: Breeds on tundra; otherwise offshore seas, sometimes oceanic.

Nesting: 2 olive-brown eggs blotched and spotted with dark brown, laid in depression among moss.

Range: Circumpolar except Europe, where it is

a scarce migrant along Atlantic coasts. Winters off coasts of West Africa, South America, and Australia.

Rather rare in European waters. Besides parasitising gulls and terns, it is also a predator, feeding on medium-sized birds and rodents. Occasional individuals have tail feathers 5–6 inches (13–15 cm) long, suggesting the Long-tailed, but the latter is small and slim with very thin tail streamers.

83, 86 **Arctic Skua**
(*Stercorarius parasiticus*)

Description: 18″ (45 cm). Overall length includes 3″ (8 cm) extension of central tail feathers. Most common skua. Light phase: dark cap; white neck and underparts, with incomplete dark breast band and some yellowish on nape; dark upperparts; *two extended central tail feathers,* which are narrow and pointed. Dark phase: brown all over, with *darker cap.* White flash on wing. Intermediate phases occur. Smaller than Pomarine, larger than Long-tailed.

Voice: Howling *yee-ow* and scolding *tuk-tuk.*

Habitat: Breeds on tundra and moorland; coastal and pelagic at other times.

Nesting: 2 olive-brown eggs spotted dark brown, laid in rounded depression in moss or grass.

Range: Circumpolar, including northern Europe. Migrates offshore to winter in Atlantic. The most commonly observed skua off Atlantic coasts.

All skuas are piratical in habits, chasing other seabirds to force them to drop or disgorge their food. Terns, in particular, fall victim to this treatment, though even birds as large as Gannets are not immune to the larger and more powerful species. Arctic Skuas are long-winged and graceful fliers, strongly resembling falcons as they twist and turn in pursuit of their victims.

84 Long-tailed Skua
(*Stercorarius longicau*

Description: 20–22" (50–55 cm).
Overall length includes
cm) extension of central ta
Flies gracefully. Adult almost
pale phase; small, clear-cut blac
yellowish nape; white underparts
(lacking breast band), except for dus
flanks and undertail; back and wing coverts greyer, with much less white on wings than other skuas. *Central tail feathers greatly extended,* very thin and flexible.

Voice: A grating *kreee* while breeding.

Habitat: Breeds on tundra and high mountain moorlands; pelagic at other times.

Nesting: 2 greenish-brown eggs marked with a few dark spots, laid in hollow in moss.

Range: Circumpolar including Scandinavia, but absent from Iceland. Winters at sea, passing south off Atlantic coasts of Europe in autumn.

The Long-tailed, like other skuas, harries terns at sea but also feeds on fish. During breeding season it is almost entirely dependent on lemmings, and its numbers and breeding success rise and fall with the cyclical population of that small arctic rodent. In non-lemming years, the Long-tailed may not breed at all.

85, 88 Great Skua
(*Stercorarius skua*)

Description: 23" (58 cm). Large, speckled, brown *gull-like* skua, with *broad wings;* heavy body; stout bill; wedge-shaped tail with two slightly protruding central tail feathers; and bold *white flashes* on wing. Its bulk, broad wings, and bold wing flashes separate it from other skuas.

Voice: A harsh *skeerr,* a scolding *tuk-tuk.*

Habitat: Pelagic most of year; in summer, high moors near seabird colonies.

Nesting: 2 olive-brown eggs spotted and

…ned dark brown, laid in simple …pression on grassy ridge.
…celand, Faeroes, and northernmost mainland and islands of Scotland. Migrates south to winter in Atlantic.

The largest of the skuas, it has often been regarded as conspecific with the skuas of the Antarctic. Antarctic populations are now considered to represent two or possibly three species: South Polar or Maccormick's Skua (*Stercorarius maccormicki*), Brown Skua (*S. loennbergi*), and Southern Great Skua (*S. antarcticus*). The last is probably closest to the Great Skua. It attacks other seabirds, forcing them to disgorge food, and also kills large numbers of seabirds at breeding colonies.

GULLS
(Laridae)

47 species: worldwide. Eleven s[illegible] breed in Europe, five others are v[illegible] Small to large water birds with sle[illegible] to stout hook-tipped bill, long wing[illegible] usually a square tail, and webbed feet. Upperparts grey or black, underparts white; head black in breeding plumage in some species. Bill and legs often brightly coloured. Plumage often different in winter. Young are brown, gradually changing to adult plumage over a period of up to four years. Sexes similar. Gregarious birds, living near both salt and fresh water, eating wide range of animal food and scavenging garbage. Strong fliers, soaring often. At home on the ocean, although usually preferring to stay fairly close to shore and inland.

46, 67 Great Black-headed Gull
(*Larus ichthyaetus*)

Description: 26" (65 cm). *Only very large gull with black head* in summer. In winter, *head heavily streaked,* usually with *dark smudge behind eye;* somewhat similar to Herring Gull, but larger, adult with *yellow bill crossed by black line,* yellowish legs, and dove-grey upperparts; *white outer primaries* have black subterminal marks. At rest, has hunched appearance and long head and bill. First-year immatures have black secondaries, black outer primaries; broad, clear-cut tail band; flesh-coloured legs; and black-tipped bill.

Voice: A nasal *kraagh.*

Habitat: Salt marshes, deltas, and islands of inland seas. In winter, on marshes, lagoons, and along rivers with sandbars and shorelines.

Nesting: 2 or 3 stone-coloured eggs streaked brown, laid in unlined hollow. Colonial nester.

Range: Breeds from Crimea east into central

Asia. Migrates south, sometimes passing along European coast of Black Sea in autumn. Vagrant to rest of Europe.

It feeds on fish and will rob birds as large as Goosanders of their prey by hovering overhead and dropping down on them when they surface.

45 **Mediterranean Gull**
(*Larus melanocephalus*)

Description: 15″ (38 cm). In summer, black (not brown) hood, red bill and legs. In winter, hood replaced by dark smudge behind eye. At all seasons adults have very pale grey mantle and wings; *primaries white*. Black-headed Gull has thinner bill, dark underside of primaries, white forewing, and black-tipped primaries. First-year immatures resemble Common Gull but have mantle very pale grey, upperwing pattern more contrasting, and bill and legs blackish. Second-year immatures look like adults except for a few black spots on tips of primaries.

Voice: *Kee-eer* or *kek-kee-kee*.

Habitat: Lagoons, marshes, seacoasts.

Nesting: 3 stone-coloured eggs with spots and streaks of dark brown, laid in grass nest lined with a few feathers on low-lying islet in marsh.

Range: Breeds in eastern Mediterranean and Black Sea east to Sea of Azov and sporadically north and west to Czechoslovakia, Holland, France, and Britain. Winters mainly in central Mediterranean; also on Swiss lakes.

Despite the Mediterranean Gull's restricted range, it reached Britain in the late 1960s and is currently spreading slowly northwest across Europe. Over most of northern Europe it remains a very scarce visitor.

42, 60, 72 **Little Gull**
(*Larus minutus*)

Description: 11″ (28 cm). Smallest European gull. *Red bill and legs* similar to Black-headed Gull, but *black (not brown) hood* in summer *more extensive*. In winter, hood reduced to dark smudge behind eye. At all seasons adults have rounded, *uniformly grey upper wing* and *uniformly blackish underwing*. Immature in flight has *bold black* W *across wings* similar to Kittiwake (but Little Gull much smaller, and *lacks neck marking* of immature Kittiwake), and white underwing. Bill black.

Voice: *K-ee* and a repeated *kek-kek-kek-kek*.

Habitat: Lakes, marshes; in winter, reservoirs, marshes, and shorelines.

Nesting: 2–3 olive-buff eggs spotted and blotched dark brown, laid in untidy nest of reeds, in marshy tussock.

Range: Breeds across Palearctic from Holland and Baltic area; also on Black Sea coasts in scattered colonies. Regular migrant in small numbers west from Denmark to winter on all European coasts except far north.

A tern-like gull that flies lightly and easily, it picks insects from the water's surface like a marsh tern. Although frequently seen inland, it usually occurs in large concentrations only on salt marshes.

43 **Sabine's Gull**
(*Larus sabini*)

Description: 13″ (33 cm). Small, tern-like gull with *forked tail*. Head slate-grey in summer, bordered by black ring; white in winter, with some dark mottling. Black bill has yellow tip. At all seasons adults and juveniles have *distinctive wing pattern:* black outer primaries contrast with white inner primaries and secondaries and grey mantle and wing coverts (brown in juvenile).

winter

Voice: A grating tern-like call.

Habitat: Pools on open tundra; pelagic outside breeding season.

Nesting: 2–3 olive-brown eggs faintly spotted and blotched dark brown, laid in tussock of grass among tundra pools.

Range: High Arctic, Canada, Alaska, and Greenland; Siberia to Spitsbergen. Frequent off Biscay and Iberia in autumn, storm-driven to southwest England and Ireland.

It spends most of its life at sea. Previously regarded as a rare wanderer to coastal Europe, it is now known to pass through the Bay of Biscay and off the coast of Portugal regularly in some numbers.

41, 70, 71 **Bonaparte's Gull**
(*Larus philadelphia*)

Description: 12–14″ (30–35 cm). Vagrant from North America resembling Black-headed Gull. Distinguished by *smaller size;* lighter, more tern-like flight; smaller, *black bill;* and *white underside of primaries.* Has *same white forewing* as Black-headed, but in that species the underside of primaries is blackish. In winter plumage, loses blackish hood. Immature has black tail band and *white underwing* with black trailing edge to primaries.

Voice: A harsh *tee-arr.*

Habitat: Lakes and rivers in forest country; coasts and estuaries in winter.

Nesting: 3 brownish-yellow eggs blotched dark olive, laid in twig nest high in tree.

Range: North America. Rare vagrant to Europe.

Bonaparte's Gulls tend to keep to themselves in their native America but mix with Black-headed Gulls in Europe. They stay mostly on shorelines in winter, seldom joining the scramble for offal or gathering at rubbish tips.

44, 61, 66 Black-headed Gull
(*Larus ridibundus*)

Description: 14–15″ (35–38 cm). The standard hooded, small gull. In summer, *chocolate hood* and *red bill and legs.* In winter, hood is replaced by dark spot behind eye and red bill becomes darker. Combination of *white forewing* and *dark underside of primaries* is diagnostic. First-year immatures have more extensive black tips to primaries, black tail band, and bold white forewing; bill flesh-coloured, with dark tip.

Voice: A nasal *kwarr.*

Habitat: Marshes, lakes, moors. In winter, along coasts, inland waters, rubbish dumps, sewage farms, reservoirs, parks.

Nesting: 2–3 olive-brown eggs boldly blotched with purple and brown, laid in untidy nest of rushes in marsh or on islands. Colonial nester.

Range: Palearctic from Iceland to Bering Sea. Breeds throughout Europe, except northern Scandinavia and Mediterranean. Winters along western coasts, inland, and throughout Mediterranean.

The most common gull over much of Europe, it is frequently found inland, where it inhabits areas as diverse as city centres and cultivated fields. It has benefited from its close relationship with man.

53, 65 Slender-billed Gull
(*Larus genei*)

Description: 17″ (43 cm). Small gull similar to Black-headed Gull, with same wing pattern, but white-headed at all seasons. Has *very elongated* forehead and bill, and *long neck. Legs and bill dark red.* First-year immatures like Black-headed; paler bill and legs and shape of head and bill are the best distinctions.

Voice: A tern-like *kaar.*

Habitat: Estuaries, lagoons, coasts, nesting on islands in dried-out lagoons and in broad rivers running through marshland.

Nesting: 2–3 cream-coloured eggs boldly blotched dark brown, laid in hollow lined with a few pieces of vegetation with rim of droppings.

Range: European breeding areas in Guadalquivir, Rhône, and Danube deltas. Also throughout the Middle East to northwest India. Rare elsewhere in Europe.

Though rare and highly localised in Europe, this species is quite numerous in other parts of its range, notably along the shores of the Persian Gulf. Its disintegrated range suggests a relict population of a once widespread bird with its centre of distribution in the Tigris-Euphrates water system.

---

54 Audouin's Gull
(*Larus audouinii*)

Description: 19½″ (49 cm). Resembles small, pale Herring Gull, but has only one small white mirror on *black wing tip. Legs slate-grey or green; bill dark red,* stout and *slightly drooping,* with black band at tip. Shape quite different from Herring Gull; in flight, *wings long and narrow* and *tail short.* First-year immature has pale grey crown, hindneck, and breast, scaly brown back and wings.

Voice: A coarse *keeow.*

Habitat: Rocky islands and islets; sandy bays, but always near rocky coasts.

Nesting: 2–3 olive eggs lightly marked with black spots, laid in scrape with lining of seaweed or grasses among rocks.

Range: Breeding confined to a few Mediterranean islands. Wanders in winter, occurring on Atlantic coast of Morocco. Vagrant elsewhere.

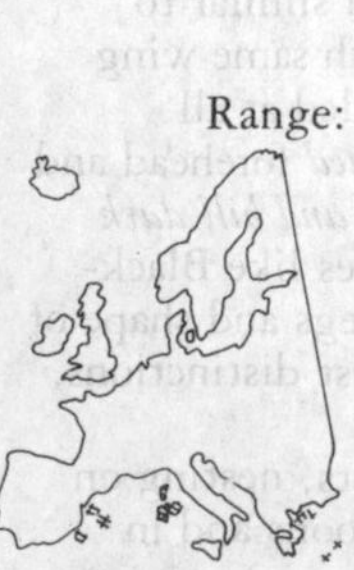

Europe's rarest gull, it is a strangely primitive-looking gull. Its distribution indicates a relict species that was once more widespread. If it is to survive, its island breeding haunts must be rigorously protected.

51, 59 **Common Gull or Mew Gull**
(*Larus canus*)

Description: 16″ (40 cm). Delicately built, medium-sized gull; adults with black-and-white wing-tip pattern similar to Herring Gull but with larger white mirrors. Separated by *smaller size, yellow-green bill without red spot,* and *yellow-green legs.* Head streaked with grey in winter. First-year immatures mainly brown, with sharply defined, rather broad, black band on white tail. Second-years have more black on wing tip than adults.

Voice: A shrill *kee-aar* and a chuckling *ka-ka-ka.*

Habitat: More frequently inland than Herring Gull. Coasts, marshes, moorland lakes, small deltas.

Nesting: 3 light green eggs variably marked with brown spots and speckles, laid in grass nest on island in lake or pool. Occasionally on shingle or in trees.

Range: Breeds across Palearctic and into Alaska and adjacent Canada. In Europe, confined to north with a few inland colonies in central Europe, but migrates to winter on all coasts including Mediterranean.

It forms a species pair with the slightly larger American Ring-billed Gull, which is a vagrant in European waters. The latter has a slightly longer, thicker bill (marked in the adult with a dark vertical bar), a paler back, and less white in the black wing tips. First-year immatures are difficult to separate, but the Ring-billed's heavier structure and thick band on bill are among the best distinctions.

48 Lesser Black-backed Gull

(*Larus fuscus*)

Description: 21″ (53 cm). *Similar to Herring Gull in size* and to Great Black-backed in colour. Adult has upperparts varying from slate-grey to black according to subspecies; distinguished from Great Black-backed by *yellow legs* and *slimmer build.* Great Black-backed is larger and has proportionately larger and heavier bill. First-year immatures mottled brown, darker than Herring Gull.

Voice: A vibrant *keeow,* a laughing *gah-gah-gah,* very similar to calls of Herring Gull but more nasal.

Habitat: Coasts and low-lying islands; also inland on moors; and on migration, on playing fields and salt pans.

Nesting: 3 green-buff eggs boldly blotched and speckled black-brown, laid in well-lined hollow among grass or other vegetation. Colonial nester.

Range: Northwestern Palearctic. Nests on northern European coasts. Migrates to western and southern Europe; also south into Africa.

It is very closely related to the Herring Gull, with which it forms a ring species, circling the entire northern hemisphere. Subspecies with varying back colour replace each other across North America and most of Asia, but in Europe the Herring and Lesser Black-backed gulls coexist without interbreeding, which places them in separate species.

49, 63 Herring Gull

(*Larus argentatus*)

Description: 22″ (55 cm). Large gull; adults with light dove-grey back and wings, *black wing tips with white mirrors,* and *yellow bill with red spot* near tip. *Legs pink* (*yellow* in Mediterranean subspecies and some Scandinavian individuals). Wing-tip pattern similar to Common Gull, but mirrors smaller on larger bird.

First-year immatures generally mottled brown, with dark primaries, secondaries, and tail band; bill dark with pale base.

Voice: Range of shrill calls including a loud *keeow* and a chuckling *hah-hah-hah.*

Habitat: Predominantly coastal, breeding on cliffs and beaches; but in winter, also inland at rubbish tips and reservoirs.

Nesting: 2–3 light olive eggs blotched black-brown, laid on cliff ledge or in scrape among dunes. Has taken to nesting on factory and house roofs in recent years.

Range: Holarctic, breeding throughout coastal Europe; also North Africa, and North America. Migrant south and west.

The Herring Gull has increased in numbers dramatically in this century and is now considered a pest in many places. Conservationists must control its numbers in some areas to prevent it from overrunning bird reserves, to the detriment of other, rarer species.

56 Iceland Gull
(*Larus glaucoides*)

Description: 22″ (55 cm). Same size or smaller than Herring Gull; very pale grey above, with *no black on wing tips.* Only Glaucous is similar, but Iceland is *much smaller,* has proportionately *smaller, neater bill, less massive head,* and *reddish eye-ring.* First- and second-year immatures resemble Glaucous, but *over half of bill is black.* Both species *lack tail band.* Long wings and buoyant flight.

Voice: Like other large gulls, but higher-pitched than Herring Gull.

Habitat: Coasts of all types, occasionally in harbours, rubbish dumps.

Nesting: 2–3 olive-coloured eggs blotched and spotted black, laid in nest of grass, moss, and seaweed on cliff ledge or island. Usually nests colonially.

Range: Breeds in Greenland and Baffin Island, but *not* in Iceland. Winter visitor to

Iceland and northwestern Britain and Ireland in small numbers. Elsewhere very rare.

It is the smaller of the two "white-winged" gulls and decidedly scarcer in Europe than the Glaucous Gull; considered tamer than the latter. Frequents rubbish tips along with other scavenging gulls.

52, 62 **Glaucous Gull**
(*Larus hyperboreus*)

Description: 25″ (63 cm). Large gull approaching Great Black-backed in size, but very pale grey above, with *no black on wing tips.* Similar to Iceland Gull but *much larger,* with *much heavier bill and head, yellow eye-ring,* and pink legs. First-year immatures lightly *mottled,* almost uniformly *grey-brown,* but without dark wing tips and tail band. Best distinguished from immature Icelands by heavier build, larger size, and *dark tip to bill.* Second-year birds are often pure white, though generally, progressively whiter plumage is acquired over 5 years before becoming fully adult.

Voice: Very similar to Herring and Iceland gulls': a shrill loud *keeow, hah-hah-hah,* etc.

Habitat: Cliffs, shores, islands; in winter, shorelines, estuaries, harbours.

Nesting: 2–3 olive-buff eggs spotted and blotched black, laid in substantial nest of moss or seaweed. Usually colonial nester.

Range: Circumpolar in high Arctic. In Europe, nests only in Iceland and Spitsbergen. Migrates south to coasts of Scandinavia, Britain and Ireland, and North Sea.

It is much more frequently observed in Europe than is the Iceland Gull. In some parts of Scotland it is regularly present throughout winter in harbours and on jetties. It feeds on carrion in the

Arctic and is also a predator, killing and eating birds, chicks, and eggs.

47, 64 **Great Black-backed Gull**
(*Larus marinus*)

Description: 26″ (65 cm). Very large gull; adults have *black back and wings,* very heavy build, and *massive yellow bill* with red spot. Legs *flesh-pink* (not yellow like Lesser Black-backed). First-year immatures speckled brown, with more contrasting pattern of light and dark than Herring Gull.

Voice: A throaty *awk.*

Habitat: More marine than most other gulls, spending much time at sea. Also coastal, but seldom inland in large numbers. Frequents rubbish tips, harbours. Breeds on offshore islands; sometimes on moors.

Nesting: 2–3 greenish-olive eggs spotted black-brown, laid in substantial nest of sticks and seaweed atop a rocky stack. Semicolonial nester.

Range: Breeding confined to coasts of northern Europe, south to northwestern France. Migrant and winter visitor elsewhere; seldom farther east than Spain in the Mediterranean.

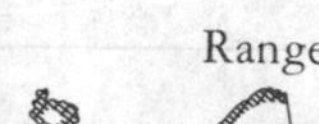

The terror of the seabird colonies, this powerful bird takes a heavy toll of Puffins and Manx Shearwaters, alongside which it frequently breeds. Like many other gulls, it has increased dramatically in this century and may now pose a threat to its prey species.

68 **Ross's Gull**
(*Rhodostethia rosea*)

Description: 12½″ (31 cm). Small gull; adults with dove-grey upperparts *without black wing tips;* head and underparts suffused with pink in summer; *black, stubby bill; narrow, black collar* in breeding season (which disappears in winter, when there is mottling around eye). *Long, wedge-*

shaped tail and long, pointed wings. Immature has a black W on wings and thin, dark band on tail tip.

Voice: More variable than most gulls: a clear *a-wow, a-wow,* a tern-like *eke-wa,* and other notes.

Habitat: Pools, lakes, and rivers on tundra; outside breeding season, at sea off pack ice.

Nesting: 3 olive-green eggs lightly blotched with dark brown, laid in nest of grasses and sedges in swamps. Usually nests colonially, often with Arctic Terns.

Range: Breeds on remote Siberian river systems; migrates north to pack ice, to Alaska, and Bering Sea. Accidental in Europe.

It is the rarest gull, and the one most sought-after by bird-watchers on both sides of the Atlantic. Its life-style seldom brings it to inhabited latitudes. When one is sighted, bird-watchers travel long distances to see it.

50, 55, 69 **Kittiwake**
(*Rissa tridactyla*)

Description: 16″ (40 cm). Medium-sized, delicately proportioned, grey-backed gull; adults with diagnostic neat, *triangular, black wing tips,* lacking white mirrors; *black legs; all-yellow bill;* and long wings. Immatures have black bill, distinctive black *W pattern* across wings in flight, *black hind-collar,* and narrow, black terminal band on slightly forked tail.

Voice: A repeated *kitti-waak, kitti-waak* on breeding grounds.

Habitat: Sheer sea cliffs; otherwise pelagic.

Nesting: 2 pale cream eggs speckled and spotted brown, laid in well-constructed nest of seaweed, grass, and mud placed on tiny ledge on sheer cliff face. Colonial breeder, usually with alcids.

Range: Breeds on coasts of northern Europe, Brittany, Britain and Ireland, Scandinavia, and Iceland across the northern Palearctic to Bering Sea; also

North America. Migrant to Atlantic coasts and western Mediterranean.

It is the noisiest member of the North Atlantic seabird colonies; the calls from which its English name derives echo around the cliffs throughout the season. It is joined in the Bering Sea by the Red-legged Kittiwake (*R. brevirostris*), a localised species confined to two island groups, where it is abundant.

57, 58 **Ivory Gull**
(*Pagophila eburnea*)

Description: 17½" (44 cm). Medium-sized, short-legged gull; adults with *black legs, short black bill with yellowish tip.* First-year immatures are white with grey face and throat, *black-speckled plumage* (a pattern created by black tips to primaries, secondaries, and the rows of wing coverts), and a narrow, black terminal band on tail. At rest, has a *pigeon-like* posture, but with *long wings.*

Voice: A range of tern-like calls including *kree-kree* and a scolding *kaar.*

Habitat: Shores and other open ground among ice; in winter, off pack ice.

Nesting: 2 stone-brown eggs blotched dark brown, laid in nest of seaweed or on ground just free of ice; usually rocky shores.

Range: Circumpolar; breeds in high Arctic islands; occasional in winter to Iceland, Scandinavia, and Shetland.

This rare little gull seldom alights on water though it spends most of its life at sea. It feeds mainly along the edge of pack ice and comes south only under extreme conditions. Feeding mainly on marine organisms, it is also fond of carrion; in Alaska it follows Eskimos on seal hunts, eating the remains of dead seals.

TERNS
(Sternidae)

43 species: worldwide. Ten species breed in Europe. Small to medium-sized water birds resembling slender gulls but with thinner, pointed bill without hooked tip, narrower wings, forked tail, and short legs; feet webbed. Sea terns are grey and white with black caps (partly lost in winter); some have crests. Marsh terns are smaller with black or dark grey body during breeding season. Many species have brightly coloured bill and legs. Sexes similar. Flight dipping, graceful, and buoyant, with much hovering over water. Sea terns plunge-dive for small fish; marsh terns feed mainly on insects, taken in the air or from the water's surface.

---

74 **Gull-billed Tern**
(*Gelochelidon nilotica*)

Description: 15″ (38 cm). Large, gull-like tern with *pale grey upperparts and rump, white underparts,* and *black cap. Feeds like a marsh tern,* often low over water, frequently hawking insects in mid-air. *Heavy, stubby, black bill* distinctive at all seasons, quite unlike thin bill of other terns. In winter, black cap reduced to *smudge behind eye.* Legs black, longer than other European terns'.

Voice: A harsh *ker-wack,* and an untern-like quacking call, *kwuck-kwuck-kwuck,* often uttered while feeding.

Habitat: Marshes, lagoons, salt pans, coasts.

Nesting: 3 (occasionally 2–5) buff-coloured eggs spotted and blotched with brown, laid in hollow lined with a few grasses, on sandbanks or mudbanks alongside water. Nests in colonies, often with gulls or Common Terns.

Range: From coastal United States, through scattered localities in Europe east into southern Siberia, and as far as Australia. A scarce migrant in Europe

away from breeding localities. Winters south into Africa and India.

The markings of the Gull-billed Tern suggest possible confusion with the Sandwich Tern, the yellow bill tip of which is difficult to see in flight. Bulky shape of its bill, head, and neck is distinctive; in fact, it often seems to have no neck and should really be called the Gull-like Tern. It habitually feeds over dry ground, catching insects in the air and on the ground.

76 Caspian Tern
(*Sterna caspia*)

Description: 21″ (53 cm). Nearly the size of a Herring Gull and the *largest tern of Europe.* Gull-like flight, but dives in typical tern manner. Underside of primaries blackish. Black cap and *huge coral-red bill* distinctive at all seasons, though cap is streaked with white in winter. Can be confused only with the rare Royal Tern, whose bill is smaller and orange.

Voice: A rasping heron-like *kraagh.*

Habitat: Beaches and small islets; outside breeding season mainly coastal, but also inland along large rivers or lakes.

Nesting: 2–3 cream-coloured eggs spotted with black, brown, and grey, laid in hollow on sand or shingle. Nests singly or in colonies.

Range: Almost cosmopolitan but absent from South America. In Europe rather scattered—Baltic and Black seacoasts; also Mediterranean coast in Tunisia. Elsewhere a scarce visitor, though regular in southern Spain. European birds winter in Africa.

The Caspian Tern plunges from considerable heights into the sea in pursuit of its prey. It seldom forms flocks outside the breeding season and when not hunting usually rests on beaches, where it may be seen singly or in pairs in company with smaller species.

75 **Sandwich Tern**
(*Sterna sandvicensis*)

Description: 16″ (40 cm). Light grey above with *black cap* that ends on nape in *ragged crest* visible only when at rest; white underparts. *Yellow tip of black, pencil-thin bill* difficult to see at a distance. In winter, forehead is white. *Larger* than other common sea terns of Europe.

Voice: A distinctive *kirrick* or *krrit.*

Habitat: Coastal, sand and shingle beaches, sometimes islands in coastal lagoons.

Nesting: 2 creamy-buff eggs variably spotted, blotched, and streaked with brown, laid in simple scrape in sand or shingle. Nests in colonies.

Range: Breeds on parts of western European coasts and at a very few spots in Mediterranean and Black seas; also in North and Central America. Migrant along coastal Europe to Africa; a few winter in Greece and Mediterranean.

This species forms tighter colonies than other European terns, several hundred pairs nesting virtually within pecking distance. Breeding Sandwich Terns are extremely noisy. Highly erratic, they will abandon a long-established ternery for no apparent reason.

77 **Roseate Tern**
(*Sterna dougallii*)

Description: 15″ (38 cm). *Much paler* than the similar Common and Arctic terns. *Bill is black* with only trace of red at base; also has *longer tail streamers,* which extend well beyond folded wings at rest. In breeding plumage, underparts suffused with light pink, looking white at long range.

Voice: A soft *chu-ic* and a harsher *aarrk,* distinctive in mixed colonies.

Habitat: Marine; nests on coastal islands often

with Common or Arctic terns in mixed colonies.

Nesting: 1–2 creamy-buff eggs speckled with brown, laid in unlined scrape on rocks or among shingle.

Range: Cosmopolitan, but colonies scattered. In Europe confined to Britain, Ireland, and Brittany. Otherwise a rare migrant along Atlantic coasts.

Despite a worldwide distribution, the Roseate Tern is scarce and elusive. In its European headquarters in Britain and Ireland, it numbers only about 2,300 pairs, over half of which breed at a single colony in County Wexford in Ireland.

78 Common Tern
(*Sterna hirundo*)

Description: 14″ (35 cm). A graceful sea tern that dives for small fish. Grey above, paler grey below, with white flash below black cap; *orange-red bill with dark tip;* orange-red legs. *Deeply forked tail does not extend beyond folded wings* at rest. Similar Arctic Tern is slightly smaller and more delicate, with shorter legs, bill entirely dark red, and tail barely longer than folded wings when perched. In flight, seen against light, *only inner primaries are translucent.*

Voice: A harsh *kree-er;* also a *ki-ki-ki.*

Habitat: Beaches and shingle banks along coasts and large rivers; in winter, predominantly coastal.

Nesting: 2–3 creamy-buff eggs spotted and blotched with browns and greys laid in simple scrape. Nests in colonies.

Range: Holarctic; summer visitor to Europe with broad but patchy distribution on coasts and inland waters; winters in Africa.

This is the "common" tern over most of temperate Europe, although it is replaced to the north by the Arctic Tern. It is a summer visitor, arriving in

April and leaving in October. Where food is abundant it sometimes forms flocks of thousands and is then harried for food by the piratical skuas. It migrates in small, low-flying flocks.

79 Arctic Tern
(*Sterna paradisaea*)

Description: 14″ (35 cm). Similar to Common Tern but slightly smaller and more delicate, with *bill entirely dark red* and *shorter legs. Tail feathers extend well beyond folded wings* at rest, and *seen against light all primaries are translucent.* Underparts grey with white flash below black cap. Adults in winter and immatures of both species have blackish bills and white foreheads.

Voice: A sharp *kee-kee;* also *kree-er* and *ki-ki-ki,* like Common Tern but more rasping.

Habitat: Beaches and shingle bars, but more maritime than Common Tern. Often nests on offshore islands. Inland only along tundra rivers and lakes.

Nesting: 2 olive-buff eggs with variable blackish-brown blotching, laid in bare or sparsely lined hollow.

Range: Circumpolar, generally north of Common Tern. In Europe, breeds in Iceland, northern Britain and Ireland, Scandinavia, and in small numbers along southern shores of North and Baltic seas; rarely south to Channel coasts. Migrates along the Atlantic coast.

Travelling farther than most other birds, Arctic Terns may cover 50,000 miles (80,000 kilometres) a year on migration, flying from the extreme north to the edge of the southern pack ice and then circumnavigating the world from west to east.

80 Little Tern
(*Sterna albifrons*)

Description: 9½" (24 cm). *Smallest of the European terns,* distinguished by its faster wing beats and frequent *hovering* like a Kingfisher. Legs yellow, *bill yellow tipped with black; forehead white.*

Voice: A shrill *kirri-kirri-kirri* and a sharper *kree-eek.*

Habitat: Nests on shingle and sandy coastlines, and in some regions along rivers and banks of inland waters. Otherwise generally maritime.

Nesting: 2–3 olive-buff eggs broadly blotched with browns and greys, laid in bare scrape among shingle or on sand.

Range: Cosmopolitan, except for South America. In Europe, found on most coasts and locally inland. Migrant along most coasts; winters off coasts of Africa.

In parts of its range, such as Britain, it is becoming an endangered species. Its scattered colonies along beaches are highly prone to disturbance by holiday makers, and efforts to persuade it away from the danger zone are not always successful.

81 Whiskered Tern
(*Chlidonias hybridus*)

Description: 9¼" (23 cm). A marsh tern; in summer, plumage *dark grey below* with lighter *grey upperwing* and *white wing linings; black crown* separated from dark grey underparts by prominent *white flash on cheek. Red bill and legs.* In winter plumage, *wings uniformly light grey above;* much *less extensive black on head* than other marsh terns; distinguished from Black Tern by *absence of shoulder smudge* and slightly longer bill.

Voice: A harsh *kee-uk* or *keer-ks.*

Habitat: Breeds in marshes and on lakes. In winter, prefers shallow fresh water.

Nesting: 3 blue-green eggs blotched with dark brown, laid on floating raft of aquatic vegetation.

Range: Patchy distribution throughout the Old World, including parts of southern Europe, especially around the Mediterranean. Rare farther north.

Rarest of the marsh terns outside its breeding range. In parts of Asia, it is a common winter visitor to lakes and marshes, where it may concentrate in large numbers.

82 Black Tern

(*Chlidonias niger*)

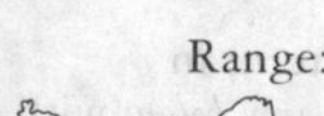

Description: 9½″ (24 cm). Typical marsh tern. In summer, *body black,* undertail white; *slate-grey upperwing and tail,* underwing entirely *silver-grey;* bill and legs dark red. Adult in winter and immatures have underparts and forehead white, and black crown. *Small, dark smudge on sides of breast.* Tail has *shallow fork* unlike sea terns'.

Voice: A high-pitched, weak cry, *kee-kee-kee.*

Habitat: Breeds on marshes and flooded lagoons with emergent vegetation. At other seasons, reservoirs, lakes, marshes, coasts, salt pans. More coastal than other marsh terns.

Nesting: 3 buff-brown eggs blotched brown or black, laid in nest of water plants, either floating or on shore.

Range: Breeds patchily through continental temperate Europe east to southern Siberia, and southern Canada through the United States. Migrates through Europe to winter mainly in Africa. Regular passage migrant in Britain.

The "standard" marsh tern of Europe, it is a light, airy bird that flies with great agility, turning this way and that low over the water's surface in search of food. It feeds by delicately picking insects from the water's surface. On migration, hundreds may be seen flying over lakes in that manner.

73 White-winged Black Tern
(*Chlidonias leucopterus*)

Description: 9¼" (23 cm). In summer, black colouration broken by *white tail, white wings* with *black wing linings* (Black Tern has silver), *red bill,* and *red legs.* In immature and winter plumages, *wings lighter than Black Tern's* and *lack dark smudge at shoulder; black cap less extensive.* In juvenile plumage, *dark mantle or "saddle"* contrasts with paler wings and *white rump.*

Voice: A harsh *keer,* similar to Black Tern.

Habitat: Shallow marshes and lagoons, lakes, reservoirs; usually fresh water.

Nesting: 3 pale brown or creamy eggs, laid in nest of gathered aquatic vegetation floating in shallow water.

Range: Yugoslavia east through Romania and southern Palearctic. Migrant south into Africa; stragglers found in western Europe.

Bird-watchers regularly find this eastern European species among the gatherings of Black Terns that pass through western Europe. In East Africa in winter, this is the common species and Black Tern the rarity.

AUKS, GUILLEMOTS, AND PUFFINS
(Alcidae)

22 species: high latitudes of Northern Hemisphere. Six species breed in Europe. Small to medium-sized seabirds with large head; short, thick neck; compact body; short, narrow wings; short tail; and webbed feet. Bill slender (guillemots) to deep (puffins). Bill sometimes brightly coloured. Legs set far back on body, aiding diving but hampering progress on land. Flight fast, with rapidly beating wings, low over water. They dive for food, mainly fish and squid, using wings underwater.

22, 25 **Guillemot**
(*Uria aalge*)

Description: 16½" (41 cm). Has slimmer head and neck, and *thinner bill* than similar Razorbill. Southern form (*U. a. albionis*) distinguished from Razorbill in summer by *chocolate upperparts,* greyish in winter. Northern form (*U. a. aalge*) is blackish-brown, closer to Razorbill. In summer, "bridled" form has thin white eye-ring and streak behind eye. Sides of head and neck white in winter, with *black line extending from eye over ear coverts.*

Voice: On nesting cliffs a continuous growling sound, *arrrr* or *murrrr.* Silent elsewhere.

Habitat: Breeds on ledges and flat tops of cliffs. Outside breeding season, in offshore waters or at sea.

Nesting: One pear-shaped egg, varying from white through browns to blues or greens, marked variously with dark lines, spots, and blotches, placed on bare rock.

Range: Holarctic, breeding on both sides of North Atlantic and North Pacific oceans; breeds on northern and western European coasts south to Portugal. Disperses from breeding areas to winter at sea, generally within same range.

The tremendous variation in the colour and markings of eggs may aid each bird in recognising its own egg in extremely crowded conditions. The eggs are broader at one end, and when the broad end is facing the edge of the cliff, the egg will roll in an arc, not off the ledge.

21 **Brünnich's Guillemot**
(*Uria lomvia*)

Description: 16½″ (41 cm). Blackish-brown above and white below; difficult to distinguish from northern race of Guillemot. *Shorter, thicker bill* with *white line at base.* In winter, black on head extends farther down onto face than in Guillemot, obscuring black streak behind eye.

Voice: Growling noises at breeding colonies, like Guillemot.

Habitat: Like Common Guillemot, nests colonially on cliffs. Pelagic at other seasons, staying farther from shore than Guillemot.

Nesting: One egg, varying from white to buff, brown, green, or blue, variably marked with dark spots, lines, and blotches, laid on bare rock ledge.

Range: Holarctic, breeding farther north than Guillemot but overlapping with it in southern part of range. In Europe, breeds in Iceland and Spitsbergen and winters south to Norway; vagrant farther south.

It hardly differs in habitat, behaviour, or voice from the Guillemot. The continuous growling, purring, and murmuring sounds made by both at their breeding colonies caused them to be called "murres" in North America.

17, 20 **Razorbill**
(*Alca torda*)

Description: 16″ (40 cm). Chunky, with heavy, rather square head, thick neck, and *deep, laterally compressed bill crossed by thin, white vertical stripe.* Black above and white below, with narrow white trailing edge to inner wing. In summer, white line from bill to eye; throat, cheeks, and sides of neck black (white in winter). Bill of immature smaller, lacking white stripe. On water, tail held higher than Guillemot.

Voice: Whirring and growling sounds on breeding grounds; otherwise silent.

Habitat: Breeds on sea cliffs and rocky coasts. At other times found along coasts or at sea.

Nesting: Usually 1, occasionally 2, oval eggs, most often white or pale brown, with dark spots and blotches, placed on bare surface in crack of cliff or hole.

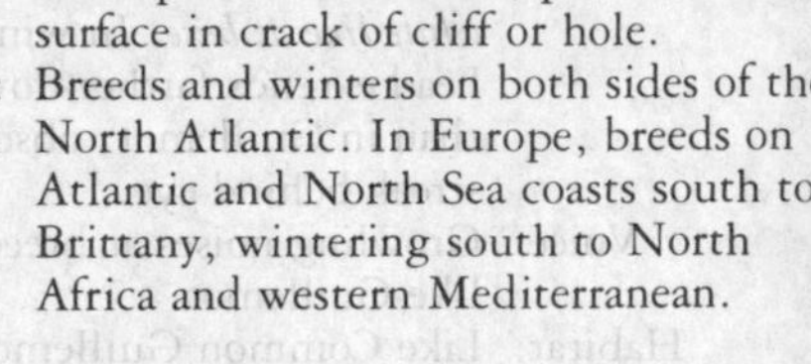

Range: Breeds and winters on both sides of the North Atlantic. In Europe, breeds on Atlantic and North Sea coasts south to Brittany, wintering south to North Africa and western Mediterranean.

It nests in large colonies, often with Guillemots, but while Guillemots nest mainly on bare, open ledges, Razorbills also often place eggs in crevices in cliffs. They also nest on rocky coasts away from cliffs, a habitat not used by Guillemots.

18 **Black Guillemot**
(*Cepphus grylle*)

Description: 13½" (34 cm). *Smaller* than Razorbill or Guillemot, with slender, pointed bill. Summer plumage unmistakable: *black body, white wing-patch,* and *red feet.* In winter, head and underparts whitish, *hind neck and upperparts barred black and white* (look grey at a distance). Juvenile similar to winter adult, but dark areas browner and wing patch barred grey.

Voice: A high-pitched, feeble whistle given on breeding grounds.

Habitat: Breeds on rocky coasts and broken cliffs; also on wooded islands. At other times lives at sea.

Nesting: 2 (sometimes 1 or 3) white eggs that

may be tinged blue-green or buffy, marked with black, brown, and grey, placed on bare ground, in crevice of cliff, or under rock.

Range: Circumpolar, breeding on arctic coasts and islands, south to northeastern North America and northern Europe. In Europe, breeds in Iceland, Scandinavia, northern and western Britain, and Ireland. Winters mainly within breeding range, but also in adjacent southern waters.

Often seen within 100 yards (90 m) of shore and much less frequently on the open sea, it is less sociable than other auks, nesting in loose groups and scattered pairs.

23, 24 **Little Auk**
(*Alle alle*)

Description: 8″ (20 cm). A *tiny, chubby* auk with round head, *short neck,* and *small, stubby bill. Squat, almost neckless* appearance on water. In summer, *head, neck, and breast blackish-brown, rest of upperparts black;* narrow white bar on trailing edge of wing, white streaks on scapulars, incomplete white eye-ring and white underparts. *In winter, neck, breast, and ear coverts white.*

Voice: Shrill chattering on breeding grounds.

Habitat: Breeds in huge colonies in high Arctic, on cliffs and in holes among rocks, chiefly on coast but sometimes on mountain screes. In winter, pelagic except when blown to shore by storms.

Nesting: 1, occasionally 2, pale blue, unmarked eggs, placed in unlined hole.

Range: High Arctic islands from northeastern Nearctic east to central Palearctic, moving south to winter at sea on both sides of the Atlantic.

Infrequently seen by European bird-watchers because of its remote breeding grounds and preference for wintering on the open ocean, it occurs in vast

numbers in its Arctic habitat and is considered one of the most abundant birds in the world. It is most often seen after severe autumn storms, when thousands may be blown ashore or even far inland. During these "wrecks" the birds linger for days in a weakened condition.

19 **Puffin**
(*Fratercula arctica*)

Description: 12″ (30 cm). *Small, chunky* auk with *large head* and spectacular *deep, triangular bill striped with red, yellow, and blue.* In summer, upperparts and *collar black,* face and underparts whitish, eye red-rimmed with fleshy wattles, legs orange. In winter, several layers of bill are shed and it becomes smaller and duller; *face becomes grey;* collar is retained, giving same head and neck pattern. Juvenile similar to winter adult, but with smaller, dark bill.

Voice: A low growling *aarr* at breeding colonies. Food-begging call of young, *chip-chip-chip.*

Habitat: Coastal, breeding on turf slopes on cliff tops and landslides and on islands; also among rocks, usually in large colonies. Winters at sea.

Nesting: 1 white egg, rarely 2, oval to elliptical in shape, sometimes with a few brown or purple markings, placed in hollow, in old burrow of rabbit or shearwater or excavated by bird itself; also in hole.

Range: Northern coasts and islands of eastern North America and western Eurasia, from Novaya Zemlya west and south to Iceland and Brittany. Winters in North Sea and in North Atlantic south to Morocco; also western Mediterranean.

Its clown-like appearance is accentuated by its ungainly waddle. It usually carries several fish (often sand eels) at a time and may arrive at its nest with half-a-dozen fish hanging from its bill, giving it a bearded appearance.

SANDGROUSE
(Pteroclididae)

16 species: warmer parts of Eurasia and Africa. Two species breed in Europe. Medium-sized terrestrial land birds resembling doves or partridges, with small bill and head, short neck and legs, and long, pointed wings. Tail varies from wedge-shaped to long and pointed; legs feathered. Plumage cryptically coloured above, sandy-brown with or without dark barring and mottling, blending with arid environment. Face and breast often boldly marked. Sexes dissimilar. Found in thinly vegetated semiarid or desert country; nest on ground.

278 Black-bellied Sandgrouse
(*Pterocles orientalis*)

Description: 13½" (34 cm). Bulky sandgrouse with comparatively *short tail,* pointed but *not elongated.* Both sexes distinguishable from Pin-tailed by *black belly,* and in flight by *black-and-white underwing.* Male has *light grey head and neck,* chestnut chin and throat with small black bib, and narrow black band across pinkish-grey breast. Upperparts mottled grey and yellow; wing similar but more orange, with dark primaries. Female has upperparts and wings closely barred black and buff, creamy throat with smaller black bib, and *rich buffy breast with black spots,* bordered below by black band.

Voice: A chuckling churr that starts explosively and trails off, *CHURRRRRrrrrr—owo;* also a more dove-like *coo-waa-oo.*

Habitat: Semidesert, steppes, stony wastes, dry hillsides, bare ground with low vegetation.

Nesting: 2–3 buff eggs heavily spotted and blotched with brown and grey, placed on ground in unlined shallow depression.

Range: Resident in Spain and Portugal, vagrant elsewhere in Europe. Also in North Africa and southwestern Asia.

Semidesert birds, they come to watering places daily in early morning and late evening, often at precisely the same time. Adults bring water to their young on their breast feathers, which are uniquely shaped for water retention.

---

279 Pin-tailed Sandgrouse
(*Pterocles alchata*)

Description: 14½″ (36 cm). Smaller and slimmer than Black-bellied, with *long, pointed central tail feathers. White belly;* in flight, shows *white centre to underwing.* Breeding male brown above with yellow spots, orange-yellow face, black throat and eyeline, pale greenish neck, and broad *rufous breast band bordered with black.* Winter male resembles female, with black and pale yellow barring above, white throat and *creamy-buff neck and breast crossed by three narrow black bands.*

Voice: Call, a crow-like *kaar* or *koor;* also cackling *kack-kack-kack-kack.*

Habitat: Sandy plains, stony steppes, dry mud flats, low vegetation at desert's edge.

Nesting: Usually 3 buff eggs spotted and blotched with brown and grey, placed on open ground in unlined shallow depression. May form loose nesting colonies.

Range: Resident in Spain, Portugal, and very locally in southern France; rare vagrant elsewhere in Europe. Also breeds in North Africa and southwestern Asia.

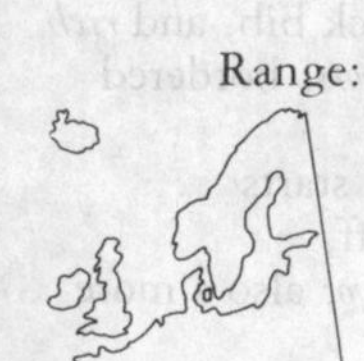

They are fast fliers, with long, pointed wings that beat rapidly. On the ground they have a dove-like appearance, but their short, stubby bill suggests a game bird. The taxonomic position of Sandgrouse is still a matter of debate.

PIGEONS AND DOVES
(Columbidae)

290 species: worldwide. Six species breed in Europe. Small to medium-sized, soft-plumaged birds with fairly short, often slender bill; small, round head; short neck; and plump body. Tail fairly long and square or graduated; legs short. Plumage mainly brown and grey in Europe, brighter in Old World tropics. Sexes similar. Flight rapid, often with clatter of wings on takeoff. Terrestrial and arboreal, feeding on seeds, grain, and fruit and drinking by sucking water through immersed bill. Nest in trees or on cliff ledges. Parents feed young "pigeon's milk" produced in their crops.

---

384 Rock Dove
(*Columba livia*)

Description: 13″ (33 cm). Same size as Stock Dove, but paler blue-grey, with *white rump, two broad black bars across pale secondaries* (Stock Dove has vestigial bars), and *white (not grey) underwing.* Feral "domestic pigeons" descended from wild Rock Doves may resemble the ancestral type, while others are varied in colours and mixtures: black, white, and cinnamon, as well as grey.

Voice: Domestic and wild Rock Doves have identical voices: several short coos followed by a long one, *u-ru-ru-COOO.*

Habitat: Mainly sea cliffs; in southern Europe also on inland cliffs. Feeds in nearby fields. Domestic pigeons chiefly in cities; also on cliffs.

Nesting: 2 white eggs, in rudimentary nest of twigs and roots, placed on ledge in sea cave or crevice in cliff face. Feral pigeons nest on building ledges, under bridges, in dovecotes.

Range: Breeds in southern Europe, coasts of Ireland, northern and western Britain, and western France; also northern Africa and southern and central Asia

east to India. Feral birds practically worldwide.

Perhaps the most completely man-adapted birds in the world, they please some, who enjoy seeing and feeding them, and annoy others, who deplore the defacement of statues and buildings caused by their droppings.

383 Stock Dove
(*Columba oenas*)

Description: 13″ (33 cm). Smaller and more compact than Woodpigeon; in flight, distinguished from Woodpigeon and Rock Dove by *pale grey panel across wing coverts. No white on rump, wings, or neck.* Breast vinaceous; green iridescent patch on neck.

Voice: Cooing song quite different from Woodpigeon: a rapid series of double notes with emphasis on first note, *COO-woo;* first note may be slurred, giving impression of 3 notes, *COO-u-woo.*

Habitat: Wooded country of all types, parkland with old trees, cliffs, sand dunes, occasionally towns. In winter, farmland and open areas.

Nesting: 2 white eggs, usually placed in tree cavity, less often in niche of cliff or building or old rabbit burrow. Nest site usually lined with twigs and roots.

Range: Western Palearctic, breeding over most of Europe except Iceland, northern Scandinavia, and a few Mediterranean areas; also North Africa and western and southwestern Asia. Eastern birds move to western Europe and the Mediterranean in winter.

Gregarious, it sometimes nests socially in small groups; sometimes found in mixed flocks with Woodpigeons in winter. Like the more abundant Woodpigeon, it feeds mainly on grain, as well as worms and snails. Unlike the Woodpigeon, it is not found in cities.

382 **Woodpigeon**
(*Columba palumbus*)

Description: 16″ (40 cm). Largest European pigeo[n], mainly grey with vinaceous breast an[d] dark tail band, readily distinguished by *white patch on neck* and conspicuous *white band across wings*. Young birds lack white neck patch.

Voice: Song, a series of distinctive 5-note phrases: first note short and introductory; second note accented and with distinct pause before next two notes—*cu-COOO-coo . . . coo-coo*. Series typically ends with single short note, *cu*, like introductory note.

Habitat: Wooded country of all types. Feeds mainly in fields and other open areas; also parks, gardens, and sometimes city squares, where it mingles with domestic pigeons.

Nesting: 2 white eggs, placed on thin platform of twigs, usually in tree or shrub, occasionally on rocks or buildings.

Range: Western Palearctic, breeding throughout Europe except Iceland and northern Scandinavia; also North Africa and western Asia. Mainly sedentary, but northern birds move south in winter.

Widespread and abundant, it has readily adapted to man, entering towns and gardens and also thriving on agricultural land, where it is generally considered a pest because it damages crops. When flushed, it rises explosively with a clatter of wings. Huge flocks of migrants occur in autumn.

386 **Collared Dove**
(*Streptopelia decaocto*)

Description: 12½″ (31 cm). Pale, washed-out plumage, dull ash-brown above, light grey-brown below, with vinaceous wash. Distinguished from Turtle Dove by *thin black half-collar on hind neck* and *plain upperparts,* and in flight by *broad* white terminal band on underside of tail and *white underwing coverts.*

Voice: Song, a series of hollow, high-pitched coos in 3-note phrases, accent on second note, with last note somewhat abrupt: *coo-COOO-cu.* Flight call, a nasal *wheee.*

Habitat: Towns, villages, farms. In original Asian habitat, palm groves and open land with scattered brush and trees.

Nesting: 2 white eggs, on thin platform of twigs, in tree or on building ledge.

Range: Breeds across much of Europe in wide band from southeast to northwest; also southwestern and eastern Asia.

This species has undergone one of the most remarkable range expansions in recent history by adapting to man-made habitats. Starting in the Balkans in about 1930 it spread rapidly north and west. The first pair nested in Britain in 1955, and it has now spread throughout Britain and Ireland.

---

387 Turtle Dove
(*Streptopelia turtur*)

Description: 11″ (28 cm). Slender dove with *black, slightly wedge-shaped tail bordered with white.* Feathers of upperparts have rufous edges, producing a *scalloped effect.* Patch of narrow black and white lines on side of neck; breast pink.

Voice: Song, a series of soft, purring coos in 3-note phrases, *urrr-turrr-turrr.*

Habitat: Open country with trees, bushes, and hedgerows; copses, plantations, heaths, parks. Often feeds on grain fields.

Nesting: 2 white eggs, on thin platform of twigs, sometimes lined with roots and plant stems, placed in bush or low tree.

Range: Breeds throughout Europe except Scandinavia, Iceland, most of Ireland, and northern Britain; also southwestern and central Asia east to Iran and Mongolia, and Mediterranean and Saharan Africa. European birds winter in northern Africa.

The slow, sleepy purring of the T Dove has given rise to its scientific name, *turtur.* It is replaced to the so of its range in Africa by the closely related Pink-breasted Dove (*S. lugens*), which has a similar purring song but a different habitat of open highland country.

---

385 Laughing Dove
(*Streptopelia senegalensis*)

Description: 10¼" (26 cm). *Smaller* and *shorter-tailed* than other doves and more richly coloured. Head greyish-pink, back rich brown, *breast reddish-brown with ring of black spots* visible at close range. In flight, piebald effect of upperwing surface produced by rich brown scapulars, *pale blue coverts,* and *black flight feathers.*

Voice: Song, variable but always a series of rapid notes that start soft, rise, and trail away at the end: *u-curru-COOK-curru* or *u-curru-curru-tu-COOK-oo.*

Habitat: In Ethiopian Region, chiefly dry thornscrub; in Middle East and Mediterranean countries, more in towns and villages.

Nesting: 2 white eggs, on thin platform of twigs and plant stems, low in bush or tree, or on building ledge.

Range: Breeds in European Turkey; also parts of southwest Asia and India; widespread in Ethiopian Region.

Its principal home is Africa south of the Sahara, where it was named Laughing Dove, its song being likened to a low, chuckling laugh. An alternate name, Palm Dove, is misleading, since it only frequents palms at oases where other trees are lacking. Typically a bird of *Acacia* scrub, it also frequents cultivated fields, gardens, and villages. It is common and widespread in India, where it is known as the "Little Brown Dove."

CUCKOOS
(Cuculidae)

125 species: worldwide. Three species breed in Europe. Small to medium-large, slender birds with somewhat decurved, often stout bill; long, graduated tail; and rather short legs. Plumage extremely variable: underparts and tail usually barred; European species mainly grey and white. Sexes similar. European species arboreal, feeding mainly on insects, especially caterpillars. Loud and far-carrying calls in breeding season. European species parasitic, laying eggs in other birds' nests.

392, 393 Great Spotted Cuckoo
(*Clamator glandarius*)

Description: 15½″ (39 cm). Magpie-sized, with *conspicuous grey crest* and *long, dark tail edged and tipped with white.* Top and sides of head dark grey; upperparts and wings dark, *boldly spotted with white;* underparts creamy-white, yellowish on throat. Juvenile has dark head, reduced crest, buffier underparts, and rufous patch on primaries.

Voice: Song, a series of rapid cackling notes descending and becoming slower at the end, *ka-ka-ka-ka-ka-ka —keow-keow-keow-kow-kow.* Also a variety of chattering and other calls, including crow-like *car.*

Habitat: Clearings and edges of woodland, open scrubby areas with scattered trees, olive groves.

Nesting: 15–16 eggs per season, pale blue-green with brown spots, deposited in nests of hosts.

Range: Summer visitor to Iberian peninsula, Mediterranean France, Italy, Sardinia, and northeast Greece; vagrant elsewhere in Europe. Also breeds in North Africa, Egypt, and Middle East and locally in Ethiopian Region. European birds winter in tropical Africa.

While the Cuckoo parasitise birds, the Great Spotted lays crows' nests, especially the Mag The Cuckoo lays only one egg in host nest, but a Great Spotted ma several in the same nest. Great Spot chicks do not eject eggs or young of host, but are raised with host's chicks.

388, 391 Cuckoo
(*Cuculus canorus*)

Description: 13″ (33 cm). Rather *falcon-like in general shape.* Adult male and female have head, throat, and upperparts grey; lower breast and belly white, with fine, dark bars; *tail long with rounded end finely tipped with white.* Juvenile underparts white with dark barring, upperparts typically reddish-brown with dark bars and white spots on nape. A rare form of adult female has reddish plumage like juvenile. Flight direct and low, on rapidly beating, pointed wings that seldom rise above the body.

Voice: Far-carrying double note, *cuck-coo.* Regular variant, a 3-note *cuck-cuck-oo,* accent on second note; when excited, several calls in quick succession. Female has long, bubbling call.

Habitat: A wide variety of habitats, including forest, moors, farmland, sand dunes.

Nesting: Parasitic. Lays a total of 8–12 eggs, depositing one in nest of each host. Eggs vary in colour and markings, often mimicking those of host species.

Range: Breeds throughout Europe except Iceland; also in North Africa and across Asia to Burma and Japan. European birds winter in tropical Africa.

This shy bird tends to remain concealed in treetops in wooded areas. In open habitats it may perch on telephone wires, walls, and other prominent places. Its habits as a brood parasite have been extensively studied. Typical hosts are wagtails, pipits, and warblers. It is often attacked by small songbirds.

Oriental Cuckoo
(*Cuculus saturatus*)

:ription: 12″ (30 cm). Slightly smaller and darker grey than Cuckoo, with buffy wash on underparts, but almost impossible to distinguish in the field except by voice.

Voice: Song, a long series of double notes, *hoo-hoo,* with a muted Hoopoe-like quality.

Habitat: Chiefly coniferous forests; also mixed forests and occasionally broad-leaved woodland.

Nesting: Parasitic. Colour and size of eggs variable, though mainly pale blue or white with indistinct dark spotting, frequently mimicking eggs of host species (most frequently warblers, flycatchers, and pipits).

Range: Eurasia, from north-central European Russia across Siberia to Kamchatka and south to India and China. Winters in the Oriental and Australasian regions.

This oriental species barely reaches Europe and migrates east in autumn from its Russian breeding ground. Very shy and difficult to see during breeding season; like most cuckoos, it is best identified by voice.

BARN OWLS
(Tytonidae)

12 species: worldwide. One species breeds in Europe. Medium-sized nocturnal birds of prey with large head, hooked bill, heart-shaped facial discs; long, rounded wings; short tail, and long legs. Toes and claws strong; outer toe reversible. Plumage soft; mainly grey, brown, or buff, often in two colour phases. Sexes similar. Barn Owl (*Tyto alba*) occurs around human habitation; other species in grassland and forest.

367, 369 Barn Owl
(*Tyto alba*)

Description: 13½″ (34 cm). Very pale owl lacking ear tufts. *Underparts vary from pure white to deep buff with black flecks. Face and underside of wing pure white;* pale orange-buff upperparts spotted with grey and white. Most often seen at night illuminated by car headlights or hunting at dawn or dusk.

Voice: A long, harsh, hissing screech; also hoarse shrieks and snoring noises.

Habitat: Frequents farms and villages, nesting in barns, church towers, and deserted buildings; also found in open country with large trees.

Nesting: 4–7 white eggs, in unlined hole of tree or building or in cliff crevice.

Range: Cosmopolitan. Breeds almost throughout Europe, but absent from Iceland, most of Scandinavia, and parts of Greece.

Though there are many gaps in its distribution, the Barn Owl has the most widespread range of any bird in the world. A strong flier, it has been able to extend its range to many islands in the Pacific and Indian oceans. Its normal diet consists mainly of mice, but it adapts readily to other available foods, including seabirds.

TRUE OWLS
(Strigidae)

130 species: worldwide. Twelve species breed in Europe. Small to large predominantly nocturnal birds of prey with large, rounded head; short neck; and strong hooked bill. Eyes very large and facing forward in flat facial discs. Wings broad and rounded; tail usually short; legs and often toes feathered. Feet strong, with hooked claws; outer toe reversible. Many species have ear-like tufts. Plumage soft and fluffy, mainly brown or grey, with barring and streaking. Sexes similar; female larger. Flight silent. Feed mainly on rodents; also birds and insects. Some species eat fish. Most hunt nocturnally. Food is swallowed whole; bones, fur, and other inedible parts are later regurgitated as pellets. The favorite perch of an owl can often be located by finding pellets on the ground below.

381 **Scops Owl**
(*Otus scops*)

Description: 7½″ (19 cm). A *small, slender owl* with *ear tufts.* Plumage grey-brown with fine spots and lines; eyes yellow. Separated by range and habitat, and ear tufts, from smaller Pygmy Owl; larger Little Owl has broader, flat-topped head, fatter body, shorter tail, and different *voice.* Ear tufts often inconspicuous.

Voice: A melancholy *pew* or *poo,* soft but penetrating, repeated monotonously.

Habitat: Partial to human habitation near trees; farms, gardens, abandoned buildings; also open woodland, olive groves.

Nesting: 4–5 white eggs, in unlined cavity in tree, wall, or building; also in old nests of other birds.

Range: Summer visitor to central and southern Europe, wintering in northern tropical Africa and some parts of Mediterranean. Also breeds in North Africa and in western and eastern Asia.

It is usually discovered by listening for its persistent song, a typical sound on warm Mediterranean nights. Closely related to the African Scops Owl (*O. senegalensis*), which has a similar, though quavering, note. Since they feed primarily on insects, most Scops Owls leave Europe in winter, though some remain around the Mediterranean.

370, 371 **Eagle Owl**
(*Bubo bubo*)

Description: 26–28″ (65–70 cm). *Huge brown owl,* largest in Europe; *prominent ear tufts* and *orange eyes.* Tawny above, with dark mottling; buffy below, with broad, black breast streaks and narrow, dark bars; belly has narrower streaks.

Voice: Song, a deep, far-carrying *boo-hu,* the origin of its scientific name. Call, a harsh *kveck.*

Habitat: Dense forests, mountain cliffs, and ravines; steep, rocky terrain.

Nesting: 2–3 white eggs, in an unlined scrape in hollow tree, on cliff ledge, or on ground in open country.

Range: Breeds locally over much of northern, eastern, and southern Europe; also in northern Africa and across Asia to Pacific, south to India and China. Rarely migrates.

Though it has a broad range, the Eagle Owl is much less numerous than its American cousin, the Great Horned Owl. It hunts at dawn and dusk, feeding on a wide variety of larger birds, especially crows and game birds, and mammals such as rats and squirrels. Opportunistic and aggressive, it will eat almost anything it can catch and has been known to take Goshawks and Capercaillie.

366, 368 **Snowy Owl**
(*Nyctea scandiaca*)

Description: 21–26″ (53–65 cm). Very *large, white* owl, with variable amounts of *narrow, dark barring and speckling.* Fully mature males are pure white; females and juveniles are barred with grey and may appear pale grey at a distance. Eyes yellow. White-breasted form of Barn Owl is much smaller, with buffy upperparts and dark eyes in a black-outlined, heart-shaped face.

Voice: A wheezy, almost heron-like coughing bark and a high-pitched screech; song, a deep *boo* repeated every 4 seconds. Silent outside breeding ground.

Habitat: Breeds on northern tundra and moorland; winters farther south in fields and open country, especially flat coastal areas and marshes.

Nesting: 4–10 white eggs, occasionally more, in a hollow scrape on tundra hummock.

Range: Circumpolar on arctic tundra. In Europe, breeds in Iceland, Scandinavia, and sometimes Shetland Isles. Winters irregularly farther south.

Feeding chiefly on lemmings and other rodents, it also takes Arctic hares, rabbits, and birds up to the size of ptarmigan and ducks. Its flight is normally a slow glide, but it can dash swiftly after birds, catching them in flight. In years when the winter lemming population is low, the Snowy Owl irrupts southward, looking for more adequate food sources. It hunts during the day.

376 **Hawk Owl**
(*Surnia ulula*)

Description: 14–16″ (35–40 cm). *Hawk-like flight silhouette and perching stance* produced by short, *pointed wings and long tail.* Dark crown patterned with fine white barring; *white facial discs boldly outlined in black.* Dark brown upperparts spotted and mottled with white; *white underparts finely barred with dark brown.*

Voice: Song, a bubbling trill. Call, a chattering, rather hawk-like *ku-ku-kick-kick-kick-kick.*

Habitat: Coniferous forests and birch woods; during winter irruptions, open country.

Nesting: 3–10 white eggs, laid in an unlined tree hole or old nest of a large bird, usually a bird of prey.

Range: Holarctic, breeding in coniferous forests from Norway across Eurasia to Pacific Siberia and from Alaska to eastern Canada. Winters in varying numbers south of its breeding range, rarely to central Europe.

Relatively easy to see, it is a diurnal hunter, habitually perching on top of a tall spruce or other prominent outpost, often flicking its tail. Its flight is swift and direct; it can catch birds in flight, but rodents are the principal diet.

---

378 Pygmy Owl
(*Glaucidium passerinum*)

Description: 6½" (16 cm). *Extremely small,* with relatively *small, rounded head* and poorly marked facial discs. Dark brown above spotted with pale buff, white below with black streaks. *Tail dark,* with narrow white bars, *frequently cocked and flicked from side to side.*

Voice: Song, a soft, piping note repeated for long periods. Several whistled calls, *kew, kuchick,* etc. Very vocal.

Habitat: Dense coniferous forests, in central Europe chiefly in mountains, elsewhere in lowlands as well.

Nesting: 4–6 white eggs, placed in unlined tree cavity or old woodpecker hole.

Range: Breeds from Norway and the Alps east across Eurasia to the Sea of Okhotsk.

The legs and feet of this tiny owl are disproportionately large and strong, making it a fierce predator able to capture prey of equal size. Though mainly nocturnal, it quite often hunts in daylight, feeding mainly on rodents, but also on small birds caught in flight. It is often mobbed by other birds.

---

379 **Little Owl**
(*Athene noctua*)

Description: 8½″ (21 cm). The common small owl of Europe, with a short tail, *squat appearance,* and *flattened top of head.* Grey-brown above and below, with white spots.

Voice: Call, a querulous, complaining *kiew;* song, a rising whistle.

Habitat: Open country with trees; farmland, forest edge, sand dunes, semideserts, barren rocky areas; also around buildings.

Nesting: 3–5 white eggs, in unlined nest in tree cavity, cliff or building crevice, or in burrow.

Range: Breeds in southern and central Europe north to Britain (where introduced), Denmark, and Latvia; also in northern Africa and southwestern and central Asia east to Mongolia.

It is probably the most frequently seen owl in Europe since it often hunts in the day and perches on fence posts and other prominent vantage points watching for its prey of rodents, insects, and occasionally small birds. It often flies from one perch to another with its peculiar dipping, bounding flight and when excited, bobs its head nervously.

---

377 **Tawny Owl**
(*Strix aluco*)

Description: 15″ (38 cm). Medium-sized *plump* owl with *large, round head, no ear tufts,* and *black eyes.* Plumage varies from rufous-brown to grey-brown, with dark streaks below and pale spotting on scapulars and wing coverts.

Voice: Call, a loud, querulous *kee-wick.* Song

consists of mellow hooting in a characteristic 3-part form: 3–4 introductory hoots (sometimes a single long hoot), a pause with a single short hoot in the middle, and a longer series of hoots run together and tremulous at the end: *hoo-hoo-hoo-hoo . . . hu . . . hoo-hoo-hu-hu-hooooooooo*.

Habitat: Open deciduous woodland, parks, farmland, gardens, often around human habitation with scattered trees, towns; occasionally open, rocky country.

Nesting: 2–4 white eggs, in unlined tree hole or old nest of bird or squirrel; sometimes rock or building crevice.

Range: Breeds throughout most of Europe except Iceland, northern Scandinavia, and Ireland; also breeds in North Africa and western and south-central Asia, east to southern China. Resident.

Strictly nocturnal, it roosts in tree branches by day and is often discovered and mobbed by small birds, which may alert the observer to this owl in daylight. Much more often heard than seen, it calls regularly throughout the year, especially in autumn and winter. Shakespeare referred to the Tawny Owl when he wrote (*Love's Labour's Lost,* v:2):

"Then nightly sings the staring owl—
Tu-who,
Tu-whit, tu-who, a merry note,"

374 **Ural Owl**
(*Strix uralensis*)

Description: 24″ (60 cm). A *large, pale* relative of the Tawny Owl, with similar *black eyes in unmarked facial disc,* but *tail longer* and *eyes relatively smaller.* Pale brown above and below, with dark streaks; wings and tail barred; head round, without ear tufts. Great Grey is larger and greyer, with yellow eyes and series of rings on facial discs.

Voice: Song, a hooting, with a 4-second pause, *huho . . . hoho, huhohe,* or a rapid series of subdued barkings, *hohohohoho*. Calls, a barking *kow* and a harsh *kee-wick*.

Habitat: Forest, chiefly coniferous or mixed; also heath forest and spruce bogs or around human habitation.

Nesting: 3–4 white eggs, in an unlined, open tree hollow, old nest of large bird, or nest box.

Range: Breeds from Norway across Eurasia to eastern Siberia and Japan; also in mountains of east-central Europe, Yugoslavia, Poland, Czechoslovakia, and Romania. Resident.

It has recently been extending its range in northern Europe. Formerly confined to deep woods, it now increasingly frequents human habitation. It takes readily to nest boxes and now prefers these where available. Vigorous in defence of its nest, its Swedish name, *slaguggla,* means "attack owl." It feeds mainly on mammals up to squirrel size, and also birds, hunting both diurnally and nocturnally.

375 **Great Grey Owl**
(*Strix nebulosa*)

Description: 27" (69 cm). *Very large* owl with long tail; grey above, mottled with white; white below, with dark streaks. *Small yellow eyes* set in *massive rounded head; large facial discs closely barred with concentric dark rings;* lacks ear tufts. Broad, white "eyebrows" and black chin. Pale wing patch shows in flight.

Voice: Song, a measured series of 9–14 deep, booming hoots, the last few downslurred and trailing away. Female has a rather high-pitched *chee-ah,* and a low, growling sound.

Habitat: Coniferous forests.

Nesting: 3–5 (sometimes up to 9) white eggs, in unlined nest on top of broken tree trunk or in old nest of large bird.

Range: Holarctic, breeding patchily from northern Norway and Sweden east

across Eurasia to Bering Sea, and in North America. Mainly resident, but during periodic irruptions winters south to southern Scandinavia, and occasionally eastern Germany.

In spite of its appearance, the Great Grey Owl weighs only half as much as the similar-sized Eagle Owl, owing much of its apparent bulk to unusually dense feathering. It lives largely on voles and shrews, feeding diurnally; in years when voles are scarce it moves south in search of them rather than shifting to different prey. A rather scarce bird, the Great Grey is not often seen.

372 Long-eared Owl

(*Asio otus*)

Description: 14″ (35 cm). *Medium-sized* brown owl with *prominent, closely set, upright ear tufts* and *orange-yellow eyes.* Buffy above, mottled with dark brown; buff below, with dark streaks and fine barring. Ears often held flat, but its *slimmer body, narrower head,* and light eyes separate it from black-eyed Tawny Owl.

Voice: Song, a low, moaning *oooo,* repeated every few seconds. A variety of barking, whistling, and wailing calls. Silent outside breeding season.

Habitat: Prefers conifers, occurring both in deep forest and small copses; will accept deciduous woods and sometimes nests on open moors and marshes.

Nesting: 4–5 white eggs, usually laid in old nest of squirrel or bird, rarely on ground.

Range: Holarctic, breeding in North America, North Africa, and Eurasia east to Pacific Siberia and Japan. Resident through most of southern and central Europe north to southern Scandinavia, and in summer north to Finland. Leaves northern areas in winter.

A nocturnal hunter and normally an inhabitant of dense woods, it is seldom observed casually. Less vocal than other owls, it is most easily seen at a nest or winter roost. It feeds on rodents, small birds, and some insects.

373 **Short-eared Owl**
(*Asio flammeus*)

Description: 15″ (38 cm). Distinguishable from other medium-sized brown owls by *habitat* and *diurnal hunting habits.* Mottled dark brown and buff above, pale buff below, with dark streaks. *Wings long and narrow, with dark carpal patches;* eyes golden-yellow; short ear tufts usually not visible.

Voice: Song, a deep hoot given during display flight. Near nest various rather harsh notes are given, *kee-weeoo, kick-wick,* etc.

Habitat: Moorland, heaths, sand dunes, marshes, and other open country.

Nesting: 4–8 white eggs, laid in unlined hollow on ground, sheltered by vegetation.

Range: Widespread, breeding in northern Eurasia, Iceland, North America, parts of South America, and on some Pacific islands. In Europe, breeds from far north, south to France (very locally), Germany, and Black Sea, wintering south to Mediterranean and North Africa.

One of the "daylight" owls and thus more frequently seen, its long wings and harrier-like gliding and wheeling flight give it a hawk-like appearance. Like the Barn Owl it is a great traveller and has extended its range to such far-off places as Argentina, Hawaii, and the Galapagos Islands.

380 **Tengmalm's Owl**
(*Aegolius funereus*)

Description: 10″ (25 cm). Small, nocturnal, forest owl. Somewhat larger than Little Owl, richer brown, with more erect posture and different shape: *head larger in proportion to body and more rounded; facial discs outlined in black, deeper, and more pointed,* giving "raised eyebrows" expression. *Legs and feet heavily feathered.* Juvenile dark chocolate-brown with white eyebrows.

Voice: A trill of hollow, popping notes slightly ascending in pitch; notes sometimes given more slowly and alternately stressed.

Habitat: Chiefly coniferous forest, sometimes deciduous, both lowland and montane.

Nesting: 3–6, occasionally up to 10 white eggs, in unlined tree cavity, sometimes nest box or old woodpecker hole. In central Europe, often uses abandoned hole of Black Woodpecker.

Range: Holarctic, breeding in Boreal forest zone across Eurasia, Alaska, and Canada. In Europe, breeds in Scandinavia and south in mountains to central Europe, Pyrenees, and northern Greece. Largely resident, extending farther south during periodic irruptions.

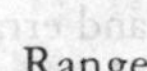

Its small size, dense habitat, and nocturnal habits make it one of the hardest European birds to observe. In summer in the far north, when nights are mostly light, it can be seen hunting, but otherwise one must locate it by listening for the call, which is seasonal.

NIGHTJARS
(Caprimulgidae)

76 species: worldwide. Two species breed in Europe. Small to medium-sized aerial, nocturnal birds with large head and eyes, tiny bill and feet, and a very wide gape (mouth) for catching insects in flight. Wings long and pointed, tail long. Plumage soft, mainly brown and grey with dark mottling, barring, and streaking, perfectly camouflaged for resting and nesting on the ground. In flight, many species show white patches on wings and tail. Sexes often somewhat dissimilar. Flight silent and erratic; birds glide and wheel as they pursue insects. Often sit on roads at night.

---

389 **Nightjar**
(*Caprimulgus europaeus*)

Description: 10½″ (26 cm). Best identified by *range* over most of Europe, where it is the only nightjar, and by *voice,* where it overlaps with the Red-necked. General colour grey-brown, mottled, streaked, and barred with dark brown and buff. In flight, male shows *white-tipped outer tail feathers* and *small white patch on outer primaries,* both lacking in the female.

Voice: Song, a sustained, dry purring *churr,* rising and falling in pitch, lasting sometimes up to 5 minutes. Flight call, *ku-ick.*

Habitat: Open country with scattered trees, with ground cover of bracken, heather, gorse, or other low bushes—open woodland, forest and meadow edges, commons, heaths, moors, occasionally sand dunes.

Nesting: 2 creamy or greyish-white eggs spotted and blotched with brown and grey, placed on bare ground in shallow scrape near bits of dead wood.

Range: Breeds throughout Europe except Iceland and northern Scandinavia, and across Asia to Lake Baikal and

Turkistan; also in North Africa. European birds winter in tropical Africa.

Although widespread, this species is seldom seen unless flushed by chance during the day or glimpsed briefly at night when illuminated in car headlights. On a warm, windless summer evening at a known breeding area, one can listen for its song, which usually starts shortly after sunset, and perhaps see it pursuing insects with its erratic, twisting flight.

---

390 **Red-necked Nightjar**
(*Caprimulgus ruficollis*)

Description: 12″ (30 cm). Larger and paler than Nightjar, with *rufous nape and prominent white throat,* and more conspicuous white patches on wings and tail.

Voice: Song consists of repetition of a clipped, hollow double note, *tutuk-tutuk-tutuk . . .* , divided by pauses into groups of variable length, sustained for long periods.

Habitat: Pine woods, dry bushy hillsides, semidesert with scattered trees and bushes.

Nesting: 2 white or greyish-white eggs, spotted and blotched with brown and grey, placed in shallow scrape on bare ground among bushes.

Range: Breeds in Iberia in all but northern section; also North Africa. Winters in tropical African savannas.

This species is a little-known bird with one of the most limited breeding ranges of any nightjar. Its wing-clapping display flight is similar to that of the Nightjar, but it appears heavier in flight; it is best distinguished by voice. It feeds primarily on locusts, grasshoppers, beetles, and moths.

SWIFTS
(Apodidae)

70 species: worldwide. Four species breed in Europe. Small to medium-sized aerial birds with tiny bill and large gape (mouth) for catching insects in flight. Long, pointed, sickle-shaped wings make them among the swiftest birds in the world—hence the vernacular name. Swifts never perch, but short legs, strong feet, and curved claws are adapted for clinging to a vertical surface, where they rest.

395 Swift
(*Apus apus*)

Description: 6½″ (16 cm). Larger than Swallow, with *long, narrow sickle-shaped wings* and *very fast flight;* action quite different, with *rapid wingbeats alternating with glides. Plumage sooty-black* except for whitish chin which is usually difficult to see. Tail short, narrow, and forked. Juvenile has fine pale feather edgings.

Voice: Call is a long, shrill scream. At nesting and roosting sites, a rapid chattering.

Habitat: Aerial, feeding over diversified habitat: towns and villages, open country, woods, lakes, rivers, mountains.

Nesting: 2–3 white eggs, in shallow cup of leaves, grass, other vegetation, and feathers, fused with saliva, placed in building crevice, old nest of other bird, tree hole, or nest box.

Range: Breeds throughout Europe except Iceland, and across Asia to Iran, Manchuria, and China; also in North Africa. Winters in tropical Africa.

Probably the most visibly abundant summer bird in Europe, the Swift constantly dashes through the air with shrill screams. It circles in large numbers over villages, towns, and even major cities. It feeds on insects taken on the wing, frequently over water, where it will often dip to the surface to snatch a drink. In 1955 a Swiss ornithologist discovered, from radar patterns followed up by observations made from an airplane, that Swifts can at times sleep in flight!

397 **Pallid Swift**
(*Apus pallidus*)

Description: 6½″ (16 cm). Paler than Swift, with *more extensive and paler throat* and paler forehead. Below, body and wing linings grey-brown, not blackish; above, secondaries paler than rest of wing. Wing tips less pointed than Swift's.

Voice: A harsh scream similar to Swift.

Habitat: Cliffs and rocky coasts; also buildings.

Nesting: 2 white eggs, in shallow cup of straw and feathers, attached to vertical rock face. Nests colonially.

Range: In Europe, summer visitor to coasts (local inland) and most islands of Mediterranean from southern Portugal to Greece, wintering in tropical Africa. Also breeds in northern Africa and southwestern Asia.

It frequently associates with its close relative the Swift, from which it can be distinguished by slower wingbeats. Swifts fly at speeds up to 60 mph (100 kph), making plumage characters hard to see.

394 **Alpine Swift**
(*Apus melba*)

Description: 8¼″ (21 cm). A large swift with 21″ (53 cm) wingspan. *General colour rather pale brown,* not black; underparts white except for brown breast band and undertail coverts.

Voice: A twittering trill, rising and falling in pitch, sometimes accompanied by short screams; very different from Swift.

Habitat: Rocky mountainsides at rather low altitudes; gorges, sea cliffs; also buildings and towns.

Nesting: 2–3 white eggs, in shallow cup of plant

material and feathers, placed in crevice or on ledge of rock face or building.

Range: Summer visitor to southern Europe (Mediterranean area and nearby mountains), wintering in tropical Africa. Also breeds in southwestern Asia south to Ceylon, and in Africa.

It has a broad but spotty distribution in Africa and Eurasia, being absent from many areas with seemingly suitable habitat. "Alpine" is a misnomer, as it is usually found at low elevations.

White-rumped Swift

(*Apus caffer*)

Description: 5½" (14 cm). A black swift, with whitish throat patch, *narrow white band across upper rump,* and *deeply forked tail.* The smaller Little Swift (*A. affinis*), of Morocco, has a shorter, square tail and broad, white rump patch.

Voice: Call, a low twittering.

Habitat: Rocky hills, cliffs, caves, buildings.

Nesting: 2–3 white eggs, laid in old swallow nest, usually relined by bird with feathers and straw. Normally waits until occupants of nest have finished breeding, but sometimes ousts them.

Range: Breeds throughout most of the Ethiopian Region; also southern Spain.

When first discovered nesting in southern Spain (Cadiz) in 1966, it was erroneously identified as the Little Swift (*A. affinis*), since the latter had been extending its range north through Morocco and had reached the Straits of Gibraltar, while the nearest known nesting area of the White-rumped Swift had been in West Africa, 1,750 miles (2,800 km) to the south. Later, the birds were photographed in flight, caught, and correctly identified as *A. caffer*. Subsequently, White-rumped Swifts were also found breeding in the mountains of Morocco.

KINGFISHERS
(Alcedinidae)

90 species: worldwide, but most numerous in tropics. One species breeds in Europe. Small to medium-sized plump birds with long, stout, pointed and often brightly coloured bill, large head, and short neck. Short, rounded wings allow fast and direct flight. Tail usually short; legs very short. Many kingfishers feed entirely on fish, caught by diving into water from perch or hovering flight; others eat insects, lizards, and frogs.

---

610 **Kingfisher**
(*Alcedo atthis*)

Description: 6½″ (16 cm). Only kingfisher in Europe. Unmistakable brilliant colouring and shape: *long, pointed black bill, large head, stumpy tail, and short wings; upperparts bright turquoise-blue, cheeks and underparts chestnut,* throat and small neck patch white.

Voice: Call, a thin, high-pitched *chee* or *chickeee;* song, a trilling whistle.

Habitat: Lowland streams, rivers, canals, ponds, and lakes; in winter, also in tidal estuaries and along rocky coasts.

Nesting: 4–8 white eggs, laid in tunnelled nest chamber in bank above water.

Range: Breeds in central and southern Europe north to Britain, southern Sweden, and western Russia. Mainly resident but retreats from northern areas in winter. Also breeds in North Africa, southern Asia, and Australasia.

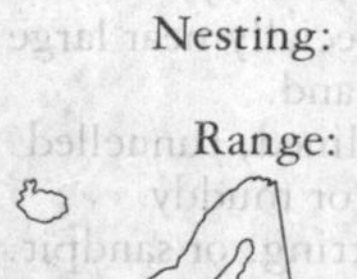

It is usually seen perching motionless on a branch or a post by water, watching for fish. It often hovers before plunging into the water. When excited, it bobs its head up and down and flicks its tail. Cold winters decimate the central European populations, which subsequently slowly recover.

BEE-EATERS
(Meropidae)

24 species: warm temperate and tropical regions of Old World. One species nests in Europe. Medium-small aerial birds with long, slender, slightly decurved bill; long, pointed, triangular wings; and long tail, often with elongated central tail feathers. Feed on insects, especially bees and wasps, captured in the air, often after quick dash from prominent perch. Flight graceful, with planing and circling, often at considerable height.

609 Bee-eater
(*Merops apiaster*)

Description: 11″ (28 cm). Unique in Europe; easily identified by liquid calls, *gaudy plumage, diagnostic shape,* and *stiff-winged, gliding flight.* Upperparts and wings a mixture of chestnut, yellow, and green; throat yellow, separated from blue-green underparts by narrow black band.

Voice: Common call, constantly used, a mellow, liquid *prrip.* Also, especially in chorus, a sharp *wick-wick.*

Habitat: Breeds in open, bushy country with scattered tall trees, especially near large rivers; also open woodland.

Nesting: 4–7 white eggs, in unlined, tunnelled nest chamber in sandy or muddy riverbank, roadside cutting, or sandpit. Nests in colonies.

Range: Summer visitor to southern and southeastern Europe, wintering in tropical Africa. Also breeds in North Africa and southwestern Asia.

Nest holes are 3–9 feet (1–3 metres) long, excavated horizontally in a bank or sloping down at an angle on flat ground. Sites are chosen with nearby available perches, such as sticks, posts, or telephone wires, from which the birds catch bees and other insects.

ROLLERS
(Coraciidae)

12 species: warm temperate and tropical regions of Old World. One species breeds in Europe. Medium-sized, stocky, crow-like birds with broad, stout bill, large head, short neck and legs, and long wings. Tail fairly long, square or forked. Sexes similar. Flight strong, with acrobatic displays. Insects and other prey captured either on the ground by sudden drop from prominent perch or in the air. Numbers gather at brush fires, feeding on insects flushed by the heat. Nest in holes.

611 Roller
(*Coracias garrulus*)

Description: 12″ (30 cm). Rather *heavy, big-headed* bird with stout bill and *build of a small crow; bright pale blue plumage with chestnut back.* In flight, broad wings are colourful mixture of pale blue, purplish-blue, and black. Tail brown, outer feathers blue. Juvenile duller, with brownish throat.

Voice: A harsh rolling screech, *krraaak* or *rrraaa;* also shorter, more clipped notes, *kakakak* or *karakak.*

Habitat: Mature forest (eastern Europe); open woodland and open country with scattered trees (Mediterranean).

Nesting: 4–7 white eggs, in unlined hole in tree, bank, old wall, ruins, or in old nest of large bird.

Range: Summer visitor to eastern and Mediterranean Europe, wintering in tropical Africa. Also breeds in North Africa and southwestern Asia.

It is named for its remarkable display flight, in which the male tumbles to earth from high in the air, twisting, turning, and "rolling" on the way. It perches prominently on a dead tree, wall, or telephone wire when hunting.

HOOPOES
(Upupidae)

1 species: warmer regions of Eurasia and Africa. Breeds in Europe. Medium-sized birds with long, slender, decurved bill; large erectile crest; broad, rounded wings; square tail; legs rather short. Sexes similar. Flight undulating and erratic. Perch and roost in trees but feed mainly on ground. Hole nesters. Nests have offensive smell due to poor sanitation and birds' musky odour.

---

613 Hoopoe
(*Upupa epops*)

Description: 11″ (28 cm). Unique, with *large erectile crest* (usually held flat), *long decurved bill, pinkish-cinnamon head and body;* tail and broad, rounded wings *boldly barred black and white,* conspicuous in flight.

Voice: Normal call, a soft, hollow, but far-carrying *hoo-poo-poo,* from which bird get its name; also chattering and cat-like mewing.

Habitat: Open country with large trees, forest edge, parkland, orchards, vineyards; often near human habitation. In African winter quarters, open bush.

Nesting: Usually 5–8 eggs, sometimes up to 12, colour variable, from pale olive-grey to yellow, green, or brown. Eggs laid in unlined tree hole, less often in wall or nest box.

Range: Summer visitor, breeding through most of Europe except Scandinavia and (very rarely) in southern England. Also breeds over most of Africa and across central and southern Asia. Winters mainly in tropical Africa, rarely in southern Spain.

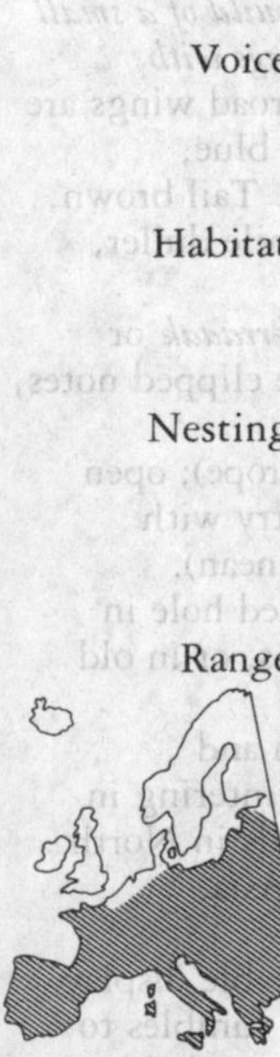

In a monotypic family, the Hoopoe is literally one of a kind. The crest is usually erected only when the bird is excited or, briefly, when alighting. A ground feeder, partial to lawns, it walks along probing for insect larvae.

WOODPECKERS AND WRYNECKS
(Picidae)

210 species: worldwide, except Madagascar and most of Australasia. Ten species breed in Europe. Small to medium-sized, mainly arborcal birds with strong feet and sharp claws for clinging to tree trunks. Usually zygodactyl (two toes pointing forward and two back), but some woodpeckers have only three toes. Woodpeckers have powerful, chisel-like bills for boring into wood to extract insects and excavate nest hole. Wrynecks have weak bills and obtain insect food from bark or on ground. Woodpeckers' tails have stiff, pointed feathers and are used as a brace when climbing trees; wrynecks' longer, rounded tails not used in climbing. Wings rounded; flight undulating in most species. Hole nesters. Sexes fairly similar; male woodpeckers more brightly coloured on head than females.

403 Wryneck
(*Jynx torquilla*)

Description: 6½″ (16 cm). Slender, with rather *long, round-ended tail;* short, straight pointed bill; and dark eye-mask. *Upperparts finely mottled and streaked grey, brown, black, and buff with bolder barring on tail; underparts buffy-white with narrow dark bars.* Well camouflaged.

Voice: Song, up to 12 high-pitched, rather nasal, monotonous notes, with a few lower introductory ones—*ker-ker-kew-kew-kew-kew. . . .*

Habitat: Open deciduous woodland, gardens, orchards, parkland, open country with large trees.

Nesting: 5–14 white eggs, in unlined tree cavity, wall, or bank crevice.

Range: Summer visitor, breeding across most of Europe except northern Scandinavia, Iceland, southern Iberia, Greece, and

most of Britain. Winters mainly in tropical Africa; a few remain in Mediterranean region. Also breeds in North Africa and in southwestern and central Asia east to China and Mongolia.

An unusual bird, this species looks like a passerine but is actually closely related to the woodpeckers, having a zygodactyl foot (the toes arranged two in front and two behind) and the ability to cling to tree trunks, though it seldom uses its tail for support. It feeds mainly on the ground, hopping along with tail slightly raised. Ants are the staple diet; it also eats beetles and gleans insects from tree bark. The name Wryneck comes from one of its displays in which the head and neck are shaken and twisted in unlikely contortions.

---

405 **Grey-headed Woodpecker**
(*Picus canus*)

Description: 10″ (25 cm). Resembles small Green Woodpecker, but with *grey head and underparts* and *thin black moustachial streak.* Male has *red on forehead only,* female lacks red. Narrow black line on lores. Juvenile browner, unspotted above, barred only on flanks, lacking red on head.

Voice: Call, not unlike "laugh" of Green Woodpecker, but mellower, becoming much slower and lower-pitched at end; drums regularly in spring, unlike Green Woodpecker.

Habitat: Similar to Green Woodpecker: deciduous woods with large clearings and open country with scattered trees, but less often near human habitation.

Nesting: 4–5 white eggs, laid in tree hole lined with wood chips. Hole excavated by both sexes.

Range: Breeds from west-central France and Scandinavia east across Eurasia to Japan and south to China and Malaysia. Sedentary.

A species of Asian origin, it has gradually expanded west into Europe and now overlaps broadly with the Green Woodpecker. Both are frequently found in the same woods, but the Grey-headed often prefers higher elevations, occurring in open deciduous forest high up on mountains, a habitat not occupied by the Green.

406 **Green Woodpecker**
(*Picus viridis*)

Description: 12½" (31 cm). Large woodpecker, *green above* and *pale green below,* with *yellow rump* conspicuous in flight. *Crown crimson,* eye area black; *moustachial streak red bordered with black* in male, all-black in female. Juvenile has pale spots above, dark bars below. Typical bounding flight of woodpecker.

Voice: Call, a series of loud, ringing notes descending in pitch, *pew-pew-pew* . . . often described as a laugh; rarely drums.

Habitat: Deciduous woods, parkland, meadows and commons with scattered large trees, orchards; from sea level to mountains.

Nesting: 4–9 white eggs, in an unlined tree hole, excavated by both birds, usually in rotten wood.

Range: Breeds almost throughout Europe except Iceland, northern Scandinavia, and Ireland; also in North Africa and western Russia, and from Turkey to Iran. Sedentary.

The Green Woodpecker usually makes its presence known with its "yaffle," as its far-carrying laugh used to be known. It feeds in trees like other woodpeckers, but also on the ground, where it hops heavily with an upright stance, searching for ants. It is sometimes found in open country far from trees.

404 **Black Woodpecker**
(*Dryocopus martius*)

Description: 18″ (45 cm). Largest European woodpecker. Plumage *black* except on head: Male has entire crown crimson, female a small crimson patch on back of head. *Eye yellow, bill ivory* with dark tip. Unlike rest of woodpeckers, *straight flight* with quick wingbeats. Characteristic silhouette (long neck and long, tapering tail) distinguishes it from similar-sized crows.

Voice: A loud, far-carrying downslurred note, *keeah,* when on tree; in flight, a strident, hollow *kruh-kruh-kruh,* each note somewhat trilled. Mating call, loud *keet-keet-keet* . . . , resembling Green Woodpecker but not descending at end. Drums vigorously.

Habitat: Mature coniferous forests, mixed forests, and beech woods, especially in mountains.

Nesting: 4–6 white eggs, in large unlined tree hole excavated by both birds.

Range: Breeds from Spain (local), central and eastern France, and Scandinavia east across Eurasia to eastern Siberia, Japan, and China. Mainly resident, but some wander in winter.

A very noisy bird, it calls loudly and has a sustained, far-carrying, sonorous drumming. The vigorous hacking sounds made while excavating grubs can be heard for a considerable distance.

409, 411 **Great Spotted Woodpecker**
(*Dendrocopos major*)

Description: 9″ (23 cm). The standard black-and-white woodpecker in Europe. Forehead buffy-white, *crown black, red band across nape in male.* Black bar across white face joins bill to nape and mantle. Upperparts, wings, and tail black, with *white patch on scapulars* and narrow white barring on flight feathers and sides of tail. Below, unstreaked buffy-white with black shoulder bar; *undertail coverts red.* Juvenile has crimson crow[n].

Voice: Usual note, a sharp *chik,* normally given singly, sometimes repeated rapidly and run together into a chatter. Drums loudly in spring.

Habitat: Coniferous and deciduous woods, open areas with hedgerows and scattered trees, parkland, orchards, gardens.

Nesting: 3–8 white eggs, in an unlined tree hole.

Range: Eurasia, breeding from Spain, Britain, and Scandinavia across northern Asia to the Pacific; also parts of North Africa. Mainly resident; some northern birds move south in winter.

The most common woodpecker in much of Europe, it is tolerant of man, living in gardens and taking suet from bird tables. It feeds mainly on the larvae of wood-boring insects, but supplements its diet with nuts and seeds, opening pine cones to get at the seeds.

412 Syrian Woodpecker
(*Dendrocopos syriacus*)

Description: 9″ (23 cm). Same size as Great Spotted, with similar black crown, large white wing patches, red nape band on male; *lacks black bar across white cheeks,* has paler, more pinkish undertail coverts, and less white at sides of tail. Syrian, Great Spotted, and Middle Spotted juveniles all have red crowns, but Syrian has *black border to red crown, pale pink breast band,* and some streaking on flanks.

Voice: Normal call, *chick* or *chwick,* less sharp than similar Great Spotted call; also a chattering *cheerrrrr,* and other more conversational notes, *tupitupitup, kewick-kewick-kewick.* Also drums.

Habitat: Open mixed woodland, parks, gardens; frequently near cultivated areas and around human habitation.

Nesting: 5–7 white eggs, placed in an unlined tree hole.

Range: Resident in southeastern Europe from Austria and Romania south to northern Greece. Also breeds in southwestern Asia from Turkey to Iran.

It is the closest European relative of the Great Spotted Woodpecker, which it replaces in parts of the Middle East. Where their ranges overlap in southeastern Europe, the Great Spotted prefers mountain forests while the Syrian remains in the more open lowlands. This species is extending its range north and west.

---

410 Middle Spotted Woodpecker
(*Dendrocopos medius*)

Description: 8½″ (21 cm). Slightly smaller than Great Spotted and Syrian woodpeckers, with similar *white wing patches* and *black back*. Differs in having *pale red crown without black border* (in other two species only juveniles have red crowns but both have black borders) and *black neck bar not extending to bill or nape.* Reduced amount of black on head and neck gives *pale-headed look.* Underparts buffy-white, *shading into pink on belly* and undertail coverts. *Flanks streaked black.*

Voice: A chattering call, *kick-kick-kick* . . . and in spring a nasal "song," *wait, wait.* . . . Seldom drums.

Habitat: Mature deciduous woods, especially oak, beech, and hornbeam, with a preference for large old trees. Not a mountain species.

Nesting: 4–8 white eggs, placed in an unlined tree hole, usually more than 12 feet (3.6 m) above the ground.

Range: Patchily distributed from southern Sweden, France, and northwestern Spain east across central and southern Europe to Greece and western Russia. Also southwestern Asia from Turkey and the Caucasus to Iran. Resident.

Though not uncommon in its preferred habitat, and with a rather broad distribution in Europe, it is nonethel difficult to find. It lives in dense woods, usually some distance from human habitation, and spends most of its time in the higher branches, where its call signals its presence.

408 White-backed Woodpecker
(*Dendrocopos leucotos*)

Description: 10″ (25 cm). Largest of the spotted woodpeckers, with a proportionately longer bill; crown red in male, black in female. *White lower back and rump* (barred black-and-white in *D. l. lilfordi* of Pyrenees and southeastern Europe). Upper back black, wing black with broad white bars on flight feathers but *no white shoulder patch.* Black neck stripe reaches bill but not nape. Underparts white, shading to pale pink on belly and deeper pink on undertail coverts, *heavily streaked with black.* Juvenile has pale pink crown and undertail coverts.

Voice: A sharp *jick* or *juck,* similar to Great Spotted. Drumming starts with single blows and then accelerates.

Habitat: Deciduous trees in pure or mixed woods; rarely coniferous forests.

Nesting: 3–6 white eggs, placed in unlined hole excavated in rotten wood of trunk or branch.

Range: Eurasia. Breeds from central Scandinavia, southern Germany, and Balkans east across north-central Asia to Sea of Okhotsk and Japan; isolated population in Pyrenees and Italy. Distribution in mountains of southern Europe patchy.

Rather uncommon, with a discontinuous distribution across Eurasia, this species apparently specialises in insects living in rotten tree trunks and hence may be unable to adapt to "managed" forests, where rotten trees are removed. It feeds chiefly on the larvae of wood-boring insects, but in late summer also eats nuts and berries.

407, 414 **Lesser Spotted Woodpecker**
(*Dendrocopos minor*)

Description: 5¾" (14 cm). Smallest European woodpecker. *Very barred appearance,* especially in flight; *black-and-white barring on back and wings; lacks white shoulder patch.* Underparts white, with black streaking on flanks. *No red on undertail coverts* (unique among spotted woodpeckers). Forehead brownish-white; male's crown dull red laterally bordered with black; female's fore-crown whitish, hind-crown black. Juveniles have some red on crown.

Voice: Normal call, a repeated, high-pitched *peee,* reminiscent of Wryneck but less ringing. Less often, a rather weak *chick,* similar to but softer than Great Spotted. Drumming weaker but faster than Great Spotted.

Habitat: Open deciduous and mixed woods; parkland, old orchards, large gardens.

Nesting: 3–8 white eggs, in an unlined tree hole, usually in rotten wood, at varying heights from ground.

Range: Breeds from Scandinavia, Britain, and Spain east across northern Eurasia to the Pacific and southeast to Iran; also North Africa. Sedentary.

An elusive treetop inhabitant, the Lesser Spotted is most often detected by its call or drumming. It moves from one branch to another with a distinctive fluttering flight. In its search for insect larvae, it often hangs from twigs that seem too slim to support its weight.

---

413 **Three-toed Woodpecker**
(*Picoides tridactylus*)

Description: 8¾" (22 cm). Mainly black and white, but plumage pattern different from spotted woodpeckers. *Dark-headed appearance: cheeks and malar stripe black;*

crown black in female, *black wi[illegible] yellow centre in male. Rump and cen[illegible] of back white* in northern birds (*P.* [illegible] *tridactylus*), *barred black-and-white* i[illegible] birds from central European mounta[illegible] (*P. t. alpinus*). *Wings and tail mainly black,* with fine white spotting on fligh[illegible] feathers and outer tail feathers. Underparts white, with *black barring on flanks.* No red in plumage.

Voice: Normal call, *kuck* or *kick,* more muted and less sharp than spotted woodpeckers. Drums slowly. Calls and drums infrequently.

Habitat: Chiefly coniferous forests, sometimes mixed or deciduous, preferring burnt-over areas with many dead trees.

Nesting: 3–6 white eggs, in unlined hole in tree trunk, usually well above ground.

Range: Holarctic, breeding from Scandinavia across northern Eurasia to Kamchatka and Japan, and in North America. Also mountains of central Europe from the Alps to the Carpathians and northern Greece.

Uncommon and difficult to see, it tends to stay in one spot for a considerable time, quietly and methodically working over trunks and branches of dead trees, stripping off the bark to reach the insects and larvae underneath. It is the only European woodpecker to have three toes; all others have four.

LARKS
(Alaudidae)

75 species: mainly Old World. Eight species breed in Europe. Small, terrestrial birds of open country, nesting on ground. Bill thin or stout, according to the species' diet; hind claw usually long. Plumage usually cryptic, brown earth colours above, paler below; sexes similar in most species. Larks walk or run on the ground and do not hop or wag tail. Many species are beautiful songsters. Often in flocks outside breeding season.

541 Calandra Lark
(*Melanocorypha calandra*)

Description: 7½" (19 cm). Large and *heavily built*, with stout, pale bill and short tail. Dark grey-brown streaked blackish above; white below, with *large black patches at sides of neck* almost meeting in centre. Breast buffy, with indistinct dark streaks. *Broad, triangular wings brown above* and *blackish below*, with *white trailing edge* conspicuous in flight.

Voice: Call, a dry, nasal *chirrup* similar to Skylark, often introduced into the song, which is a continuous stream of bubbling notes, some musical and liquid, others rattling and trilling, incorporating mimicry.

Habitat: Arid stony regions, dry pastures, grassy steppes with low vegetation, cultivated ground, wasteland.

Nesting: 4–7 off-white eggs heavily spotted brown, in cup nest of dead grass with lining of finer materials, placed in hollow, usually sheltered by vegetation.

Range: Breeds in Mediterranean Europe north to southern France, coastal Yugoslavia, Romania, and the Ukraine; also in North Africa and southwestern Asia. European birds resident.

An extremely fine singer, the Calandra Lark's abilities have been overshadowe by its two better-known relatives, the Skylark and the Woodlark. It is particularly skilled at imitating a variety of other birds. When singing, it usually circles high in the air.

540 **Short-toed Lark**
(*Calandrella brachydactyla*)

Description: 5½" (14 cm). Small, *pale sandy* lark with *short, yellowish bill* and no crest, often with *flat-headed* appearance. Underparts whitish with pale buffy band across breast, *usually unstreaked,* but juveniles and a few spring adults have fine streaks on breast, *not extending to flanks. Small black patch at sides of breast* (often not visible). A dark brown bar across centre of wing is often apparent. In flight, dark brown tail contrasts with pale upperparts. In the hand, *long tertials* covering all but one or two primary tips are diagnostic.

Voice: Normal calls, a grating *tchirrup* or *krri-krrip* and a hard *chititip;* also a plaintive *pee-yi* or *pee-yu*. Song, a repetition of short, variable phrases, some rattling, some more liquid, usually given in high, undulating flight.

Habitat: Open sandy and stony ground, dunes, dry salt marshes and mud flats, steppes.

Nesting: 3–5 eggs varying in colour from white to yellow and olive, speckled with brown and grey, in cup of dry grasses and roots, lined with down, hair, and feathers, placed on ground, usually sheltered by vegetation.

Range: Summer visitor to Europe; range extends from Spain and southern France to Balkans and Romania; winters in Africa. Also breeds in North Africa and central Asia from Turkey and southern Russia to Manchuria.

A large gap separates its range from the formerly conspecific Red-capped Lark (*Calandrella cinerea*) of eastern and southern Africa. There are also notable plumage differences, the Red-capped

Lark having a bright red cap and neck patch and marked white eye-stripe.

539 **Lesser Short-toed Lark**
(*Calandrella rufescens*)

Description: 5½" (14 cm). Similar to Short-toed Lark but *darker and greyer,* with *much streaking on breast and flanks,* lacking dark breast patch and wing bar; *tertials much shorter*.

Voice: Call, a grating *prrrit*. Song, faster, rolling, and more musical than Short-toed, with much longer phrases, including some mimicry, given closer to ground in less undulating flight.

Habitat: More arid and stony country than Short-toed; edges of deserts, steppes, dry pastures, wasteland.

Nesting: 3–5 eggs, ground colour varying from white to yellow and olive, speckled brown and grey, in grass nest placed on ground by tuft of vegetation.

Range: Summer visitor to southern Spain north to Ebro delta; vagrant elsewhere in Europe. Winters in Africa. Also breeds in southwestern and central Asia east to Manchuria, and in North Africa.

As with the Short-toed Lark, this species is replaced in eastern Africa by a closely related bird (Somali Lark, *C. somalica*) with which it is sometimes considered conspecific. Both are highly gregarious, often forming large mixed flocks in winter.

528 **Crested Lark**
(*Galerida cristata*)

Description: 6¾" (17 cm). *Similar to Skylark* but plumage generally more uniform, less streaked, and *shape different* (most obvious in flight), with *plumper body, broad, rounded wings,* and *short tail. Crest, longer and more pointed,* always conspicuous. Bill somewhat longer, slightly decurved. *Outer tail feathers buff,* not white. *Underside of wings orange-buff*. Lacks white trailing edge to inner wing.

Voice: Call, a liquid *twee-whee-tu*, with emphasis on the second note. Song, less musical, more disjointed, with shorter phrases than Skylark; often mimetic.

Habitat: Open arid country, stony wastes, sand dunes, arable land, sometimes grassland, often in dry wasteland near human habitation and industry.

Nesting: 3–5 greyish-white or buff-white eggs speckled with brown and grey, in loosely constructed ground nest of dry grasses lined with fine grass and hair, placed in depression.

Range: Resident throughout most of continental Europe north to southern tip of Scandinavia and Estonia. Also in southwestern and central Asia east to northern India and Korea, and in northern Africa.

It perches more often than the Skylark on bushes, fences, buildings, and sometimes trees, regularly singing from these perches rather than in flight. Occasionally it sings on the wing but does not have the Skylark's soaring display flight.

527 **Thekla Lark**
(*Galerida theklae*)

Description: 6¼″ (16 cm). Very similar to Crested Lark; slightly smaller, *shorter bill;* greyer, *less sandy above,* and whiter, less buffy below; breast streaking marks more distinct. Underwing grey rather than buff.

Voice: A liquid, musical song, sometimes uttered in short phrases, but often in continuous stream, with much mimicry but without grating trills of Skylark.

Habitat: Rocky hillsides and other broken ground, thick ground vegetation; occurs at higher elevations than Crested and not around human habitation.

Nesting: 3–6 eggs, indistinguishable from Crested Lark, in shallow ground nest of grass and plant stems, lined with finer material.

Range: Resident in southern Spain, Portugal, extreme southern France, and Balearic Islands. Also in North Africa, Ethiopia, Somalia, and Northern Kenya.

Larks are notoriously difficult to identify, because they have similar plumages and spend much time on the ground, obscured from view among the vegetation. Thekla and Crested larks are best distinguished by differences in habitat, behaviour, and voice. Thekla has a more musical song and sings more often from the air in a circular display flight.

538 Woodlark
(*Lullula arborea*)

Description: 6″ (15 cm). Smaller than Skylark, with finer bill; *much shorter, white-tipped tail;* and pinkish legs. Rounded crest often not visible; *buffy eye-stripes meet on nape.* Brown above, with dark streaks; buffy-white below, streaked on breast; *black-and-white mark near bend of wing.* Juvenile spotted above and on breast.

Voice: Call, a liquid *tilooeet.* Song, a succession of variable phrases of 10–20 repeated notes, pure, mellow, and fluty, descending and accelerating within the phrase, *tee-yu, tee-yu, tee-yu . . . looee, looee, looee . . . twee, twee, twee . . . lulululululu. . . .*

Habitat: Open country with scattered trees, forest edge, scrubby hillsides, heaths, weedy farmlands, olive groves.

Nesting: 3–5 greyish-white eggs spotted brown and grey, in nest of grass and moss lined with fine grass and hair, placed on ground under shelter of vegetation.

Range: Breeds throughout southern and central Europe, north to southern Britain and southern Scandinavia, retiring from northeastern part of range in winter. Also breeds in western Asia from Russia and Turkey to Iran, and North Africa.

Its song is considered one of the loveliest in Europe, and though not as effervescent or powerful as the Skylark's, it is richer and more melodious, with a hint of melancholy. In its song flight, the bird rises in widening spirals, then flies in broad circles over its territory, singing continuously, eventually descending in the same manner. It also sometimes sings from a bush or tree, often at night.

529 Skylark
(*Alauda arvensis*)

Description: 7″(18 cm) Most common European lark; rather large, brown above with black streaks, buffy-white below with streaked breast. *Short crest.* Distinguished from all larks except Calandra by *white trailing edge of inner wing;* from Woodlark, Crested, and Thekla larks by longish tail with *conspicuous white outer tail feathers.* Juvenile scaly above with short tail and no crest.

Voice: Call, a liquid, rather metallic *prrrip* or *chirrrup.* Song, bubbling and effervescent, a continuous outpouring of high-pitched trills and warblings, lasting up to 5 minutes.

Habitat: Grasslands, grain fields, pastures, moorlands, sand dunes, salt marshes, alpine meadows.

Nesting: 3–5 greyish or greenish-white eggs thickly spotted with olive or brown, in a shallow grass nest lined with finer grasses and hair, placed in hollow on ground among vegetation.

Range: Breeds throughout Europe except Iceland and northern Scandinavia, retiring from northeastern areas in winter. Also breeds in North Africa and in southwestern and north central Asia.

The Skylark rises from the ground with a special fluttering flight, singing as it ascends to great heights, hovering and circling. It sings through most of the descent, at the end plummeting silently to earth with folded wings.

526 **Shore Lark or Horned Lark**
(*Eremophila alpestris*)

Description: 6½″ (16 cm). Slim, with *yellow forehead, face, and throat; black cheeks and breast band.* Male has black band on forehead and two erectile "horns" (lacking in winter). Pinkish-brown above, white below, with contrasting *blackish tail, conspicuous in flight.* Female has less black. In winter, both sexes have black areas mottled with yellow. Juvenile speckled above and below, with yellow about face.

Voice: Various thin calls: *tsweep, chup,* and *tsiti.* Song, a rather tuneless jingle, starting with separate notes and accelerating into a trill, usually given in flight.

Habitat: Breeds on bare stony ground above tree line in mountains and at lower levels on dry, grassy tundra of the high Arctic. Winters along coasts and on adjacent open ground.

Nesting: 2–5 greenish-white eggs with pale brown spots and often blackish lines, in loose cup nest of dry grass, lined with down and hair, in hollow on ground sheltered by vegetation.

Range: Holarctic, breeding from Scandinavia across arctic Russia to eastern Siberia, and from Balkans and Turkey through Middle East to Himalayas and Manchuria. Also breeds in Morocco and North America. Birds from northern Europe winter along southern shores of North and Baltic seas.

This species and Temminck's Horned Lark of North Africa and the Middle East are unique in having males with "horns" on their heads during the breeding season. The horns are normally raised only during courtship or aggressive displays.

SWALLOWS AND MARTINS
(Hirundinidae)

80 species: worldwide. Five species nest in Europe. Small, slim aerial birds with long, pointed wings and forked or notched tail. Bill very small but mouth wide, adapted for catching insects in flight. Neck and legs short, feet weak. Sexes similar. Expert fliers. Gregarious, most nesting colonially and forming large flocks on migration. Many nest on man-made structures. Often perch on wires.

396, 399 Sand Martin
(*Riparia riparia*)

Description: 4¾″ (12 cm). Smallest and most slender swallow in Europe. Brown above, pure white below, with contrasting *brown breast band.* Tail slightly forked, lacking white spots of Crag Martin; flight more rapid, wings narrower than Crag Martin.

Voice: A dry, rather nasal twitter, prolonged into a loose song during breeding season.

Habitat: Open country, usually near fresh water, nesting in cliffs, riverbanks, roadsides, quarries, ravines.

Nesting: 3–7 white eggs in a loose nest of straw, plant stems, and feathers in a nest chamber at the end of a 2–3′ (60–90 cm) tunnel, excavated by both sexes in bank of earth or sand.

Range: Holarctic. Summer visitor to all of Europe except Iceland, extreme northern Scandinavia and Corsica, wintering in tropical Africa. Also breeds in North Africa, most of northern and central Asia, and North America.

Often nests in quite large colonies, but its distribution is somewhat patchy, being limited by nest-site availability. It does not enter towns and villages like other swallows.

Crag Martin
(*Ptyonoprogne rupestris*)

Description: 5¾″ (14 cm). Larger and chunkier than Sand Martin with broader wings and tail. Brown above, *light brown below* with dark streaks on throat but *no dark breast band;* darker on belly and undertail coverts. *Blackish underwing linings* contrast with paler flight feathers. *Row of white spots near tip* of almost *square tail*. Juvenile similar to adult but tinged rufous.

Voice: Normal call, a short, dry *trrit;* also slurred notes, *chwee* or *weeoo*.

Habitat: Mountain cliffs up to about 6,500′ (2,000 m), gorges, ravines, rocky outcrops, sea cliffs, sometimes buildings in towns.

Nesting: 4–5 white eggs with a few small red and grey spots, in half-cup nest of mud lined with down, feathers, and plants, stuck to vertical rock face under overhang. Nests colonially.

Range: Breeds in southern Europe north to France and Austria; also in northwestern Africa and across central Asia to Manchuria and China. Winters in Mediterranean area.

It is the European representative of a closely knit group of brown, rock-loving martins, also including the Pale Crag Martin (*P. obsoleta*) of North Africa and the Middle East, the African Rock Martin (*P. fuligula*) of Africa south of the Sahara, and the Dusky Crag Martin (*P. concolor*) of India. All nest in similar situations, though Indian and African birds are more partial to houses.

401, 402 **Swallow or Barn Swallow**
(*Hirundo rustica*)

Description: 7½″ (19 cm). The common swallow of Europe, easily identified by *long, deeply forked tail with elongated outer tail feathers* and *ring of white spots* around base of fork. Dark, glossy blue above and creamy-white below; *brick red forehead and throat; dark blue breast band.* Length of outer tail feathers variable. Juvenile duller, with yellow-brown throat and shorter tail.

Voice: Call, a high, thin *tswit,* rapidly repeated and becoming a twitter. Song, a bustling medley of liquid, twittering notes, often ending with a dry, "watch-winding" trill. Sings from rooftops and telephone wires, as well as in the air.

Habitat: Open country, especially farmland, usually near water. During breeding season in vicinity of buildings, bridges, and similar nest sites.

Nesting: 3–6 white eggs lightly spotted with brown and grey, in an open cup of mud strengthened with straw or plant fibres, lined with feathers, situated in building or under bridge, placed on a support and usually attached to a vertical surface.

Range: Summer visitor, breeding throughout Europe except Iceland and northern Scandinavia; wintering in Africa. Also breeds in North Africa, across Asia east to the Pacific and in North America.

The abundant and familiar Swallow originally probably nested in caves, but today rarely uses such natural sites, having long since adapted to man-made structures. It nests in barns, garages, and other buildings as long as there is constant access to the outside, quickly becoming accustomed to people, animals, and vehicles.

---

400 Red-rumped Swallow
(*Hirundo daurica*)

Description: 7″ (18 cm). Similar to Swallow but tail lacks white spots; streamers a little shorter. Flight more leisurely. Crown and upperparts glossy blue-black; flight feathers and tail dull blackish; *rump reddish-buff with whitish-buff uppertail coverts; thin collar and eye-stripe chestnut;* underparts uniformly buff except for black undertail; *lacks dark throat.*

Voice: Call, a grating *queek* or *quake.* Song, slower, deeper, and less liquid than Swallow, given in short bursts rather than a continuous stream but includes a similar "watch-winding" trill.

Habitat: Open rocky country, cliffs, caves; also buildings and bridges; usually near water.

Nesting: 3–5 white eggs, sometimes with fine red-brown spots, in a flask-shaped nest with entrance tunnel, made of mud and grass, lined with feathers and wool, attached to overhanging surface.

Range: Widespread in the Old World, breeding from Spain, extreme southern France, Italy, and Balkans, south over much of Africa and east to Japan, China, and India. Spreading in Europe. European birds winter in Africa.

It readily adapts to man-made structures, but is not dependent on them like the Swallow, also using caves, overhanging rocks, and other natural nest sites. Its nest is closed, attached to a cave roof, building ceiling, underside of bridge, or other horizontal surface.

398 House Martin
(*Delichon urbica*)

Description: 5″ (13 cm). Blue-black above with *conspicuous white rump;* pure white below. Tail rather short, with shallow fork. Juveniles browner on upperparts.

Voice: Call, a chirpy *pirrit;* alarm call, a high-pitched *seep.* Song low and twittering.

Habitat: Nests principally around human habitation; also cliffs, quarries, and in open rocky country, up to 4,900–6,600′ (1,500–2,000 m) in mountains.

Nesting: 4–5 (sometimes 2–6) white eggs, in a half-cup nest of mud mixed with grass, lined with feathers and dry grass, attached to vertical surface just under overhang, leaving only narrow entrance hole at top.

Range: Summer visitor to North Africa and western and central Eurasia, breeding throughout Europe except Iceland and northern tip of Scandinavia. Replaced in eastern Asia by Asiatic House Martin (*D. dasypus*), often considered conspecific. European birds winter in Africa.

A common and familiar bird, closely associated with man, it nests colonially under the eaves of houses and around buildings in towns and cities. In early evening, it often rises high in the air, circling in large flocks with Swifts. Its flight is distinctive, sailing and fluttering rather than swooping and twisting like a Swallow or dashing like a Swift.

PIPITS AND WAGTAILS
(Motacillidae)

50 species: worldwide, but mainly Old World. Eight species breed in Europe, one other a visitor. Small, slender, mainly terrestrial birds with longish tail constantly wagged. Pipits outwardly resemble larks, having plain brown plumage, often spotted or streaked; wagtails are black, white, grey, or yellow. Sexes similar or dissimilar. Flight undulating; walk or run on ground. Many species have aerial song flight. Gregarious after breeding season. Feed mainly on insects and spiders.

---

537 Richard's Pipit
(*Anthus novaeseelandiae*)

Description: 7″ (18 cm). *Large pipit,* with *long, pale yellowish-pink legs* and *long tail.* Upperparts brown with dark streaks, *breast and flanks buff, usually with bold blackish streaks;* belly white. Moustachial stripe black, bill somewhat shorter and stouter than Tawny Pipit. *Long hind claw,* twice as long as that of Tawny Pipit.

Voice: Call, similar to Tawny Pipit but harsher, a loud, rasping *schreep.* Song, usually given in song flight high in air, a repetition of monotonous phrases, *cheer-cheer-cheer, chi-chi-chi-chi.*

Habitat: Wet grasslands on its Asian breeding grounds; in similar open country, especially near coast, when it wanders to Europe.

Nesting: 4–6 eggs varying in colour from grey-green to dull pink, thickly spotted with olive, brown, or grey, in nest of grass and moss placed in hollow on ground under grass tussock.

Range: Breeds from Siberia south to India, China, Malaysia, Australia, and New Zealand; also in Africa. Annual visitor to western Europe, especially Britain.

The formal scientific descriptior based on a bird from New Zealar hence its Latin name. Though onl vagrant in Europe, through much c Africa it is the most common pipit.

536 Tawny Pipit
(*Anthus campestris*)

Description: 6½" (16 cm). A rather large but slim, wagtail-like pipit, with long legs and long tail. *Light sandy-brown above,* with only *indistinct streaks; sandy-buff below, with no streaks.* Well-marked pale buff eyebrow; legs yellowish or pale flesh-coloured. Juvenile closely resembles Richard's Pipit but slightly paler.

Voice: Call, a ringing *tslee-up;* and a variety of other notes, more strident than other pipits': *tseep, tsup.* Song, a loud *chivee-chivee-chivee,* usually given during descent from display flight.

Habitat: Dry open country with scattered scrub, wasteland, sand dunes, vineyards, and other cultivation in arid areas.

Nesting: 4–5 whitish eggs spotted with brown and violet, in nest of grass and weeds, lined with hair, placed in depression under protective vegetation or lump of earth.

Range: Summer visitor, breeding from southern Europe north to southern shores of the Baltic Sea and southern Sweden. Also breeds in North Africa and southwestern Asia. Winters in northern tropical Africa and Middle East.

Its cryptic colouration helps the bird blend with its dry, sandy habitat. Once thought of as a great rarity in England (though now found to occur annually), it became the subject of a 1940s British movie, *The Tawny Pipit,* a melodrama showing the electrifying effect of the appearance of such a rarity.

530 **Tree Pipit**
(*Anthus trivialis*)

[D]escription: 6″ (15 cm). Warm brown above, with dark streaks; *buff-white below; yellowish suffusion* on breast, with bold blackish streaks on breast and flanks; buff eyebrow; white outer tail feathers; *flesh pink legs*. Very similar to Meadow Pipit; best distinguished by voice.

Voice: Call, a harsh *teez,* very different from softer, squeaky notes of Meadow Pipit. Song, usually given in song flight, a series of repeated musical phrases and trills, ending with characteristic double notes, *seea-seea-seea* . . .

Habitat: Breeds in parklands, heaths, and other types of open country with scattered trees; also at edges of woods and in clearings. On migration also in open country.

Nesting: 4–6 speckled, blotched, or streaked eggs of variable colour, usually brown, grey, or reddish, laid in grass and moss nest lined with fine grass and hair, placed in depression on ground.

Range: Breeds throughout northern and central Europe (except for Iceland and Ireland), south to northern Spain, Italy, and northern Greece; also in southwest and central Asia, east to eastern Siberia. Winters in tropical Africa and India.

Tree Pipits have the short, curved hind claw characteristic of birds that perch in trees, while Meadow Pipits have the long, straight hind claw of ground birds. During its song flight, it flies up from its tree perch for 100′ (30 m) or so and then sings as it planes down in parachute fashion, with spread tail and raised wings.

531 **Meadow Pipit**
(*Anthus pratensis*)

Description: 5¾″ (14 cm). Upper parts brown with olive or greenish tinge, streaked darker; underparts greyish-white with blackish streaks on breast and flanks. Eyebrow whitish; outer tail feathers whit… *dark pinkish-brown in adult, flesh p… juvenile.* Juvenile similar to adult … with yellowish tinge.

Voice: Call, a high, thin, squeaky *sip* or *sip-* (or, with a stretch of the imagination, *pipit*), often repeated; also a louder *tissip*. Song, usually given in song flight, an accelerating series of high tinkling and piping notes ending in a trill.

Habitat: Breeds in open country where there is some grass—pastures, moors, heaths, sand dunes. In winter, appears in lowlands, marshes, water meadows, sewage farms, and along the coast.

Nesting: 3–6 eggs variable in colour, usually some shade of brown or grey, sometimes spotted, in grass nest placed on ground near protective vegetation.

Range: Breeds widely in northern and central Europe but not in the south, and across Russia to western Siberia. Winters in southern Europe and North Africa; some western European birds resident.

Meadow and Tree Pipits are best distinguished by voice. To learn the calls, remember that a Meadow Pipit says *pipit* and Tree Pipit says *tree.* During song flight it rises from the ground about 100′ (30 m) and then glides back down again, singing all the way.

532 Red-throated Pipit
(*Anthus cervinus*)

Description: 5¾″ (14 cm). Similar in size and shape to Meadow and Tree pipits, but has *bolder and blacker streaks above and below. Rump boldly streaked* (uniform in Meadow and Tree pipits). In breeding season, *throat and breast become rust-red,* extent and intensity varying individually. Legs pale yellowish or pinkish.

Voice: Normal call, a characteristic fine *tseeze,* somewhat resembling call of Tree Pipit but much higher and more drawn out. Alarm, a short *chup*. Song, a series of different phrases, some trilling, some buzzy, usually given in song flight.

Habitat: Tundra, marshes, and wet meadows, often with dwarf vegetation, cultivation near water. Frequently close to coast.

Nesting: 5–6 eggs, ground colour varying from grey-blue and olive-grey to buff, variably marked with spots or hairlines, in grass nest lined with finer grass, placed in depression in shelter of grassy hummock.

Range: Breeds from northern Scandinavia east across arctic tundra of Asia to Bering Straits. European breeders winter in Africa.

When not in breeding plumage, the Red-throated Pipit can be easily overlooked among migrating flocks of more common pipits.

533, 534, 535 **Rock and Water Pipits**
(*Anthus spinoletta*)

Description: 6½″ (16 cm). Water Pipits (*spinoletta* group) in breeding plumage grey-brown above, with some darker streaks; *white below, with pinkish flush on breast and no streaking;* eyebrow and outer tail feathers white. In winter, brown above; white below, with some streaking on breast. Rock Pipits (*petrosus* group) *darker* than Water Pipits, olive-brown above, and *much more heavily streaked below;* outer tail feathers grey; winter and summer plumages similar.

Voice: Call, a high *tsip* or *seep,* less thin and squeaky than Meadow Pipit; song similar to Meadow Pipit, but less musical—a series of rather dry repeated phrases—given in similar song flight, rising from and returning to ground.

Habitat: Water Pipits breed on alpine meadows and bare or rocky mountain slopes above tree line; Rock Pipits nest along rocky coasts. In winter, both occur in a variety of damp situations: wet grasslands, edges of lakes, fresh and salt marshes, sewage farms, sandy and muddy coasts.

Nesting: 4–6 greyish-white eggs thickly spotted with brown and grey, in a grass and moss nest, lined with fine grass, placed in cliff hole or in hollow in ground under vegetation.

Range: Water Pipit: high mountains of central and southern Europe, dispersing north and south of breeding areas in winter. Rock Pipit: coasts of northern and western Europe, wintering on coasts of western and southwestern Europe. The species also breeds across Asia to the Pacific, and in North America.

The pipits are an Old World group that has colonised the New World at least twice. The latest invader is the Water Pipit, which has evolved into a well-marked subspecies, *A. s. rubescens,* formerly known as the American Pipit. In North America it occupies both lowland tundra and alpine meadows.

518, 519, 520, 522, 523 **Yellow Wagtail**
(*Motacilla flava*)

Description: 6½″ (16 cm). Yellow-green above and yellow below. Females duller than males; both sexes duller in winter. Juveniles browner than females, with buffy throat and dark brown bib. Breeding males differ in head colour. British race, *M. f. flavissima,* has yellow-green crown and cheek patch and yellow eyebrow; Balkans race, *M. f. feldegg,* has black crown and sides of head. Other races have crown and nape various shades of grey; grey to blackish face patches, with or without white eyebrow.

Voice: Call, a ringing *tsweep;* also *tswip* and *tsirr.* Short song consists of call notes interspersed with more musical ones.

Habitat: Water meadows, salt marshes, damp grasslands, cultivated fields near water; often associated with cattle.

Nesting: 4–6 whitish or pale buffy eggs finely speckled buff or brown, in ground nest of grass and roots, lined with hair, in depression among thick vegetation.

Range: Breeds throughout Europe (but local in interior) except for Iceland and northern and western parts of British Isles; also in Morocco, Egypt, and Asia east to the Pacific and western Alaska. Summer visitor; winters in Africa and southern Asia.

Winter males, females, and juveniles of the many European races are extremely difficult to separate in the field, and most observers call any member of this complex simply a Yellow Wagtail. The male in spring displays in a courtship flight with fluffed-out feathers, shivering wings, and spread tail.

---

521 Grey Wagtail
(*Motacilla cinerea*)

Description: 7″ (18 cm). Slimmer and more graceful than other wagtails, and with *longer tail.* Male in breeding plumage, *blue-grey above* with *yellow-green rump,* white eyebrow and moustachial streak, *black throat,* and *bright lemon yellow underparts.* Female similar but with whitish throat. In nonbreeding plumage, both sexes have creamy-white throats and whitish-buff underparts. Undertail coverts bright lemon yellow. Juvenile pale buff below, with faint streaking at sides of breast, but with *yellow lower belly and undertail coverts.*

Voice: Call, similar to *chissick* of White Wagtail but thinner, shorter, higher-pitched, more metallic *tizzy* or a single *dzit;* also a less grating call, *ching* or *chipp.* Song, a series of shrill notes, *tsee-tsee-tsee, zee-zee-zee,* etc., delivered from perch or in flight.

Habitat: Breeds principally along fast-flowing rocky mountain streams, but also in lowlands where water flows swiftly. In winter, along rivers and canals, margins of lakes and ponds, and around sewage farms.

Nesting: 4–6 buff or grey-white eggs often with dark streaks, in a nest of moss, twigs, leaves, and grass, lined with hair, placed in cliff hole, wall, or bank cavity.

Range: Breeds in Europe, north to Scotland and southern Sweden, Poland, and southwest Russia; also in North Africa, and across Asia to the Pacific.

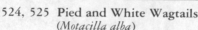

Like the White Wagtail, it tolerates man, readily nesting on man-made structures such as bridges, weirs, and walls of old mills; in winter, may occur by ponds in parks.

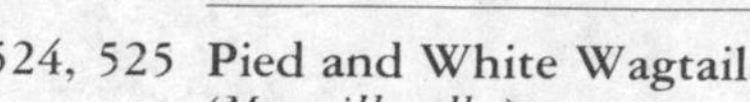

524, 525 **Pied and White Wagtails**
(*Motacilla alba*)

Description: 7″ (18 cm). Breeding adults have black crown, nape, throat, and upper breast; white forehead, face, sides of neck, and underparts; black wing with double white wing bar; black tail with white outer feathers. Back and rump pale grey in White Wagtail, *M. a. alba* (continental Europe), black or dark grey in Pied Wagtail, *M. a. yarrellii* (Britain and Ireland). In winter, throat white, breast white with crescent-shaped black band. Juvenile grey-brown above, with white throat, dark breast band, and greyish-white underparts. Plumage varies according to season, sex, and age in both races, making racial identification difficult.

Voice: Call, a loud, sharp *chissick;* sometimes just a single note, *chick.* Song, a rambling twitter incorporating call notes as well as more musical ones.

Habitat: Open country, usually near water, often around human habitation; in winter, especially on cultivated ground.

Nesting: 4–7 pale-bluish or greyish eggs, in nest of moss, leaves, twigs, and grass, lined with hair and feathers, placed in cavity in cliff, bank, wall, or tree.

Range: Breeds throughout Europe. Partial resident in west and south, summer visitor in north and east; many migrate to Africa for winter. Also breeds in Morocco and across Asia to Pacific.

This attractive bird is familiar and popular and a frequent subject in Oriental art. In Africa it is considered good luck if the closely related African Pied Wagtail, *Motacilla aguimp,* nests in the village, and bad luck if it doesn't.

WAXWINGS
(Bombycillidae)

3 species: temperate regions of Northern Hemisphere. One species breeds in Europe. Small arboreal birds with conspicuous crest, short bill, plump body, and short tail and legs. Soft, silky plumage mainly grey, brown, and cinnamon, with waxy red tips to secondaries. Sexes similar. Posture upright; flight direct and rapid. Gregarious, forming large flocks in winter. Feed chiefly on berries, and in breeding season also on insects caught in air. Remarkably tame.

612 **Waxwing**
(*Bombycilla garrulus*)

Description: 7″ (18 cm). Plump and short-tailed, with *prominent crest.* General colour pinkish-brown, paler below; *throat and narrow eye-line black; lower back, rump, and uppertail coverts grey; tail broadly tipped yellow.* Wing dark with white and yellow markings; undertail coverts rusty-brown. Juvenile brown, streaked paler below, with short crest, black eye-line with white border above and below. Shape in flight similar to Starling.

Voice: Call, a high-pitched, thin trill, *tsirrrr* or *sreeeee.* Song, a succession of trills mixed with chirping and other notes. Birds in flocks often call together, producing loud chorus.

Habitat: Breeds in northern coniferous and birch forests; in winter, found in parks, gardens, hawthorn hedges, berry-bearing trees, and bushes.

Nesting: 4–6 pale grey or grey-blue eggs with fine blackish markings, in nest of twigs, lichens, and moss, well-concealed on horizontal branches of conifer or birch.

Range: Breeds from northern Scandinavia and Russia east to eastern Siberia; also northwestern North America. Winters

south in varying numbers to Britain, France, Germany, and Romania.

Though known to few Europeans in its northern breeding range, the Waxwing in its periodic winter irruptions is found throughout northern and central Europe. It regularly comes into towns and villages in search of berries, being particularly fond of rowan, mistletoe, *Cotoneaster*, and *Pyracantha*.

DIPPERS
(Cinclidae)

5 species: temperate regions of Eurasia and New World. One species breeds in Europe. Small aquatic birds with stout body, short wings and tail, and long legs. Plumage dense. In constant bobbing motion—hence the common name. They swim on surface and underwater, using wings, and when submerging either wade or dive into water from surface or from rock. Able to walk underwater.

484 Dipper
(*Cinclus cinclus*)

Description: 7″ (18 cm). *Plump, short-tailed* bird; *blackish-brown above;* head lighter; *throat and breast white.* Belly blackish-brown; British and central European race has chestnut band on upper belly. Juvenile greyish-brown above, whitish below, with darker mottling.

Voice: Calls, a loud *zit-zit* and a metallic *clink-clink.* Song, high-pitched and wren-like, with sustained warbling notes mixed with grating ones.

Habitat: Breeds along fast-flowing streams of mountains and hills, usually resident; in winter, occasionally found along lowland streams and lakeshores.

Nesting: 3–6 pure white eggs, in large, globular nest of moss and grass, lined with dead leaves, placed on rock face or in crevice, under bridge or waterfall; riverbanks.

Range: Breeds in most of Europe except Iceland and some lowland areas in north. Also breeds in North Africa and parts of Asia. Mainly resident; some altitudinal and local movements in winter.

It is usually seen perched on a rock in midstream, bobbing up and down, or flying low over the water on rapidly whirring wings. It dives to feed on stream bottoms, mainly on larvae of aquatic insects.

WRENS
(Troglodytidae)

60 species: all except one in New World. One species breeds in Europe. Small to very small land birds with slender bill, short, rounded wings, and tail typically short and often cocked. Plumage mainly brown with dark barring on wings and tail; often black and white stripes on face. Sexes similar. Usually solitary or in pairs. Most species rather shy, skulking in low vegetation. Wrens are among the world's most brilliant songsters. Most are hole nesters; often polygamous.

---

460 Wren
(*Troglodytes troglodytes*)

Description: 3¾″ (9 cm). *Tiny, plump* bird, with *very short tail frequently cocked.* Warm brown above, paler buffy-brown below; *faint bars* on flanks, wings, and tail; indistinct pale eye-stripe. Juvenile similar, but more mottled below.

Voice: A hard, grating *tick,* repeated singly or in groups of 2 or 3; in alarm call, *ticks* are accelerated into scolding trill. Has amazingly loud song for such a small bird, a varied succession of high, clear, almost piercing notes interspersed with trill, usually lasting 5 seconds or longer.

Habitat: Variable. Typically low, thick cover in woods, heaths, parks, hedgerows, and gardens; also open rocky situations on mountain slopes, cliffs, rocky coasts, offshore islands.

Nesting: 5–6 white eggs with red-brown spots, in domed nest with side entrance, constructed with moss, grass, and leaves and lined with feathers, placed in low vegetation, rock crevice, or tree hole.

Range: Breeds throughout Europe, including Iceland, except in northern Scandinavia: also breeds in North Africa, Asia, and northern North America. Mainly

resident, but northernmos[illegible] south within breeding range[illegible]

Of the 60 species of wrens, this[illegible] only one to occur in the Old Wo[illegible] It is a recent invader from North America, and finding no competitor[illegible] from its own family, it has spread int[illegible] a wide range of habitats from which it is excluded in the New World.

ACCENTORS
(Prunellidae)

12 species: temperate regions of North Africa and Eurasia. Two species breed in Europe. Small, streaked, sparrow-like birds but with thin bill. Plumage mainly brown and grey; sexes similar. Most species montane and only partly migratory, remaining in mountains all year. Terrestrial, creeping along ground with shuffling walk and short hops. Often flick wings and tail.

586 Dunnock or Hedge Accentor
(*Prunella modularis*)

Description: 5¾″ (14 cm). A very plain grey and brown bird with *thin bill. Head grey,* with brown crown and ear coverts; *upperparts rich brown* streaked black; *underparts grey,* with some streaking on flanks; narrow, buffy wing bar. Juvenile duller and more spotted, especially around head.

Voice: Call note, a thin, high-pitched *tseep.* Song, a flat, tuneless jingle lasting about 5 seconds.

Habitat: Thick undergrowth and bushes in woods and gardens, hedgerows, scrubby hillsides, alpine shrubbery, and coniferous scrub.

Nesting: 3–6 deep bright blue eggs usually unmarked, in nest of twigs, grass, and roots lined with moss, hair, and wool, placed in thick bush.

Range: Western Palearctic, breeding throughout Europe except Mediterranean region and extreme north; also in western Russia, Caucasus, Turkey, and northern Iran. Mainly resident but northern birds move south in winter as far as North Africa.

The archetypical "little brown bird," it is often mistaken for a female House Sparrow by the beginner until the thin bill and grey underparts are noticed. It feeds mainly on the ground, always near cover, turning over dead lea… search of beetles, caterpillars, wor… and spiders. In winter, it feeds ma… on seeds. Abundant in many areas, … a regular inhabitant of gardens.

585 Alpine Accentor
(*Prunella collaris*)

Description: 7″ (18 cm). A large, colourful version of the Dunnock, with grey head and underparts, *white throat spotted with black,* and *orange-chestnut streaking on flanks.* Upperparts grey-brown, with darker streaking; has thin, *double white wing bar* and prominent dark bar across greater coverts; *tail tipped with white.* Juvenile duller, with grey, unspotted throat.

Voice: Calls, a dry *jrrrt* or *jujut* and a shriller *chrreee.* Song resembles Dunnock's but louder, more tuneful. Sings from ground or in short song flight.

Habitat: Breeds on rocky mountain slopes, with or without scrubby vegetation, between tree limit and snow line. Winters in similar habitat at lower elevations, usually in mountains, sometimes lowlands.

Nesting: 3–5 pale blue eggs, in cup nest of grass and roots, lined with moss, lichens, and feathers, placed in crack or hollow in rocks, sometimes under sheltering vegetation.

Range: High mountains of central and southern Europe from Spain to Romania and Balkans; also in northwest Africa and discontinuously across Asia from Turkey to Himalayas, China, and Japan.

Quiet and inconspicuous, it has cryptic colouration that enables it to merge into its rocky habitat. It is familiar to skiers at alpine resorts, where it frequents huts on the upper slopes, picking up table crumbs.

THRUSHES
(Turdidae)

310 species: worldwide, except New Zealand. Twenty-three species breed in Europe, one other is a visitor. Small to medium-sized land birds with rather slender bill. Plumage of adults highly variable; juveniles are spotted. Arboreal and terrestrial, found in both wooded and open country, feeding on insects, worms, and berries. Most species migratory. Usually solitary but some (especially larger species) flock on migration and in winter. Thrushes are among the world's finest songsters.

---

497 Rufous Bush Robin
(*Cercotrichas galactotes*)

Description: 6″ (15 cm). *Upperparts warm buff* (grey-brown in eastern race (*C. g. syriacus*); darker centres to flight feathers and lighter margins to wing coverts. Rump warmer brown, merging into *rufous tail broadly tipped with black and white.* Underparts light buff. Head marked with *creamy eye-brow, thin black eye-stripe,* and brown ear patch. Long legs; horn-coloured bill; sloping fore-crown. *Long tail frequently cocked.*

Voice: Harsh *tec*. Song, a musical twittering warble uttered from prominent perch or in parachute-like song-flight descent.

Habitat: Scrub, olive groves, palms, cacti; often associated with prickly pear.

Nesting: 4–5 white eggs spotted with brown, laid in untidy cup low in bush or prickly pear.

Range: Breeds in Spain, Greece, and southern Yugoslavia, North Africa east to southern Siberia, and Middle East to Pakistan. Also Africa in belt south of the Sahara. Summer visitor to Mediterranean, wintering in tropical Africa. Vagrant farther north.

Its propensity to nest among prickly pears is an interesting adaptation, sinc

these plants were firs
the New World only 5
This is the northernmost
genus that is widespread i
where the birds are known as
robins.

470, 489 **Robin**
(*Erithacus rubecula*)

Description: 5½" (14 cm). Small, rather long-legged brown bird with *striking orange-red breast and face.* Upperparts dull khaki; line separating breast and upperparts dull blue-grey; belly white. Sexes alike. Juvenile has same chunky shape but has brown spots and pale bars above and below.

Voice: A repeated *tick;* song, a series of high-pitched warbles, trembled notes, and fluty trills.

Habitat: Woods, hedges, bushes, gardens.

Nesting: 5–6 white eggs speckled with brown, laid in neat cup hidden in bush or on ledge, shelf, or open-fronted nest box.

Range: Europe, except for farthest north, through Russia to western Siberia and southeast to Iran. A partial migrant, birds from north and east wintering west to Britain and France or south to North Africa.

A secretive forest bird over much of its range; in the Mediterranean region, the Robin is mostly confined to what little natural woodland remains. It has learned to live alongside man in Britain and other parts of western Europe, becoming a tame and familiar garden bird.

499 **Thrush Nightingale**
(*Luscinia luscinia*)

Description: 6½" (16 cm). Upperparts brown, becoming more rufous on tail, but generally *darker and less warm brown than similar Nightingale;* underparts dull white, lightly *mottled brown on breast and flanks.* Legs and bill dark; thin, inconspicuous, cream-coloured eye-ring.

ice: Song begins with flute-like *peu-peu-peu* like Nightingale and has similar virtuosity and variety, but also shows some of the loudness and hard notes of Great Reed Warbler. Does not build up to a crescendo.

Habitat: Swampy thickets of alder and birch, damp undergrowth in woods and beside water.

Nesting: 5 variable blue-grey to buff eggs, faintly mottled, laid in cup hidden among leaf litter on ground.

Range: Summer visitor to eastern Europe from southern Finland to Yugoslavia, west to southern Sweden and Denmark, and east to Romania. Migrates southeast to winter in East Africa.

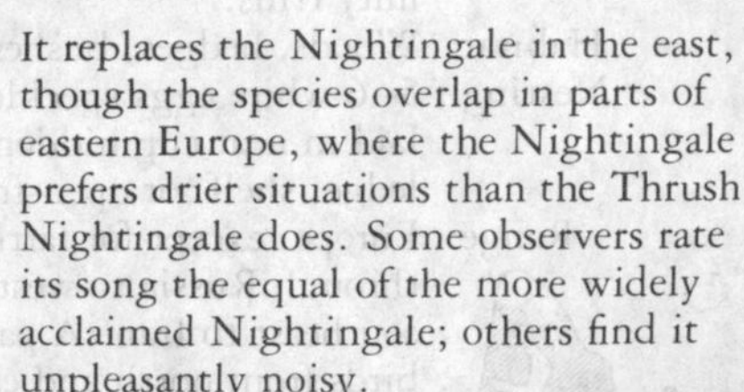

It replaces the Nightingale in the east, though the species overlap in parts of eastern Europe, where the Nightingale prefers drier situations than the Thrush Nightingale does. Some observers rate its song the equal of the more widely acclaimed Nightingale; others find it unpleasantly noisy.

498 Nightingale
(*Luscinia megarhynchos*)

Description: 6½" (16 cm). A secretive bird; more often located by song than by sight. Upperparts warm brown; *tail rufous contrasting with upperparts* but not as red as Redstart's tail. Underparts dull cream with *uniform* darker wash on chest, but *no mottling.* Faint, pale eye-ring. Frequently feeds on ground with upright posture like Robin, often with tail cocked. Juvenile spotted above and below.

Voice: Song preceded by a flute-like *peu-peu-peu* rolling into a beautiful liquid warbling ending in a crescendo. Call notes, a whistling *whit* and a harsh *queck;* a low *turr* of alarm.

Habitat: Deciduous woods, copses, hedgerows.

Nesting: 4–5 greyish-blue eggs cover… red-brown markings, laid in c… ground hidden in ivy or leaf litt… among shrubs.

Range: Temperate and Mediterranean Euro… from Britain east to southwestern Siberia and Afghanistan. Summer visitor, wintering in tropical Africa.

The voice of this magnificent songster can be mistaken only for that of the similar Thrush Nightingale, which replaces this species in the east. Part of its reputation may be due to its propensity to sing at night, when its voice is not hidden among the songs of other birds.

467, 468 **Bluethroat**
(*Luscinia svecica*)

Description: 5½" (14 cm). Varying throat and breast colourations. Europe has red-spotted form, *L. s. svecica* (Scandinavia) and white-spotted form, *L. s. cyanecula* (central and southern Europe). All subspecies brown above, with prominent *whitish eyebrow. Tail often held cocked,* showing *rufous sides to base.* In male, *chin and upper breast blue,* bordered below with *black, white, and red breast bands.* In middle of blue throat is *white or red spot.* Female similar, but with only *a little blue* on throat; black moustachial stripe, broadening into *spotted black necklace* on breast.

Voice: A harsh *tack* and softer *wheet.* Song, warbling with some metallic, high-pitched discordant notes. Highly mimetic.

Habitat: Damp thickets, hedges, ground vegetation, bushy scrub, tundra with dwarf shrubs.

Nesting: 5–7 pale green-blue eggs speckled with light brown, laid in cup on ground or at base of bush.

Breeds disjointedly in western Europe (Spain, France), and from central Europe across Palearctic to Bering Sea and northwestern Alaska. Migrant, wintering in Mediterranean region and from Africa to Asia.

This secretive little bird is fond of dark, damp places, but it can also be found in dry bush country. It frequently feeds on the ground at the base of dense vegetation.

---

469 Red-flanked Bluetail
(*Tarsiger cyanurus*)

Description: 5½″ (14 cm). Male, *metallic navy blue above,* with *royal blue* eyebrow, rump patch, and shoulders. *Throat pure white,* rest of underparts silver-grey, with bright *orange wash along flanks.* Female brown above, with white throat and eye-ring and *orange flanks.*

Voice: A *tic-tic.* Song, pleasant with repeated phrases in the middle.

Habitat: Coniferous forests with damp thickets in Europe. In winter, parkland and deciduous forest along streams.

Nesting: 3–5 white eggs, sometimes speckled with brown, laid in cup of grass and moss hidden in bank.

Range: Breeds from eastern Finland across Asia to Japan. Migrates southeast to Asia; vagrant to Europe outside breeding range.

It perches in trees, swoops to the ground in search of prey, and quivers its tail like a Redstart. It also skulks among thick vegetation like a Bluethroat, coming out into paths and clearings to feed.

473, 476 Black Redstart
(*Phoenicurus ochruros*)

Description: 5½″ (14 cm). Colour highly variable, but in Europe usually constant. Male has *dull sooty-black upperparts,* black wings with *bold* ... *face and breast* tha... belly and white on ... and *rust-red tail.* Faint ... Female *dull sooty-brown,* ... *tail.* Resembles Redstart be... below. Constantly quivers tai... Redstart.

Voice: Song, a vibrant warble with squea... metallic whistles. Calls, a *tsip* and a rapid *tick-tick-tick.*

Habitat: Cliffs, walls, rocky outcrops, burnt-over ground, demolished city centres, and industrial wasteland.

Nesting: 4–6 white eggs, laid in loose cup in rock crevice or on ledge.

Range: Breeds in temperate and Mediterranean Europe north to England and southern Scandinavia, east to central Asia. Partial migrant, leaving much of Europe, except the south and west, to winter in northern Africa.

This most adaptable of birds is known in Germany as the "house redstart," indicating a certain intimacy with man, whereas in other parts of the Continent it inhabits rocky outcrops and cliffs. It colonized Britain just before World War II, where it took first to cliffs, then to blitzed sites in London. Recently it has moved to railway sidings. It also breeds in many large European cities.

474, 475 **Redstart**
(*Phoenicurus phoenicurus*)

Description: 5½" (14 cm). A slim bird that *constantly quivers its rust-red tail;* can be confused only with Black Redstart or Nightingale. Male has *dove grey crown and mantle,* white forehead, and short white eyebrow; grey-brown wings; *black chin, neck, lores, and ear coverts. Underparts rust-red,* becoming buff-white on lower belly. Female brownish above, and creamy-buff below, with *light eye-ring, rust-red tail.*

…-tuc or *wheat* call note; song, a …ng melody of warbled metallic …es.

…Woodland edges both coniferous and deciduous, parks, orchards, stone walls, ruins.

…sting: 6–7 pale blue eggs laid in cup in tree hole or hole in wall, building, broken tree stump, or nest box.

Range: Breeds across almost all of Europe, east to Iran and central Siberia; also North Africa. Summer visitor migrating south to tropical Africa.

This species is plentiful wherever nest holes are available. The cutting out of dead trees to "tidy up" woodland has eliminated many nest holes, with a resultant decline in numbers, possibly aggravated by drought conditions in winter quarters.

492, 493 **Whinchat**
(*Saxicola rubetra*)

Description: 5″ (13 cm). Upperparts striped dark; *white bar across wing;* prominent *whitish eyebrow,* dark ear coverts, and *white or creamy moustachial streak. Underparts rufous-orange extending to chin. Tail dark with triangular white patches at sides of base.*

Voice: A snappy *tic-tac* and a soft *peu.* Song, a squeaking warble similar to Stonechat.

Habitat: Open country, heaths, mountain grassland, wasteland; on migration, also on cultivated land.

Nesting: 5–7 pale blue eggs speckled with red-brown, laid in cup hidden on ground beneath small bush.

Range: Breeds in Europe except extreme north and south extending east into central Siberia and Iran. Winters in tropical Africa.

Though superficially like the Stonechat, it lacks dark chin and has a light eyebrow, field marks that clearly distinguish it. Additionally, it always seems slimmer and more elegant than its plump relative. It perches openly on low ground cover.

472, 491 **Stonechat**
(*Saxicola torquata*)

Description: 5″ (13 cm). Plump chat; *dark brown above,* with indistinct mottling on mantle, whitish rump, and *white bar* across wing. *Black head and chin* (brown in female) almost separated from mantle by *broad, white incomplete collar* (less distinct in female). Underparts rufous-orange, becoming whiter on belly. Unlike Whinchat, lacks eyebrow and white on tail.

Voice: A metallic *whit-sac-sac.* Song, a tinkling warble with repeated notes, produced from high perch or in flight.

Habitat: Commons and heaths, particularly with gorse, broken areas with hedges, and embankments; agricultural land in winter and on migration.

Nesting: 5–6 light blue eggs speckled with brown, laid in cup on or near ground sheltered by dense bush.

Range: Though absent from much of Scandinavia and Russia, breeds across Palearctic from Atlantic to Pacific; also breeds in Africa south of the Sahara. Partial migrant, wintering in Mediterranean. Resident in western Europe and Mediterranean.

Though still numerous in many parts of its range, it has seriously declined in others, partly due to changing agricultural techniques that allow the ploughing of marginal land. It perches in a highly visible position on top of a bush, telephone wire, or fence post, often flicking its wings and tail and uttering its grating call. The name derives from the call, which resembles the sound of two stones being struck together.

495 **Isabelline Wheatear**
(*Oenanthe isabellina*)

Description: 6½" (16 cm). *Large, strikingly pale buff-coloured* wheatear; sexes alike. Resembles female Wheatear, but best identified by paler wings and ear coverts; broader black terminal band on tail; *larger bill;* neat black line between eye and bill; and more *upright stance.*

Voice: A nasal *jeee,* and chirping and whistling notes, all unlike other chats. Song, sustained and variable, including mimicry.

Habitat: Dry grasslands, bare hills, and semideserts, preferring sandy areas in winter.

Nesting: 4–6 light blue eggs, laid in cup of grasses in natural hole, cleft in bank, or mammal hole.

Range: From Greece, Turkey, and southern Russia east through Middle East to Pakistan, central Siberia, and Mongolia. Winters in Africa and Oriental region.

The male has a remarkable display flight in which it flutters in the air around the female and then suddenly drops like a stone. It then leaps up and down around its mate with drooping wings and tail fanned. It usually sings from a rock.

479, 494 **Wheatear**
(*Oenanthe oenanthe*)

Description: 5¾" (14 cm). Male has *dove grey crown and mantle;* broad, black mark through eye extends over ear coverts. Wings black, and *white tail has broad, black terminal band* extending toward white rump on central feathers. Underparts white, washed light orange on breast. Female has brownish upperparts and dark (not black) mask and wings; generally buff-brown, paler below; with *white rump;* tail pattern like male. Male much browner in winter, more like female.

Voice: A harsh *chack* and a penetrating *heet*. Song, a warble of sweet and harsh notes, often given in flight.

Habitat: Open country, moorland, heaths, commons, grassy downs, dunes, tundra, and rocky terrain above tree line.

Nesting: 5–6 pale blue eggs, laid in cup in hole among rocks or in mammal hole.

Range: Almost circumpolar: absent only from north-central Canada. Summer visitor throughout Europe, migrating south to tropical Africa.

One of the most successful members of its genus, it is the only wheatear to have colonised the New World. It has invaded North America from both east and west, into Greenland and Baffin Island, inland to Quebec, and through Alaska to the Yukon. Except for a few stragglers, both populations return to the Old World, the Greenland subspecies making a transatlantic crossing toward Africa and Iberia in winter.

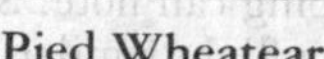

Pied Wheatear
(*Oenanthe pleschanka*)

Description: 5¾" (14 cm). Male, boldly patterned black and white; *black chin, throat, face, mantle, and wings;* white crown, nape, breast, and belly. Rump and tail white, with narrow, black terminal band and central tail feathers. Female buff-brown, with tail pattern of male (narrow, black terminal band and much more white than other female wheatears).

Voice: A harsh *zac*. Song, a varied warble, with much mimicry.

Habitat: Rocky hillsides, bare rocky plains, and cliffs, usually with scattered bushes.

Nesting: 4–6 light blue eggs speckled with rufous-brown, laid in cup in hole or rock crevice.

Range: Shores of Black Sea in Romania and Bulgaria to southern Siberia, Iran,

Afghanistan. Summer visitor to Europe, migrating south to Africa.

Though it is readily separated from other European wheatears, it is similar to several species that breed outside European boundaries but may occur as vagrants. The Mourning Wheatear (*O. lugens*) has a broader tail band, is buffish (not white), and is found across North Africa; and Finsch's Wheatear (*O. finschii*) has a buff (not black) back and occurs in Turkey.

480, 481, 496 **Black-eared Wheatear**
(*Oenanthe hispanica*)

Description: 5¾" (14 cm). Male dimorphic, having a black mask or black throat. Wings black; body and underparts vary from whitish to deep orange-buff (never grey), forming *striking pattern of dark and light*. Tail has narrower black terminal band and *more white at sides* than Wheatear. Female resembles Wheatear, but is distinguishable by darker cheeks and wings.

Voice: A rasping call note. Song uttered in display flight similar to Wheatear: a series of grating and warbling notes in short phrases.

Habitat: Stony ground, often high mountainsides, arid plains, dry riverbeds. On migration, also on cultivated land.

Nesting: 4–5 pale blue eggs lightly speckled with reddish-brown, laid in cup in hole or under a stone, sometimes at base of bush.

Range: Mediterranean Europe and North Africa east through Turkey to Middle East and Iran. Summer visitor, vagrant in northern Europe.

It is similar in its pale black-throated form to the Desert Wheatear, but the Black-eared's tail is extensively white, while the Desert's tail is almost entirely black.

Desert Wheatear
(*Oenanthe deserti*)

Description: 5¾" (14 cm). Light sandy-buff wheatear that varies considerably in colouration geographically. Male's upperparts rich sandy to light buff; *rump white; tail solid black,* which best separates it from similar Black-eared Wheatear. *Face and throat black,* not connecting to black of wings; underparts sandy-buff to off-white.
334 Female similar to other wheatears, but also distinguished by black tail.

Voice: A quiet whistle; song, a series of short, plaintive phrases often uttered in flight.

Habitat: Rocky or sandy ground with scant vegetation. In winter and on migration, also among crops.

Nesting: 4–5 light blue eggs speckled with brown, laid in cup in natural or man-made hole.

Range: Breeds from North Africa east through the Middle East to Afghanistan and Mongolia. Partial migrant, vagrant north or west to Europe.

It is an irregular vagrant as far north and west as Britain, and may be overlooked in the Mediterranean. Preferring flat, hard ground in North Africa, it may also be found in Iberia in similar habitat.

---

485 **Black Wheatear**
(*Oenanthe leucura*)

Description: 7" (18 cm). *Very large, all-black* wheatear, marked with *white rump, white undertail coverts,* and *black-and-white tail pattern.* Female sooty-brown.

Voice: A *pee-pee* call note. Song, a short, rich warble of melodious notes.

Habitat: Dry semidesert, mountain slopes, sea cliffs.

Nesting: 3–6 light blue eggs speckled rufous-brown, laid in cup hidden in hole on or near ground. Builds a small wall of pebbles across the entrance.

Range: Southern Spain and extreme southern France; also northeast Africa. Resident.

Unlike any other European wheatear in colouration, it does resemble the White-crowned Black Wheatear of North Africa, which is accidental in Europe. Though many males of that species have a white crown, females and immatures have a black one. However, the African bird is smaller and has completely white outer tail feathers, while the Black Wheatear's are black-tipped.

---

471 Rock Thrush

(*Monticola saxatilis*)

Description: 7½" (19 cm). Short-tailed thrush. Male is boldly coloured: *Head, chin, and throat light blue;* wings sooty-black; mantle dark blue-black; *rump white.* Tail has dark centre with *rust-red outer tail feathers. Underparts rust-red.* Bill and legs dark. Female *light brown, underparts marked with darker streaks and crescents;* tail rufous.

Voice: A *chack-chack* call note; song, a flute-like warble, repeated and uttered in flight.

Habitat: Rocky areas in mountains and down to sea level in east, but less often on coasts than Blue Rock Thrush.

Nesting: 4–5 light blue eggs, laid in cup hidden in hole among rocks or in wall.

Range: Breeds in southern Europe north to France, Switzerland, and Poland and east to northern China. Summer visitor wintering in Africa; vagrant in north.

It tends to inhabit higher regions than the Blue Rock Thrush in the western parts of its range, but even there it may be found on bare cliffs on migration. At all seasons it is a shy bird, easily overlooked.

477, 478 **Blue Rock Thrush**
(*Monticola solitarius*)

Description: 8″ (20 cm). Male marked with various *shades of blue,* paler on the head, becoming darker on back and breast; wings and tail blackish. Black bill and legs. At a distance, appears all black. In flight, *shape similar to Starling,* with triangular pointed wings and short tail. Female grey-brown, underparts marked with bars and spots, dark brown tail.

Voice: Call note, *chack-chack.* Flight song, loud, slow, and repetitive with a flute-like quality.

Habitat: Rocky outcrops near seacoasts and in mountains. Frequents ruins in many parts of the world, and even some European cities, such as Rome.

Nesting: 4–5 light blue eggs, laid in cup hidden in rock cleft or hole in wall.

Range: Southern Europe and North Africa east across central Asia to China and Japan. Mainly resident in southern Europe.

Though it perches openly on the tops of rocks, the Blue Rock Thrush usually attracts attention by its song. Its dark colouring and habit of staying stock-still make it difficult to spot even when its whereabouts are known.

483, 488 **Ring Ouzel**
(*Turdus torquatus*)

Description: 9½″ (24 cm). Remarkably similar to Blackbird, but male has broad, *white crescent on chest,* faint scaly pattern on mantle and underparts, and *pale edgings to inner wing feathers* noticeable in flight and when perched. *Bill yellowish.* Female similar to female Blackbird, but greyer, with *dull white crescent* on chest and silvery wings and feather margins.

Voice: A piping call and a Blackbird-like *tack-tack,* often becoming a chatter. Song, repeated phrases of piping notes interspersed with chuckling.

Habitat: Mountain slopes and moors, usually at some altitude, among junipers and other hardy shrubs, but also above tree line.

Nesting: 4–5 pale blue eggs spotted with rufous-brown, laid in cup against bank, under ledge, or in shrub.

Range: Breeds in Scandinavia, northwestern Britain and Ireland, and mountains of central and southern Europe, east through Turkey to Iran. Winters in Mediterranean basin.

The "blackbird" of the uplands, this summer visitor to the hill districts of Europe is an early migrant and appears in even the most unlikely of habitats. The silvery wings distinguish it from the Blackbird even at a considerable distance.

486, 505 **Blackbird**
(*Turdus merula*)

Description: 10″ (25 cm). Male *all-black* with *yellow bill* and *yellow eye-ring.* Female dark brown above, *paler below with indistinct dark mottling,* but never has clear-cut breast spots like Song and Mistle thrushes.

Voice: A scolding *tak-tak* and a rattle of alarm. Song, a series of mellow, fluty whistles combined in a variety of phrases.

Habitat: Woods, hedgerows, scrub, gardens, playing fields.

Nesting: 4–5 pale blue eggs thickly speckled with rufous, laid in nest cup of grass and mud placed in fork of tree, shrub, or ledge of building.

Range: Europe, except for extreme north, across central Asia to China. Mainly resident, but partial migrant south to North Africa.

One of the most abundant European birds, it appears in gardens, parks, golf courses, and other areas where short grass provides ideal foraging. It "listens" for worms in typical thrush fashion before darting forward to grab its prey; it also feeds on berries and fruit. Originally a forest dweller, it has greatly increased its population by adapting to suburban conditions.

490 **Fieldfare**
(*Turdus pilaris*)

Description: 10″ (25 cm). Between Song and Mistle Thrush in size; *head, nape, and rump dove grey,* light eyebrow and dark lores. Mantle and wings chestnut-brown, contrasting with grey rump in flight. Tail black; *breast orange-buff, with black streaks* that become "arrows" on white flanks; belly and underwing coverts white; bill yellow, tipped black; legs black.

Voice: A clear, raucous *chack-chack.* Song, a medley of chuckling notes.

Habitat: Woods, particularly birch, at or near tree line; forest clearings, parks, and gardens. In winter, grassland, hedgerows, and farmland.

Nesting: 5–6 pale blue eggs spotted with rufous-brown, laid in mud-lined cup placed in tree fork. Nests in colonies.

Range: From Scandanavia, northern Britain, and eastern France east to central Siberia. Migrates south and west from northern Europe, reaching Iceland, Ireland, and northern shores of Mediterranean.

This characteristic winter visitor to most of Europe arrives in late October and departs by mid-March. In winter, it forms large flocks, often with Redwings, roaming the countryside in search of berries and fruit. It also consumes slugs, worms, insects, and spiders.

501 **Song Thrush**
(*Turdus philomelos*)

Description: 9″ (23 cm). *Upperparts sandy-brown;* chest and flanks warm yellowish-buff, becoming white on belly *heavily spotted* with dark brown. Distinguishable from Redwing by lack of prominent eyebrow and by orange-buff, not rust, underwing.

Voice: A sharp *stit*. Song, a flute-like whistle, with each note or combination repeated 3 or 4 times.

Habitat: Woodland, hedgerows, gardens, parks.

Nesting: 4–6 light blue eggs with black spots in mud-lined nest close to trunk of tree or shrub, or against a building.

Range: Breeds throughout temperate and northern Europe, except extreme north and Mediterranean area, through Russia to central Siberia. Partial migrant south to Mediterranean region.

Although a winter visitor to western and southern Europe, as well as a local breeding bird, the Song Thrush never forms closely knit flocks as the Redwing and Fieldfare do. It may feed alongside these birds and even gather in a small group on a field, but each individual seems to be independent.

500 Redwing
(*Turdus iliacus*)

Description: 8¼″ (21 cm). Resembles slightly larger Song Thrush, but has *bold, creamy eyebrow* and moustachial stripes framing dark ear coverts. Underparts whitish, boldly spotted with dark brown; flanks and underwing *rust-red*.

Voice: Call note, a high-pitched *tsseep;* also a harsher *nuck*. Song, usually includes a phrase repeating 4 or 5 flute-like notes.

Habitat: Young coniferous forests, birches, willows, alders, scrub, and dwarf tundra vegetation. In winter, frequents fields and hedgerows.

Nesting: 4–5 pale blue eggs speckled rufous, in cup nest against tree trunk, in shrub, or on ground.

Range: From Iceland, northern Scotland, and Fenno-Scandia east to central Siberia. Winters south to western and southern Europe, North Africa, Middle East.

Huge numbers of Redwings, often w Fieldfares, move into temperate Europ for the winter. They generally take to the hedgerows when they arrive in autumn, but as the earth gets wetter they find a plentiful supply of animate food on the ground. They are particularly vulnerable to freezing conditions, and extreme cold weather will cause them to migrate south or west even in midwinter.

---

502 Mistle Thrush

(*Turdus viscivorus*)

Description: 10½" (26 cm). Obviously *larger and longer-tailed than Song Thrush. Grey-brown* above with *thin pale edgings to wing feathers. Creamy-white* below, *boldly spotted* with blackish marks. Lacks Song Thrush's orange-buff on breast, and has greyer upperparts. Tail has *pale* outer feathers and corners, obvious in flight, and white underwing coverts.

Voice: A dry *churr.* Song, like Blackbird but louder and less varied, with a distinctive melancholy quality. Lacks repetition of Song Thrush.

Habitat: Woodlands with open glades and large trees; also parks, orchards.

Nesting: 4–5 pale blue-washed eggs spotted with brown, in bulky cup set in major fork of large tree.

Range: Europe, except for Iceland and northern Scandinavia, extending east through Russia and Turkey to central Siberia and Afghanistan. Partial migrant, northern birds wintering south to Mediterranean.

Known by the country name of "Storm-cock," it sings earlier than most other European birds and also breeds earlier. It camouflages its nest in a major fork of a large tree, often at some height from the ground.

WARBLERS AND GOLDCRESTS
(Sylviidae)

300 species: worldwide but mainly Old World. Thirty-six species breed in Europe, two others are visitors. Small birds with slender bill and weak flight. Plumage rather drab, chiefly brown, green, or grey; sexes similar except in *Sylvia.* Juveniles not spotted. Active, arboreal birds feeding on insects and spiders gleaned from vegetation. Most species nesting in temperate regions are migratory. Many are excellent singers.

459 Cetti's Warbler
(*Cettia cetti*)

Description: 5½″ (14 cm). Warbler with uniformly brown upperparts; prominent, rounded tail; and *unmistakable song. Dark reddish-brown above,* with short, whitish eyebrow; silky-white below with buffy wash on flanks and undertail coverts.

Voice: Song begins with startlingly sudden *pwit,* followed by a half-second pause, and a series of equally explosive notes, *pitchewitchewit.* Has a memorable, vigorously fluty quality.

Habitat: Tangled vegetation along edges of marshes, reedbeds, bushes in wet gullies.

Nesting: 4 bright reddish eggs, laid in deep, untidy cup at base of bush, or in deep vegetation up to 3′ (1 m) from ground.

Range: Mediterranean basin extending north to France and Britain and east into southern Siberia and through Middle East to Afghanistan. Resident, and partial migrant into North Africa.

A skulking bird, it is seldom seen before its strident song draws attention to its presence. It has expanded its range spectacularly from the Mediterranean basin through France to southern England in recent years.

464 Fan-tailed Warbler or Zitting Cisticola
(*Cisticola juncidis*)

Description: 4″ (10 cm). Very small, boldly *striped above with light brown and black;* white below, with tawny wash on breast and flanks; *distinctly striped crown.* Best identified in distinctive song flight. *Rufous rump and short, rounded tail* tipped black-and-white.

Voice: Song flight, *tsip-tsip-tsip-tsip,* repeated at length, with dip in hovering flight at each call. May also sing from reed top.

Habitat: Marshy scrub, edges of reedbeds, grain fields and other dry localities.

Nesting: 4–6 variable light eggs, plain or spotted with brown, laid in deep pear-shaped nest made of vegetation bound together with spiders' webs.

Range: Mediterranean region, Africa south of the Sahara, India east to Japan, and south to Australia. Has recently spread north through western France to Brittany. Resident; very rare vagrant away from breeding areas.

It is the only member of the genus *Cisticola* to occur in Europe. Its African name, Zitting Cisticola, more accurately describes it and shows its relationships.

---

465 Grasshopper Warbler
(*Locustella naevia*)

Description: 5″ (13 cm). Streaked warbler similar to Sedge Warbler, but with *indistinct eyebrow* and *distinctive song.* Upperparts *olive-brown, streaked dark;* rump only lightly streaked. Faintly streaked on breast.

Voice: A *distinctive, high-pitched trilling* similar to the winding of a fishing reel, continuing for long periods; similar to songs of Savi's and River warblers.

Habitat: Tangled vegetation in or along marsh edges; also drier land such as heaths, young conifer plantations, and crops.

Nesting: 4–6 white eggs speckled purple-brown,

laid in neat cup hidden in dense vegetation.

Range: Breeds from northern Spain, Ireland, and southern Sweden across most of temperate Europe east to central-southern Siberia. Absent from Mediterranean. Migrant south to Africa and Asia.

A skulking species, the Grasshopper Warbler is more often heard than seen, disappearing into thick vegetation when disturbed. Its nest is notoriously difficult to find. In many parts of Europe it is the only "reeler."

444 River Warbler
(*Locustella fluviatilis*)

Description: 5″ (13 cm). Unstreaked olive-brown above, creamy-white below, with *grey streaking on throat and breast*. Lack of strong rufous colouration and streaked white throat separate it from Savi's Warbler.

Voice: A repeated cricket-like reeling in which *two notes are fast and the next two slower,* producing an effect like the puffing of a distant steam engine.

Habitat: Thickets in wet, dense woodlands and scattered bushes in damp pastureland.

Nesting: 5–6 white eggs speckled red-brown, laid in loose cup on ground.

Range: Breeds from Austria and Germany through eastern Europe into western Siberia. Migrates through Middle East into Africa. Rare in western Europe.

A skulking reeler, the River Warbler is very reluctant to fly. It is most likely to be identified by its song. Its plumage varies, with some dark brown rather than olive-brown individuals.

447 Savi's Warbler
(*Locustella luscinioïdes*)

Description: 5½″ (14 cm). Uniform, featureless warbler with uniformly rich brown

upperparts; creamy-buff below w buffy wash on flanks and across br Short, pale eyebrow; broad, rounde tail. White throat visible when singing. Similar in shape to Grasshopper Warbler but slightly larger, and *uniform, not streaked, above and below.*

Voice: Song, lower-pitched and faster than Grasshopper Warbler, usually in shorter bursts. Starts with series of ticking notes that merge into a continuous buzz.

Habitat: Reedbeds almost exclusively; rarely sedges with scattered bushes. More aquatic than Grasshopper Warbler.

Nesting: 4 white eggs with brown speckling, in neat cup in large loose nest of vegetation placed on or just above swampy ground among reeds or sedges.

Range: Breeds across temperate Europe from England, Spain, and Holland to southwest Asia; also in North Africa. Summer visitor migrating south to Africa. A very rare breeder in southern England.

Often sits high among reed tops and produces its song in full view. Its reeling voice and the lack of streaking facilitate identification.

461 Moustached Warbler
(*Acrocephalus melanopogon*)

Description: 5″ (13 cm). Similar to Sedge Warbler, but *more rufous and more boldly striped* above. *Crown almost black,* accentuated by *broad, white eyebrow* that *widens behind eye* and *ends squarely.* Unstreaked rump. Underparts much like Sedge, but *throat pure white.*

Voice: Song, resembles Sedge Warbler's but lacks rattling and jarring notes. Often introduced or interrupted by a series of flute-like ascending notes, like a Nightingale. Contact note, a *churr.*

Habitat: Reedbeds and marshy edges.

Nesting: 3–6 white eggs speckled light olive-green, laid in deep cup hidden among marsh vegetation.

Range: Breeds in Mediterranean Europe (but not Balkans) east to southern Russia and Iran; also Tunisia. Resident in western Mediterranean; summer visitor in eastern part of range, wintering just south of breeding range.

The Moustached Warbler is similar to Sedge Warbler, but the black crown and white eyebrow are usually distinctive features. When alarmed, often cocks tail.

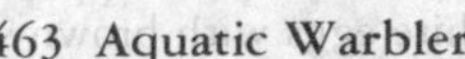

463 Aquatic Warbler
(*Acrocephalus paludicola*)

Description: 5″ (13 cm). Streaked warbler, with *distinctive head pattern* of broad, creamy eyebrow and blackish crown with *clear-cut creamy median stripe.* Upperparts and *rump* boldly *streaked black on rufous-buff,* far more contrasty than similar Sedge Warbler. Underparts warm buff, marked with few *streaks on breast and flanks.*

Voice: Similar to Sedge Warbler but shorter and not so varied.

Habitat: Marshes with thick vegetation, especially sedges. Generally avoids reedbeds except on migration.

Nesting: 5–6 white eggs speckled olive-green, laid in cup hidden among shrubs.

Range: Breeds mainly in eastern Europe west to Holland and northern Italy, extending into adjacent areas of Russia. Migrant south to Africa; irregular visitor to western Europe.

The Aquatic Warbler's head pattern makes it one of the easiest of the "marsh" warblers to recognize in spring. In autumn it can be confused with young Sedge Warbler, which has similar, though less clear-cut, striped pattern on the crown.

462 **Sedge Warbler**
(*Acrocephalus schoenobaenus*)

Description: 5″ (13 cm). Most common *streaked* "marsh" warbler. Upperparts warm brown, with dark streaking; rump unstreaked. Underparts warm creamy-buff. Pronounced *creamy eyebrow.*

Voice: Calls, a loud *tuc* and a harsh *churr.* Song, a varied range of harsh and sweet notes, frequently mixed with imitations of other species. Often sings in flight.

Habitat: Aquatic vegetation, thickets, bushes, reedbeds, generally more varied than Reed Warbler.

Nesting: 5–6 pale green eggs speckled olive, laid in deep cut in reeds, sedges, or bushes.

Range: Breeds over much of Europe (but absent from Iberia and most of Mediterranean), east through Russia to central Siberia. Winters in Africa.

The Sedge Warbler is the standard streaked "marsh" warbler. Others are less or more boldly streaked above; some have a less pronounced eyebrow, and others have one that is even more pronounced. It spends much time creeping about in low, tangled vegetation but will also perch freely on exposed reed stems, bushes, and tall plants.

Paddyfield Warbler
(*Acrocephalus agricola*)

Description: 5″ (15 cm). Closely resembles Reed, Blyth's Reed, and Marsh warblers but *paler and more rufous above,* with *prominent white eyebrow* and *shorter bill.* Legs pale horn.

Voice: Sweet song rather like Marsh Warbler, but lacking harsh notes. Call, *chik-chik.*

Habitat: Not confined to reedbeds; found among reeds, sedges, willows, and low bushes along streams and lakes, and in gardens and other damp situations.

Nesting: 4–5 pale green eggs, speckled and blotched with green and grey, laid in a neat cup of grass and reed fibre, bound to 3 or 4 supporting reeds or branches.

Range: Breeds in northeast Bulgaria, Romania (Danube delta), and from southern Ukraine and Crimea to central Siberia and Mongolia; winters in southern Asia. Vagrant in western Europe.

The Paddyfield Warbler appears to be extending its range westward, as it has recently been discovered breeding on the coast of Romania (Sulina) and in extreme northeast Bulgaria (Lake Sabla). Very rare elsewhere in Europe, it moves southeast from its breeding grounds to winter in Afghanistan, India, China, and southeast Asia.

431 Blyth's Reed Warbler
(*Acrocephalus dumetorum*)

Description: 5″ (13 cm). Difficult to distinguish from Reed Warbler, and especially Marsh Warbler. *Upperparts greyish olive-brown,* becoming greyer through summer. Underparts creamy-brown. Rump often somewhat rufous. Autumn birds warmer brown and even more like Reed Warbler.

Voice: A *chick-chick;* also *tup-tup.* Rich though discontinuous song, like Marsh Warbler, with much mimicry, but with slower speed and tendency to repeat phrases 3 to 8 times like Song Thrush. Song frequently uttered after dark.

Habitat: Similar to Marsh Warbler: bushy, marshy ground with trees; woodland edges, overgrown gardens.

Nesting: 4–5 variably greenish-cream eggs with spots of olive-green or brown, laid in deep cup among thick vegetation.

Range: Breeds from southeastern Finland across Soviet Union to Caspian region. Winters in Asia; vagrant to rest of Europe.

The greyish tinge to the upperparts, together with similar habitat, makes distinction of Blyth's Reed Warbler from the Marsh Warbler particularly difficult unless the song is heard.

443 Marsh Warbler
(*Acrocephalus palustris*)

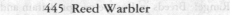

Description: 5″ (13 cm). Upperparts *greenish olive-brown,* with *brown rump* (Reed Warbler is olive-brown above, with rufous rump). Creamy underparts, with whiter throat. Difference in plumage slight; combination of *voice* and habitat best means of distinguishing from Reed Warbler. Legs flesh-yellow, not brown.

Voice: Varied and musical, with fine phrases, liquid trills, and a harsh *za-wee.* Imitates other sounds and songs. Often sings from trees, sometimes at night.

Habitat: Dank areas of bushes, undergrowth, edges of fields, ditches, much less confined to water and reeds than Reed Warbler.

Nesting: 4–5 pale greenish-grey eggs blotched dark green, laid in cup well hidden among bushes.

Range: From Britain (local) and eastern France through central Europe into Russia and south to Iran. Winters in East Africa.

The pure, liquid warbling, varied song without repetitive phrases, and expert imitations of the Marsh Warbler are the surest means of separating Marsh Warbler from Reed Warbler.

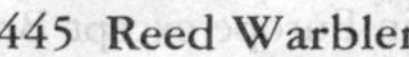

445 Reed Warbler
(*Acrocephalus scirpaceus*)

Description: 5″ (13 cm). The standard *unstreaked* marsh warbler. Rich *brown above,* with rufous tinge to rump; *creamy below,* becoming more buff on flanks and undertail coverts. Richer and warmer in colouration than either Marsh Warbler or Blyth's Reed Warbler, but with a white throat. Best distinguished by voice.

Voice: Series of grating croaks and repetitive phrases interspersed with a few liquid notes. Lacks melodic qualities of Marsh and Blyth's Reed warblers and variety and harshness of Sedge Warbler.

Habitat: More aquatic than other marsh warblers and more confined to pure reedbeds.

Nesting: 4–5 greenish-white eggs heavily blotched olive-green, laid in deep cup suspended among reeds. Semicolonial; nests some distance apart.

Range: Breeds in southern and temperate Europe east to southern Siberia and Iran; also North Africa. Migrates south to tropical Africa.

The slow, deliberate song, lacking the merest semblance of sweetness, is diagnostic.

446 **Great Reed Warbler**
(*Acrocephalus arundinaceus*)

Description: 7½″ (19 cm). Resembles Reed Warbler, but much larger, near to Song Thrush in size. *Warm brown above* with more rufous rump and *clear-cut eyebrow;* creamy-buff below.

Voice: Like Reed Warbler, but louder, slower, and harsher. Strident, with repeated, grating *karra-karra-keek-keek* phrases interrupted by shrill notes.

Habitat: Reedbeds with bushes and open water; on migration, will occupy any available aquatic habitat.

Nesting: 4–6 pale green eggs marked with brown, laid in deep cup suspended among reeds.

Range: Breeds in Europe except Britain and most of Scandinavia east across north-central Asia to Japan; also in North Africa. European birds winter in Africa.

A distinctively loud bird, it often sings atop a reed. It is usually easily distinguished by size from other European warblers, but vagrants may include the almost identical Clamorous Reed Warbler (*A. stentoreus*).

Olivaceous Warbler
(*Hippolais pallida*)

Description: 5¼" (13 cm). *Grey-brown* bird similar to Garden Warbler, but with *whitish "face" and eye-ring* and longer, *more dagger-like bill. Smaller* and more compact than Olive-tree Warbler and lacks pale wing patch. Lacks olive or yellow colouration in all plumages. Short wing only reaches base of tail.

Voice: Song sustained, recalling Sedge Warbler: loud and harsh notes interspersed with more liquid ones. Call note, *chak-chak*.

Habitat: Variable, including gardens, orchards, bushy hillsides, and damp valleys.

Nesting: 3–4 pale grey eggs speckled black, laid in neat cup among outer twigs of bush.

Range: Breeds in southeast Spain and from Yugoslavia and Hungary through Middle East to Afghanistan and northern and Saharan Africa. Winters in tropical Africa.

It is the most widespread of the "grey" *Hippolais* in Europe, despite its spotty distribution. Boldness and deliberateness characterise the genus, helping to distinguish it from other groups of warblers.

Olive-tree Warbler
(*Hippolais olivetorum*)

Description: 6" (15 cm). *Largest Hippolais* warbler. *Brownish-grey* above, with short, whitish eyebrow and eye-ring. Underparts dull greyish-white. Pale edges to secondaries and tertials form *light patch on wing* lacking in similar species except smaller Icterine Warbler. *Long dagger-like bill*. Legs blue-grey; wing long, reaching well beyond base of tail.

Voice: Grating song reminiscent of Sedge Warbler but less strident. Slower and deeper than other *Hippolais*.

Habitat: Olive groves and thorny scrub.

Nesting: 4 pale pink eggs sparsely spotted black,

laid in deep cup in tree or bush.

Range: Breeds in Balkans, Turkey, and eastern Mediterranean, reappearing in northern Iran. Migrates to eastern Africa.

It is shy and secretive like the other members of its genus and a true test of identification ability. It could be confused with immatures of the similarly sized Barred Warbler, but the latter lacks a huge bill and has a longer tail.

---

438 Icterine Warbler
(*Hippolais icterina*)

Description: 5¼" (13 cm). Medium-sized and stocky; with *deliberate* movements, lacking the nonstop action of a *Phylloscopus*. Adults *olive-green above*, with yellowish "face" and eye-ring; *yellow below*, with *bluish legs*. Bill long and dagger-like. Unlike very similar Melodious Warbler, edges of secondaries pale yellow, forming *pale panel on folded wing*, and *long wings* reach well beyond base of tail. Immatures often lack olive-green and yellow colouration, generally greyer with yellow wash on breast.

Voice: Loud, varied song mixed with musical and chattering notes. Similar to Marsh Warbler, but more strident and with repetitive phrases.

Habitat: Hedges, woods, gardens, parks.

Nesting: 4–5 dull pinkish eggs spotted black, laid in deep cup situated in fork of tree.

Range: Breeds from eastern France and southern Scandinavia east across Europe into Russia as far as Urals. Migrates to eastern tropical Africa; irregular farther west in Europe.

It is one of two predominantly yellow-and-green *Hippolais* warblers. The Melodious Warbler replaces it to the west. *Hippolais* warblers are characterized by square, not notched, tail and long dagger-like bill.

437 Melodious Warbler
(*Hippolais polyglotta*)

Description: 5″ (13 cm). Adults *olive-green above* and *yellow below;* very similar to Icterine Warbler, but lacking pale panel on folded wing; shorter *wings do not extend beyond base of tail* when perched. Yellowish "face" and short eyebrow. Immatures less olive-green above, and yellow often reduced to a wash on breast.

Voice: More musical than Icterine, with few harsh notes, and generally quieter, less strident, but more hurried. Call, a House Sparrow-like *churrup* that also appears in song.

Habitat: Hedges, bushes beside streams, woodland clearings.

Nesting: 4–5 dull pink eggs sparsely spotted black, laid in deep cup built into a fork of bush or tree.

Range: Replaces Icterine Warbler in the southwest from France and Italy through Iberia to North Africa. Migrates into tropical West Africa.

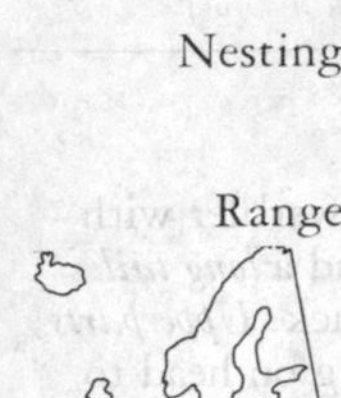

In the breeding season, the Icterine and Melodious warblers are generally geographically distinct, but they do overlap in northeastern France.

---

457 Marmora's Warbler
(*Sylvia sarda*)

Description: 4¾″ (12 cm). Similar to Dartford Warbler, but *underparts grey* (not chestnut-brown). *Male slate-grey* above, with touch of dark brown on wings. *Underparts slate-grey,* shading lighter from breast to belly and undertail coverts. *Female slate-grey above, pinkish below,* with prominent dark spots on chin. Both sexes *cock long tail;* both have red eye-ring. In autumn, juveniles similar to juvenile Dartfords but are paler above and below.

Voice: A harsh *tsig* or *tsick,* unlike Dartford's call. Song, a Whitethroat-like chatter, but sweeter.

Habitat: Scrub and maquis, usually on slopes and near the sea.

Nesting: 3–4 white eggs speckled rufous, laid in neat cup in dwarf shrub near ground.

Range: Confined to Tunisia and the islands of western Mediterranean, Balearics, Corsica, Pantelleria, and Sardinia. Resident, but some migration to North Africa.

Closely related to the Dartford Warbler, it lives in similar habitats and is easily overlooked or misidentified. During the breeding season, it will perch in the open occasionally. Its range is one of the most restricted of any European bird.

455 Dartford Warbler
(*Sylvia undata*)

Description: 5″ (13 cm). Dark scrub warbler with short, rounded wings and a *long tail frequently cocked* above back. *Upperparts dark grey-brown* extending on head to below eye and over cheeks. *Below, rich chestnut-brown,* speckled white on chin. Belly and undertail coverts off-white. Legs yellow-horn; eye-ring and iris (in many males) red. Sexes similar; juveniles in autumn grey below, slightly darker than similar Marmora's Warbler.

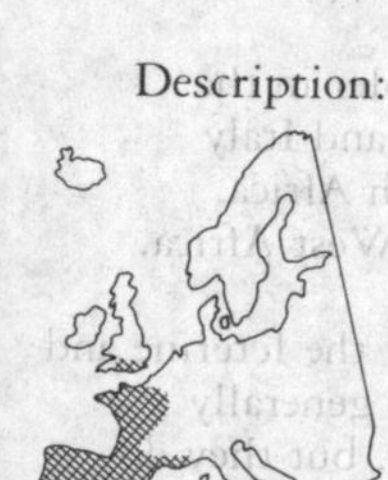

Voice: Call, a harsh *churr, tuk,* and often combinations of the two. Song, a short, grating Whitethroat-like chatter, sometimes uttered in song flight.

Habitat: Heath and scrubland with gorse; or maquis in Mediterranean zone.

Nesting: 3–4 white eggs speckled dark brown, laid in cup hidden in dense vegetation near ground.

Range: From North Africa to southern England through Spain and Portugal, but not Balearics, France, and Italy; resident.

A skulking warbler, it is difficult to locate except when singing in spring. One of the few resident warblers of

Europe, the small British population is almost wiped out periodically by severe winters.

450 **Spectacled Warbler**
(*Sylvia conspicillata*)

Description: 5″ (12 cm). Like a diminutive Whitethroat, but male has slightly darker *grey head with prominent white eye-ring,* grey back, *rufous-edged flight feathers,* pink-buff underparts, white throat and white outer tail feathers. Pale yellow legs. Female similar, but paler brownish-grey above. Female Whitethroat is larger and buffish-brown on back, and female Subalpine has faint moustachial stripe.

Voice: A quiet *tech-tech* or harsh rattle. Song similar to but sweeter, more warbling, and less grating than Whitethroat; similar song flight; also sings from prominent perch.

Habitat: Low scrub in both coastal and inland areas.

Nesting: 4–5 pale tinted eggs speckled olive-grey, laid in a cup at base of bush.

Range: Resident in North Africa and parts of Near East. Summer visitor to western Mediterranean Europe from Spain to Italy.

A true scrub warbler, it is seldom found near tall trees or bushes. The thorny maquis in which it nests is the understory of what were once extensive evergreen forests in the Mediterranean region.

458 **Subalpine Warbler**
(*Sylvia cantillans*)

Description: 4¾″ (12 cm). Male *dark grey above,* with dark brown edges to flight feathers, and white outer tail feathers. Deep *orange-red below,* with prominent *white moustachial stripe.* Female resembles female Spectacled Warbler or female Whitethroat: dull brown-buff above, with broad rufous margins to flight feathers, white outer tail feathers; pale pinkish-cream below, *lacking white throat,* with hint of *white moustachial stripe.*

Voice: Contact note, *tech-tech;* a slow and sweet Whitethroat-like warble, with fewer harsh notes.

Habitat: Scrub maquis, scattered woods, bush country, old walls, and hedges.

Nesting: 3–4 white or pale washed eggs with light spots, laid in cup hidden low in shrub or creeper.

Range: Summer visitor to Mediterranean basin from Spain to Turkey and Syria and from Morocco to Libya. European birds winter in West Africa. Vagrant farther north.

In some areas, such as Corfu, it replaces the Sardinian Warbler at higher altitudes, where vegetation becomes pure maquis. Elsewhere it occurs to sea level but invariably in broken rocky country. It has a dancing song flight similar to Whitethroat's, though it is generally a skulker.

453 Sardinian Warbler
(*Sylvia melanocephala*)

Description: 5¼" (13 cm). Most common and widespread Mediterranean scrub warbler. Male slate-grey above, with *black cap extending below eye and over ear coverts.* Both sexes have bright *red eye-ring.* Throat white, *underparts silver-grey,* tail edged and tipped with white. Female lighter grey than male and lacking black cap.

Voice: A harsh and repeated *chack-chack* and a grating *churr.* Song, a grating, chattering warble mixed with *chacks.*

Habitat: Scrub, olive groves, Mediterranean forest, pine woods, even suburban gardens.

Nesting: 3–4 white or lightly washed eggs variously speckled, laid in neat cup near ground in brambles or dwarf vegetation

Range: Resident from Spain and Mediterran east through Turkey and Middle East and from Morocco to Egypt. Partial migrant south and east of breeding range.

The Sardinian is the typical scrub and bush warbler over most of Mediterranean Europe. It usually disappears deep into vegetation, but during the breeding season it may sing from prominent perches or be seen in a dancing display flight similar to Whitethroat's.

454 Rüppell's Warbler
(*Sylvia rueppelli*)

Description: 5½" (14 cm). Male has *black head, throat, and breast* broken by *white moustachial stripe*. Upperparts dark slate grey; underparts pale buffy-pink. Female resembles female Sardinian Warbler, but grey above, buffy-pink below, with well-defined white moustachial streak. Both sexes have *red eye* (Sardinian has red eye-ring), white outer tail feathers, and *red legs*.

Voice: Call, a rattling *chac-chac-chac* like Sardinian Warbler. Song, a musical Whitethroat-like chattering, with harsh chucks between bursts of song.

Habitat: Rocky Mediterranean scrub from sea level to considerable altitude, usually close to sea.

Nesting: 5 pale green eggs heavily speckled olive, laid in cup placed in bush, often of broom.

Range: Breeds in Greece, Turkey, eastern Mediterranean. Migrates south to winter in northeastern Africa. Vagrant elsewhere in Europe.

Rüppell's Warbler is restricted to the eastern Mediterranean. It can easily be confused with the Sardinian Warbler. It often sings in a display flight with slow, deliberate wing flaps.

452 Orphean Warbler
(*Sylvia hortensis*)

Description: 6″ (15 cm). *Large, blackish-capped* scrub warbler with prominent *pale yellow eye.* Similar to Sardinian Warbler (which has a red eye-ring), but larger. Black extends below eye. *Upperparts dark brown,* underparts warm pinkish-buff. White outer tail feathers. Head of female dark brown.

Voice: Song, a much more pleasant warble with more frequent repetition of phrases then other *Sylvia* species. Also a harsh, loud alarm note.

Habitat: Scrub in wooded areas, olive groves, and gardens; also open scrub-covered hillsides.

Nesting: 4–5 white eggs lightly spotted olive-brown, laid in cup of twigs placed in outer branches of tree or large bush.

Range: Summer visitor to Mediterranean basin extending east through Middle East to Iran. European birds winter in Africa. Rare farther north. Absent from Corsica, Sardinia, and Sicily.

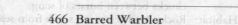

A typically skulking *Sylvia* warbler, it is usually located by its thrush-like song. It occasionally perches in the open while singing.

---

466 Barred Warbler
(*Sylvia nisoria*)

Description: 6″ (15 cm). *Large grey warbler,* adults with *fine barring on underparts. Bright golden eye;* tail has white outer feathers and is frequently flicked. Juveniles in autumn more uniformly grey, tinged brown, and *lacking barring* except on undertail. At all ages has *white outer tail feathers* and *two white wing bars. Eye dark* on immatures at least until late autumn.

Voice: Harsh *chack* and *charr.* Song, a mixture of melodic phrases and harsh chattering, sometimes uttered in display flight.

Habitat: Woodland clearings, thickets, and

hedges, often associated with thorns.

Nesting: 5 pale grey eggs speckled slightly darker, laid in deep cup placed in fork of thornbush.

Range: Breeds in central Europe as far west as eastern Switzerland, east to central Siberia; winters in Africa. Regularly wanders west, particularly in autumn.

Size alone separates this bird from almost all other European *Sylvia* warblers. In all plumages it looks chunkier and more robust than other similar grey warblers.

451 Lesser Whitethroat
(*Sylvia curruca*)

Description: 5¼" (13 cm). Resembles Whitethroat, but *grey above and whiter below. Wings grey,* completely lacking rufous. *Darker grey ear coverts* give *masked effect.* Legs and bill dark; outer tail feathers white.

Voice: Call, a hard *tac* note. Subdued, warbling song ends with a far-ranging dry rattle.

Habitat: Thickets, bushes, hedges, areas with taller trees than those frequented by Whitethroat.

Nesting: 4–6 white eggs speckled olive, laid in thin cup in bush or young conifer set in dense cover.

Range: Breeds from Britain, France, and Scandinavia east across most of the Soviet Union to Manchuria and south to Iran. Migrates southeast from Europe through Greece; a rarity in Ireland and Iberia.

There are several subspecies of Lesser Whitethroat in different parts of its range. Hume's Lesser Whitethroat (*S. c. althaea*) of the Taurus Mountains to the Himalayas, is much darker grey on back and crown and is sometimes regarded as a full species. The Desert Lesser Whitethroat (*S. c. minula*) of the Persian Gulf lacks dark ear coverts.

448, 449 **Whitethroat**
(*Sylvia communis*)

Description: 5½" (14 cm). Broad, *reddish-brown edges to wing feathers*. Male has *grey head* and buffy-pink underparts contrasting with *prominent white throat,* often puffed out. *Female has grey-brown head,* buff breast, and less pronounced white throat. Both have white outer tail feathers. Only the smaller Spectacled Warbler shares these features in Europe, but male has darker lores and more prominent white eye-ring. Legs and base of bill straw-coloured or pinkish-buff.

Voice: A harsh *chuck* or *charr.* Song, a creaky, grating chatter often uttered in song flight or atop a prominent bush.

Habitat: Thickets, bushes, hedges, often with brambles and nettles.

Nesting: 4–5 pale green eggs speckled olive-buff laid in cup among bushes or grasses.

Range: Breeds throughout Europe, except extreme north, east to central Siberia and Afghanistan; also North Africa. Migrates south to winter in tropical Africa.

It is the most numerous and widespread member of the genus *Sylvia* and a standard with which to compare others. Its chattering song flight is a typical sight and sound of the European spring. Though quite capapable of skulking like any *Sylvia,* this is one of the most bold, alert, and active members of the genus.

432 **Garden Warbler**
(*Sylvia borin*)

Description: 5½" (14 cm). A uniform, comparatively *featureless* warbler, with *short, stubby bill* and round head. Can be mistaken for an Olivaceous Warbler, but has short bill and dark "face." Light greyish-brown above, dull buff-white below. Has a narrow, *light eye-ring*.

Voice: A sweet Blackcap-like song, but more sustained and without loud notes of that species. A *chuck* call note.

Habitat: Thickets, overgrown woods with extensive undergrowth, bushes and hedges with brambles.

Nesting: 4–5 white eggs often tinged buff or olive, with buff blotches and spots, laid in cup constructed in bush or among dense vegetation.

Range: Breeds across most of Europe, except for areas with Mediterranean climate and vegetation, east through Russia to central Siberia. Migrant to Africa.

Despite its name, it only sometimes occurs in gardens with abundant, thick shrubby undergrowth. Unlike the Blackcap it will sometimes occupy bushy areas lacking in trees.

456 Blackcap
(*Sylvia atricapilla*)

Description: 5½" (14 cm). Greyish, with distinctive *black cap not extending below eye.* Upperparts slate-grey; *underparts light grey* in male, pale buff-grey in female. Male has distinctive *sooty-black cap* (*not glossy*) contrasting with grey of nape; female has *rust-coloured cap.* No white in tail; eye brown.

Voice: A repeated *tac-tac.* Song, a sweet, melodic warbling, with more vibrant loud notes than similar song of Garden Warbler. Tends to start softly and become louder.

Habitat: Woodland with undergrowth, thickets, hedges, orchards, gardens.

Nesting: 5 white eggs often washed with buff and spotted reddish-brown, laid in neat cup in low bush.

Range: Breeds through most of Europe east to Iran and central-southern Siberia. Partial migrant, most migrating south to Africa, some remaining in southern and western Europe as far north as Britain.

The male can be confused with Marsh or Willow tits but lacks the white cheeks and black bib of those species. The contrast between its black crown and grey neck and upperparts distinguishes it from any other *Sylvia* warbler. Not particularly shy, it is quite common in town and city gardens in Mediterranean region.

439 **Greenish Warbler**
(*Phylloscopus trochiloides*)

Description: 4¼″ (11 cm). Similar to Chiffchaff, but upperparts olive-green, underparts much whiter, and *eyebrow always better marked* (but not as long as Arctic Warbler's). Short, thin, *whitish wing bar* may become abraded and disappear. *Legs invariably dark.*

Voice: A liquid *chiweet,* recalling Pied Wagtail. Strident song resembles Wren's but is shorter.

Habitat: From sea level to 11,000′ (3,300 m) in coniferous and deciduous woodlands, scrub with trees. In winter, forest edges, parks, orchards.

Nesting: 3–4 smooth white eggs, laid in domed nest, among vegetation on ground or built into bank or wall.

Range: Breeds from southern shores of Baltic east across Asia to the Pacific, extending south through central Asia to Himalayas. Winters in India and Malaysia. Vagrant west to western Europe.

Difficult to identify; the single white wing bar and well-defined eyebrow help to separate it from all other European warblers.

441 **Arctic Warbler**
(*Phylloscopus borealis*)

Description: 4¾″ (12 cm). Resembles Greenish Warbler, but slightly larger; *long, yellowish-white eyebrow* reaches nape; upturned at rear; and has stouter, more dagger-like bill. *Short, thin, pale wing bar,* often abraded. Rarely, a second wing bar is visible. *Legs pale horn.*

Voice: A loud *tswee-ep* or *chik.* Song, a rapid *ziz-ziz-ziz,* repeated a dozen or so times, followed by a conclusive *tseer.*

Habitat: Woods with undergrowth, especially pines, birch, and willow. Found among trees in winter.

Nesting: 5–6 white eggs spotted brown, laid in domed nest on ground.

Range: Breeds from northern Scandinavia across arctic and subarctic Asia to western Alaska; also in Japan. Occasional vagrant to western Europe.

Scarce throughout Europe, it breeds in Scandinavia but migrates east about 8,000 miles (13,000 km) to winter on the Pacific coast of Asia in China and Indonesia.

Pallas's Warbler
(*Phylloscopus proregulus*)

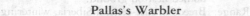

Description: 3½" (9.5 cm). *Tiny* leaf warbler with upperparts olive-green, underparts white, washed with yellow on flanks. Bold *crown-stripe* and *prominent, broad eyebrow* give head a striped pattern. Darker wings have *two broad wing bars;* prominent, square *yellow rump patch.*

Voice: A canary-like *tweet.* Song, a series of pleasant notes each repeated 4 or 5 times.

Habitat: Coniferous and mixed forests in summer; in winter and on migration, woodland, parks, and scrub.

Nesting: 4 white eggs blotched reddish, laid in domed nest constructed among outer conifer branches.

Range: Breeds in eastern half of Siberia south to central China with isolated population in Himalayas. Winters in southern China and northern India. Vagrant west as far as Britain.

It often hovers as it picks insects from the outer branches of trees, displaying the yellow rump that separates it from Goldcrest and Firecrest, to which it is similar in both its plumage and its ever-active behaviour. It often associates with tit flocks in winter quarters.

Yellow-browed Warbler
(*Phylloscopus inornatus*)

Description: 4″ (10 cm). Small leaf warbler, olive-green above, with slightly lighter rump and whitish below. *Long, prominent creamy eyebrow,* bordered by well-marked dark *stripe through eye. Two broad, yellowish wing bars.* Legs pale.

Voice: A strong *wheet* and a disyllabic *tiss-yip.* Song, a repeated plaintive version of the call note, ending in a buzz.

Habitat: Conifer and mixed forests; on migration and in winter, wooded and bush country.

Nesting: 4–5 white eggs speckled brown, laid in domed nest on ground.

Range: Breeds in east-central Siberia, wintering south into India, Burma, and southern China. Annual vagrant west to western Europe, especially to Britain.

It occurs with great regularity in western Europe. Two currently favoured explanations for this phenomenon are: population explosions in the breeding areas, and reverse migration, which takes young birds along on the exact reverse of the route that leads to winter quarters.

433 Bonelli's Warbler
(*Phylloscopus bonelli*)

Description: 4½″ (11 cm). Greyish-olive upperparts, *greyish head,* and silky-white underparts; wings brown, with prominent yellow panel on closed wing created by yellow edges of secondaries and tertials. Rump yellow (less obvious on young), but does not form a clear-cut rump patch and is difficult to see. Faint eyebrow; legs brown.

Voice: Call, a *clooee* or *clweet.* Song, a Wood

Warbler-like rattle, but shorter and no accelerated at the end.

Habitat: Mature woods, both pine and deciduous with sparse ground cover, parks, birch scrub in highland areas.

Nesting: 4–6 white eggs heavily speckled red-brown, laid in domed nest placed against bank.

Range: Breeds in southwestern Europe and European shores except for some islands of Mediterranean, east to Syria, and in North Africa. Migrates to Africa, rare farther north.

Because of its habitat, which often includes hills and mountains, it is a late nester throughout its range. The female constructs the neatly camouflaged nest and incubates the eggs alone.

436 Wood Warbler
(*Phylloscopus sibilatrix*)

Description: 5″ (13 cm). *Larger* and more brightly coloured than most leaf warblers. Bright *yellow-green upperparts and wings.* Yellow throat and eyebrow; *pure white belly.* Pale horn-coloured legs. Proportionately longer wings and shorter tail than other leaf warblers.

Voice: Call, *peu.* Song begins with series of clicking notes which accelerate into rapid, vibrant trill.

Habitat: Deciduous woods in western Europe with little undergrowth; beech or oak often dominant.

Nesting: 6–7 white eggs speckled rufous-brown, laid in domed nest hidden on ground.

Range: Temperate Europe from Britain and France to Russia, north to southern Norway and south to Italy. Avoids Mediterranean coast. Migrates southeast through Greece and Middle East to winter in tropical Africa.

It is more arboreal than other leaf warblers, feeding higher in the trees. It is numerous on migration through

Greece and other parts of southeast Europe.

434 **Chiffchaff**
(*Phylloscopus collybita*)

Description: 4¼" (11 cm). Very similar to Willow Warbler; best differentiated by song. *Upperparts olive-brown, underparts white, diffused with yellow-buff. Legs dark or black.* Overall colour usually more buff than Willow Warbler and eyebrow less marked.

Voice: Contact call, *hooet,* with more stress on second syllable and stronger than that of Willow Warbler. Song, a distinctive *chiff-chaff-chiff-chaff* (hence its name) repeated on two notes, but sometimes two *chaffs* or *chiffs* consecutively.

Habitat: Woodland, glades, forest edges with thick undergrowth. More often found among trees than Willow Warbler.

Nesting: 4–9 white eggs speckled dark brown, laid in domed nest on or near ground in thick vegetation.

Range: Breeds in temperate and subarctic Palearctic region from western Europe to northeastern Siberia; also in North Africa. Leaves eastern part of range in winter, moving south and west to North Africa and Mediterranean region.

It arrives in northern temperate Europe earlier than almost any other summer visitor. When birds are not singing, bird-watchers often lump this species with Willow Warblers as "Willow-Chiffs," a useful term when limited views prevent positive identification.

435 **Willow Warbler**
(*Phylloscopus trochilus*)

Description: 4½" (11 cm). Standard *Phylloscopus* warbler. *Olive-brown above,* with *yellow eyebrow. Underparts white,* with varying amounts of *yellow* on breast. *Legs pale horn.* Juveniles more yellow below tha[n] adults. Very similar to Chiffchaff, bu[t] leg colour, "cleaner" (less buff) greenish and yellow colouration, and song are distinctive.

Voice: A soft contact note, *hooet.* Song, a series of mellow liquid notes on a descending scale, ending with a flourish.

Habitat: Woods, heaths with trees and bushes; not as confined to woodland as Chiffchaff.

Nesting: 6–7 white eggs spotted reddish-brown, laid in domed nest set against low bank or mound.

Range: Breeds in temperate and boreal Palearctic region from Ireland almost to Bering Straits. Absent from southern Europe; winters in Africa.

Its song identifies this warbler, but silent birds need close examination. Willow warblers are always "cleaner-looking" than Chiffchaffs, with a clearer eyebrow that extends farther behind the eye. Leg colour is not totally reliable: Chiffchaffs never have pale legs, although those of Willow Warbler may be dark.

440 Goldcrest
(*Regulus regulus*)

Description: 3½" (9 cm). Apart from rarer Firecrest, this is Europe's smallest breeding bird, resembling plump, short-tailed warbler. Olive-green above, pale buffish below. Prominent, *double white wing bar;* bold light tips to tertials. *Face lacks bars and stripes,* unlike Firecrest. Male has bright *yellow-orange crown stripe bordered with black.* Female's crown stripe yellow.

Voice: A thin, high-pitched *see-see-see.* Song, a thin, fairy bell-like *see-see-see-see-sississi-sip.*

Habitat: Woodland, mostly coniferous, but also mixed; in winter, hedges and scrub.

Nesting: 7–10 white eggs speckled brown, laid in tightly woven cup suspended from end of branch high up in spruce.

Range: Throughout most of Europe in boreal,

temperate, and mountain zones, across Palearctic to Japan. Partial migrant but resident over most of Europe.

It roams over woodlands with titmice during the winter. Hard winters may decimate the population, but its powers of recovery are remarkable. It constantly flutters from twig to twig in its search for insects.

442 Firecrest

(*Regulus ignicapillus*)

Description: 3½″ (9 cm). Similar to Goldcrest, but bronzed-green on shoulders and whiter below. Double wing bar, light tips to tertials, and orange crown stripe (yellow in female) like Goldcrest. Diagnostic *whitish eyebrow* and *black eye-stripe* give a quite different head pattern than Goldcrest.

Voice: Call, similar to Goldcrest, but sharper, with upward inflexion. Song also similar, but with repetition of one note slightly ascending in pitch and lacking flourish at end.

Habitat: Coniferous and mixed woods; less dependent on conifers than Goldcrest. Often frequents scrub, burnt-over bracken, and other undergrowth.

Nesting: 7–11 white or pinkish eggs speckled dull brown, laid in neat cup suspended near tip of conifer branch, occasionally in creepers or juniper.

Range: Temperate continental Europe, North Africa, and Turkey. Rare in Denmark and otherwise absent from Scandinavia. Partial migrant from continental parts of range.

Its range has expanded in recent years and it now can be found breeding in southern England.

FLYCATCHERS
(Muscicapidae)

110 species: widespread in Old World. Five species breed in Europe. Small birds with broad, flattened bill adapted for catching flying insects. Legs rather short. Plumage highly variable; sexes similar or dissimilar; juvenile spotted. They perch upright on a prominent vantage point, making sallies after passing insects or dropping to the ground to catch prey, often returning to the same favoured perch. Feed entirely on insects and spiders.

---

517 Spotted Flycatcher
(*Muscicapa striata*)

Description: 5½″ (14 cm). Dull grey-brown above, with pale edges to wing feathers; *lacks any prominent area of white on wing. Forehead whitish with fine dark streaks.* Underparts dull grey-white, with *dark streaking on breast.* Appears long-tailed and *sits very upright on perch.*

Voice: A harsh *teee.* Song, a series of 5 or 6 hurried and squeaky notes.

Habitat: Forest edges and glades, gardens, parks, orchards.

Nesting: 4–5 pale blue eggs blotched with brown, laid in neat cup resting on ledge or against tree trunk.

Range: Breeds throughout Europe and from North Africa to south-central Asia. Absent from Iceland. Summer visitor; winters in tropical Africa.

It readily takes to gardens and will nest in open-fronted nest boxes. It habitually chooses a favorite perch from which it darts out after passing insects, catching them with an audible snap of its bill, returning to the same perch.

506 **Red-breasted Flycatcher**
(*Ficedula parva*)

Description: 4½″ (11 cm). Small flycatcher that habitually *cocks its rather long tail.* Brown above, washed greyish on head. *Prominent thin, creamy eye-ring.* Tail black, with *prominent white oval patches at sides of tail-base.* Adult male has *throat and breast orange-red,* shading to white on belly. Females and immatures washed with buff on throat and breast. Juveniles mottled and scaly, with white tail patches.

Voice: A *chick* call, a Wren-like rattle. Song, a quiet *peu-peu* among Wood Warbler- and Redstart-like phrases. Very variable.

Habitat: Deciduous forests and woods; frequents bushy areas on migration and in winter.

Nesting: 5–6 white eggs speckled with rufous-brown, laid in cup built against tree, or in tree or wall hollow.

Range: Breeds from central Europe across northern Eurasia to the Pacific; also south into the Caucasus and Iran. Migrates south to winter in southern Asia; rare visitor to western Europe.

Often more secretive than Pied or Spotted flycatchers, perching in cover. During breeding season it is rather shy, feeding mainly within the foliage of the upper branches of trees, seldom using an exposed perch like the Spotted Flycatcher does.

Semi-collared Flycatcher
(*Ficedula semitorquata*)

Description: 5″ (13 cm). Male black above and white below, with white patch at base of bill and *bold white area on wing* similar to Collared Flycatcher but with *half-collar on side of neck.* Rump grey. Female shows more white on wing than female Pied, but is similar to female Collared except that it lacks a faint collar.

Voice: Call, a dry, hard *check;* song, a variable

5- to 8- syllable *tsiro-tsiro-tjia-tjia-t*, similar to Collared.

Habitat: Deciduous and coniferous woods.

Nesting: 6–7 light blue eggs, in nest of leaves in tree hole, often old woodpecker hole.

Range: Eastern Bulgaria and northern Greece through Turkey to the Caspian region and Iran. Migrant through Greece to tropical Africa.

Intermediate between Collared and Pied flycatchers, it was until recently considered a subspecies of the Collared. In 1958 a field study of nesting Semi-collared flycatchers in western Macedonia showed that their social behaviour differed considerably from both Pied and Collared, resulting in their elevation to a full species.

513 Collared Flycatcher
(*Ficedula albicollis*)

Description: 5″ (13 cm). Male black above and white below, similar to Pied Flycatcher but with forehead showing more white and *complete white collar around neck.* Also *greyish-white rump* patch and much *more extensive area of white on wings.* Female

♀ similar to female Pied, but with *much more white on wings,* hint of silver on rump, and sometimes indistinct collar.

Voice: Song, shorter and higher-pitched than Pied, *sit-sit-sit-sueesi.*

Habitat: Same as Pied Flycatcher; deciduous and coniferous forests.

Nesting: 6–7 pale blue eggs, laid in cup of leaves in tree hole.

Range: Patchy distribution from northeastern France as far north as southeast Sweden; Italy east through Balkans to southern Russia. Migrates to tropical Africa, passing regularly through Greece.

It occurs quite commonly as a migrant in southeastern Europe, especially in the Greek islands. In Crete it is sometimes more common than the Pied Flycatcher in spring. In areas where all

three "pied" flycatchers occur, the identification of females and juveniles is difficult.

512, 514 Pied Flycatcher
(*Ficedula hypoleuca*)

Description: 5″ (13 cm). *Male in summer is black* above (with white spot on forehead at base of bill) and white below; *wing bar,* tertial edgings, and outer tail *white.* Female brown above, buffish below, with wing and tail pattern similar to male. In autumn, male and immatures resemble female. Wing pattern and plain chest distinguish female and immatures from Spotted Flycatcher. Juveniles mottled and scaly, similar to young Spotted, but with white on wings and tail.

Voice: A shrill *wit* or *tick.* Song, a repeated (often double) note, followed by a trilling conclusion.

Habitat: Deciduous and coniferous woodlands, gardens, often near water; orchards; almost any bush on migration.

Nesting: 4–7 pale blue eggs, laid in tree hole or nest box.

Range: Breeds from northern Europe and Russia southwest to the Mediterranean in Spain and North Africa. Migrant farther south in Africa.

It sits upright and makes sallies after flying insects. Unlike the Spotted Flycatcher, it is less inclined to return over and over to the same perch after catching a fly.

BABBLERS
(Timaliidae)

282 species: mainly Old World (one species in North America). One species breeds in Europe. Widely diversified family of small to medium-sized perching birds, most abundant in southern Asia, occupying a wide variety of habitats, though mainly arboreal. Plumage variable; sexes similar or dissimilar; bill varies from small and thin to long and curved. Wings rather short and rounded; flight weak. Many species very noisy, giving the family its name. Mainly insectivorous.

427, 430 **Bearded Tit or Bearded Reedling**
(*Panurus biarmicus*)

Description: 6½″ (16 cm). Tail, 3″ (8 cm). *Small body and long tail.* Male has *pale-grey head* with bold *black moustachial streak;* otherwise tawny-brown except for whitish throat and breast, black undertail coverts, and narrow black and white bands on wing. Bill yellow; legs black. Female paler, with brown head, and lacking black moustachial streak and undertail coverts. Juvenile has black back, wing patch, and sides of tail.

Voice: Distinctive call, a ringing, metallic *ching;* also a variety of squeaky wheezes and twittering notes.

Habitat: Extensive reedbeds, swamps, or areas adjacent to lakes or streams.

Nesting: 5–7 white eggs with fine brown streaks and specks, in an open nest of dead reed leaves lined with flowering reed heads, placed low in reeds or aquatic vegetation.

Range: Breeds in widely scattered localities in central and southern Europe from England and Spain east to western Russia and Greece; also in Asia east to Manchuria. Northern population partially migratory.

Though called a tit, it is in fact a babbler. Supposed tit-like actions resemble those of other small Asian babblers. It is usually seen laboriously flying just over the reed tops, with rapidly beating wings and long, spread tail moving from side to side. Active and agile, it moves easily through the reed stems.

LONG-TAILED TITS
(*Aegithalidae*)

7 species: Eurasia and North and Central America. One species breeds in Europe. Small family closely related to true tits (*Paridae*). Small, long-tailed birds with tiny bill and tit-like action. Feed chiefly on small insects and their larvae. Nest is large and domed, with side entrance.

---

426 Long-tailed Tit
(*Aegithalos caudatus*)

Description: 5½″ (14 cm). Tail 3″ (8 cm). Shape distinctive, with *tiny body* shorter than *long tail.* Plumage a mixture of *black, white, and pink,* but very variable. West European birds have white head, with broad black stripe over eye; pink and black upperparts; black wings with white edgings to secondaries; black tail with white outer feathers; white underparts, with pinkish wash on flanks and belly. Northern birds have pure white head and whiter underparts. Some Mediterranean birds have grey backs or brown eye-stripes. Young birds browner, with shorter tails, and lacking pink.

Voice: A dry, rattling trill, *tsirrrrrup;* a thin *see-see-see,* like that of other tits; and a low *tupp.* No real song, but call notes sometimes run together in a bubbly subsong.

Habitat: Undergrowth in broad-leaved and mixed woodland, scrub, thickets, copses, hedgerows, bushy heaths. In winter, more in woodland.

Nesting: 8–12 white eggs with pale red spotting, in domed oval nest of moss, lichens, and cobwebs, lined with feathers, in a thorny bush, sometimes in narrow fork of tree.

Range: Breeds throughout Europe, except Iceland, northern Scandinavia, and some Mediterranean islands; also breeds across Asia to Japan. Mainly resident.

It flocks with other tits in winter, but more typically travels in family parties, following one another from tree to tree in a long string. More of a woodland bird than other tits, it is less inclined to come into gardens.

TITS
(Paridae)

65 species: Eurasia, Africa, and No America. Nine species breed in Euro Small to very small arboreal birds wit short bill and rather short, rounded wings. Flight weak. Plumage variable, often with black on head; some species crested. Sexes similar. Active, restless birds, often hanging acrobatically from twigs while feeding. Travel in mixed flocks after breeding season. Mainly insectivorous; also take seeds and nuts, coming regularly to bird feeders and becoming very tame. Hole nesters.

420 Marsh Tit
(*Parus palustris*)

Description: 4½″ (11 cm). *Glossy black crown and nape, small black bib;* uniformly brown upperparts, wings, and tail; off-white cheeks and underparts with buffy wash on flanks. Best distinguished from similar Willow Tit by voice.

Voice: Common call, *pitchoo-oo,* with many variations; other calls are the usual thin *see-see-see* common to many tits, and a scolding *chickadeedeedee.* Song, repeated liquid musical notes uttered singly or in phrases.

Habitat: Deciduous woods, hedgerows, thickets, scrub; not high in mountains.

Nesting: 7–8 white eggs with a few red-brown spots, in a moss nest lined with hair, placed in tree hole.

Range: Breeds from southern Scandinavia, Britain, and northeast Spain across most of central and southern Europe, except Mediterranean zone, east across central Russia to the Urals; also in eastern Asia.

Despite its name, this is not a marsh bird, preferring woodlands, and in most areas is not attracted to parks or gardens. Usually travels singly or in pairs.

Sombre Tit
(*Parus lugubris*)

Description: 5½" (14 cm). Resembles large Marsh or Willow Tit. Grey-brown above, dull white below with grey-brown rather than buffy flanks. *Crown dull brownish-black, black bib more extensive* than in Marsh or Willow tits, cheeks somewhat whiter and more contrasting.

Voice: Wide vocabulary, including strong, ringing calls: *pyee-pyee-pyee-pyee; chur-wee-wee-wee; widdi-widdi-widdi;* a quick *chizzy-chaa;* and a harsh, grating scold similar to Great Tit, often prefaced by introductory *zi-zi-zi.*

Habitat: Deciduous and mixed woods, orchards, thickets, and evergreen oak scrub in rocky country, both in lowlands and mountains.

Nesting: 5–7 white eggs with fine reddish spots, in nest of dried plants and wool, lined with feathers, placed in tree hole.

Range: Breeds from Yugoslavia and Romania south through the Balkans; also in southwest Asia from Asia Minor to Iran.

A lively, restless bird with a loud voice, it tends to keep to the treetops in woodland, though in Greece it is found in low scrub on rocky hillsides. Not social, it usually travels singly or in pairs.

---

421 Willow Tit
(*Parus montanus*)

Description: 4½" (11 cm). *Crown dull sooty-black,* without gloss; black bib more extensive than Marsh Tit. Upperparts and tail brown, wings *usually with a pale patch on secondaries.* Cheeks and underparts off-white; flanks tend to be richer buff than Marsh Tit. Differences slight; best distinguished by voice.

Voice: Typical call, a nasal, grating *chaa* or *chay,* sometimes preceded by *chick* or *chicky;* also a thin, buzzy *eez-eez-eez* and a very high, thin *zi-zi-zi.* Two songs, a rich warble and a repeated plaintive note, *piu piu-piu*.

Habitat: Deciduous, mixed, and coniferous woods; in the breeding season, shows preference for damp, marshy places, but in winter often in drier areas. In central Europe, also breeds in montane mixed and pure coniferous woods up to tree line.

Nesting: 8–9 white eggs variably spotted with red-brown, in nest of hair and wood fibre, placed in hole in rotting wood excavated by the female.

Range: Breeds from Britain and eastern France east and north across central Europe and Scandinavia; largely absent from Mediterranean countries. Also breeds across northern Asia to the Pacific.

The Willow Tit was formerly thought to be conspecific with the Black-capped Chickadee of North America, although the vocal repertoires of the two are very different. The Willow Tit's habit of excavating its own nest clearly distinguishes it from the Marsh Tit.

---

425 **Siberian Tit**
(*Parus cinctus*)

Description: 5¼" (13 cm). Large tit with rather loose plumage, giving it a slightly disheveled look. *Crown and nape brown; large black bib blends with breast* rather than being sharply delineated. Rich brown above, cheeks and underparts dingy white, *flanks rufous-brown,* a richer colour than other tits. Juvenile similar but with neater appearance.

Voice: A slow *chee-ee* or *dee-dee,* similar to Willow Tit's *eez-eez* but more drawn-out, sometimes prefaced with *chick* or *chicka* to produce a lazy *chicka-deee-deee-deee.*

Habitat: Northern birch or mixed coniferous birch forests.

Nesting: 6–10 white eggs with red-brown spots, in a moss nest lined with hair, placed in tree hole.

Range: Breeds in northern and central Scandinavia and northern Russia, east across Siberia to Alaska and northwest Mackenzie.

It is not common and is usually much less numerous than other tits in its range. One of several Asian species that has recently invaded North America, where it is known as the Gray-headed Chickadee, it is not doing particularly well, being greatly outnumbered by the local Boreal and Black-capped chickadees. It wanders widely in winter.

---

429 Crested Tit
(*Parus cristatus*)

Description: 4½″ (11 cm). Distinguishable from all other tits by *scaly black-and-white crest.* Cheeks dingy white; *black line through eye onto cheek;* black line on side of neck joins small black throat patch. Upperparts brown, underparts white, flanks buffy.

Voice: A distinctive low, purring trill. Also a thin *see-see-see,* like that of other tits.

Habitat: Chiefly coniferous woods, especially pine; also mixed woods and locally even in pure deciduous woods, especially in winter.

Nesting: 5–6 white eggs with area of reddish spots, in moss nest lined with hair, placed in hole or crack or old conifer stump.

Range: Breeds in Scotland and from central Scandinavia south through most of Europe to Spain, northernmost Italy, and north-central Greece. Absent from Mediterranean islands. Also breeds across central Russia to Urals.

Crested Tits are quite common in coniferous forests and, like other tits, can be readily "squeaked up" by an observer. Often associates with Coal Tits.

419 **Coal Tit**
(*Parus ater*)

Description: 4½″ (11 cm). Smallest tit; tail shorter than other tits'. Crown and throat black, with white cheeks and *conspicuous white nape patch.* Olive-grey above; white below, with buffy flanks; double white wing bar. Juvenile has dull underparts, cheeks, and nape.

Voice: A wide variety of notes, many of them higher-pitched versions of Great Tit's calls; a high, thin *tsoo* or *tsui,* interspersed with brief twitters. Also a little churring scold and a thin *see-see-see.* Song, a clear, bell-like *teacher, teacher,* quite variable but always 2 or 3 notes, *pee-too, pee-too; ti-pui, ti-pui,* delivered more quickly than similar song of Great Tit.

Habitat: Chiefly coniferous woods, but also mixed and deciduous woods, parks, and gardens.

Nesting: 7–11 white eggs variably speckled with red-brown, in hole nest lined with moss, hair, and feathers, close to ground in tree stump, among tree roots, in crevice in wall, or in hole in bank.

Range: Breeds throughout Europe, except northern Scandinavia and northern Russia. Also breeds in North Africa and across Asia to the Pacific and south to Himalayas and southern China.

It is common in coniferous woods, often visiting gardens and parks. After breeding season, it joins mixed flocks of other tits, Goldcrests, and leaf warblers. Like the Blue Tit, it is a bark-gleaner, creeping along trunks and branches, probing for insects.

423, 424 **Blue Tit**
(*Parus caeruleus*)

Description: 4½″ (11 cm). *Crown, wings, and tail blue,* back dull green, *underparts yellow.* Narrow white border surrounding blue crown; cheeks and nape patch white.

Thin, black eye-line, black chin, and collar all connect. Juvenile has yellow cheeks and nape patch.

Voice: Typical call, a rounded 4-note phrase, the last note lower, *tsee-tee-tee-tsu.* Harsh scolding churr, like Great Tit, but higher-pitched. A variety of other notes, including a thin *see-see-see,* like that of other tits. Song, a musical trill with 2 or 3 introductory notes, *tsee, tsee, tsuhuhuhuhu.*

Habitat: Broad-leaved and mixed woodland; uncommon in conifers. Open bushy country, thickets, hedgerows, gardens, parks. In winter, often in reedbeds.

Nesting: 7–14 white eggs variably spotted with light chestnut, in moss and grass nest lined with hair and feathers, placed in tree hole or wall crevice; also in nest box.

Range: Breeds throughout Europe, north to southern Scandinavia and central Russia. Also in North Africa, western Russia, and southwestern Asia. Mainly resident, but in some winters northern populations move south.

An engaging little bird, it is noted as much for its fearless behaviour as for its abundance. Like Great Tit, it is well-known in Britain for its habit of prising the tops off milk bottles and drinking the cream. Its diet varies, but it prefers bark-gleaning, creeping along trunks and branches in search of insects and hanging acrobatically from the smallest twigs.

Azure Tit
(*Parus cyanus*)

Description: 5¼″ (13 cm). Suggests a very pale Blue Tit, but larger and with longer tail. *Head and underparts pure white, upperparts grey-blue; two broad white wing bars form inverted* V; conspicuous white outer tail feathers; narrow, dark line through eye joins similar line across nape; small, suffused blue patch on breast. Juvenile has grey crown and greyer upperparts.

Voice: Call, a low rattle like Long-tailed Tit. Alarm, a loud *cherpink.* Song, a loud trill.

Habitat: Chiefly willow and other trees and scrub at edges of streams and lakes. Also birch woods, but avoids dense forests.

Nesting: 9–11 white eggs with fine reddish spots, in nest of moss, grass, and hair, lined with fine hair, placed in tree hole.

Range: Breeds from western Russia across Siberia to northern Manchuria. Vagrant only to western Europe.

The Asiatic counterpart of the Blue Tit, it is known in Russia as the White Bluetit. It is extending its range west into Europe and has hybridized to some extent with the Blue Tit where their ranges overlap. Secretive, it lives in dense marshy thickets rather than boldly inhabiting woods and gardens like the Blue Tit.

---

422 **Great Tit**
(*Parus major*)

Description: 5½″ (14 cm). *Large, stocky* tit, with black crown and throat, white cheeks, and *black bib extending as line down centre of yellow underparts.* Yellow-green back becoming *yellower on nape;* wings, rump, and tail largely blue-grey. Juvenile duller, with black parts dark brown and cheeks yellow.

Voice: Varied repertoire of calls, many like other tits but louder, including a husky, churring scold, a thin *see-see-see,* a Chaffinch-like *pink-pink,* and a dry *char.* Song, also variable but generally a series of 2- or 3-syllable ringing bell-like phrases: *teacher, teacher; pity-wee, pity-wee, pity-wee.*

Habitat: Woodlands, thickets, hedgerows, parks, gardens, and other open bushy areas.

Nesting: 5–11 white eggs variably spotted with red-brown, in moss nest lined with hair or down, placed in tree hole or wall cavity; also in nest box or other man-made object.

Range: Breeds throughout Europe, except Iceland and extreme northern Scandinavia. Also breeds in North Africa and extensively in Asia, east across Siberia to Japan and south through Orient to Sri Lanka and Indonesia.

It is familiar in parks and gardens and around bird feeders. It travels in large family parties after the breeding season and joins mixed flocks with other tits. Though arboreal, it tends to feed lower than other tits, often in bushes and on the ground.

NUTHATCHES
(Sittidae)

22 species: Eurasia and North America. Three species breed in Europe. Small birds with long, straight bill; short neck, tail, and legs; and long toes, which aid in climbing. Noted for their ability to climb downward head first on tree trunks and rocks. Plumage grey or blue above, white to chestnut below; sexes similar. They glean insects from bark and also feed on seeds and nuts, cracking open nutshells with their stout bills. Hole nesters.

Krüper's Nuthatch
(*Sitta krueperi*)

Description: 5″ (13 cm). Very like Corsican Nuthatch, but slightly larger, with *grey nape* and *broad, red-brown breast band*. Distinguished from Nuthatch by black crown, smaller size, white stripe over eye, and white flanks and belly.

Voice: Call, a harsh, jay-like scold similar to Corsican Nuthatch, and a soft *pwit*. Song, a high-pitched, yodelling trill, *toodloodloodloodl* . . . , or a slower *toopi, toopi, toopi*. . . .

Habitat: Forests of pine, cedar, and juniper, in hills and mountains. Sometimes nests in chestnut trees at edge of coniferous forest.

Nesting: 5–6 white eggs with fine reddish speckling, in tree hole or cavity behind bark.

Range: Breeds in Lesbos, Turkey, the Caucasus, Transcaucasia, and northern Syria. Resident. Has been observed near Salonika (Macedonia).

A recent addition to the European avifauna, Krüper's Nuthatch was discovered on Lesbos in 1960. It is closely related to the Corsican Nuthatch, with a similar voice and habitat.

Corsican Nuthatch
(*Sitta whiteheadi*)

Description: 4¾" (12 cm). Small nuthatch with distinctive head pattern. Male has *black crown and nape* and *black line through eye* separated by broad, *white eyebrow.* Upperparts blue-grey, tail with white corners; underparts off-white. Female duller with grey crown and less conspicuous eye-stripe. Juvenile resembles female.

Voice: A penetrating, ringing trill somewhat variable in pace and pitch, and a jay-like screech similar to that of the Rock Nuthatch. Also twittering and scolding notes.

Habitat: Montane forests and groves, only in Laricio pines, between 2,500–5,400′ (750–1,600 m) altitude.

Nesting: 5–6 white eggs finely speckled with red, in a nest of bark, moss, and grass, lined with hair, placed in a tree cavity that it excavates.

Range: Endemic to the island of Corsica.

Because of similarity in size and head pattern, this species was once considered conspecific with the North American Red-breasted Nuthatch (*Sitta canadensis*), in spite of the tremendous gap in their ranges. Both are partial to coniferous forests, but their voices are totally different, a major reason for separating the two.

---

416 **Nuthatch**
(*Sitta europaea*)

Description: 5½" (14 cm). *Blue-grey above* with *black line through eye,* white cheeks and throat, *chestnut flanks.* Remaining underparts vary from white in northern birds to deep buff in southern and western ones. White-tipped outer tail feathers usually seen only in flight or display.

Voice: Has wide vocabulary. Call, a strong, ringing *wit-wit-wit,* with variations; also some shrill notes, *tsirrr, tsitt.* Song, a repetition of a single loud note at varying speeds and pitches: *pee-pee-pee, tutututututu, kwi-kwi-kwi-kwi.*

Habitat: Completely arboreal, preferring mature deciduous trees, in forests, woods, parks, and gardens, usually not higher than 4,900′ (1,500 m).

Nesting: 6–11 white eggs spotted red-brown, in a nest of bark and leaves in tree hole plastered with mud around entrance.

Range: Breeds from England and southern Scandinavia south and east throughout Europe, except for some Mediterranean islands. Also breeds locally in Morocco, across Asia to the Pacific and south to India and southeast Asia.

It climbs on tree trunks and branches, probing for insects on the surface and prying under the bark with its long bill. It produces a loud, woodpecker-like tapping when it cracks hazelnuts with its bill. Not gregarious, they usually travel in pairs but in winter sometimes join mixed flocks of tits, Goldcrests, and treecreepers.

---

415 **Rock Nuthatch**
(*Sitta neumayer*)

Description: 5½″ (14 cm). Resembles a pale Nuthatch, light grey-blue above, *tail plain grey with no white* on outer tips; black line through eye; throat and *breast white; belly, flanks, and undertail coverts pale brownish-buff,* lacking chestnut wash.

Voice: Richer repertoire than Nuthatch; voice also richer and more powerful. Most calls are trilling, and may be high or low in pitch, shrill or fluty, fast or slow: *tui-tui-tui-tui, teeteeteetee, peeu-peeu-peeu.* A harsh jay-like screech.

Habitat: Mountain slopes, cliffs, ravines, stony hillsides, and other rocky places.

Nesting: 6–10 white eggs with small reddish spots, in a round mud nest with a short tubular side entrance and a lining of moss, hair, and feathers, placed in rock crevice.

Range: Western Yugoslavia to western Bulgaria and Greece. Also breeds in southwestern Asia from Asia Minor to Iran.

It behaves like other nuthatches, but climbs on rocks instead of trees. It is also found on stone walls and around old buildings. The visitor to Delphi in Greece will often find these birds among the ruins.

WALLCREEPERS
(Tichodromadidae)

1 species: Eurasia. Breeds in Europe. A monotypic family related to both nuthatches and treecreepers, with some characters of each. Wallcreeper has curved bill of treecreeper but climbs more like a nuthatch.

418 Wallcreeper
(*Tichodroma muraria*)

Description: 6½″ (16 cm). Bill, 1″ (2.5 cm). Unique in *shape, plumage,* and *behaviour. Long, curved bill; broad, rounded wings; short tail.* Wings black, with *large bright crimson patch and double row of white spots* across primaries; tail black, *with white terminal fringe.* Upperparts grey; throat and breast black in summer, greyish-white in winter; belly dark grey.

Voice: A variety of high, clear, ringing, partly trilled notes, uttered singly or in twos and threes: *toy; toy-tsee; toi-tsee-tweeeu; chick-err-tsee-woy,* etc. Also a distinctive 3-note phrase: a short, low, introductory note, followed by two long, clear whistles, the first rising in pitch and the second falling.

Habitat: High mountains in summer, usually from 3,300–7,300′ (1,000–2,200 m), on cliffs, rock faces, rocky gorges, and ravines. Lower in winter, when found in rocky valleys and foothills; also frequently on walls and buildings.

Nesting: 4 white eggs with a few red-brown spots, in nest of moss, roots, and grass, lined with wool and hair, placed deep in rock crevice.

Range: High mountains of central and southern Europe from northwest Spain to Romania and Greece. Also in mountains of Asia, east to Himalayas and China.

The special structural adaptations of this bird to its harsh environment have made it a subject of debate among taxonomists. It recently has been placed in a family of its own (Tichodromadidae). It goes from the bottom to the top of a wall face or cliff looking for insects, then flies down and starts up again.

TREECREEPERS
(Certhiidae)

5 species: temperate Eurasia and North America. Two species breed in Europe. Small arboreal birds with slender, curved bill; rather long tail used as a brace in climbing, the feathers with pointed tips. Long toes and sharp claws also aid in climbing. Plumage streaked brown above, whitish below; sexes similar. Treecreepers use their bills to probe into bark cracks and crevices, searching for insects and spiders.

417 Treecreeper
(*Certhia familiaris*)

Description: 5″ (13 cm). *Brown above,* with pale spots and streaks; white below; rufous wash on rump, pale eye-stripe, and pale wing bars. *Curved bill.*

Voice: Call notes, a high, thin *seee* and a shorter *tsit*. High-pitched accelerating song somewhat resembles the Goldcrest's, but notes more distinct and stronger; several introductory notes are followed by a jumble of shorter notes, ending with more long notes, often on an upbeat: *seee-seee-tsi-tsee-tsoo-tisisisi-tsee-tsui*.

Habitat: Woodland of all types. In central and southern Europe, chiefly in mountains, where it prefers coniferous and mixed woods; farther north, in lowlands; in Britain and Ireland, common in deciduous woods, parks, and gardens.

Nesting: 6 white eggs spotted with red-brown at large end, in a nest of twigs and moss, lined with feathers and bark, placed in tree-trunk crack or behind loose bark.

Range: Breeds from southern Scandinavia, Britain and Ireland, eastern France, and the Pyrenees, east across central and northern Europe and north-central Asia to the Pacific; also in North America.

Treecreepers work their way up tree trunks and along the underside of branches in short, jerky movements, like miniature woodpeckers. When they reach the top of one trunk, they fly down to the bottom of the next and start working up again. In winter, they often flock with tits and Goldcrests.

Short-toed Treecreeper
(*Certhia brachydactyla*)

Description: 5″ (13 cm). Distinguished from Treecreeper by *brownish flanks,* less rusty rump, less distinct eye-stripe, and slightly longer and more curved bill.

Voice: Call, a distinct *ting*!, resembling call of tit, very different from high, thin call of Treecreeper. Song, high-pitched, buzzy, and rapid: *tsee-tsee-didireetoo-see-too-tsee* and variations; sometimes a shorter *tee-tee-doodawy-tee.*

Habitat: Deciduous woodlands, copses, parks, gardens; also coniferous woods at high elevations in Pyrenees and Mediterranean region.

Nesting: 6–7 white eggs with reddish spots, in a nest of twigs, roots, and moss, lined with feathers and fine bark, and placed behind loose bark or in tree-trunk crack.

Range: Resident in central and southern Europe from Spain and France to extreme western Russia, south to Italy, Sicily, and the Balkans; also in North Africa and Asia Minor. Recently, a few have occurred in England.

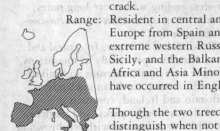

Though the two treecreepers are hard to distinguish when not calling, in many parts of Europe only one of them occurs and they can be identified by range alone. Where they overlap, in central and east Europe, they tend to separate altitudinally, the Treecreeper living more in the mountains and the Short-toed in the lowlands.

PENDULINE TITS
(Remizidae)

9 species: Eurasia, Africa, and North America. One species breeds in Europe. Very small birds with thin, finely pointed bills. Their actions and behaviour resemble that of closely related true tits. They inhabit scrub and open bushy country rather than woodland. Strong, globular nest with a tubular side entrance.

428 Penduline Tit
(*Remiz pendulinus*)

Description: 4¼" (11 cm). Small tit with *pale grey head and throat, black mask, chestnut back,* and pale buff underparts. Juvenile lacks black mask and chestnut back.

Voice: Call, a thin, plaintive but rather penetrating whistle, a down-slurred *seee;* also a shorter tit-like *si-si-si* or *tsi-si-si.* Song, a series of liquid, rather canary-like trills interspersed with call notes.

Habitat: Bushes, scrub, and trees, especially willow and alder, in flooded marshes and lake edges and along riverbanks.

Nesting: 6–8 white eggs in domed nest of plant fibres and seeds suspended from small twigs at end of branch, usually over water. Nest has a tubular side entrance.

Range: Breeds patchily from eastern Spain and southern France to Italy and the Balkans; in east-central Europe west to Denmark and eastern France; and in Asia east to Manchuria and northern China. Gradually extending its European range to the north and west. European birds are partially migratory.

Its remarkable nest is an intricately woven structure up to an inch thick that takes both birds about two weeks to build. A curiously local bird with a spotty distribution, it is most common along large rivers (chiefly the Danube in Europe) and around their deltas.

ORIOLES
(Oriolidae)

28 species: mainly tropical regions of Old World. One species breeds in Europe. Medium-small arboreal birds with rather stout bill and short legs. Feed on both insects and fruit.

608 Golden Oriole
(Oriolus oriolus)

Description: 9½″ (24 cm). Male *bright yellow* with black lores, *black wings* with small yellow spot at base of primaries, and *black tail with broad yellow corners.* Female and juvenile yellowish-green above, with darker wings and tail; greyish-white below, with fine streaks. *Bill pink,* legs dark grey.

Voice: Call of male, also used as song, 2 downslurred, whistled notes, mellow and fluty yet far-carrying: *weela-weeo* or, with a stretch of imagination, *or-i-ole.* Both sexes have a harsh, jay-like scold, *skaaa;* also other grating notes.

Habitat: Broad-leaved woodland, well-timbered parkland, sometimes coniferous forest; lines of trees along rivers, orchards, gardens.

Nesting: 3–4 creamy-white eggs with a few bold, blackish spots, in nest of grass stems, strips of bark, and other materials, lined with grass heads, and slung between two branches.

Range: Breeds in most of central and southern Europe (except southern Greece) north to southern Finland and southern Sweden and Britain (very local). Also breeds in North Africa and Asia east to central Siberia and northern India. European birds winter in eastern Africa.

Strictly arboreal, it haunts the highest branches, making even the brightly coloured male difficult to see; his presence is often detected only by his fluty whistle. Its flight is often deeply undulating, like that of a woodpecker.

SHRIKES
(Laniidae)

74 species: chiefly Old World (two r North America). Five species breed ir Europe. Medium-small birds with larg head; strong, hooked bill; and long, graduated or rounded tail. Sexes fairly similar; juveniles barred. Solitary, aggressive birds that hunt insects, small birds, and rodents from an exposed perch, frequently making "larders" of prey impaled on thorns. Flight direct and undulating. Generally rather silent, but song quite musical and calls harsh.

508, 516 Red-backed Shrike
(*Lanius collurio*)

Description: 6¾″ (17 cm). Male has *blue-grey crown, nape, and rump, predominantly chestnut back and wings.* Broad black line from bill through eye to ear-coverts, separated from crown by narrow white line. Throat white; underparts white, with pinkish wash. Tail black, with white edges broadening at base. Female rich brown above; broad brown stripe through eye; underparts buffy-white, with dark scalloping. Juvenile similar to female but with dark scalloping on upperparts.

Voice: Call, a nasal, grating *shaaaak* and other harsh or clucking notes. Song, a long, bustling, subdued chatter incorporating both squeaky and warbled notes and imitations of other birds.

Habitat: Open country with scattered thickets, gorse-covered heaths, bushy commons, hedgerows, orchards, disused railway cuttings.

Nesting: 5–6 pale eggs variably coloured brown, pink, cream, or green, usually with red-brown spots, in large nest of moss, grass, and plant stems, lined with fine roots and hair, placed in dense bush.

Range: Breeds from northern Spain and most Mediterranean islands north to southern England and southern Scandinavia; also

in Asia east to central Siberia. European birds winter in Africa.

A typical shrike in its habits, it positions itself on an exposed perch and watches for passing prey while twisting its tail in different directions and scanning the air like a flycatcher. Insectivorous and carnivorous, it sometimes accumulates larders of prey items impaled on thorns or barbed wire.

---

511 **Lesser Grey Shrike**
(*Lanius minor*)

Description: 8″ (20 cm). Smaller than similar Great Grey Shrike, with longer wings, shorter tail, and stubbier bill. *Forehead black; no white eyebrow* above black mask. Back and rump grey; wing black with broad white bar; tail black with conspicuous white outer tail feathers; underparts white with *pink tinge.* Female similar, but with less black on forehead. Juvenile yellowish-brown above, buffy below, with dark mask not extending onto forehead.

Voice: A harsh *shek* or *shaak* and a variety of chattering, strident, and whistled notes. Song varied, incorporating mimicry and grating call notes.

Habitat: Breeds in open country with some bushes and trees, grasslands, cultivated fields, gardens, and edges of woods. Winters in dry thorny scrub in Africa.

Nesting: 5–7 blue-green eggs with brown blotches, in nest of twigs and stems lined with feathers, roots, and hair, placed fairly high up in tree. Sometimes nests in loose colonies.

Range: Summer visitor to southern and eastern Europe, breeding from extreme northeastern Spain, central France (local), and southern Germany east to north-central Italy, Balkans, and central Russia; also parts of Asia. Winters in tropical Africa.

It tends to hover more than other shrikes and has a direct, less undulating flight. It perches with a more upright stance than Great Grey Shrike. It eats chiefly insects and is less inclined to have larders than other shrikes.

509 Great Grey Shrike
(*Lanius excubitor*)

Description: 9½" (24 cm). Largest European shrike. *Forehead, crown, back, and rump grey, scapulars white.* Broad black stripe from bill through eye onto ear coverts, *bordered above by narrow white line.* Wing black, with single or double white patches. Long, graduated tail black, with conspicuous white edges and tips. Underparts white (washed pinkish in race *meridionalis* in Iberia and southern France). Female often faintly barred on breast. Juvenile grey-brown above; whitish below, with dark barring.

Voice: A harsh *shek* or *shack,* sometimes given in quick succession to produce a chatter; also a variety of other harsh and whistled notes. Song, a rambling series of grating and musical notes.

Habitat: Breeds in more wooded country than other shrikes, frequenting forest edge, open woodland, orchards, and gardens. In winter, in more open country but always near scattered bushes or other perches.

Nesting: 5–7 grey or buff eggs with olive or grey blotches, in a bulky nest of twigs and grass, lined with roots, hair, and feathers, placed in thornbush or sometimes a tall tree.

Range: Breeds from Spain, central France, and Norway east across much of Eurasia to the Pacific; also northern Africa and North America. Mainly resident but northernmost birds move south in winter.

This aggressive bird has the broadest distribution of any shrike, tolerating a wide range of temperatures and habitats. It includes many birds in its diet.

507, 515 **Woodchat Shrike**
(*Lanius senator*)

Description: 6¾" (17 cm). Distinguished from other shrikes by *chestnut crown and nape* and *white rump contrasting with black back.* Forehead and mask black; wing black with *broad white patch on coverts* and white wing bar (lacking in some Mediterranean island populations); tail black with white edges and tip; underparts white. Female similar but duller. Juvenile light brown with dark barring, distinguished from similar juvenile Red-backed Shrike by pale coverts and rump.

Voice: A variety of harsh chattering calls. Song vigorous and sustained, with much mimicry interspersed with its own grating notes.

Habitat: Open country with scattered trees and bushes, orchards, olive groves, gardens, bushy commons.

Nesting: 5–6 pale green eggs with brown and grey markings, in a nest of roots and weed stems lined with hair and feathers, usually placed on an outer tree branch.

Range: Breeds throughout southern Europe north to northern France, central Germany, and central Poland; also in North Africa and from Asia Minor to Iran. Winters in tropical Africa.

Its white underparts make it very conspicuous when perching in the open, although it often perches in more concealed situations than other shrikes. It feeds on small birds and their young, as well as on beetles, moths, and grasshoppers.

510 Masked Shrike
(*Lanius nubicus*)

Description: 6¾" (17 cm). Male *black above,* with *white forehead and eyebrow;* black mask; white patch on wing coverts, wing bar, and edges of tail; white below, except for *orange-pink flanks.* Female paler, with dark grey-brown upperparts. Juvenile brown above, with pale forehead and shoulder patch; white below, with dark barring.

Voice: Call, a harsh, shrill *kaaa* or *keer.* Song, a disjointed series of tuneless, scratchy notes, with occasional liquid note and sometimes repeated phrases.

Habitat: Open woodland, scrub, open country with scattered bushes, olive groves, gardens.

Nesting: 4–6 pale creamy or buff eggs with heavy brown and grey spots, in nest of twigs and stalks lined with fine roots, placed on tree branch.

Range: Breeds in southeastern Europe from Greece north to southern Yugoslavia, eastern Bulgaria, and Turkey; also from Asia Minor to Iran. Winters in Arabia and Africa.

It is slimmer and appears longer-tailed than other shrikes. Its diet includes insects—chiefly grasshoppers, beetles, bees, and wasps—and, occasionally, nestlings of small birds. It perches less conspicuously than other shrikes.

CROWS, MAGPIES, AND JAYS
(Corvidae)

107 species: worldwide, except New Zealand. Eleven breed in Europe. Medium- to large-sized land birds, largest of the Passeriformes (perching birds). Bill and legs strong, plumage varying from all-black in typical crows to diverse and colourful in jays and magpies; sexes similar. Bold, aggressive, and wary, they are among the most intelligent birds in the world. Highly adaptable, found in a wide variety of habitats, and omnivorous. Voice harsh. Most species build large stick nest in tree or on cliff.

606 Jay
(*Garrulus glandarius*)

Description: 13½″ (34 cm). Plumage variable geographically. European birds have *pinkish-brown bodies* (greyer above on Continent, pinker in Britain and Ireland); black-and-white crown feathers that can be raised in *crest; broad, black moustachial streak; white rump;* black tail; and mainly black wing, with *blue-and-white patches* and brown shoulder. Bill dark, eyes pale blue.

Voice: Usual call, a harsh, raucous screech, *skaaaak*. Also has varied repertoire of mewing, cawing, grating, and clicking notes. No true song, but a weak, disjointed subsong mixing burbling, creaking, and warbling notes. Also a mimic.

Habitat: Woodlands of various types, open country with scattered trees, orchards, gardens, sometimes even city parks, but always near trees, especially oaks.

Nesting: 5–7 pale green or olive eggs with small dark spots, in stick nest lined with fine roots, well hidden high in tree.

Range: Breeds almost throughout Europe except northern treeless areas; also in

North Africa and across central Asia to Pacific. Mainly resident in Europe.

Though common and quite conspicuously coloured, this jay is very wary, especially when nesting, and is more often heard than seen. When flying away, the white rump and contrasting black tail are conspicuous. It hops along branches and on the ground, frequently flicking its tail. Its flight is heavy and undulating.

607 **Siberian Jay**
(*Perisoreus infaustus*)

Description: 12″ (30 cm). Top and sides of head dark brown, rest of body dull grey-brown, with rufous wash on lower belly and undertail coverts. Wing brown, with *reddish patch at base of primaries; rump reddish;* centre of tail grey-brown, *outer feathers reddish.* Reddish underside of tail and underwing coverts conspicuous in flight. Smaller than Jay, with slimmer body and bill and longer, graduated tail.

Voice: Calls, *kook-kook, whisk-ee,* and a harsh *chair.*

Habitat: Dense coniferous northern forests; also birch woods. In winter, frequents edges of human habitations.

Nesting: 4 pale bluish eggs spotted with brown and grey, in nest of twigs and bark lined with lichen and feathers, placed in conifer, usually near trunk.

Range: Breeds in northern and central Scandinavia and northern Russia, east across forested parts of northern Siberia to Pacific.

It nests early, in April or even March, long before the snows have melted. In winter, it stays largely within its breeding range but becomes somewhat nomadic, frequenting human settlements in search of scraps and handouts. Pairs mate for life.

604 Azure-winged Magpie
(*Cyanopica cyana*)

Description: 13½″ (34 cm). *Top and sides of head black; throat white.* Body pinkish-grey, paler below; *long, graduated tail pale blue; wings largely pale blue,* with some black on primaries and pinkish-grey on shoulders.

Voice: Normal call, a dry *zhreeee,* sometimes rising in pitch, but also other notes including crow-like *caw,* double *kee-aw,* and some shriller, more liquid notes.

Habitat: Open woodland, especially pine; olive and cork oak groves, orchards, gardens.

Nesting: 5–7 pale creamy-buff or creamy-olive eggs, in well-camouflaged nest of sticks and roots lined with plant fibres and hair, placed in fork of tree or on branch.

Range: Resident locally in central and southern Spain and Portugal. Also breeds in China, Mongolia, Japan, and parts of eastern Siberia.

A gap of about 5,000 miles (8,000 km) separates the populations of Spain and China. The species' range must have been continuous from China to Spain in the not-too-distant past. It is gregarious, constantly roving about in small, noisy bands. Often bold and confiding, it is plentiful in parks and suburban gardens in Tokyo.

603 Magpie
(*Pica pica*)

Description: 18″ (45 cm). Tail (8–10″ (20–25 cm). Adult unmistakable, with *pied plumage* and *long tail*. Head and body black except for white belly; wing black; scapulars and primaries largely white. Purple and green sheen on wings and tail.

Voice: Normal call, a hard, rattling chatter of variable length; also a nasal, questioning *renk?* In spring, gives a more liquid *chook-chook;* occasional *babbling* subsong.

Habitat: Open country with trees, hedgerows, thickets, scrub, copses. Edges of woods, but not dense woodland.

Nesting: 5–8 greenish eggs spotted brown and grey, in large domed stick nest lined with earth and roots, usually placed in tall tree.

Range: Breeds almost throughout Europe, but absent from Iceland, parts of northern Scotland, and some Mediterranean islands. Also breeds in North Africa, western half of Asia, and western North America.

A very common bird, it is viewed by man with mixed emotions. While hunted by gamekeepers because it eats the eggs and young of game birds and by farmers because it sometimes eats grain, it is also known to be beneficial, eating rats, mice, and harmful insects. It is attracted by shiny or colourful objects, which it appropriates for its nest.

---

605 **Nutcracker**
(*Nucifraga caryocatactes*)

Description: 12½" (31 cm). Body dark *chocolate-brown, covered with white spots;* cap darker, unspotted; *undertail coverts white.* Wings black; *tail black, with broad, white terminal band.* Long black bill. Sexes alike. Juvenile less spotted and paler brown. In flight, rather short tail and broad, rounded wings give it characteristic shape; flight rather heavy and laboured.

Voice: Normal call, a high-pitched, rasping *chair.* Also has rattling alarm call and variety of croaks, clicks, caws, and other grating notes. No true song, but a weak subsong of babbling, warbling, and clicking notes.

Habitat: Coniferous forests, with preference for Swiss pine (*Pinus cembra*). In central Europe, only in mountains; but in northern Europe and Asia, also in lowlands.

Nesting: 3–4 pale blue-green eggs with fine brown and grey spots, in grass-lined nest of sticks, moss, and lichens, on conifer branch usually near trunk.

Range: Breeds in mountains of central and southeastern Europe, and from southern Scandinavia across Asia to Japan.

It feeds principally on seeds of conifers, but is also fond of hazelnuts, which it cracks open with its sharp bill, and takes some beetles and other insects. It also stores food for winter use. Siberian birds irrupt westward at regular intervals, reaching Britain and other parts of western Europe.

---

597 **Alpine Chough**
(*Pyrrhocorax graculus*)

Description: 15″ (38 cm). *All-black,* less glossy than Chough and shorter-tailed; *bill yellow, less curved, and much shorter; red legs.* Juvenile somewhat duller, with blackish legs.

Voice: Two basic calls, with variations: a ringing, metallic trill, *trrreee,* and a pure, shrill, high-pitched *tee-lu* or *chee-oop.* The two are sometimes joined, *trreee-yup.*

Habitat: High mountains, up to snow line, nesting on cliffs and feeding on nearby slopes. In winter, descends into valleys and often found around human habitation. More strictly montane than Chough, seldom occurring in lowlands or on coast.

Nesting: 4 creamy-white eggs covered with small dark brown spots, in bulky stick nest lined with fine grasses and placed in hole or crevice in cliff.

Range: Mountainous regions of central and southern Europe from Spain to Balkans; also in Corsica and North Africa and in southwestern and central Asia, east to Himalayas.

Flocks are found around alpine towns all winter, looking for food. In the

Himalayas they frequent the h mountain villages, and Everest c have reported them around their at 26,000 feet (8000 m). Fond of soaring, they can be seen in large flo circling slowly in the air, making use thermals and occasionally engaging in extravagant aerobatics.

---

596 Chough or Red-billed Chough

(*Pyrrhocorax pyrrhocorax*)

Description: 15″ (38 cm). *Entirely black,* glossed dark blue, with *long, thin, decurved red bill* and *red legs.* Juvenile has orange-yellow bill, not quite as long as adult's but longer and more decurved than bill of Alpine Chough.

Voice: Thin, drawn-out cawing notes, *kaaa, kyaaa,* or *kyaw;* also high-pitched gull-like mewing, *kee-ah,* and a low *kwuk-uk-uk;* often says its name, *k'chuf.*

Habitat: Cliffs, both in hills and mountains and on seacoasts. Feeds in nearby fields. Resident throughout its range.

Nesting: 3–4 whitish eggs, in bulky nest of sticks and sturdy plant stems, lined with hair, placed in rock crevice or on ledge of cave or cliff. Sometimes nests in small colonies.

Range: Local on rocky western coasts of British Isles and Brittany and in scattered coastal and mountainous areas in southern Europe from Spain and Alps to Greece. Locally common, but range discontinuous because of habitat requirements. Also breeds in North Africa, Ethiopia, and across southern Asia to Himalayas and western China.

It frequently engages in aerobatics, diving with closed wings and swooping up again in a broad arc, and even rolling over on its back. Fond of soaring, it keeps its primaries spread, with tips curved upward.

601 **Jackdaw**
(*Corvus monedula*)

Description: 13″ (33 cm). Mainly black, with *grey nape and ear coverts.* Dark grey below, *eye greyish-white;* bill short; forehead steeper than other crows, giving head more rounded look.

Voice: Quite different from larger crows. Normal call, a high-pitched yelp, *jack!,* often lengthened into *jack-a-jack.* Also *kyow,* and varied notes incorporated into a low subsong in spring.

Habitat: Open woods and parkland with large old trees, coastal inland cliffs, farm buildings, church towers, houses.

Nesting: 4–6 pale blue eggs lightly spotted with black and grey, in stick nest lined with hair and grass (hole nests have lining only), sometimes in the open but usually in cavity in tree, cliff, or building.

Range: Breeds in central and southern Europe, north to central Scandinavia and north-central Russia. Also breeds in North Africa and in southwestern and central Asia east to Lake Baikal.

Very sociable, usually nesting in loose colonies and forming large flocks after the breeding season, roosting together at night. They frequently indulge in aerobatics.

598 **Rook**
(*Corvus frugilegus*)

Description: 18″ (45 cm). All-black, with purplish gloss. Distinguished from Carrion Crow by *pale whitish patch of bare skin around base of bill; thinner, straighter,* more pointed *bill;* steep forehead, giving head an angled look; and *shaggy thighs.* Juvenile less glossy, with no grey on face; distinguished from Carrion Crow by more slender bill.

Voice: Wide vocabulary includes the normal call, *kaaaa* or *caw,* higher-pitched and more drawn out than *kaa* of Carrion

Crow, and varied croaks, squaw... yelps.

Habitat: Agricultural country with rows of... copses, and small woods.

Nesting: 3–5 pale green eggs, in bulky nest o... sticks and earth, lined with grass, leaves, and moss, in colony or rookery in tops of large tree. Sometimes previous year's nest is reused.

Range: Very common, breeding in western, central, and eastern Europe, north to southern Scandinavia and northern Russia, but not in Mediterranean region, where it occurs only in winter. Also breeds across central Asia to Pacific. Mainly sedentary, but northernmost birds move south in winter.

Highly gregarious, it nests socially in rookeries and forms huge flocks after the breeding season. A large rookery often seems chaotic, with birds squabbling over nest sites, stealing sticks from each other's nests, and threatening their neighbours.

600, 602 Carrion Crow (including "Hooded Crow")

(*Corvus corone*)

Description: 18½" (46 cm). *All-black,* with *heavy, black bill* feathered at the base. Bill and lower slope of forehead give head flatter shape than that of Rook, which has thinner, straighter bill and angular forehead. Lacks whitish on face, unlike Rook; young Rook lacks whitish face but has thinner bill. *"Hooded Crow"* (*C. c. cornix*) *has grey, not black, body.* Intermediates also occur.

Voice: Normal call, a short, deep, gutteral *kaa,* usually repeated 3–4 times in quick succession, quite different from Rook's higher-pitched, more drawn-out call. Also has vocabulary of other notes, several higher in pitch.

Habitat: Open country with a few trees, including farmland, grasslands, moors, parks, even in cities. Not usually in dense woods. Often feeds on lakeshores and along coasts. Occurs up to 6,500′ (2,000 m) in mountains.

Nesting: 4–6 blue or green eggs heavily spotted with dark brown, in bulky nest of sticks and mud lined with hair, usually in fork of tree but also on coastal cliff ledges.

Range: Breeds throughout Europe and discontinuously across northern and central Asia to Japan; also in Egypt. Mainly resident, but northernmost birds move south or west in winter.

The "Hooded Crow" (*C. c. cornix*) is now classified as a subspecies of the Carrion Crow. They are identical in every respect except plumage. The black form inhabits southern Scotland, England, France, Spain, Holland, Belgium, and western Germany, while the black-and-grey form occupies the rest of Europe.

---

599 **Raven**
(*Corvus corax*)

Description: 25″ (63 cm). *Large and thick-set,* with longer neck than other crows and a *long, wedge-shaped tail.* Glossy black, with *heavy, black bill;* loose feathers give throat a shaggy look. Juvenile somewhat browner and lacking gloss.

Voice: Normal call, a deep, guttural croak repeated 2 or 3 times, *krrro, krrro, krrro* or *krruk, krruk,* different from other crows, though Rooks occasionally produce rather similar croak. A variety of other calls during the breeding season.

Habitat: Open rocky country of various types, from coastal cliffs to high mountain slopes; also densely wooded country.

Nesting: 4–6 light blue or green eggs spotted dark brown, in bulky stick nest lined with grass, moss, and hair and placed on cliff ledge or in tree.

Range: Holarctic. Resident over greater part of

Europe but abse
Britain, France, G
west-central Europea
breeds in northern Afr
to Pacific, and from Nor
south to Guatemala.

Omnivorous and a scavenger, it
attack sick and disabled animals ar
eats small rodents, eggs, and someti
birds. A fine acrobatic flier, it may be seen tumbling, flying upside down, and nose-diving in spring courtship display.

LINGS

rnidae)

111 species: Old World. Three species breed in Europe. Small to medium-sized, plump birds with rather long straight bill and usually short tail. Plumage variable, often black or blue with metallic gloss; sexes similar or dissimilar. Noisy, active birds, gregarious outside breeding season. European species largely terrestrial, others arboreal. They run or walk on the ground but do not hop; flight is swift and direct. Omnivorous. Hole nesters.

487, 503, 504 **Starling**

(*Sturnus vulgaris*)

Description: 8½″ (21 cm). Plump and compact, with *long bill, short tail,* and short, pointed, *triangular wings.* In spring, adult blackish, with green and purple iridescence; lightly speckled above but plain below. In winter, heavily spotted white all over. Bill yellow in spring, dark in winter. Sexes similar. Juvenile unspotted grey-brown, with pale throat and dark bill.

Voice: Huge repertoire of notes, chuckling, whistling, bubbling, clicking, woven into long, rambling song. Especially characteristic are downslurred whistle, *peee-ooo,* and grating *charrr.* Also mimics other birds.

Habitat: Farmland, gardens, parks, and other man-made habitats. In the breeding season, favours deciduous woodlands.

Nesting: 5–7 whitish eggs, in untidy grass or straw nest lined with feathers, placed in almost any hole, especially in trees or buildings.

Range: Breeds throughout Europe except the Iberian peninsula; also in Asia, east to Lake Baikal. Resident and migratory, retiring from northern parts of breeding range in winter and moving south to Spain, North Africa, and Middle East.

It is one of the world's most familiar birds. When roosting on city buildings, as they do around Trafalgar Square, London, they become a considerable nuisance, defacing buildings with their droppings.

Spotless Starling
(*Sturnus unicolor*)

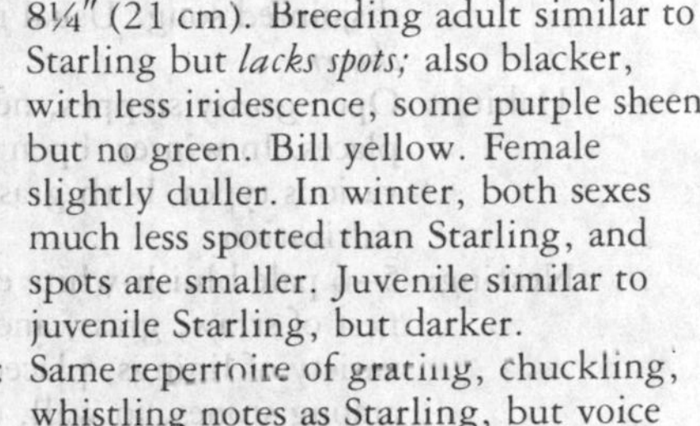

Description: 8¼″ (21 cm). Breeding adult similar to Starling but *lacks spots;* also blacker, with less iridescence, some purple sheen but no green. Bill yellow. Female slightly duller. In winter, both sexes much less spotted than Starling, and spots are smaller. Juvenile similar to juvenile Starling, but darker.

Voice: Same repertoire of grating, chuckling, whistling notes as Starling, but voice somewhat more powerful. Tends to emphasise downslurred *peeee-ooo* more. Also a fine mimic.

Habitat: Similar to that of Starling, favouring man-made habitats. Nests on buildings and cliffs and locally in woods, flocking on cultivated land in winter.

Nesting: 4 pale blue eggs, in untidy nest of plant material, lined with feathers and hair, placed in tree hole or crevice in rock or building. Nests colonially.

Range: Resident on Iberian peninsula, Corsica, Sardinia, and Sicily; also in western North Africa.

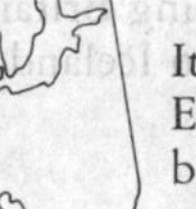

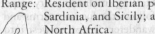

It replaces the Starling in southwest Europe and North Africa as a breeding bird. When the two species occur together in winter flocks, identification can be difficult. No hybridisation is known between these species.

482 Rose-coloured Starling
(*Sturnus roseus*)

Description: 8½″ (21 cm). Summer adult has *pink body; glossy black head, neck, wings, and tail;* and *bushy crest.* Chunky shape. In winter, pink and black areas mottled with brown. Bill yellowish-pink in summer, brown in winter. Legs pink. Juvenile lacks crest and is paler than juvenile Starling; light sandy-brown, with somewhat darker wings and tail, and further distinguished by pink legs and yellowish-pink base to bill.

Voice: Similar to Starling: varied grating, chattering, and whistling notes sometimes strung together into a disjointed song. Usual note, a harsh *churrr.*

Habitat: Open grassy steppes, nesting in rocky places. In winter, open country of various types, both grassland and cultivation.

Nesting: 5–6 pale bluish-white eggs, in untidy nest of straw, grass, and twigs with a variety of linings, placed in hole, either among stones, in wall, or even in the ground.

Range: Breeds in southeastern Europe in countries bordering Black Sea (rare in Bulgaria), west to Hungary and sometimes Yugoslavia and Italy. Also in southwestern Asia and east to south-central Siberia. Winters mainly in India.

Except for its beautiful plumage, the Rose-coloured Starling is similar to the Starling in almost every respect. It follows the locust swarms and is thus a wanderer, irrupting west into Europe irregularly and reaching Britain, Scandinavia, and even Iceland.

SPARROWS
(Passeridae)

42 species: Old World. Five species breed in Europe. Small, stout-billed birds with mainly brown or grey plumage; sexes similar or dissimilar. Terrestrial, feeding mainly on seeds. Closely related to the weaverbirds but with a different nest, bulky and untidy, usually in a hole. Largely sedentary.

576, 587 **House Sparrow**
(*Passer domesticus*)

Description: 5¾″ (14 cm). Male has *grey crown bordered with chestnut* at back and sides; *black bib;* dingy white cheeks and underparts. Back rich brown with black stripes; rump grey; wing brown, with distinct white wing bar. Head colours duller in winter. Female and young nondescript: dingy white below; brown above, with dark streaks; buffy, less prominent wing bar; indistinct, pale eyebrow. Males of the race Italian Sparrow (*P. d. italiae*) have chestnut crown, more black on breast, and whiter cheeks and underparts.

Voice: Varied chirps and cheeps; also a hard, grating twitter. Male in spring has double note, *chissit,* incorporated into series of chirps and cheeps to form a rough song. Males may sing in chorus.

Habitat: Human habitations and nearby cultivated land, including parks, houses, farmyards, roadsides, grainfields.

Nesting: 3–5 greyish-white eggs covered with dark blotches and spots, in loose, untidy grass or straw nest placed in building crevice or in dense vegetation; often nests colonially.

Range: Breeds throughout Europe, except Iceland, and in western and northern Asia east to Manchuria; also in northern Africa. Hybridises with Spanish Sparrow in Sicily and southern Italy.

Successfully introduced in many parts of the world, and perhaps the world's most familiar bird, the lowly House Sparrow is more closely attached to man than is any other species. It is now one of the most abundant birds in North America, where it was unknown until a few birds were released in Central Park, New York City, in 1850.

---

588 Spanish Sparrow
(*Passer hispaniolensis*)

Description: 5¾″ (14 cm). Male similar to Italian race of House Sparrow (*P. d. italiae*), with *chestnut crown and nape,* white cheeks and underparts, but with *much more extensive black* on throat and breast and *black streaks on flanks;* also heavier black markings on back. Female and juvenile resemble female House Sparrow, but with some faint streaks on flanks, whiter cheeks, and darker backs.

Voice: Varied chirps and cheeps, like House Sparrow, but deeper, fuller, and richer. Song also similar, a series of call notes.

Habitat: Open bushy areas, woodlands, olive groves, trees along watercourses.

Nesting: 5–6 white eggs with grey or dark purple spots and blotches, in loose domed nest of grass and straw, lined with feathers and hair, placed in tree.

Range: Breeds in southern Spain, Sardinia, and Balkans; also in North Africa and southwest Asia. Hybridises with House Sparrow in Sicily and southern Italy. Partial migrant to Africa and Asia.

It hybridises with its close relative the House Sparrow in some parts of its range, but elsewhere it may nest side by side without interbreeding. Generally they choose separate nest areas, the Spanish typically nesting colonially in trees, often along rivers, or in nest of stork or raptor. Where the House Sparrow is absent, the Spanish Sparrow may replace it and build its nests around houses.

589 Tree Sparrow
(*Passer montanus*)

Description: 5½" (14 cm). Smaller and slimmer than House Sparrow; *chestnut crown and nape,* smaller black bib, whiter cheeks with *black cheek patch,* almost complete white collar; rump yellowish-brown, not grey. Sexes alike; juveniles resemble adults.

Voice: Varied chirps and cheeps, generally similar to House Sparrow but shorter and higher-pitched. Hard, *teck* flight note is distinctive. Song, a repeated series of call notes.

Habitat: Regionally variable. In western Europe, less attached to man than House Sparrow, preferring open woodland, lines of trees, orchards, and large gardens. Especially partial to pollarded willows. In far north, nests on open tundra; in southern and eastern Europe, found more frequently around buildings.

Nesting: 4–6 brownish-white eggs with fine markings, in loose, untidy nest of grass or straw, placed in tree hole or building crevice. Often forms loose nesting colonies.

Range: Breeds in most of Europe but absent from northern Scandinavia and parts of England, Scotland, Ireland, and Mediterranean region. Also breeds across most of northern and central Asia, east to Pacific and south to Indonesia.

Where their ranges overlap, the Tree Sparrow prefers open wooded situations, while the House Sparrow lives exclusively around human habitation. Where the Tree Sparrow occurs alone, it fills the niche of the House Sparrow. In the Orient, where the House Sparrow is absent, the Tree Sparrow is the common city sparrow.

577 **Rock Sparrow**
(*Petronia petronia*)

Description: 5½" (14 cm). Pale brown, short-tailed bird resembling female House Sparrow but with different head pattern: pale eyebrow and crown stripe, and brown cheek patch and stripe on sides of crown. Upperparts light brown with darker streaking; *tail, with white spots at the tip,* conspicuous in flight; dingy white below, with indistinct mottling and streaking; *pale yellow spot on breast* visibile only in fresh plumage at close range. Sexes alike. Juvenile paler, with no yellow on throat. *Pale bill.* Undulating flight and broad wings unlike House Sparrow.

Voice: Various chirping notes, more ringing and nasal than those of House Sparrow: *chee-u-wee, pee-dyu, per-dee-du.* No true song, just a succession of notes.

Habitat: Rocky mountain slopes, stony ground, ruined buildings, villages, marshy edges, occasionally farmland.

Nesting: 5–6 white or greenish-white eggs with dark spots and blotches, in domed nest of stems and roots lined with feathers, placed in hole in rock, tree, wall, or building. Often nests in colonies.

Range: Breeds in southwestern Europe from Spain and south-central France through Italy to Balkans; also on Atlantic islands, North Africa, and Asia east to Mongolia and northern China.

While not as dependent on man as the House Sparrow is, it often occurs near human habitations and readily accepts old buildings, bridges, stone walls, and other man-made edifices as nest sites. Though largely sedentary, in winter there is some altitudinal migration to lower slopes.

583 **Snowfinch**
(*Montifringilla nivalis*)

Description: 7" (18 cm). Adult male has *grey head, black throat,* rich brown upperparts, and creamy-white underparts. *Wing white with black primaries, tail largely white with black centre.* Female has browner head, less white in wing and tail; juvenile like female but duller. Bill black in spring adults, orange-yellow in winter adults and juveniles.

Voice: Call, a grating, nasal *tsweek*. Song, a rather pleasing medley of twittering and chirping notes, including repetition of *tweet-sit-jidder* or *tweet-sit*.

Habitat: A true high mountain species, inhabiting bare rocky and stony mountain slopes above 6,000′ (2,000 m), moving somewhat lower in winter. Often around human habitation.

Nesting: 4–5 white eggs, in nest of grass, moss, and feathers, lined with feathers and hair, placed in a hole in rock or building.

Range: Breeds in Pyrenees, Alps, mountains of northern Italy and Balkans, and east across southwest and central Asia to Mongolia and Tibet. Resident.

It is familiar to skiers at alpine resorts, where with the Alpine Accentor it frequents the huts on the upper slopes in winter, picking up table crumbs. In male's display flight, it planes with spread wings and tail, showing its extensive white, then spirals down to earth. It often sings during this flight, but will also sing from the top of a boulder.

FINCHES
(*Fringillidae*)

124 species: worldwide, except Australasia. Nineteen species breed in Europe. Very small to medium-small arboreal birds feeding mainly on nuts and seeds. Bill usually stout and conical; some have massive head and bill and thick neck. Plumage often bright, especially in male; sexes dissimilar. Many species have song flight and prolonged, pleasant song. Cup-shaped nest built by female.

552, 558 **Chaffinch**
(*Fringilla coelebs*)

Description: 6″ (15 cm). Male has *blue-grey crown and nape, chestnut mantle, greenish rump, and pinkish-brown underparts.* Female much duller, olive-brown above and greyish below. Distinct *white shoulder patch, narrower white wing bar, and white sides of tail* in both sexes. Juvenile like female.

Voice: Common calls a loud *pink, pink,* a flight note, *tsup,* and a loud warning *wheet;* also a variety of other notes. Cheerful, bustling song, a descending, slightly accelerating series of 10–12 notes ending in a flourish, *chu-wee-o.*

Habitat: A wide range, including woods, hedgerows, farmland, gardens, and parks. In winter, more open country.

Nesting: 4–5 eggs, greenish-blue to light brown with dark spots and streaks, in very neat nest of grass, bark, root fibres, moss, and lichens, lined with hair, placed in bush or small tree.

Range: Breeds almost throughout Europe except Iceland and extreme northern Scandinavia; also Atlantic islands, North Africa, and western Asia. Partial migrant, northern birds wintering south to North Africa and Middle East.

This is one of the most abundant and familiar birds in Europe. Its song is extremely variable, with pronounced accents and dialects in different parts of its range. Its plumage also varies; the all-blue form on the Canary Islands is considered a separate species, the Canary Islands Chaffinch (*Fringilla teydea*).

551, 555 **Brambling**
(*Fringilla montifringilla*)

Description: 5¾" (14 cm). Male has *black head and mantle, conspicuous white rump, orange breast and shoulder.* In winter, head and mantle became dark, mottled brown. Female brown above with dull orange breast, much less orange on shoulder, and *white rump.* Immature resembles female.

Voice: Call, nasal *tsweek* or *scape;* flight note, *chucc-chucc.* Usual song, a series of notes resembling Greenfinch's *dzweee,* but more tuneful.

Habitat: Breeds mainly in birch woods but also at edges of coniferous forests and in willow scrub. In winter, on farmland and in woods, especially beech.

Nesting: 5–7 eggs, light blue with dark spots and streaks, laid in nest of coarse grasses, root fibres, and lichen, lined with feathers and down, placed well off the ground in a tree, especially birch.

Range: Breeds from Scandinavia and northern Baltic States across northern Asia to Kamchatka and Mongolia. Scattered breeding records from Britain, Denmark, and central Europe. Winters in central and southern Europe, south to Mediterranean islands and North Africa.

A close relative of the Chaffinch, the two often occur together in large mixed flocks in winter. They feed on weed seeds and grain, with a special predilection for beechmast. Spotting the less numerous Bramblings among a large flock of Chaffinches is easiest when they are in flight, because their white rumps become conspicuous.

564 **Serin**
(*Serinus serinus*)

Description: 4½" (11 cm). A *small,* streaky green finch with *tiny stubby bill* and *bright yellow rump.* Male has *bright yellow head with dark cheeks and crown;* breast yellow *streaked with black.* Female less yellow, duller, and more streaked. Distinguished from Siskin by shorter bill, brighter-yellow rump, and *no yellow at sides of tail.* Juvenile like female but more heavily streaked; lacks yellow on rump.

Voice: Flight note, a rather liquid twitter; anxiety note, *tsooeet.* Song, a rapid cascade of sibilant, jingly notes with musical quality.

Habitat: Small copses and rows of trees, orchards, vineyards, gardens, city parks, and suburbs.

Nesting: 4 pale blue eggs streaked and spotted with purple and brown, laid in a nest of grass stems, moss, and lichen, lined with hair, concealed in bush or tree.

Range: Breeds in continental Europe north to southern tip of Sweden and Baltic States; also Turkey and North Africa. Has recently bred in England. Partial migrant, northern birds wintering south to North Africa and Middle East.

A bird of the woodland edge, the European Serin now seems to prefer man-made habitats that provide some trees. Its exuberant song, given from a treetop or in flight, is one of the dominant sounds of spring in Mediterranean countries.

563 **Citril Finch**
(*Serinus citrinella*)

Description: 4¾" (12 cm). A *small yellow-green* finch with *grey nape and sides of neck,* yellowish-green rump, and *unstreaked underparts.* Wing black with two greenish-yellow wing bars; dark tail lacks yellow. Female duller and greyer. Juvenile grey-brown and heavily streaked. Distinguished from Siskin and Serin by grey neck and unstreaked underparts; from Greenfinch by smaller size, different wing pattern, and lack of yellow on tail.

Voice: Call, a plaintive, piping *tsu-u;* twittering flight call produced by repetition of metallic *tweck.* Song, a mixture of musical notes and creaky twittering. Sings in circling aerial display.

Habitat: Mostly mountains. Breeds in open rocky slopes with scattered conifers (mainly spruce) at upper edge of tree line, in Spain also in birch-holly woods and in Corsica in tall heath not far above sea level. In winter, moves to lower mountain levels.

Nesting: 4–5 pale blue eggs with red-brown streaks and spots, laid in nest of grass and lichens, lined with thistledown and other materials, placed well up in tree.

Range: Breeds in mountains of central and southern Europe from northwest Spain to Germany and northern Italy; also Balearic Islands, Corsica, and Sardinia. Sedentary.

This is one of the very few species endemic to the continent of Europe. A true mountain species on the mainland, on islands it has adapted to lower levels and is equally at home in trees or on the ground among rocks. It feeds mainly on conifer seeds.

566, 567 Greenfinch
(*Carduelis chloris*)

Description: 5¾″ (14 cm). Chunky, short-tailed, big-headed bird, with heavy, pale bill and pinkish legs. Male *olive-green, with yellow-green rump and large, well-defined yellow patches on primaries and at base of tail, very conspicuous in flight.* Female browner, with less yellow; juvenile browner still, streaked above and below, with brown rump and yellow wing and tail patches.

Voice: Common call, both in flight and perched, a hard, dry *titititi.* In breeding season, male gives a long-drawn nasal *dzhweee.* Song, a succession of these two calls, sometimes mixed with more musical warbling and twittering notes.

Habitat: Edges of woods, farmland with hedges, orchards, olive groves, gardens, parks. In winter, on cultivated land and open areas near coast.

Nesting: 4–6 off-white to pale blue eggs with red-brown and violet markings, in nest of twigs and moss lined with roots, hair, or feathers, placed in hedge.

Range: Breeds throughout Europe except Iceland and northern Scandinavia; also North Africa and western Asia. Mainly resident, but northernmost birds winter south to North Africa and Middle East.

A very common and familiar bird, it is quite at home near man. In spring and summer, males perch on treetops to sing, from time to time taking off in a curious, butterfly-like display flight, with slowly flapping wings.

---

550 Goldfinch
(*Carduelis carduelis*)

Description: 4¾″ (12 cm). Adult unmistakable, with *red face, black-and-white head,* and *black wings with broad, yellow stripe* conspicuous in flight. Upperparts brown, *rump white, tail black* with white near tips. Mainly white below, with some brown on breast and flanks. Sexes similar. Juvenile has plain brown head, but wings similar to adult. Flight undulating, bouncy, and erratic.

Voice: Call, a liquid *tswitt-witt-witt* but unique tinkling quality; also a harsh *geez.* Song, tinkling call notes interwoven with canary-like twittering.

Habitat: Forest edge, orchards, hedges, gardens, parks. In winter, more open country.

Nesting: 4–6 very pale blue eggs with a few red-brown spots and streaks, in nest of grass, moss, and lichens, lined with wool and down, on tree branch.

Range: Breeds over most of Europe, but absent from Iceland and most of Fennoscandia (except south) and rare in northern Scotland; also North Africa and Asia east to Iran and Himalayas. Partial migrant, northern birds wintering south to North Africa and Middle East.

Popular in some countries as a cage bird, it was often featured in medieval tapestries and Renaissance paintings. Outside the breeding season, it spends much of its time in small groups feeding in patches of weeds, especially thistles, often hanging from plant heads, like a tit.

562, 571 Siskin
(*Carduelis spinus*)

Description: 4¾" (12 cm). A small yellow-green finch, about the size of Serin but with longer bill and yellow patches on sides of tail-base. Male has *black crown and chin, yellow rump and sides of tail,* and *black-and-yellow wing.* Female lacks black on head, has less yellow, is whiter below and more streaked.

Voice: Call, a characteristic wheezy, downslurred *tseeoo,* also *tsooeet* with a similar creaky tone. Song, a long, bustling twitter of sweet musical notes, ending in a buzzy *jeeeee.*

Habitat: Breeds mainly in coniferous woods, in Central Europe chiefly in mountains. In winter, prefers birches and alders, often along streams.

Nesting: 3–5 pale blue eggs with pale red spots and streaks, in nest of dead twigs, lichens, moss, and grasses, placed high in a conifer, often near the end of a branch.

Range: Breeds discontinuously from Britain, Ireland, and Scandinavia and Pyrenees east across Europe to western Siberia and Iran; also in eastern Asia. Partial migrant, wintering south to Mediterranean region and Middle East.

It forms loose flocks in winter, often joining Redpolls. Active and restless while feeding, it often hangs from an alder catkin like a tit and has recently acquired a taste for peanuts put out for tits in gardens. It sings from treetops and in display flights, circling above trees with fluffed-up plumage and slow wingbeats.

546, 575 **Linnet**
(*Carduelis cannabina*)

Description: 5¼″ (13 cm). Breeding male has *grey head, red forehead and breast,* whitish throat with dark streaks, *chestnut back,* and *white edgings to primaries and tail* visible both in flight and at rest. Bill dark grey-brown. In winter, breast brownish-pink, underparts buffy with darker streaking. Female duller brown, more streaked, and lacking red at all seasons. Juvenile similar to female but more heavily streaked.

Voice: Call, *tsooeet;* in flight, a dry, rapid twitter. Song variable in form, a pleasant musical twittering combining both liquid and nasal notes.

Habitat: Low bushes and scrub, especially gorse; heath, forest edge, gardens, orchards. In winter, weedy fields, rough open ground, grassy country.

Nesting: 4–6 pale blue eggs spotted purplish-red, in nest of grass, moss, and plant stems, lined with hair, placed low in bush.

Range: Breeds throughout Europe, except Iceland and northern Fennoscandia; also North Africa and Asia east to western Siberia and Turkestan. Partial migrant, northern birds wintering south to North Africa and Middle East

Males often sing in chorus, and breeding in loose colonies is frequent, though pairs regularly nest singly. It forms large flocks in winter, sometimes with other species. It feeds mainly on weed seeds.

572 Twite
(*Carduelis flavirostris*)

Description: 5¼″ (13 cm). Streaked brown finch, darker above and warmer below than similar Linnet, with less white on wings and tail. *Throat unstreaked warm buff* (whitish and streaked in Linnet); *bill yellow in winter, grey in summer* (Linnet's bill dark all year; Redpoll's bill yellow all year). Male has *pink* rump; female rump buff with dark streaks. Juvenile similar to female.

Voice: Call, a distinctive nasal *chweet, tsooeek,* or *twa-it,* hence the name Twite. Flight twitter, like Linnet but harder. Song, rather like Linnet but more twangy and metallic, a jumble of liquid and nasal notes.

Habitat: Open, often rocky country in hills and lowlands, heathery moors, grassy uplands. In winter, lowlands, cultivated ground, especially near coast, salt marshes.

Nesting: 5–6 blue eggs with a few dark spots and streaks, in nest of grass, moss, and twigs lined with hair, wool, or feathers, placed on or near ground in low vegetation.

Range: Breeds in Britain, Ireland, and Norway and discontinuously across central Asia from Turkey to China. Partial migrant, wintering south to coasts of North and Baltic seas.

A close relative of the Linnet, it is more northern in distribution and prefers open country rather than trees. It sometimes sings in chorus, like Linnet, and similarly breeds in loose colonies.

548 Redpoll or Common Redpoll
(*Carduelis flammea*)

Description: 5–6″ (13–15 cm). Small, streaked, grey-brown finch, with *red forehead, black chin,* and *two pale wing bars.* Male in breeding season acquires *pink breast and rump;* otherwise, sexes alike. Juvenile lacks red and has poorly marked chin. Races differ considerably in size and colour: Lesser Redpoll (*C. f. cabaret*) of Britain, Ireland, and mountains of central Europe is smallest and darkest; Mealy Redpoll (*C. f. flammea*) of northern Europe is intermediate in size and palest; Greenland Redpoll (*C. f. rostrata*), a winter visitor from Greenland, is largest, and almost as dark as *C. f. cabaret*.

Voice: A dry, hard flight call, *chit-chit-chit-chit,* and nasal *tsweet.* Song, a series of flight calls interspersed with brief, rattling trills and more melodious rolling notes.

Habitat: Birch and mixed woods, clumps of alder and willow, sometimes coniferous forest and plantations; also beyond timberline on open tundra with dwarf scrub. In winter, mainly in birches and alders.

Nesting: 4–5 pale blue eggs spotted and streaked with light brown, in nest of twigs, roots, and bark, lined with down and feathers, placed in fork of tree or bush.

Range: Holarctic, breeding in Iceland, Britain, Ireland, mountains of central Europe, and from Scandinavia across northern Asia to Bering Sea, and in North America. Winters south to northeast Spain, northern Italy, and northern Balkans.

In spring, several males may sing together in a special display flight, circling over the trees with slow wingbeats. When feeding on their favourite diet of birch and alder seeds, they often hang upside down like tits to reach the catkins.

549 **Arctic Redpoll**
(*Carduelis hornemanni*)

Description: 5″ (13 cm). Very similar to Redpoll, but with *pale, frosty look,* especially on head and nape; paler grey back with dark streaks; *white, unstreaked rump* (streaked in Redpoll); whiter underparts; and more prominent, pure white wing bars. Pink breast of male much paler.

Voice: Almost identical to Redpoll; but *chit-chit-chit* flight call is rather sharper and slower. Same nasal *tsweet* and twittering song.

Habitat: Open tundra with dwarf birch and willow. In winter, much as Redpoll, chiefly in birches and alders.

Nesting: 5 pale blue eggs spotted and streaked with light brown, in nest of twigs, roots, and bark, lined with down and feathers, placed on or near ground among rocks or in dwarf vegetation.

Range: Circumpolar, breeding in Lapland, extreme northern Asia, and North America from Alaska to Greenland. Winters fairly regularly south to southern Finland and central Scandinavia, irregularly further to countries bordering North and Baltic seas.

As its name suggests, the Arctic Redpoll nests farther north than most Redpolls and does not come as far south in winter. It frequently joins in winter flocks with Redpolls where their ranges overlap, when the pure white rumps of the Arctics distinguish them.

542, 559 **Two-barred Crossbill or White-winged Crossbill**
(*Loxia leucoptera*)

Description: 5¾" (14 cm). *Male red,* brighter and more rosy than Crossbill. *Female olive,* more streaked than female Crossbill, rump paler and brighter yellow. Both sexes have distinctive *black wing with two broad white wing bars.* Juvenile heavily streaked all over, wing bars less prominent than on adult.

Voice: Flight call, also given while perched, a dry *chif-chif,* less metallic than similar call of Crossbill. Also, a soft *peet* or *twee.* Song, a series of rapid trills, varying in speed and pitch.

Habitat: Coniferous forests, especially larch.

Nesting: 3–4 pale blue eggs with a few dark spots, in nest of twigs, grass, lichens, and moss, lined with hair, fine grasses, and feathers, placed on conifer branch.

Range: Breeds irregularly in northern Scandinavia and Finland, regularly from northern Russia to eastern Siberia, in North America, and in Hispaniola. Wanders irregularly in winter to central Russia, southern Scandinavia, and Baltic States, more rarely elsewhere in Europe.

Crossbills feed principally on conifer seeds; their bills are specially adapted for extracting seeds from the cones. The bill is opened, inserted into a cone, and then closed. As it closes, the tips of the mandibles cross and press in different directions, thus forcing the cone open. Two-barred Crossbill's bill is the slimmest of the three species. It prefers cones of spruce and larch, which are easier to open than pine.

547, 568 **Crossbill**
(*Loxia curvirostra*)

Description: 6½″ (16 cm). Heavy-headed, with short, deeply forked tail, and *crossed bill. Adult male brick red,* brightest on rump; *young male orange-brown; female olive-green,* with yellowish rump and underparts. Juvenile olive and heavily streaked. Scottish race, *L. c. scotica,* with heavier bill, is sometimes considered a separate species.

Crossbill

Voice: Common call, a hard *jip-jip.* Song, a rambling medley of call notes, sweet warbled phrases, and a variety of short notes and phrases, including *jee-jee* and *ti-chee.*

Scottish Crossbill

Habitat: Coniferous forests, mainly spruce and fir, occasionally pine and larch. Sometimes in clumps of conifers in parks and gardens.

Nesting: 3–4 pale green eggs with a few spots and streaks, in large, loosely constructed nest of pine twigs and grass lined with hair and feathers, placed on branch of conifer.

Range: Breeds from Scandinavia, Britain, central France, Iberia, and North Africa discontinuously across central and southern Europe to Greece, Turkey, and the Caucasus, and across Asia to the Pacific and Indochina; also North and Central America.

Because of their preferred diet of conifer seeds, crossbills are dependent on the success of the cone crop. In good seasons they may stay within their breeding range most of the year, but when cones are sparse they are forced to leave, resulting in periodic large irruptions of crossbills into southern and western Europe.

---

544 **Parrot Crossbill**
(*Loxia pytyopsittacus*)

Description: 6¾" (17 cm). Largest crossbill, with *huge head* and *very heavy bill.* Plumage similar to Crossbill: adult male brick red, brightest on rump, young male orange-brown. Female olive-green with yellowish rump and underparts. Juvenile olive and heavily streaked.

Voice: Almost identical to Crossbill, the flight call being a somewhat deeper and rounder *chup-chup,* the song somewhat stronger.

Habitat: Coniferous forests, principally pine. Usually spends winter in breeding range, much less prone to wander than other crossbills.

Nesting: 2–4 pale green eggs with a few black spots and streaks, in nest of twigs, grass, pine needles, and moss, placed on pine branch.

Range: Breeds in Norway, Sweden, Finland, Estonia, and northwest Russia. Mainly resident, wintering irregularly south to central Europe.

This species is much less common than other crossbills and is rarely found in mixed flocks because of its strong preference for pines. It has the same parrot- or tit-like action as other crossbills, hanging upside down from a pinecone while extracting seeds.

Trumpeter Finch
(*Bucanetes githagineus*)

Description: 5½" (14 cm). Plump, with *short, thick bill; large, rounded head;* short tail. Breeding male has *pearl grey head; pale pink face, rump, and underparts;* earth-brown back, with pinkish wash. Wings and tail dark brown, with pink edgings. Female lacks grey on head and is much browner, less rosy; juvenile pale sandy-buff. *Bill orange-red in breeding male,* orange-brown in winter male and female, yellow-brown in juvenile.

Voice: Short, nasal call likened to sound of a child's trumpet.

Habitat: Dry, rocky slopes and ravines, stony hills and uplands, and edges of deserts.

Nesting: 4–6 pale blue eggs with a few small blackish marks and specks, in grass cup nest lined with wool and hair, under a stone or shrub or in a rock crevice.

Range: Breeds in southeast Spain, northern Africa, and southwestern Asia. Mainly resident.

Apparently expanding its range northward, the Trumpeter Finch invaded southern Spain in the 1960s, where it previously occurred only as a vagrant. Now fairly numerous in some coastal areas of Almería province, it is found in dry, rocky areas similar to its African habitat. Recent records from Mallorca, the Channel Islands, England, and Scotland further mark the spread of this species.

545 **Scarlet Rosefinch or Common Rosefinch**
(*Carpodacus erythrinus*)

Description: 5¾″ (14 cm). Male has *bright rosy-red head, breast, and rump;* extent of red varies individually. Wings dark brown with *two indistinct, pale wing bars;* tail dark brown and forked; belly white; *heavy brown bill.* Female and juvenile nondescript streaky brown, best identified by bill and wing bars, sluggish movements, and chunky shape.

Voice: Call, *twee-eek* or *tiu-eek,* rather soft. Song, 4 or 5 piping notes, *tiu-tiu-fi-tiu.*

Habitat: Prefers swampy areas with bushes, thickets along streams, undergrowth in damp woods; also gardens and orchards and in Asia around mountain villages and cultivated areas.

Nesting: 4–5 deep blue eggs with a few spots and streaks of blackish-brown, in grass nest lined with roots, placed fairly low in bush.

Range: Breeds from Sweden (scarce), southern Finland, Baltics, eastern Germany, Poland, and western Russia across northern Asia to Kamchatka and from Turkey through mountains of central Asia to western China. Winters in southern Asia.

The only European member of a genus widespread in Asia and North America, it is gradually extending its range westward in Europe. It is still only a summer visitor, retreating in winter to its ancestral home in Asia. American rosefinch species are probably descended from Asian birds that crossed at the Bering Straits.

543, 557 **Pine Grosbeak**
(*Pinicola enucleator*)

Description: 8″ (20 cm). A *large* finch with a *long tail. Male rosy-red,* with some grey on lower back and belly and black streaks on upper back; wing black, with *two conspicuous white wing bars.* Female *gingery-yellow.* Young male yellowish-chestnut. Bill stout.

Voice: Call, a liquid *pleep* and a downslurred *tew,* the latter often preceded, especially in flight, by 1 or 2 shorter notes, *tee-tew* or *tee-tee-tew.* Song, a rich, lilting warble.

Habitat: Northern coniferous forests; also birch and mixed woods.

Nesting: 4 greenish-blue eggs with dark spots and blotches, in nest of birch and spruce twigs lined with fine roots and grasses, placed in birch or conifer.

Range: Northern Scandinavia and Russia, wandering irregularly south of breeding range in winter but seldom as far as central or western Europe. Holarctic, also breeding in northern Asia and North America.

It is a tame bird and sociable in winter, when feeding flocks can be located by their frequent calls. It uses its heavy bill to crush the stones of fruit and also feeds on buds and seeds. The bill is not large in proportion to the size of the head and body, so the bird does not have a particularly large-billed appearance.

553, 556 **Bullfinch**
(*Pyrrhula pyrrhula*)

Description: 5¾–6¼" (14–16 cm). Male has *glossy black cap, rosy-red underparts,* grey back, *white rump* conspicuous in flight, and black tail. Wings black with broad white wing bar. Black bill thick but short. Female greyish-pink below, otherwise like male.

Voice: Call, a low, soft, rather melancholy *whew* or *pew.* Song poorly developed, a disjointed succession of low warbling and creaky notes.

Habitat: Thick cover such as woodland, scrub, parks, gardens, orchards, copses, thickets, hedgerows in western European lowlands. In eastern Europe and mountains of central Europe, favours conifers.

Nesting: 4–5 light blue eggs with a few dark brown spots, in a nest of fine twigs and moss lined with fine roots, placed in a thick hedgerow or bush.

Range: Breeds in most of Europe except southern Iberia, Mediterranean climatic zone, and northern Scandinavia, and east across north-central Asia to Japan. Mainly resident, but some birds move south of breeding range in winter; mountain birds move to lowlands in Alps.

A rather shy and secretive species, it generally travels in pairs but is also found in family parties after the breeding season. It is very partial to the buds of fruit trees in spring, particularly when the ash crop fails, and is sometimes regarded as a pest.

---

554 Hawfinch

(*Coccothraustes coccothraustes*)

Description: 7″ (18 cm). Chunky, thick-set finch, with *huge bill, large head and neck,* and *short tail.* Male has tawny head; black lores and throat; grey collar; chocolate-brown back and tail *broadly tipped with white;* pale rump. Underparts rich pinkish-brown; *wing black with broad white patch* and brown shoulder. Bill grey-blue in summer, dull yellow in winter. Female like male but has ash-grey panel on secondaries. Juvenile has yellowish throat and bill and barred underparts.

Voice: Call, a short, sharp *tick* or *ptik,* given both in flight and at rest; also, especially in spring, a thin, harsh whistle, *tzeep* or *tseeip.* Weak, halting song, not often heard, *cheek-cheek-tur-wee-wee.*

Habitat: Mature woodland, chiefly deciduous; parks, orchards, large gardens.

Nesting: 5 pale blue, grey, or green eggs with a few bold blackish spots and streaks, in a shallow nest of grass, roots, and lichen built on layer of twigs, placed on horizontal tree branch.

Range: Breeds from southern Scotland, southern Sweden, and central Russia south to the Mediterranean (patchy); also in North Africa and across central Asia to Japan.

Shy and wary, it spends much of its time feeding in the treetops, where it easily goes unnoticed when not calling. It will also feed on the ground on fallen fruit and seeds, using its enormous bill to crack nuts, kernels, and fruit stones.

BUNTINGS
(*Emberizidae*)

324 species: worldwide. Fourteen species breed in Europe. Small, terrestrial birds with stout bills adapted to a diet of seeds; found in a wide variety of open country habitats. In Europe, sexes dissimilar except for Corn Bunting; males rather brightly coloured, females dull and streaky. Song buzzy and unmusical in most European species. Cup-shaped nest built by female.

591, 594 **Lapland Bunting**
(*Calcarius lapponicus*)

Description: 6″ (15 cm). Male has *black head, throat, and upper breast; chestnut nape; buffy-white line from eye curving around cheek onto side of neck.* White below, with black streaking on flanks; upperparts brown, with darker streaks; outer tail feathers white. *Bill yellow.* In winter, loses most of the black, retaining grey patch on lower throat and some chestnut on the nape. Female streaky brown above, with paler, less extensive chestnut nape; buffy-white underparts, with paler streaking on breast and flanks. Winter female and juvenile have pale median stripe on crown; almost no chestnut on nape; two indistinct, buffy wing bars; pale chestnut coverts. Tail short.

Voice: A hard *tititick* and a liquid *teeoo.* On breeding grounds, an alarm note, *teeler* or *teeleeoo,* is given at intruder's approach. Song, a short, sweet, bubbling jingle, given in flight.

Habitat: Breeds on open, rough tundra above tree line; winters on rough, open areas near coast; also on moors and inland hills.

Nesting: 5–6 greenish-grey to olive-brown eggs with dark streaks and spots, in deep cup of grass and moss, lined with feathers and fine grasses, placed in hollow hidden by vegetation.

Range: Holarctic, breeding in arctic and subarctic Eurasia and North America; in Europe, confined to Fennoscandia, absent from Iceland. Occurs in winter on North Sea coasts and in southwestern Russia.

It is difficult to observe on the ground among stubble and grass clumps. In flight, it may be picked out of mixed flocks by its call notes.

580, 581, 582 **Snow Bunting**
(*Plectrophenax nivalis*)

Description: 6½″ (16 cm). Breeding male *entirely white except for black back, centre of tail, and primaries.* In winter, back becomes brown with black streaks; crown, ear coverts, and patch at sides of breast orange-brown. Female's head and back grey-brown in summer; similar to male in winter but with more orange-brown on head and underparts and less white in wings. Immature browner still, with brown wings.

Voice: Common flight call from flocks, a dry, rolling twitter and a clear *tew.* Song, given in flight or from low perch, a high-pitched, loud, sweet warble.

Habitat: Breeds in open stony and rocky country, on flat tundra, or in high mountains. In winter, along seashore and open country near coast; sometimes inland on open high ground.

Nesting: 4–6 off-white eggs with red-brown spots, in nest made of tundra plants, lined with feathers, fur, and fine grasses, concealed among stones.

Range: Holarctic, breeding in Iceland, Scandinavia, northern Scotland, and Arctic and subarctic Asia and North America. Winters south to central Europe.

Whitest of the wintering buntings; at a distance, flocks resemble shimmering, swirling snowflakes. Once on the ground, their drab brown and white plumage blends into the sand dunes and shingle; in the arctic spring their black and white plumage is equally camouflaged among the dark rocks and patches of melting snow.

570 **Yellowhammer**
(*Emberiza citrinella*)

Description: 6½" (16 cm). Male has *mainly yellow head* and *chestnut rump;* streaks on head, back, and flanks. Female duller, less yellow, and more streaked; juvenile duller still, with almost no yellow. Both distinguished from female and juvenile Cirl Bunting by chestnut rump. All have conspicuous white outer tail feathers.

Voice: A nasal *twink,* a hard *twick,* and a more liquid *twitup.* Song, a buzzy *jijijijijijiji—jeeee,* usually rendered "little-bit-of-bread-and-no—cheese." The final "cheese" is sometimes dropped.

Habitat: Farmland with hedgerows, open country with bushes and scrub, woodland edges. In winter, mainly on cultivated land, especially stubble fields.

Nesting: 3–5 white to pale purple or light red-brown eggs marked with fine, dark lines, in grass nest lined with fine grass or horsehair, placed on or near ground and often partly concealed.

Range: Breeds throughout Europe, except Iceland, and areas bordering Mediterranean; also in western Asia to Iran and central Siberia. Partial migrant, wintering south to Mediterranean region and Middle East.

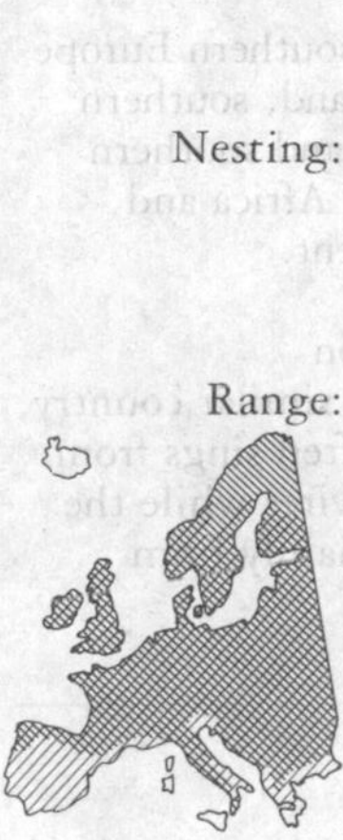

It is common and familiar with a lazy song typifying a warm summer afternoon. In winter, it feeds in mixed flocks with finches and other buntings, eating grain and seeds as well as insects.

569, 574 **Cirl Bunting**
(*Emberiza cirlus*)

Description: 6½" (16 cm). Male has distinctive *yellow face, dark crown, black eye-line and throat,* and *olive-green breast band.* Back and *patch at sides of breast chestnut,* underparts yellow. All ages have *olive-brown rump* and white outer tail feathers. Female and juvenile similar to Yellowhammer: dull brown, finely streaked above and below, with traces of yellow on throat and abdomen; best distinguished by olive-brown rump (chestnut in Yellowhammer).

Voice: A thin *zit;* flight call, *sissi-sissi-sip;* and a churring alarm note. Usual song, a short, hard trill on one pitch.

Habitat: Farmland, especially pastures, hedgerows, open country with scattered trees and bushes. In winter, in open fields.

Nesting: 3–4 green or blue eggs with black streaks and hairlines, in nest of moss, roots, and grass, lined with fine grass and horsehair, placed on ground or in thick bush or hedge.

Range: Breeds in western and southern Europe north to southern England, southern Germany, Yugoslavia, and southern Bulgaria; also in North Africa and western Turkey. Resident.

It and the more common Yellowhammer inhabit similar country, but the Cirl Bunting often sings from tall trees or telephone wires while the Yellowhammer sings mainly from bushes.

590 **Rock Bunting**
(*Emberiza cia*)

Description: 6¼" (16 cm). Male has *silver-white head, with black stripes* on side of crown and through eye and black moustachial stripe, the latter two connected around cheeks; *silver-grey throat and upper breast; light rufous underparts.* Upperparts chestnut, with dark streaking on back but *not on rump. Flicks tail,* showing conspicuous white in outer feathers. Female browner and duller, head stripes prominent but browner; grey throat; some streaks on breast and flanks. Juvenile like dull female, separated from other juvenile buntings by pale rufous underparts and dark bill.

Voice: A thin *zit,* like that of Cirl Bunting; a twittering flight call, *tootootooc;* also a long, high-pitched *seeee.* Song, high-pitched and buzzy, several short notes followed by a longer one, *zi-zi-zi-zirr.*

Habitat: Rocky and sunny hillsides with some brush and scattered trees; also vineyards and gardens in hilly districts.

Nesting: 4–6 pale grey to pale brown eggs with hairlines round large end, in nest of grass and bark strips lined with roots and horsehair, placed on ground among rocks, sometimes in low bush.

Range: Breeds discontinuously across southern and central Europe from Iberia to southern Germany, Italy, Romania, and Balkans; also in North Africa and Asia east to Himalayas and central China. Sedentary.

Though an alpine bird in central Asia, it is more of a midmountain bird in Europe, not usually found above 6,000 feet (2,000 m). It remains in the mountains in winter, only moving down the slopes when forced to by severe weather.

Cinereous Bunting
(*Emberiza cineracea*)

Description: 6½" (16 cm). Adult male has top of *head greyish-green, becoming brighter lemon yellow on face* and still *brighter yellow* on *throat.* Sides of neck and breast grey-brown, rest of underparts dull white. Grey-brown above, with streaking on back; rump paler and unstreaked. Tail brown, with broad white patch on two outermost feathers, visible only when tail spread. Female has greyer, finely streaked head, paler and less extensive yellow on throat. Juvenile like female, but head even greyer, throat pale sulphur yellow, and more extensive streaking on head and breast.

Voice: Call, *kip.* Song, grating, bunting-like, with 3 succinct introductory notes, followed by *deedloo* or *deedawit; dee-dee-dee-deedloo.*

Habitat: Sparsely vegetated dry stony hillsides and rocky mountain slopes, up to tree limit. On migration and in winter, occurs in deserts.

Nesting: 4–6 pale blue or beige eggs covered with blackish spots and hairlines, in open cup nest of dead leaves and grasses, lined with small roots and hair, placed on sloping ground up against a stone and concealed by vegetation.

Range: In Europe, only on Lesbos in Aegean. Also breeds in southwestern Asia. Migrates through Middle East to winter in Sudan, Eritrea, and Arabia.

An uncommon bird about which very little is known, it has an amazingly restricted world distribution, being found mainly in two widely separated areas, western Turkey and western Iran.

---

578 **Ortolan Bunting**
(*Emberiza hortulana*)

Description: 6½″ (16 cm). A bunting of subdued colouration; male has *greyish-green head and breast, pale yellow throat,* and greyish-green moustachial stripe. Underparts pinkish-brown; upperparts brown streaked with black. Narrow, *pale yellow eye-ring;* bill and legs pink. White outer tail feathers. Female similar to male but duller; head less greenish; fine streaks on head and breast. Juvenile duller and browner than female, more streaked.

Voice: *Tsee-ip; jup;* and a piping *tseu.* Song, buzzy but quite melodious; variable in form, usually 6–8 notes, the last 2–4 notes dropping in pitch.

Habitat: A wide variety of open country with scattered bushes and trees; mountains, stony hillsides, cultivated lowlands. In winter, more open dry country.

Nesting: 4–6 pale blue to pinkish-grey eggs with dark, scattered spots, in nest of dried grass and fine roots, often lined with hair, placed in vegetation on or near ground.

Range: Breeds from Iberia, France, and Scandinavia east to western Siberia and through Middle East to Afghanistan. Winters in Mediterranean region and northern Africa.

The word "Ortolan" is derived from its Latin name, *hortulana,* which means "of a garden." In Russia the bird is known as Garden Bunting, although gardens are only one habitat it uses.

584 Cretzschmar's Bunting

(*Emberiza caesia*)

Description: 6¼" (16 cm). Similar to Ortolan Bunting, but *male has blue-grey* (not grey-green) *head and breast,* and *orange-rufous* (not yellow) *throat and moustachial stripe.* Underparts pinkish-brown, upperparts brown streaked with black; bill and legs fleshy pink. Female duller, with less grey and some streaks on breast; distinguished from female Ortolan by buff, not yellow, throat. Both sexes duller in winter. Juvenile streaky brown, very like juvenile Ortolan but richer, rufous-buff below; distinguished from juvenile Rock Bunting by pink (not blackish) bill and *more brown on rump.*

Voice: Call, a loud *tyup* or *tyip.* Song, high, clear, and sweet, alternating between a thinner, more nasal *dwee-dwee-dwee-dwee* and a rounder, purer *tuwi-tuwi-tuwi-tee.*

Habitat: Bare rocky hillsides with scattered vegetation, semiarid lowlands with a few low bushes.

Nesting: 4–6 pale grey, blue, or purple eggs with fine specks and a few larger spots, in nest of plant stems lined with grass and hair, placed among vegetation on ground.

Range: Breeds in easternmost Yugoslavia and Greece; also in southwestern Asia from Turkey south to Israel. Winters in northeast Africa.

Very much a ground bird, it seldom flies into a bush or tree unless alarmed. A common breeder in Cyprus, it is also an abundant migrant there in spring and autumn.

593 **Rustic Bunting**
(*Emberiza rustica*)

Description: 5¾″ (14 cm). Breeding male has *black head,* with *white stripe behind eye,* white throat, *chestnut breast band and streaked flanks,* and *pure white underparts.* Rich brown above, with darker streaks; white outer tail feathers. Black parts brown in female and winter male. Both are best distinguished from female Reed Bunting by *chestnut* streaking on breast and flanks, *pale spot on ear coverts, pale patch on nape,* and *ticking call note.* Juvenile resembles female.

Voice: A sharp *tick* similar to but louder than that of Little Bunting. Song, brief, varied, and musical.

Habitat: Swampy undergrowth at edge of forests, wet moors with scattered trees, thickets along streams.

Nesting: 4–5 greenish-grey to bluish-green eggs spotted greyish-olive and violet, in grass nest placed on or near ground in bush or vegetation.

Range: Breeds from northern Scandinavia and Finland across Siberia to Kamchatka, wintering in China and Japan.

It is common, even abundant, in parts of Siberia, its principal nesting ground. Its summer diet consists mainly of insects and other small invertebrates. It frequently raises its crown feathers, producing a small crest.

579 **Little Bunting**
(*Emberiza pusilla*)

Description: 5¼″ (13 cm). Smallest European bunting. Male has *chestnut crown-stripe broadly edged with black,* and black-bordered chestnut ear coverts. Upperparts brown streaked with black; underparts white with *narrow black streaks* on breast and flanks; moustachial streak black. White outer tail feathers. Female similar but duller; juvenile duller still and more streaked.

Voice: A distinctive Robin-like *tick.* Song, brief and musical, with a Robin-like quality.

Habitat: Tundra scrub, especially near water; also undergrowth in more forested regions and birch growth in marshy lowlands.

Nesting: 4–5 green, grey, or brown eggs spotted dark brown, in nest of grass, moss, and dead leaves, lined with fine grass, placed on ground in depression among bushes.

Range: Breeds from northern Finland across northern Siberia to Pacific; winters in south-central Asia, from northern India to China and Southeast Asia.

Four European buntings (Little, Rustic, Yellow-breasted, and Black-headed) share a similar migration pattern, heading east rather than south from their nesting grounds and spending the winter in various parts of the Orient. This habit makes them rare or accidental in Europe west of their nesting areas.

561, 565 **Yellow-breasted Bunting**
(*Emberiza aureola*)

Description: 5½″ (14 cm). Male in breeding plumage has dark chestnut crown and upperparts; *black forehead, face, and throat;* yellow underparts, with *narrow chestnut breast band.* Wing has *white patch and narrower white bar* conspicuous in flight. In winter, pale tips of feathers obscure some of the black and chestnut, but breast band and wing bars still present. All ages have some white in tail. Female and juvenile pale yellow below, *streaked only on sides;* further distinguished from Yellowhammer by *pale crown-stripe.*

Voice: A sharp *tick* and a soft *trssit.* Song, a melodious warble like Ortolan, only faster and more liquid.

Habitat: Chiefly damp thickets of birch and willow and bushy meadows near water; also dry scrub and steppes. More open country in winter.

Nesting: 4–5 grey-green eggs streaked dark brown, in nest of dead grass lined with finer grass, placed in low bush or dense vegetation.

Range: Breeds from Finland and Russia across Siberia to Manchuria and Kamchatka; winters in southern Asia.

This strikingly handsome Asian bunting barely reaches Europe in summer to breed. In autumn it flies east to its wintering grounds in the Orient and is only a straggler to western Europe.

592, 595 **Reed Bunting**
(*Emberiza schoeniclus*)

Description: 6″ (15 cm). Male has *black head and throat, white moustachial stripe and collar,* and white underparts, with black streaks on flanks. Back dark brown streaked with black, *rump grey.* White outer tail feathers conspicuous in flight. Female has brown head with pale eyebrow, *well-marked black and white moustachial streaks,* buffy-white underparts, and brown rump. Juvenile like female. Head and throat of winter males are black mottled with brown.

Voice: A loud, grating *tseep.* Short, 2-speed song, with slow introductory notes and faster terminal ones, a monotonous, repeated *tseep, tseep, tseep, tississi.* Often sings from conspicuous perch.

Habitat: Almost any kind of marshy place. In winter, on farmland and open country away from water.

Nesting: 4–5 eggs, usually brownish-olive, with a few dark streaks and spots, in nest of coarse grass lined with fine grass, horsehair, or reed flowers, usually placed on or near ground in vegetation.

Range: Breeds throughout Europe except Iceland and a few areas bordering Mediterranean; also breeds across northern Asia to eastern Siberia and Japan. Partial migrant, wintering south to North Africa and Middle East.

While the male is easy to identify, the female is a classic "little brown job"; beginners should become thoroughly familiar with it before attempting to identify rarer buntings.

560 **Black-headed Bunting**
(*Emberiza melanocephala*)

Description: 6½″ (16 cm). Male has *black hood,* chestnut upperparts, *yellow collar,* and *unstreaked yellow underparts.* Duller in winter, head browner. Unlike other yellow buntings, lacks white in tail. Female has faintly streaked brown head, pale chestnut back and rump, unstreaked yellowish-white underparts, *pale yellow undertail* coverts. Female Red-headed Bunting (*E. bruniceps;* accidental), similar but has somewhat greener upperparts. Juvenile like female, but duller brown above.

Voice: A nasal, bunting-like *zitt;* also quieter notes, *chup* and *zee.* Song, 2–5 introductory notes, *chit-chit-chit* . . . followed by sweet, hurried warble; sings from exposed perch.

Habitat: Open country with scrub, bushes, and scattered trees; hedgerows, gardens, olive groves, vineyards. In winter, in cultivated areas and scrub jungle.

Nesting: 4–5 light greenish-blue eggs spotted brown and violet, in rough nest of dead vegetation, lined with fine grasses and hair, placed in bush or clump of low vegetation.

Range: Breeds from Italy, Yugoslavia, and Balkans to Caucasus and Iran; winters in India.

It travels up to 4,000 miles (6,500 km) to reach its spring breeding grounds in southeastern Europe. In India, it often forms huge mixed flocks with the Red-headed Bunting, doing much damage to grain crops. It is the characteristic roadside bunting in Greece and Turkey.

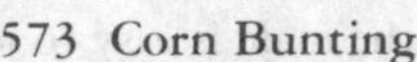

573 **Corn Bunting**
(*Miliaria calandra*)

Description: 7″ (18 cm). Largest bunting; looks plump, with *large, round head* and *stout bill*. Uniformly buff, with dark streaking on breast and upperparts; *no wing bars or white on tail.* Bill and legs pale. Sexes alike. Flight direct and rather heavy.

Voice: A harsh *dzip;* autumn flight call, *tip* or *tippy-tip*. Song very distinctive; begins as a rattle and accelerates into a discordant jingle.

Habitat: Open country with scattered bushes; farmland, grassland, dry open steppe, rough ground both inland and coastal.

Nesting: 4–6 pale grey to light brown eggs with dark lines and spots, in loose grass nest lined with finer grasses and roots located in long grass, weeds, or scrub.

Range: Breeds in central and southern Europe north to Scotland, southern Sweden, and Estonia; also in North Africa and southwestern Asia. Partial migrant, wintering south to Egypt and southern Middle East.

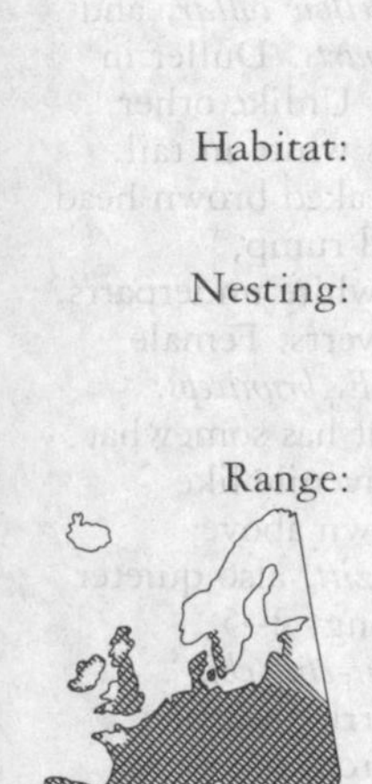

It is visually undistinguished but easily spotted during breeding season, when it perches prominently on a telephone wire or bush top and sings its characteristic song, which has often been likened to the jangling of a bunch of keys.

Part III
Appendices

LIST OF ACCIDENTAL SPECIES

Accidentals are birds that have strayed from their normal breeding or wintering areas or their migration routes and have occurred at least once, but less than 30 times in Europe in the last 50 years. This list, arranged in taxonomic order, thus includes birds such as Pallas's Sandgrouse that were once more common but are now rare vagrants.

Accidentals reaching Europe come from 4 main sources: oceanic islands, mainly in the Atlantic (O); North America (NA); Asia (As); Africa (Af). "New" birds continue to arrive from North America and Asia, but the combined barriers of the Sahara and the Mediterranean make the influx from Africa rather small.

Pied-billed Grebe, *Podilymbus podiceps* (NA)
Wandering Albatross, *Diomedea exulans* (O)
Southern Giant Petrel, *Macronectes giganteus* (O)
Capped Petrel, *Pterodroma hasitata* (O)
Bulwer's Petrel, *Bulweria bulwerii* (O)
White-faced Petrel, *Pelagodroma marina* (O)
Madeiran Petrel, *Oceanodroma castro* (O)
Magnificent Frigatebird, *Fregata magnificens* (O)

American Bittern, *Botaurus lentiginosus* (NA)
Least Bittern, *Ixobrychus exilis* (NA)
Schrenck's Little Bittern, *Ixobrychus eurhythmus* (As)
Green Heron, *Butorides (virescens) striatus* (NA)
Chinese Pond Heron, *Ardeola bacchus* (As)
Western Reef Heron, *Egretta gularis* (Af)
Bald Ibis, *Geronticus eremita* (Af/As)
Lesser Flamingo, *Phoenicopterus minor* (Af)
Black Duck, *Anas rubripes* (NA)
Redhead, *Aythya americana* (NA)
Ring-necked Duck, *Aythya collaris* (NA)
Spectacled Eider, *Somateria fischeri* (As)
Bufflehead, *Bucephala albeola* (NA)
Hooded Merganser, *Mergus cucullatus* (NA)
Pallas's Fish Eagle, *Haliaeetus leucoryphus* (As)
American Kestrel, *Falco sparverius* (NA)
Sora Rail, *Porzana carolina* (NA)
Allen's Gallinule, *Poryphyrula alleni* (Af)
American Purple Gallinule, *Porphyrula martinica* (NA)
American Coot, *Fulica americana* (NA)
Sandhill Crane, *Grus canadensis* (NA)
Houbara Bustard, *Chlamydotis undulata* (As)
Lesser Sand Plover, *Charadrius mongolus* (As)
Greater Sand Plover, *Charadrius leschenaultii* (As)
Caspian Plover, *Charadrius asiaticus* (As)
White-tailed Plover, *Chettusia leucura* (As)
Western Sandpiper, *Calidris mauri* (NA)
Long-toed Stint, *Calidris subminuta* (As)
Least Sandpiper, *Calidris minutilla* (NA)
Sharp-tailed Sandpiper, *Calidris acuminata* (As/NA)
Stilt Sandpiper, *Micropalama himantopus* (NA)
Little Whimbrel, *Numenius minutus* (As)
Eskimo Curlew, *Numenius borealis* (NA)

Solitary Sandpiper, *Tringa solitaria* (NA)
Spotted Sandpiper, *Actitis macularia* (NA)
Willet, *Catoptrophorus semipalmatus* (NA)
Laughing Gull, *Larus atricilla* (NA)
Franklin's Gull, *Larus pipixcan* (NA)
Grey-headed Gull, *Larus cirrocephalus* (Af)
Ring-billed Gull, *Larus delawarensis* (NA)
Royal Tern, *Sterna maxima* (NA/Af)
Lesser Crested Tern, *Sterna bengalensis* (Af)
Forster's Tern, *Sterna forsteri* (NA)
Bridled Tern, *Sterna anaethetus* (O)
Sooty Tern, *Sterna fuscata* (O)
Brown Noddy, *Anous stolidus* (O)
Crested Auklet, *Aethia cristatella* (O)
Parakeet Auklet, *Cyclorrhynchus psittacula* (O)
Spotted Sandgrouse, *Pterocles senegallus* (Af)
Chestnut-bellied Sandgrouse, *Pterocles exustus* (Af)
Pallas's Sandgrouse, *Syrrhaptes paradoxus* (As)
Rufous Turtle Dove, *Streptopelia orientalis* (As)
Black-billed Cuckoo, *Coccyzus erythrophthalmus* (NA)
Yellow-billed Cuckoo, *Coccyzus americanus* (NA)
Marsh Owl, *Asio capensis* (Af)
Egyptian Nightjar, *Caprimulgus aegyptius* (Af)
Common Nighthawk, *Chordeiles minor* (NA)
Needle-tailed Swift, *Hirundapus caudacutus* (As)
Little Swift, *Apus affinis* (Af)
Pied Kingfisher, *Ceryle rudis* (Af/As)
Belted Kingfisher, *Ceryle alcyon* (NA)
Blue-cheeked Bee-eater, *Merops superciliosus* (Af/As)
Yellow-shafted Flicker, *Colaptes auratus* (NA)
Yellow-bellied Sapsucker, *Sphyrapicus varius* (NA)

Acadian Flycatcher, *Empidonax virescens* (NA)
Bar-tailed Desert Lark, *Ammomanes cincturus* (Af/As)
Desert Lark, *Ammomanes deserti* (Af/As)
Hoopoe Lark, *Alaemon alaudipes* (Af/As)
Dupont's Lark, *Chersophilus duponti* (Af)
Bimaculated Lark, *Melanocorypha bimaculata* (As)
White-winged Lark, *Melanocorypha leucoptera* (As)
Black Lark, *Melanocorypha yeltoniensis* (As)
Blyth's Pipit, *Anthus godlewskii* (As)
Olive-backed Pipit, *Anthus hodgsoni* (As)
Pechora Pipit, *Anthus gustavi* (As)
Citrine Wagtail, *Motacilla citreola* (As)
Brown Thrasher, *Toxostoma rufum,* (NA)
Catbird, *Dumetella carolinensis* (NA)
Siberian Accentor, *Prunella montanella* (As)
Siberian Rubythroat, *Luscinia calliope* (As)
Siberian Blue Robin, *Luscinia cyane* (As)
White-throated Robin, *Irania gutturalis* (As)
Moussier's Redstart, *Phoenicurus moussieri* (Af)
White-crowned Black Wheatear, *Oenanthe leucopyga* (Af/As)
White's Thrush, *Zoothera dauma,* (As)
Siberian Thrush, *Zoothera sibirica* (As)
Wood Thrush, *Hylocichla mustelina* (NA)
Hermit Thrush, *Catharus guttatus* (NA)
Swainson's Thrush, *Catharus ustulatus* (NA)
Grey-cheeked Thrush, *Catharus minimus* (NA)
Veery, *Catharus fuscescens* (NA)
Tickell's Thrush, *Turdus unicolor* (As)
Eye-browed Thrush, *Turdus obscurus* (As)
Dusky/Naumann's Thrush, *Turdus naumanni* (As)
Black-throated/Red-throated Thrush, *Turdus ruficollis* (As)
American Robin, *Turdus migratorius* (NA)

Pallas's Grasshopper Warbler, *Locustella certhiola* (As)
Lanceolated Warbler, *Locustella lanceolata* (As)
Gray's Grasshopper Warbler, *Locustella fasciolata* (As)
Thick-billed Warbler, *Acrocephalus aedon* (As)
Booted Warbler, *Hippolais caligata* (As)
Desert Warbler, *Sylvia nana* (Af/As)
Radde's Warbler, *Phylloscopus schwarzi* (As)
Dusky Warbler, *Phylloscopus fuscatus* (As)
Red-breasted Nuthatch, *Sitta canadensis* (NA)
Isabelline Shrike, *Lanius isabellinus* (As)
Daurian Jackdaw, *Corvus dauuricus* (As)
Red-eyed Vireo, *Vireo olivaceus* (NA)
Pallas's Rosefinch, *Carpodacus roseus* (As)
Evening Grosbeak, *Hesperiphona vespertina* (NA)
Black-and-white Warbler, *Mniotilta varia* (NA)
Tennessee Warbler, *Vermivora peregrina* (NA)
Parula Warbler, *Parula americana* (NA)
Yellow Warbler, *Dendroica petechia* (NA)
Black-throated Green Warbler, *Dendroica virens* (NA)
Yellow-rumped Warbler, *Dendroica coronata* (NA)
Blackpoll Warbler, *Dendroica striata* (NA)
American Redstart, *Setophaga ruticilla* (NA)
Ovenbird, *Seiurus aurocapillus* (NA)
Northern Waterthrush, *Seiurus noveboracensis* (NA)
Yellowthroat, *Geothlypis trichas* (NA)
Hooded Warbler, *Wilsonia citrina* (NA)
Summer Tanager, *Piranga rubra* (NA)
Scarlet Tanager, *Piranga olivacea* (NA)
Rufous-sided Towhee, *Pipilo erythrophthalmus* (NA)
Fox Sparrow, *Zonotrichia iliaca* (NA)
Song Sparrow, *Zonotrichia melodia* (NA)

White-crowned Sparrow, *Zonotrichia leucophrys* (NA)
White-throated Sparrow, *Zonotrichia albicollis* (NA)
Slate-colored Junco, *Junco hyemalis* (NA)
Black-faced Bunting, *Emberiza spodocephala* (As)
Pine Bunting, *Emberiza leucocephalos* (As)
Meadow Bunting, *Emberiza cioides* (As)
Yellow-browed Bunting, *Emberiza chrysophrys* (As)
Chestnut Bunting, *Emberiza rutila* (As)
Pallas's Reed Bunting, *Emberiza pallasi* (As)
Red-headed Bunting, *Emberiza bruniceps* (As)
Rose-breasted Grosbeak, *Pheucticus ludovicianus* (NA)
Blue Grosbeak, *Guiraca caerulea* (NA)
Indigo Bunting, *Passerina cyanea* (NA)
Bobolink, *Dolichonyx oryzivorous* (NA)
Northern Oriole, *Icterus galbula* (NA)

THE ART OF BIRD-WATCHING

You can watch birds just about anywhere, including urban areas, and the equipment required is minimal. The only essentials are a field guide and a pair of binoculars; additional equipment is optional.

While a field guide is intended for use when the bird is in front of you, or at least fresh in the memory, it should also be studied at home. As you enjoy the photographs, study the shapes, postures, and plumage of different types of birds and become familiar with the categories in which they are arranged. Try to memorize the principal field marks—many birds are not identified because an observer fails to notice leg colour, bill shape, or some other key feature. When you see a new bird, make a note of such features as the size and shape of the bill (whether long or short, slender or stout, curved or straight), the tail (long or short, rounded, squared, wedge-shaped, notched, or forked), and the wings (long or short, rounded or pointed). Note any distinctive markings such as a crest, or eye-rings, or wing bars, or a flashing white patch in the wings, tail, or rump. Many species have colour patterns that identify them at a glance, by studying the pictures in this book in advance, you may be able to identify many species at first sight.

The second essential is a pair of binoculars; the range of available makes and models of binoculars is immense. Every pair of prismatic binoculars is marked with a code of two figures, e.g., 10 × 40; the first number, 10, is the magnification, that is, 10 times (10×), and the second number, 40, is the diameter of the object lens (the one at the front) in millimetres—40 mm. For bird-watching the magnification should be between 7× and 10×, and the diameter of the object lens between 30mm and 50mm. This comparatively narrow range eliminates many instruments not suited to a bird-watcher's needs. Higher magnification brings objects closer, but it also reduces the area that can be seen (field of view), thus making it more difficult to locate the object, especially a fast-moving bird. The larger the object lens, the larger the field of view, but the heavier the binoculars. Another important factor is the light-gathering power of the binoculars; the larger the object lens, the more light is admitted. Ideally the diameter of the object lens should be five times the magnification: with a magnification of 8, the diameter should be 5 × 8 = 40.

Bird-watchers soon discover that for identifying ducks on a large reservoir or sandpipers on mud flats even a 10-power binocular is inadequate. Although it may be a nuisance to carry, a telescope is indispensable for viewing distant birds. The most useful magnification is 30× since this is about as large as can be achieved without loss of light-gathering power or increased vibration. The telescope should be mounted on a tripod since it is difficult to keep it steady by hand.

Many bird-watchers carry a field notebook. Details of each field trip may be logged, including date, time, route taken, companions, and weather. Keep a list of birds observed, with numbers, and make notes and drawings if possible.

Train yourself to move quietly and unobtrusively through the countryside; be alert and observant and avoid chatting with your companions. Wear dull-brown or greenish clothing that blends with your surroundings, and at all times obey the laws and codes. Remember that there are other people with an interest in the countryside besides bird-watchers.

GLOSSARY

Accidental	A species that has appeared in a given area only a very few times and whose normal range is in another area. Also known as a vagrant.
Aquatic	Frequenting water.
Arboreal	Frequenting trees
Axillaries	The feathers of the "armpit," where the underside of the wing joins the body.
Carpal patch	A patch of feathers at the "wrist," or bend of the wing.
Cere	A fleshy, featherless area surrounding the nostrils of hawks, falcons, pigeons, and a few other groups of birds.
Circumpolar	Of or inhabiting the Arctic (or Antarctic) regions in both the eastern and western hemispheres.
Colonial	Nesting in groups or colonies rather than in isolated pairs.
Commensal	Living near or with another organism.
Conspecific	Belonging to the same species
Cosmopolitan	Worldwide in distribution, or at least occurring on all continents except Antarctica.

Coverts Small feathers that overlie or cover the bases of the large flight feathers of the wings and tail or that cover an area or structure (e.g., ear coverts).

Crepuscular Active at dawn and dusk.

Crest A tuft of elongated feathers on the crown.

Crown The top of the head.

Cryptic Form or colouring that serves to conceal.

Decurved Curved downward.

Dimorphic Having two colour forms.

Diurnal Active during the day.

Eclipse plumage A dull-coloured plumage acquired by most ducks immediately after the breeding season and worn for a few weeks; males then acquire more brightly coloured plumage.

Endemic Restricted to a certain area.

Eyebrow A conspicuous stripe of colour running above but not through the eye. Also known as the supercilium.

Eye-stripe A stripe that runs horizontally from the base of the bill through the eye.

Feral Escaped from captivity and now wild.

Field mark A characteristic of colour, pattern, or structure useful in distinguishing a species in the field.

Flight feathers The long, well-developed feathers of the wings and tail, used during flight. The flight feathers of the wings are divided into primaries and secondaries.

Frontal shield A fleshy, featherless, and often brightly coloured area on the forehead of coots, gallinules, and a few other groups of birds.

Fulvous Tawny, dull yellowish-red.

Gape The mouth opening.

Holarctic Occurring in both Palearctic and Nearctic regions, i.e., in northern and temperate regions of both New and Old Worlds.

Immature A young bird in a plumage stage between juvenile and adult.

Intergrade An intermediate or transitional form.

Irruption An irregular, large-scale migratory movement.

Juvenile A young bird in the first feathered plumage.

Lek A place where males of some bird species, especially game birds, gather and perform courtship displays in a group rather than courting females individually and in isolation from one another; females visit a lek to mate, but generally they build their nests elsewhere.

Lore The area between the eye and the base of the bill, sometimes distinctively coloured.

Mandible One of the two parts of a bird's bill, termed respectively the upper mandible and the lower mandible.

Mantle The back of a bird together with the upper surface of the wings; the term is used especially in groups of birds like gulls and terns in which these areas are of one colour.

Migrant A bird that regularly passes through an area on its way to or from its normal breeding range.

Mirrors White spots or areas in the black wingtips of gulls.

Montane Pertaining to mountains.

Moult The process of shedding and replacing feathers.

Moustachial streak A streak of colour running from the base of the bill back along the side of the throat.

Nocturnal Active at night.

Ochreous The colour of ochre; yellowish-brown.

Omnivorous Eating almost any kind of plant or animal food.

Pelagic Frequenting the open ocean.

Phase A distinctive plumage colour in certain groups such as hawks and owls that is unrelated to race, age, sex, or season.

Plume A feather larger or longer than the feathers around it, generally used in display.

Polygamous Mating with more than one member of the opposite sex.

Primaries The outermost and longest flight feathers on a bird's wing.

Race A geographical population of a species, slightly different from other populations of that species; also called a subspecies.

Range The geographical area or areas inhabited by a species.

Raptor A bird of prey.

Resident Remaining in one place all year; non-migratory.

Ringing The marking of birds by placing rings of metal or coloured plastic on their legs for future recognition as individuals.

Riparian Of or inhabiting the banks of a river or stream.

Rufous Reddish colour.

Scapulars A group of feathers on the shoulder of a bird, along the side of the back.

Scrape A shallow depression made by a bird on the ground to serve as a nest.

Secondaries The large flight feathers along the rear edge of the wing, inward from the primaries.

Sedentary Remaining in one place; non-migratory.

Shoulder The point where the wing meets the body. The term is also loosely applied to the bend of the wing.

Spatulate Spoon-shaped.

Speculum A distinctively coloured area on the wing of a bird, especially the metallic-coloured patch on the secondaries of some ducks.

Subadult An immature bird about to reach full maturity; a term usually used of birds that take more than a year to acquire adult plumage.

Subspecies A geographical population of a species that is slightly different from other populations of that species; a race.

Supercilium A conspicuous stripe of colour running above but not through the eye. Also known as the eyebrow.

Superspecies A group of closely related species whose ranges do not overlap.

Tarsus	The lower, usually featherless, part of a bird's leg above the feet.
Taxonomy	The science of classifying organisms according to their natural relationships.
Terrestrial	Frequenting the ground.
Territory	Any defended area.
Tertials	The innermost flight feathers on a bird's wing, immediately adjacent to the body. They are often regarded simply as the innermost secondaries. Also called tertiaries.
Thermals	Currents of warm, rising air used by hawks and other soaring birds to assist flight.
Vagrant	A species that has appeared in a given area only a few times and whose normal range is in another area. Also known as an accidental.
Vinaceous	Dark red, wine-coloured.

CONSERVING BIRD LIFE

The decline in bird populations in Europe has generally been caused by the destruction of a bird's environment—as in the draining of swamps or the cutting down of forests—or by offshore oil spills, pesticides, and hunting by man.

Although the destruction of wetlands or forests is difficult to control, organizations for the saving of marsh areas, as in Spain's Coto Doñana, have occasionally been effective. The use of harmful pesticides can be curbed by law. To reduce the possibility of oil spills, laws controlling safe tanker construction and operation should be encouraged in every possible way. Meanwhile, techniques are being explored to clean up spills and to rescue birds that have been contaminated.

Every country in Europe has some legislation that protects birds from hunters. But the enforcement ranges from negligible to adequate. In general, northern European birds are better protected than in southern Europe. The tradition of hunting over the open countryside is very strong, and "sport" is in most areas the primary aim. In a few countries wild birds are taken for food, but usually for gourmets rather than as a source of necessary protein. Because of the lack of adequate laws and enforcement in southern Europe, a heavy toll is also taken of migrants that breed in the north and pass through the Mediterranean on their way to Africa.

British bird-protection laws are fairly typical of northern Europe. In Britain, as a rule, all birds and their eggs are protected at all times. The few exceptions include pest species such as the Woodpigeon and the Starling, game birds in season, some migratory wildfowl, and Gannets on the islet of Sula Sgeir that have been taken by the men of Noss for centuries. Some birds may not even be photographed without permission from the Nature Conservancy Council. Although the penalties for breaking the law are high in certain cases, they are not nearly as severe as those in the United States.

The last 20 years have seen a dramatic decline in the number of certain European birds such as the Peregrine and other birds of prey. Pesticides and chemical poisons are responsible for part of this decrease, but direct persecution has also taken a toll.

Oil pollution is cutting into the populations of Guillemots, Razorbills, Puffins, and other northern seabirds. Large spills make the headlines, but the pollution is more or less constant. One wonders which will run out first, the oil or the auks.

Among the British ornithological societies of interest to bird watchers are: The British Ornithological Union, which holds regular meetings and publishes an outstanding journal, *The Ibis;* the British Trust for Ornithology, an organisation of amateur ornithologists that concentrates on cooperative field work; and The Royal Society for the Protection of Birds, a fast-growing society of bird conservationists that maintains a string of important reserves and publishes *Birds* magazine.

PICTURE CREDITS

The numbers in parentheses are plate numbers. Some photographers have pictures under agency names as well as their own. Agency names appear in boldface.

Ardea London
(166, 303, 340, 361, 424, 494, 531) Dennis Avon and Tony Tilford (390, 433, 434, 464, 517, 530, 552, 572, 573) J. A. Bailey (13, 55, 60, 62, 72, 106, 214, 220, 244, 251, 254, 398, 399, 402, 407, 409, 414, 416, 417, 419, 421, 422, 426, 435, 463, 498, 518, 529, 538, 546, 553, 556, 558, 575, 578, 589, 601, 610) F. Balát (130, 334, 506) Ian Beames (25, 85, 194, 197, 238, 242) Gert Behrens (268) Per-Göran Bentz (513, 527) Hans and Judy Beste (87) Brian Bevan (451, 456, 492, 493, 509, 574, 587) R. J. C. Blewitt (3, 127, 263, 276, 311, 322, 323, 324, 338, 367, 369, 382, 383, 389, 411, 470, 512, 600) Arne Blomgren (374, 413, 557) Anthony and Elizabeth Bomford (395) J. B. and S. Bottomley (9, 47, 66, 76, 84, 97, 105, 112, 116, 117, 133, 143, 150, 229, 230, 271, 280, 281, 283, 341, 356, 386, 472, 491, 565, 566, 603, 606) A. D. Brewer (140) G. J. Broekhuysen (298) G. K. Brown (46, 53, 65, 67, 89, 92, 93, 94, 107, 110, 111, 120, 129, 147, 148, 171, 179, 233, 264, 306, 321, 358, 359, 364, 384, 471, 495, 523, 525, 532, 535, 595, 613) L. H. Brown (180, 186) Roberto Bunge (29) Kevin Carlson (123, 128, 154, 239, 250, 318, 461, 466, 481, 519, 522) Graeme Chapman

(77, 312) F. Collet (550) Werner Curth (178, 291, 309, 396, 401, 405, 406, 486, 554, 586, 609) M. D. England (27, 73, 132, 164, 168, 181, 182, 199, 209, 217, 222, 319, 357, 400, 430, 437, 450, 452, 453, 459, 469, 477, 478, 480, 485, 496, 497, 507, 590, 608, 611) André Fatras (10, 28, 45, 74, 81, 152, 165, 173, 175, 187, 196, 313, 314, 320, 325, 377, 379, 387, 410, 420, 445, 446, 460, 462, 473, 476, 500, 502, 528) J. P. Ferrero (158) Kenneth W. Fink (4, 34, 41, 43, 48, 52, 71, 103, 174, 192, 198, 203, 204, 205, 207, 211, 213, 216, 219, 223, 224, 227, 232, 234, 236, 237, 241, 243, 245, 253, 257, 258, 260, 284, 293, 295, 591) Paul Germain (32, 36) John Gooders (63, 151, 300, 360) Su Gooders (167) M. E. J. Gore (96, 109, 156) D. W. Greenslade (249) Don Hadden (537) Per Klaesson and Bengt Olsson (376) Edgar Jones (329) C. R. Knights (23, 118, 126, 289, 465) M. Krishnan (170) Jens-Peter Laub (18, 19, 91, 134, 200, 210, 212, 504, 505, 508, 516, 521) Ake Lindau (61, 162, 310) Trevor Marshall (142, 366, 425) P. Morris (22, 30, 33, 201, 215) C. K. Mylne (20, 59, 489) R. F. Porter (185) Ralf Richter (6, 80, 137, 141, 153, 157, 161, 163, 429, 436, 479, 499, 501, 520) S. Roberts (39, 136, 191, 208, 228, 285, 346, 368, 388, 448, 449, 488, 547, 562) Bryan L. Sage (1, 5, 26, 56, 78, 88, 135, 145, 159, 160, 259, 594, 596, 597) Robert T. Smith (44, 50, 51, 83, 121, 188, 189, 273, 403, 412, 432, 440, 442, 455, 458, 474, 475, 514, 524, 570, 571, 576, 592, 612) Peter Steyn (183, 270, 337) W. Stribling (2) Bruno Sundin (235, 378, 408, 441, 544, 593) John E. Swedberg (172) A. D. Trounson and M. C. Clampett (8, 102, 108) Richard Vaughan (40, 49, 64, 69, 90, 95, 98, 99, 144, 146, 190, 240, 269, 274, 327, 328, 423, 468, 483, 487, 490,

503, 515, 533, 551, 567, 581, 582, 598) Richard Waller (184) Adrian Warren (297) Alan Weaving (330, 381, 385) Wardene Weisser (177, 277) J. S. Wightman (86, 122, 124, 149, 262, 282, 331, 393, 415) Robin Williams (101) Tom Willock (373)

Per-Göran Bentz (256)
Ola Bondesson (79, 356)
Arthur Christiansen (266, 339, 380, 404, 427, 605)
Herbert Clarke (12, 104, 247)

Bruce Coleman, Inc.
Ron Austing (542, 559) Jen and Des Bartlett (225) B. J. Coates (294) Harry N. Darrow (16) Kenneth W. Fink (206, 226) Gösta Håkansson (42) Edgar T. Jones (548) F. W. Lane (604) H. Reinhard (286, 370, 371, 372, 563, 564) Joseph Van Wormer (568) Gary R. Zahm (292)

Bruce Coleman, Ltd.
Oto E. Duscher (540) Juan A. Fernandez (316) Dennis Green (304)

Harry N. Darrow (24, 70, 100, 119, 131, 139, 155, 231, 549)
Thomas H. Davis (58, 68, 138)
Etienne Edberg (169)
Jan Elmelid (444, 579)
Kenneth W. Fink (193, 221, 246)
Dick Forsman (17, 125, 561)
Claus Frahm (54, 352, 353, 354, 355, 363)
D. A. Gill (57)
Per Schiermacher Hansen (348, 394)
Olle Hedvall (375, 545)
Björn Helander (350)
Eric Hosking (265, 267, 279, 307, 317, 391, 438, 447, 510, 539, 555, 580, 599, 602)

Jacana
Bos (583) J. P. Champroux (315) J. L. S. DuBois (278, 541) Ermie (299) R. Konig (301) Jean-Claude Maes (308,

428) C. Nardin (332, 392, 443) Pierre Petit (536) Pissavini (585) Bernard Rebouleau (195) Jacques Robert (305, 577) Trotignon (335) Varin-Visage Collection (218, 272, 275, 290, 326, 362, 365, 418) René Volot (543, 569) Ziesler (467)

Lars Jonsson (176, 252, 336, 344, 345, 347, 351, 397, 431, 439, 454, 457, 482, 511, 534, 584, 588)
Michael Kleinbaum (115)
Peter Lindberg (302)
S. J. Miller (288)
Tomas Moll (342)

National Audubon Society Collection/Photo Researchers, Inc.
Helen Cruickshank (11, 114) Robert J. Erwin (82) Russ Kinne (248) Leonard Lee Rue III (202) Charlie Ott (287) Hope Ryden (349) Bill Wilson (35, 37, 113)

Natural History Photographic Agency
J. Jeffrey (484)

Naturfotograferna
Arne Blomgren (21) Peter Lindberg (333) Bengt Lundberg (607) Björn-Eyvind Swahn (7, 75, 560)

Klaus Malling Olsen (261)
Bengt Olsson and Per Klaesson (31, 296, 343, 526)
Leonard Lee Rue III (255)
Arnold Small (14, 15)
Bruno Sundin (38)

INDEX

Numbers in boldface type refer to plates. Numbers in italics refer to pages. Circles preceding English names of birds make it easy for you to keep a record of the birds you have seen.

Z

ACKNOWLEDGEMENTS

The authors would like to express their gratitude to Paul Steiner and the staff of Chanticleer Press for the tremendous amount of work they put into the preparation of this book. We would like especially to thank Milton Rugoff, Gudrun Buettner, Susan Rayfield, Richard Christopher, Carol Nehring, Helga Lose, and Ray Patient. Our greatest debt, however, is to Olivia Buehl, the project editor.
We are particularly grateful to Lars Svensson whose knowledge of the birds not only of Scandinavia but all of Europe enabled him to make many invaluable suggestions on text, pictures, and captions. François Vuilleumier was also very helpful in checking all the range maps and text. We are also indebted to Peter Grant and Cloe Mifsud for their helpful comments, and to Sallyann Keith for many useful suggestions. R. F. Porter has been of assistance in identifying photographs of birds of prey.

THE AUTHORS

Stuart Keith, born and educated in England, is a Research Associate at the American Museum of Natural History in New York. The founding president of the American Birding Association, he has written many scientific and popular articles on birds. He has led bird-watching tours in Europe, Africa, and Madagascar, and is an authority on birds of Eastern Africa. He holds the record of 5,450 species sighted and is listed in *Guinness Book of World Records* as the World Champion Bird-watcher.

John Gooders is an ornithologist whose books include *Where to Watch Birds in Europe* and *Where to Watch Birds* (Britain). He has edited two multi-volume encyclopedias, *Birds of the World* and *The Encyclopedia of Birds,* and has written numerous scripts for television wildlife films. His travels as a bird-watcher have taken him from Ecuador to Zaire.

STAFF

Prepared and produced by Chanticleer Press, Inc.

Publisher: Paul Steiner
Editor-in-Chief: Gudrun Buettner
Managing Editor: Susan Costello
Guides Editor: Susan Rayfield
Project Editor: Olivia Buehl
Production: Helga Lose, Amy Roche
Art Director: Carol Nehring
Picture Library: Edward Douglas
Drawings: Lars Svensson
Range Maps: John Gooders, Malcolm Gipson
Map of Europe: Paul Singer
Visual Key: Olivia Buehl, Carol Nehring, Susan Rayfield

Design: Massimo Vignelli